THE SUNDAY PAPER

THE HISTORY OF COMMUNICATION

Robert W. McChesney and John C. Nerone, editors

A list of books in the series appears at the end of this book.

The Sunday Paper

A MEDIA HISTORY

Paul Moore and Sandra Gabriele

UNIVERSITY OF ILLINOIS PRESS
Urbana, Chicago, and Springfield

Library of Congress Cataloging-in-Publication Data
Names: Moore, Paul S., 1970– author. | Gabriele, Sandra,
    1972– author.
Title: The Sunday paper : a media history / Paul Moore and
    Sandra Gabriele.
Description: Urbana : University of Illinois Press, [2022]
    | Series: The history of communication | Includes
    bibliographical references and index.
Identifiers: LCCN 2021062784 (print) | LCCN 2021062785
    (ebook) | ISBN 9780252044496 (cloth) | ISBN
    9780252086564 (paperback) | ISBN 9780252053498
    (ebook)
Subjects: LCSH: American newspapers--History—19th
    century. | American newspapers--History—20th century.
    | American newspapers--Social aspects.
Classification: LCC PN4864 .M66 2022 (print) | LCC PN4864
    (ebook) | DDC 071.309/034—dc23/eng/20220125
LC record available at https://lccn.loc.gov/2021062784
LC ebook record available at https://lccn.loc.gov/2021062785

CONTENTS

ACKNOWLEDGMENTS

Our work on this book began fifteen years ago. We were each planning to start separate projects on weekend newspapers when colleagues put us in touch. A few messages later, an incredible partnership was born, characterized by generosity and trust. Although it took twice as long as we imagined, *The Sunday Paper* is twice as ambitious as we could have achieved apart. Our original title was *Animating Modernity*, aiming to tell how Sunday papers became a weekly reflection on the constant novelty of the modern world, stewarding new forms of mass media and consumption. It became clear in our earlier research (Paul's work on movie publicity, and Sandra's on women's weekend journalism) that the leisure of Sunday reading spawned a unique media form. But American scholars seemed to take the Sunday paper for granted as an unremarkable fact of American life that often went without comment. Our fascination perhaps arose because the Sunday paper didn't really have an equivalent in Canada. Our Saturday papers had color comics, extra sections, and flyers, but weren't the same overstuffed abundance of popular culture.

When we started in 2007, we would never have guessed how newspapers would be a thing of the past by the time we finished, including the great American Sunday paper. But we already knew the art, fiction, and fun of Sunday papers had always been precarious and ephemeral. Many microfilmed papers were missing Sunday comics, magazines, song sheets, and posters; some were missing the Sunday edition altogether. In the archives, much of the Sunday paper had disappeared without a trace except for Saturday issues' publicity of what was to come. We knew Nicholson Baker had helped rescue whole volumes of print copies of U.S. newspapers from the British Library. Visiting the resulting collection at Duke University Library's American Newspaper Repository was among our first research trips. Many days were later spent in newspaper reading rooms at the Library of Congress and New York Public Library. There was also a foray to Princeton to get on-demand access to old periodicals stored in the Research Collections and Preservation Consortium, and where we got a chance to see banks of scanners at work digitizing American print culture's past. Over a decade later, those online sources allowed us to add final details from across the border, locked down during a pandemic. Of course, the power of digital circulation has also brought the Sunday paper to its knees, certainly as a national pastime in the way we recount.

Our research was funded through a grant from the Social Sciences and Humanities Research Council of Canada (2008–2012), a Ryerson Institutional Grant (2007), and a University of Windsor Humanities Research Group Fellowship (2009), among other forms of funding and institutional support from Ryerson and Concordia Universities. Thanks to all the research assistants over the years who helped in various stages. At a crucial moment of synthesis in 2012, we both had the rare chance to teach graduate seminars on the topic. Early versions of those ideas were presented to the History Division of the International Communication Association, the International Association for Media and History, and the Canadian Communication Association, among others. Danny Nassett at University of Illinois Press kept the door open until we were ready to step through it. He and his stellar staff at the press were incredibly helpful and thorough. John Nerone, History of Communication Series co-editor, was an early booster at the proposal stage. Richard Abel, Aurora Wallace, and Michael Stamm offered critical input and encouragement exactly when it counted.

Half a career and many professional and personal milestones have passed in those fifteen years, too. Offices, institutions, and job titles have come and gone as each of us has served terms as chair, director, associate dean, or vice provost and on executives of academic associations.

PAUL: Much more than thanks are owed Sandra for co-piloting this once-in-a-lifetime camaraderie in the archives and on the page. Our book would not have nearly the same ambition and integrity without our collaboration. Thanks are owed my dean, Pamela Sugiman, and my chair, Alan Sears, for supporting the final stages of editing. Final thanks to Andrew, who accompanied every step.

SANDRA: Above all else, I want to thank Paul for his friendship, compassion, and patience. My life has been enriched by his smarts and kind soul. To my colleagues in the provost office at Concordia who took over my responsibilities during the last push of writing and editing, a sincere thank you. Through the years of development, Darren, my unwavering partner in life, has encouraged, edited, and enabled its completion. Thank you, my love. For always shouting, "Go mom, go!" whenever I most needed to hear it, I am grateful to my boos, Max and Gus. I dedicate this book to my family, near and far, who remind me every day of what really matters. *Senza famiglia niente è possibile.*

INTRODUCTION

The Sunday paper was the stage on which the drama of American modernity unfolded. From the 1890s to the 1920s, the Sunday paper found its form and function as an intermedial variety of information, entertainment, and advice for modern living, shamelessly adopting and transfiguring other media forms in its endless quest to expand its readership. For instance, the *Chicago Inter-Ocean* depicted its Sunday classified section as a vaudevillian stage, "The People's Exchange," with readers of all classes, genders, and ages (even the family dog) entering through the proscenium arch of a printed page.[1] But if we consider it as more than a metaphor—as a technique for producing not just new kinds of engagement but new kinds of readers as well—this illustration transforms the newspaper into a lived place where readers could imagine entering into the convivial interpersonal exchange of modern life for the trifling expense of a newspaper. The high value this low cost provided was a favorite theme for the *Inter-Ocean* and other metropolitan papers, insistently reminding readers that, for mere pennies, the Sunday issue was "more than a newspaper and better than a magazine."[2] The word "better" flags how newspapers were contesting other media for the mass public's imagination, but "more" signals how the Sunday paper provided an excess in both form and content beyond the weekday routine of news reading. "Instead of paying twenty-five cents for a magazine, ten cents for a comic weekly and five cents for a newspaper, making a total of forty cents in all," explained the leading New York paper, "get the three combined for five cents in *The Sunday World*."[3] The Sunday paper truly had an ability to mobilize all the new forms of media and modernity itself as it unfolded.

At the height of the era of sensationalist "yellow journalism," Joseph Pulitzer's *New York World* used theatrical forms to promote its Sunday edition as an entertaining diorama. As an audience of Sunday paper readers sat in anticipation of the coming show, the *New York World* lined up a backdrop of posters for an ensemble of eleven forthcoming feature stories to create a playbill of coming attractions (see fig. 1).[4] Nearly a quarter of a century later, William Randolph Hearst's *San Francisco Examiner* used a more elaborate version of the same theme to promote "The Want Ad Page—The Newspaper Stage," drawing on the Shakespearean aphorism "All the World's a Stage," with a seated theatrical audience watching a spread of newspaper pages coming alive through the melodrama of thirty ordinary interpersonal transactions, ranging from buying a used car to applying for a job.[5] In 1914, to promote its new Sunday directory of programs playing at hundreds of Chicago movie theaters, the *Record-Herald* lauded the innovation as "Making 'Movie' History," illustrating a crowd entering a newspaper by passing through the entrance to a theater.[6] A few days later, the paper made the links between newspaper and box office explicit by underlining the relationship between reading and seeing: "Everybody's Going! First they read the great short story in *The Record-Herald*—then they go to see it dramatically depicted in moving pictures."[7] If the weekday newspaper carried news to the reader, the weekend edition transfigured that news for them into a range of new media formats, transforming the reading experience and creating new kinds of reading subjects. All of these scenes depicted the cultural work of the newspaper:

FIGURE 1. "The Sunday World's Stage," *New York World*, August 28, 1897, 11.

the way into this new, modern cultural experience was not just metaphorically but also literally and materially *through* the hybrid media forms that comprised the Sunday edition.

In 1898 Richard Felton Outcault, already famous as creator of the Yellow Kid cartoons, first for Joseph Pulitzer's *New York World*, then for William Randolph Hearst's *New York Journal*, drew a full-page illustrated color cover for the "Sunday Magazine and Woman's World" section of the *World* (see plate 1).[8] In the illustration, a young woman in bloomers and high-top lace-up boots, hands clenched in action, hurtles through the opening of the newspaper page.[9] She is simultaneously an idealized reader and the object of the illustrated sensational stories in the magazine section. Such printed "supplements to *The World*" in Sunday papers extended the sphere of experience (in Marshall McLuhan's sense) as technologies of sensory mediation, making modern subjects of their readers and tying syndicated regional publishers into continental media networks.[10] Their aesthetic features employed a logic of popular art appreciation, gendering and racializing their reading publics even as they transformed them into seeing and listening publics for audiovisual media.

The modern newspaper's foundations were in hot type and rotary printing presses, technologies that exceeded the capacity of manual printing by hundreds of copies per minute, working faster than mere human senses could perceive. But the Sunday paper extended these technologies beyond type and image. On Sunday the paper strove to overcome the constraints of newsprint entirely. It embraced *circulation* as a modern ideal, transforming journalism from paper and ink into a dizzying array of new material formats: inserts and supplements of varying shapes and sizes but also moving picture newsreels and wireless radio broadcasts. The resulting intermedial forms, along with new kinds of relations to the paper they produced through such extended techniques of reading as seeing, listening, touching, cutting out, and putting together, suggest that the Sunday paper transformed people with a diverse range of interests into a carefully delineated mass media readership. Each member of the family had their own section, and each of them handled the paper according to a different set of techniques, unfolding and collecting and making it their own as it remade them into modern citizens. The forms and formats that made up the assemblage that became known as the Sunday paper is what this book explores.

Kevin Barnhurst and John Nerone have highlighted *The Form of News* as "the persistent visible structure of the newspaper . . . the way the medium imagines itself to be and to act."[11] Not simply the contextual framework for journalism, the *form* of news "proposes ideal relationships between the world and the public."[12] In the case of Sunday papers, a persistently distinct form emerged around 1888 in New York and soon after in other metropolitan cities in the United States. With a unique form separate from everyday newspapers, offering something other than "news," the Sunday paper structured a different relationship between its world and its public. From the society and fashion pages to sporting and business reports, theater reviews and listings, and feature stories about contemporary culture, Sunday supplements took advantage of a day of leisure to reflect upon pastimes and amusements. Syndicated serial fiction and relatively lavish illustration further sustained a unique character for leisure reading on the day of rest. Advance publicity and self-referential promotion added an element of planning and anticipation.

The Sunday Paper is an argument for shifting the topography of journalism and newspaper history and placing it more squarely within media history. The central premise of the book is that the Sunday paper animated modernity for its readership. Publishers and editors continually presented their Sunday editions as the center of all communications media, both in form and content, as the engine driving a transnational public focused on popular culture as much as civic culture. By and large, the mass reading public for Sunday papers was central to the development of a novel form of cultural citizenship—one that was identified not with a formal, democratic nation but rather with modern media in a more general and performative way, through acts of engagement with popular culture. Of course, this is also a uniquely American media history of how modernity became inseparable from its mediated environment *as it developed in America*. The Sunday paper's collection of popular practices allowed people to engage with the simultaneous problems of collectivity and incredible social difference through the accessibility, immediacy, and connectivity of secular weekend leisure. The overall effect is a "socially prismatic" cultural form that provides something for everybody under one banner; its paradoxically routine novelty maps the relation between any particular reader and the entire social field of modernity, always implicitly limited to America.[13] Framing the Sunday paper as a medium in its own right, rather than merely a branch of journalism, presents the considerable advantage of emphasizing not just the relation of the Sunday paper to other media but also the larger question of the centrality of *mediation* to American modernity.[14] As such, our focus throughout the book is on the changing form and formats that characterized the emergence of the Sunday newspaper.

If newspaper *form*, in the way Barnhurst and Nerone use the term, concerns the ideological relations proper to a given medium (that is, its imaginary—the way it would like to be seen and the way that we see it[15]), then media *format*, as Lisa Gitelman and Jonathan Sterne define it, describes both the physical arrangement of the medium (size, weight, folds of paper, and so on[16]) and the "social and material relations" imbricated within those arrangements as it is "worked on" and "works for" a range of subjects, technologies, and other social actors.[17] One of the reasons this distinction is important is because much of Sunday newspapers' contents was quite literally provided as supplements, as separate objects that transfigure the content of everyday newspapers and other media entirely to some novel format. Magazine, poster, and song sheet formats could be folded in as Sunday supplements, while, later, moving picture and wireless hybrid "newspaper" forms exceeded print altogether. Because of its deft use of a variety of novelty formats, the Sunday paper became a distinct media form, encouraging its readers to think of it and themselves and the larger culture in novel ways. The experience of reading the Sunday paper was thus sensational, sensual, and synaesthetic.[18]

The all-encompassing intermedial purview of the Sunday paper also aimed to transform a domestic day of leisure into a lifetime of immersion in public culture, domesticating practices of public and collective leisure reading.[19] As the Sunday newspaper became a forum for popular culture in the 1890s, it continually assumed new mediated forms and formats that effectively transformed the printed page into other media. The relationships between the various media forms in the Sunday paper's publicity network are sufficiently complex that no one specific form or title was the primary site for encountering the novelties of popular culture. In their steadfast commitment to showcasing new technologies and to finding new ways to mediate experience, Sunday newspapers sought to position themselves to their readers as a crucial nexus in this mediated network, even if they weren't the only cultural purveyors hard at work in this domain.[20]

For example, it is not difficult to imagine that a radio listener might feel that their enjoyment in hearing a program was enhanced by the advance information in the Sunday radio department of the newspaper to such an extent that their experience was incomplete without both used in tandem. Conversely, the newspaper reader interested in the contents of the radio page without being able to hear the nightly broadcast (the position we are in today, of course, as readers of yesterday's newspapers) might still feel knowledgeable about the events described, despite knowing their reading experience was incomplete without listening. The mass broadcast of the radio program was largely designed to be accompanied by the mass reading of the newspaper and supplemented in turn by the mass viewing of newsreels at a theater. In this example and dozens more, the following chapters provide a glimpse of a new mandate-in-formation for newspaper information; the Sunday newspaper aimed to take reading beyond the page and transform the knowledge people gleaned from reading into social and cultural activities, especially those centered on popular culture and consumption.

SUNDAY SUPPLEMENTS
AND THE FORMS OF MASS CIRCULATION

What was a Sunday paper? For Americans of a certain age, and a certain class, the Sunday paper provided a leisurely, reflective review of the past week's news or an insider's preview of cultural events. Others spent time with the crossword puzzle or sitting down with the book review or magazine section—each could easily be kept aside for the entire week. In fashion pages and wedding announcements, Sunday newspapers supported the vestiges of an old-fashioned notion of "society" through a display of modest publicity connected to social standing and rituals rather than celebrity. For younger Americans of the same era, the Sunday paper offered content of a different cultural register altogether: color comic strips; games and puzzles; coupons to clip, save, and mail to exchange for a "free" giveaway. The Sunday paper was so large and voluminous it needed to be organized: managed over time, across a family of people, ordered according to self-aware interests. Some aspects of the Sunday paper blurred together with other media. The serial story or feature article from a magazine arrived as a tabloid-size Sunday supplement that might be kept and collected, while the radio and television guide or movie directory might be set aside for easy reference for just the coming week. What all of these resonances convey is a connection between the leisurely pace of weekends and reading reflectively about all aspects of popular culture. The Sunday paper provided a panoramic view of mass society, connecting the home to the city, region, nation, and beyond as a lived community as well as a consumer market.[21] Ironically, one of the least important things the Sunday newspaper provided was news. That was the domain of the other days' papers; on Sunday, news took second billing and the supplement took center stage.

Journalism historians have paid a great deal of attention to the sensationalism of the "new journalism" and the yellow press of the late nineteenth century.[22] In the last years of the 1890s, strident progressive interventions in news events, antics of stunt reporters, wild illustrations, and color comic supplements of Sunday editions were central to the fierce competition between Joseph Pulitzer's *New York World* and William Randolph Hearst's *New York Journal.* Their fight over newspaper circulation ultimately defined American journalism negatively, as counterpoint to a more restrained objectivity that took hold in the subsequent century.[23] But the difference between the middle-of-the-road objectivity of the establishment press and the populist muckraking yellow papers was not whether they published on Sunday nor even whether they published heavily illustrated, color, and comic supplements in voluminous Sunday editions. On the contrary, Sunday papers with pictorial magazine supplements and color comic sections soon became the nationally syndicated standard for papers of all stripes.

Consider, for example, the *Philadelphia North American,* in 1901 the self-proclaimed "oldest daily newspaper in America."[24] Throughout the nineteenth century, it was a stodgy, serious, business-minded paper strictly issued from Monday to Saturday, paying minimal attention to items concerning the wider popular culture, with little to appeal specifically to female or juvenile readers. On September 29, 1901, after moving into a towering new office building and purchasing the latest printing presses and news circulation technologies, the *North American* issued its first regular Sunday edition (see fig. 2). The newspaper made great efforts to retain the distinction and esteem it had previously garnered by refraining from the yellow kind of Sunday publishing. Its advance promotion claimed it was to be "a sensible Sunday newspaper," with "no silly heroics—no exaggerated trifles—no exploitation of things shocking or offensive; nothing but sane and sensible and new features to entertain, inform, and instruct. That's the platform."[25] And yet the new *Sunday North American* included exactly the same elaborately illustrated, color, and comic supplements that had been vilified when associated with Hearst and Pulitzer just a few years earlier. In addition to thirty-two pages of news, the now-weekly *Sunday North American* launched with four separate, distinctly purposed color supplements: a four-page comic section, with color cartoons and comic strips drawn in-house; a twelve-page color magazine section full of features, profusely illustrated in color and halftoned pictures; an eight-page color women's supplement with helpful hints about fashion, home-keeping, and children's stories to read at bedtime; and a final page of music and lyrics, printed to cut and fold in order to create a tabloid-size keepsake of illustrated sheet music. By 1901 these features defined the form: "funny pages" of color comics, a women's section, a literary feature magazine, and a collectible song sheet, each often tabloid-size, sometimes bound, and sometimes printed on high-quality, low-acid paper stock instead of newsprint. In the previous decade, each was introduced separately

FIGURE 2. "The Sunday North American," *Philadelphia North American,* September 28, 1901, 5.

by other metropolitan Sunday papers, but by the twentieth century, the *North American* needed to include them all together to fit the form.

In addition to magazines, comics, and song sheets, Sunday papers also occasionally included a string of novelty print supplements: paper dolls, cutout toys, dress patterns, and, especially, lithographed posters. Some novelty supplements used "magic" invisible inks that needed to be either wet, heated, or viewed with special glasses. The tactility of separate sections; contests, coupons, and cutouts; the sensuality of color and fine paper inserts; the espousal of serial comic characters; an emphasis on aesthetic appreciation—all of these elements conspired to make the Sunday paper a key weapon in the battle for greater circulation. Newspaper publishers were no longer competing strictly among each other but also against magazines, moving pictures, and, eventually, radio. Alongside these new media, Sunday editions of newspapers introduced magazine supplements in the 1890s, collaborations with moving picture producers and wireless experimenters in the early 1900s, sponsored newsreels in the 1910s, and were among the earliest and most prominent owners of broadcast radio licenses in 1922. The *Detroit News* owned one of the first commercial radio stations but still continued to depict the Sunday edition as synonymous with harmonious domesticity. Ads promoting the Sunday paper in 1922 show two girls on the floor dissecting one section with scissors and paste, Junior reading his tabloid children's fiction section next to Father reading the full-sized news, while Mother looks through her magazine section at the dining room table: "You're going to have some fun with the new Sunday News magazine."[26] Rather than competition, a radio playing music would only further supplement the Sunday scene of the family at ease.

Economic and exploitative profiteering were always at play, of course, but the Sunday paper's engagement with the apparently endless proliferation of new media forms facilitated the sense that they were creating a semipermanent people's archive of popular culture. Newspapers offered affordable almanacs and encyclopedias, and they expedited compilations of ephemera into souvenir portfolios for repeated appreciation. Such publications worked against the notion that a daily newspaper was instantly replaceable with the next edition, even as the forms and features of the Sunday paper stoked the appetite for more additions to the collectors' pile. If there is nothing older than yesterday's daily news, it was also true that there was nothing as collectible as last week's Sunday supplement, which documented modernity's variety, provided it in a form worth savoring, and instilled a sense of its desirability. This logic could not, at that time, extend to ordinary people's experience of moving picture viewing and radio broadcast listening. However, many newspapers' involvement in the documentation, production, ownership, and transmission of movies and radio soon ensured that the Sunday paper was the locus for conceiving of other media as a supplement to its print sections.

The Sunday paper offered publishers a means for coordination and even overt collaboration with these other forms of media. Techniques of syndication developed in Sunday editions made the newspaper central to constructing continent-wide media networks and transformed the press from a social institution in the political public sphere into the material basis for habits and pastimes at the center of popular culture in a media society—at least on Sundays. Newspapers didn't abandon the weekday commitment to civic culture, but their Sunday editions mediated that role differently, as popular mass culture. At the turn of the century, the animated variety of early cinema was characterized as a "visual newspaper," recognizing the all-encompassing context of print at the time.[27] And yet the illustrated variety of the Sunday paper could just as convincingly be characterized as "material moving pictures," especially if we take comics, posters, and magazine supplements as central to its colorful, playful, and interactive features. Indeed, the entire first decade of film has been termed a "cinema of attractions" to emphasize an aesthetic and social grammar in a cultural series with novelty amusements of all sorts.[28]

The Sunday paper can likewise be productively taken as a "newspaper of attractions," supplementary to weekday news. An advance listing of *Sunday New York Herald* features was presented, in one case, as if promoting a theatrical spectacle: "Programme of the High Class Entertainment . . . Admission five cents."[29] Offering leisure as a weekend feature atop the routines of daily life, the Sunday edition addressed the mass public through a grammar of material forms and aesthetic conventions all of its own. Its very garishness, shifting material form, and extensive features on modern living and technological change were justified as a public service helping readers to become deeply connected to a broader technological and cultural imaginary. Under this rhetoric of popular education and public service—providing something for everyone—the standard five-cent price of the Sunday paper ostensibly brought its attractions within the budget of any working family. Its profitability lay partly in the collected nickels of mass circulation.[30] Profits also derived largely from advertising, from the lucrative accounts of department stores to the want ads in the classified section, each of which brought in a few pennies. Dating back to the popular penny press of the 1830s, the economics of American newspaper circulation laid the ground for the nickel-and-dime prices of subsequent mass-cultural pursuits—the Sunday newspaper's rivals as popular pastimes—from novels to confections to amusement parks, but especially the magazine and the nickelodeon picture show. The nickel cost of a metropolitan Sunday paper—more or less constant from the late 1880s until the First World War—aligned the seventh-day edition with an emerging secular commercial culture of mass amusements exploiting economies of scale to make fortunes penny by penny.

THE SUNDAY PAPER, POPULAR CULTURE, AND MODERN LIFE

Laying the cornerstone of the Pulitzer Building—future home of the *New York World*—in October 1889, New York governor David Bennett Hill offered a speech that framed American journalism in superlative terms.[31] Recalled for special occasions by the *World* for years to come, and reprinted nationally at the time, Hill proclaimed that "the modern newspaper is truly one of the wonders of the age. It reflects the varied life of humanity and is a faithful recorder of everyday history. . . . The newspaper of modern times is more and more usurping the place of the lecturer, the orator and the teacher."[32] This special role for the popular press as a public institution helped achieve social cohesion by providing a popular culture in late nineteenth-century American cities. Histories of American mass culture have long recognized the place of newspaper reading in providing a secular, all-encompassing pastime and guide to everyday life. Gunther Barth argued generally that newspapers and journalism in turn-of-the-twentieth-century America were the foundation for the establishment of a common culture for "city people."[33] In a similar vein, Julia Guarneri focused especially on the illustrated features of the Sunday paper to argue for American newspapers' central role in "making metropolitans."[34] Both echo a theme dating to the early Chicago-school sociology of Robert Park and Anselm Strauss, who proposed that newspapers provided a lexicon and grammar for navigating the divided space and cultural heterogeneity of the modern metropolis.[35]

Integration had its limits, and race was one of them, to be sure. Commercial culture maximized mass circulation by blurring class boundaries, but this semblance of mass inclusion was built upon overt racism—in newspapers as crassly as anywhere else. The commercialization of the entirety of America under the auspices of a mass society came at the cost of abandoning the promise of emancipation for all citizens, gained only recently at great cost with the Civil War. Despite the gains of formal freedoms, African Americans were subject to new forms of systemic segregation in urban spaces and labor practices and to minstrelsy in the content of entertainment. Jackson Lears, among others, has placed racial segregation and discrimination at the core of U.S. mass society at the turn of the twentieth century. "The common American idiom that united disparate ethnic groups in a mass culture," he wrote, "depended for its coherence on the exclusion of African Americans, or on their ritual humiliation if they appeared in public at all."[36] The constant stereotyping, Henry Louis Gates Jr. argues, anchored Jim Crow segregation in white supremacy because "the collective image of the black person in American popular culture functions like a visual mantra reinforcing the negativity of difference."[37]

Sunday color comics, in particular, constantly published what Jean Lee Cole notes as among the most "shocking examples of virulent racism and xenophobia."[38] Every Sunday morning, African Americans and other racialized groups were viciously lampooned and caricatured in the halftoned four-color comic pages.[39] Consider one example from 1897, practically at the origins of the comic supplement, when Hearst's Sunday "American Humorist" published a collage of racist stereotypes depicting "How They Publish the Comic Supplement in the Jungle."[40] Just months after the Supreme Court had entrenched racial segregation in its *Plessy v. Ferguson* decision, this comic strip was remarkably self-aware that many comics were offensive and reliant on hateful stereotypes. The cartoon Africans, with their stereotypical blackface figures, were depicted as happily in the midst of printing a yellow-colored "Jungle Supplement" of cave drawings, using an elephant in their pressroom, and delivering papers by riding a giraffe labeled "The Jungle Colored Supplement's Special Train." And yet the jungle comic "editor" had posted a warning to the illustrators: "Not responsible if the readers rise *en masse* and vent their wrath on the artists." As we shall see in chapter 4, self-aware promotion of the spectacle of Sunday circulation was common, which further demonstrates how this comic relief came at the expense of a racist exaggeration that contrasted with the objective and realistic journalistic norm.

To participate in American modernity, even on its margins, black readers and audiences were often relegated to "laughing at themselves," as Jacqueline Stewart discusses in relation to similar stereotypes circulating on screen in early movie theaters.[41] In discussions of the Sunday paper's sensational journalism, popular fiction, and, especially, comic strips and music supplements, such racism is always in the background. Although this book does not spotlight stereotyping and caricatures, they are ever present in the pages of Sunday supplements—not only racist depictions of African Americans but also of Indigenous American Indians, Asian Americans, and heavily accented immigrants of all types, people with physical and mental disabilities, and women of all types.[42] The weekly little victories of smart-alecky kids in the funny pages kept social and racial hierarchies firmly in place in its guise of providing a common culture of entertainment for everybody, a culture that relentlessly and ruthlessly reinforced racist, classist, anti-immigrant, sexist, and heteronormative differences.[43]

The paradox is partially explained in considering the unprecedented remarkable scale Sunday newspaper circulation attained and the complex industrial network required to achieve it, especially considered collectively. Neil Harris proposed a central role for pictorialism and printing technologies in distributing urban ideals on a mass scale, pinpointing developments such as halftone, color printing, illustration, and copyright in bridging the divide between late nineteenth-century urban cultural institutions and twentieth-century national mass media. Harris noted how gatekeeping urban institutions, such as libraries, museums, opera houses, and literary magazines, worked to facilitate social segmentation in the Progressive Era, abandoning an earlier, antebellum-era American urban culture that was genuinely and remarkably integrating, "characterized by an emphasis on popular distribution, an openness of management, and a willingness to accept commercial profit as a legitimate goal."[44] On the one hand, Harris was acutely concerned with the impact of pictorialism in print culture, but he demarcates the advent of Hollywood movies and network radio and television as the "challenge to the carefully gathered treasures of the older cultural institutions. The ability to popularize on a huge scale objects of art, images, and living styles helped thrust urban culture into a new stage."[45] But the same effect occurs earlier and just as completely in the mass circulation of the Sunday paper, exactly through its capacity to provide a serial pictorial form on a national scale, using techniques of cultural circulation and serialized subscriptions to syndicate popular culture for a mass public.

Using a similar periodization, William R. Taylor marks the 1920s as a transformative moment when New York commercial culture became a national popular culture with network radio and the Hollywood studio system.[46] Taylor's history of commercial mass entertainment as inherent in metropolitan urban life aims to glimpse "the complex ways in which urban audiences consumed these cultural forms."[47] Popular pastimes were more than commercial diversion; mass culture helped many individuals to navigate the modern city and its polyglot masses. Taylor calls this a "socially prismatic" capacity at a metropolitan scale—an amorphous ability to simultaneously address a diverse mass as individuals with culturally divergent interests.[48] But the Sunday paper's earlier variety of syndicated popular culture did this in a "geographically prismatic" way, merging all regions under one mass culture as well.[49] With the Sunday paper, the logics of urban modernity were broadly cast beyond the city limits to become metropolitan in scope, in aggregate extending to the entire continent as a network of metropolitan regions. Radio broadcast signals would make this self-evident, but rail-based "fast mail" delivery, telegraphed newswire services, and syndicated print features allowed newspaper circulation to achieve the same scale with nearly the same simultaneity, distributing millions of papers each Sunday morning.[50] The newspaper took on different media forms in its Sunday supplements, and it experimented with new economies of circulation, hoping that film and radio might finally unshackle the newspaper's circulation and cultural influence from the limitations of print distribution. Newspaper circulation was based in technologies linking the twin tasks of news gathering and distributing papers.[51] Week after week, paper after paper, the newspaper often paid particular attention to its own increasingly complex system for gathering news—from restless reporters on the ground to hot air balloons soaring high above—but it also continually explained to readers how their experience relied on the work of newsboys, newsdealers, fast trains, and automobile vans that promised to deliver papers efficiently and expeditiously.

In the decades surrounding the turn of the century, multiple papers competed for Sunday circulation in all of America's metropolitan cities. Up to four Sunday papers existed concurrently in Boston, San Francisco, and St. Louis; five in Chicago; and six in Philadelphia. For a five-year period from 1891 to 1896, eleven different Sunday papers vied for the attention of New Yorkers—not counting those printed on Saturday evenings or in languages other than English. Competing Sunday editions could differ in form and content starkly because of their supplements. Daily papers focused primarily on news and appeared more alike each other, day in, day out, encouraging routines of morning or evening reading. On Sundays, however, each paper offered an exclusive bonus in prizes, posters, comics, fiction, or pictorial supplements. Many households would purchase more than one Sunday paper—or opt in and out more impulsively—a phenomenon noted by William R. Scott in a textbook on "scientific" techniques for newspaper circulation. Prodding and responding to the whims of popular demand for novelties fell to circulation managers—a new profession spurred especially in the 1890s by the metropolitan Sunday paper. "Few circulation managers realize fully the extent to which readers are governed in the selection of a paper by special features," Scott explained. "No great American city's composite population could be served by one or a few papers. The conglomeration of nationalities and the gradations of mental tastes require variety of news treatment."[52]

Throughout the 1880s, price wars were still common and Sunday prices still varied between one and five cents, still proportionate more to the esteemed quality of literary content than simply reflecting the quantity of amusing features. In 1880 the higher five-cent price of a Sunday edition of the *New York Herald* or the *Chicago Tribune* reflected the exclusive copyrighted character of its reading matter. In the early 1880s the more popular illustrated style of a Sunday *New York World* cost only three or four cents, its lower price still part of its mass appeal. Around 1890 five cents became not only a remarkable uniform price for these and most other multi-sectioned metropolitan Sunday papers but also a remarkably stable price that lasted into wartime paper shortages of the late 1910s. A few exceptions stuck to lower prices as their competitive edge instead of adding more content for a nickel. In New York the Sunday edition of the *New York News* was only two cents, "emphatically the people's paper . . . rich in reading matter, instructive as well as entertaining."[53] Not to be confused with the later illustrated tabloid, the *Sunday News* of 1890 was only sixteen plain text pages, facing tough competition from illustrations, cartoons, and celebrity stunt journalists. Similarly, the three-cent *Sunday Star* kept its price when it transformed into the *Sunday Advertiser* in 1893 without adding significant new features. In Philadelphia the *Sunday Item* was a simple one-cent paper with double the circulation of any other Sunday edition in the city, and the two-cent price of the Sunday edition of the *Philadelphia Record* also resulted in a relatively large circulation for its relatively modest content.

Despite mass readerships, these exceptions did not withstand the new expectations of funny pages and magazine sections. Low prices kept circulations high for a few years, but these papers either shut down or joined the syndicated supplement bandwagon in the 1900s. Besides these exceptions, almost all of the key players on the Sunday supplement stage kept a constant price of five cents for three decades or more, right up until newsprint shortages spiked during World War I, resulting in a push up to seven or ten cents for most Sunday papers between 1918 and 1920. For more than two decades until then, in the crowded competitive field of big city Sunday papers, the battlefield was the terrain of circulation; with the price anchored to five cents, the weapons were special supplements and extra content. Flooding the streets with more copies or with extra content, offering a souvenir keepsake, or connected to a coupon-clipping contest, all of these served the goal of racking up higher circulation figures.

Fueling the fire of increased circulation, which far exceeded population growth in the late nineteenth century, was a confluence of factors linked to the development of the wood-pulp newsprint industry. In tandem with new modes of journalism, production capacity expanded greatly as printing press speeds accelerated.[54] The cost of newsprint fell dramatically, and perhaps no other single factor permitted the expanded circulation and size of the Sunday paper and its sensational features and illustrated form. Long ago Harold Innis provided a succinct synopsis of the effect of these economic and technological conditions, saying they "stimulated a search for inventions designed to increase circulation, particularly in metropolitan areas. . . . It made possible the modern newspaper."[55] Innis's focus was constraints on public opinion, and he concluded with a critique of the enhanced role of advertising, which lent newspapers bias toward mass-produced, mass-distributed goods, but mass-printed, mass-circulated newspapers preceded standardized brand consumption.

To read the newspaper circa 1900 was to witness its production and circulation even as the multi-sectioned Sunday paper produced and circulated modern experience. The Sunday paper's form and content was continually framed through technologies, starting with the fast printing press that produced it and extending to diverse modes of communication playing a part in either allowing its features to be more realistic in their sensationalism or facilitating the wide circulation of printed copies across vast regions of the continent. Altogether, the Sunday edition was positioned at the center of emerging networks of mediated communication. Sunday papers circulated well beyond the cities named in their mastheads.

Although weekday editions often had a metropolitan reach into commuter suburbs, many Sunday editions had regional readerships stretching hundreds of miles into neighboring cities. Markets for New York Sunday papers in the 1890s approached a national scale. A newspaper's popular illustrated Sunday items could thus be read widely and become nationally known, even in the years before syndication became standardized for illustrated magazine, comic, and puzzle features. Joseph Pulitzer's *New York Sunday World* printed a map of its continental circulation for a special edition in 1893 to honor the tenth anniversary of Pulitzer's ownership; there were subscribers in all states and territories, Canada, and Mexico (see fig. 3).[56] Circulation to the immediately adjacent states of New Jersey and Connecticut was

FIGURE 3. "*The New York World* Where It Circulates," *New York World*, May 7, 1893, 39.

predictably high, but there were more than four thousand subscribers in Pennsylvania and almost as many in Massachusetts; according to the *World*'s map, nearly one in six copies of the newspaper were delivered outside the state of New York.

The full-page illustration of the *World*'s circulation map was no mere table of figures; the map was embedded within a globe crowned by the signature domed Pulitzer Building as papers flew like leaflets dropped from a hot air balloon across the continent and around the globe. In light of newspapers' later forays into wireless and ownership of early radio stations, the *World*'s circulation in the 1890s could be taken as a form of broadcasting, or at least striving for broadcasting attributes of simultaneity and immediacy across its mass readership. The constraint of doing so in print was thus a limitation to achieving its own circulatory ambitions. The material conditions of circulating newsprint, in turn, were presented as a constant point of fascination in features revealing to readers the basis of their collective readership. In pursuit of increased circulation, all other media converged upon the newspaper; the address to a mass readership across cities and regions was presented as the quintessence of modern networked communication. No mere beneficiary of technology, other media supplemented weekend newspapers' aim of permeating across cultural domains. As Bruno Latour eloquently argues, any attempt to build a collective, including the writing of a history, must continually begin again, following different trails each time in order to try to include all of the things omitted in the last attempt.[57] The great cultural reach of newspapers prompted many publishers to actively facilitate and participate in a nascent national popular culture emerging through magazines, moving pictures, and radio, each improving upon the others' capacity for circulation of mediated experience in slightly distinct ways. This entire mediated environment eventually stretched out to embrace not just the technological mass communications of broadcasting but also the accessible luxury of department stores, the inclusive entertainment of movie palaces and amusement parks, and the mechanized mobilities of the bicycle and automobiles. Lavishly illustrated newspaper articles portrayed each new idea as a progressive step toward perfect communication, blurring the lines between the wireless spectrum and the contemporary interest in spiritualism; triumphalist narratives contended that soon people would be able to communicate even with the dead to create an infinitely expanding audience.[58]

IN THE PUBLIC INTEREST:
A NEWSPAPER FOR SUNDAY LEISURE

However self-evident it might seem, it's worth pointing out that the Sunday paper was published on Sunday. The arguments, intrigue, and social turmoil over the moral standing of the Sunday paper and its relation to Sabbatarianism have a long, colorful history.[59] Distinctions between reading, selling, and producing newspapers on Sunday were once matters of great seriousness. In the United States a "Sunday paper" was the seventh-day edition of a *daily* newspaper, usually a morning paper, that also printed Saturday and Monday editions.[60] This is distinct from popular and illustrated *weekly* papers and magazines that were intended for Sunday reading, many even including "Sunday" in their titles, yet sold and delivered on Saturdays. These weekly papers and magazines avoided the scrutiny and scorn of Sabbatarians because they weren't delivered or purchased on Sundays and did not inhibit church attendance. Throughout the nineteenth century, another handful of "Saturday" and "Sunday" weekly newspapers relied on home subscriptions and postal delivery; the *Saturday Globe* and the *Sunday Grit* indicated Utica, New York, and Williamsport, Pennsylvania, on their respective nameplates, but they were nationally distributed like magazines, heavily illustrated with feature stories and leisure reading. These were similar to a class of weekly papers in Britain early in the nineteenth century. Even today some prominent British Sunday papers appear only once a week, without daily editions that share the same masthead. In addition to weekly papers, most metropolitan newspapers in the U.S. published weekly "farm" editions, a condensed compilation of a week's worth of news, delivered by the postal service to distant subscribers across the continent. Such practices made the border between newspaper and magazine difficult to discern, requiring consideration of not just periodicity and price but also form, content, and the location of readerships.

Beginning in the 1880s, Sabbatarian sermonizers lay the blame for the Sunday news-reading habit on the "demoralization attending the Civil War," which led to "an almost insane desire to read the news."[61] Increased wartime demand for constantly updated reporting was seen to mask publishers' pursuit of profits and to allow for a greater degree of leniency in the laws prohibiting Sunday circulation and loosening cultural norms that discouraged secular leisure reading on the Sabbath. The causal link between the Civil War and Sunday papers has often been taken for granted, but Ronald Rodgers's detailed account of the Sabbatarian "struggle for the soul of journalism" more subtly concludes that "the Civil War and the accompanying recognition of the popular mass demand for news" laid a foundation for the Sunday paper to flourish.[62] To be sure, many papers did issue special Sunday editions as war extras in 1861 (see fig. 4). This fact was recalled in later decades when permanent seventh-day editions proliferated.[63] The common notion that Sunday editions arose in response to public demand for news during the Civil War masks the complex and gradual emergence of the editorial distinctiveness of the Sunday edition and its equally complex and gradual assumption of a position of cultural prominence. The more important shift began in the 1870s and reached fruition in the late 1880s.

Starting the first Sunday issue in Philadelphia in 1878, the *Times* simply pointed to the existing norm in other major cities: "In New York, Boston, Cincinnati,

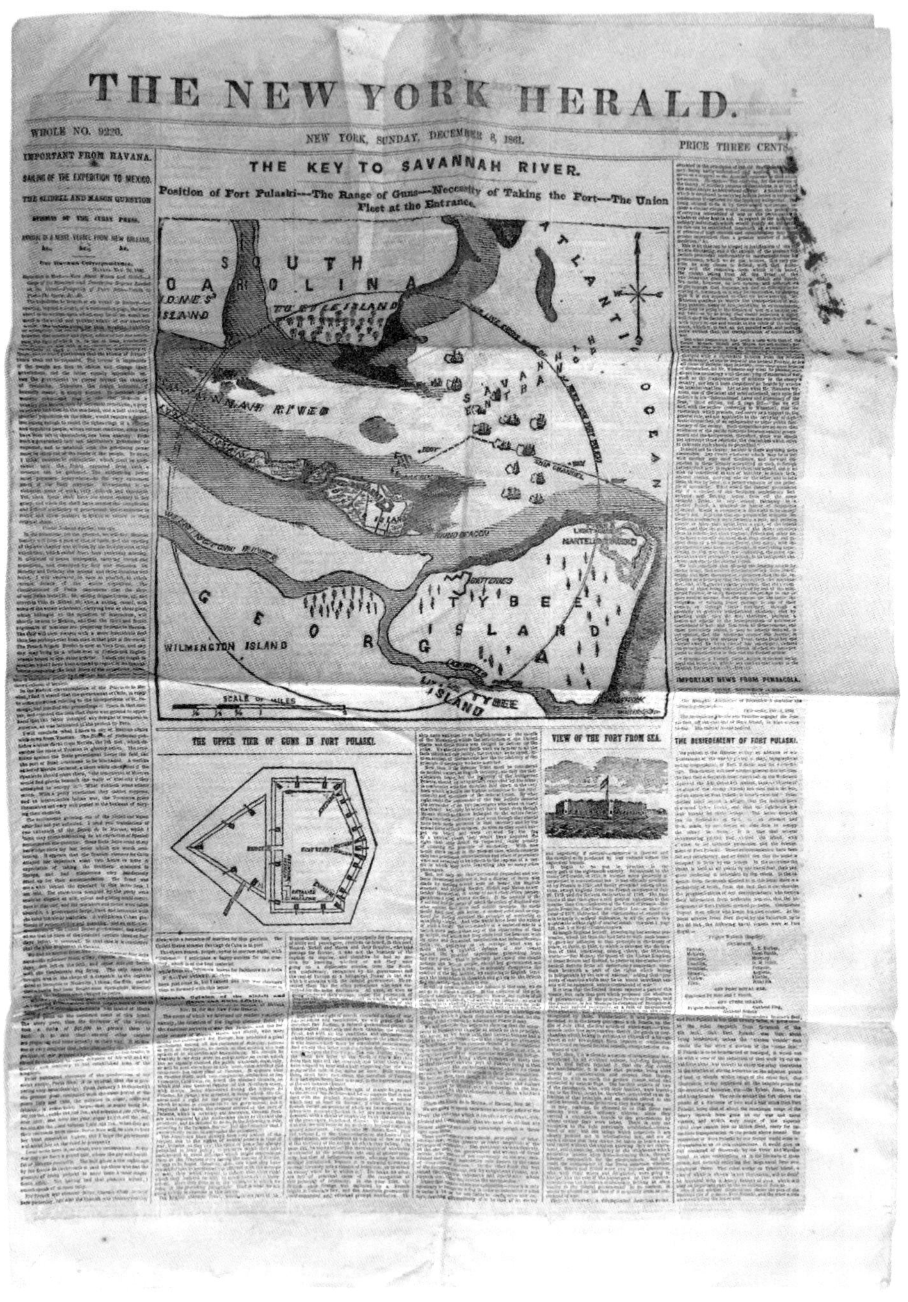

FIGURE 4. An example of illustrated Sunday news coverage during the Civil War. *New York Herald*, December 8, 1861, 1. (Authors' collection.)

Chicago, St. Louis, San Francisco, Louisville and New Orleans, the Sunday editions of the leading daily journals are their ablest, most entertaining and most instructive publications . . . a notable evidence of the progress and elevation of American journalism."[64] New York's holdout was the *Tribune,* not beginning a Sunday issue until 1879, several years after the death of its founder, Horace Greeley. The change arose from undeniable public interest: "Our patrons have long urged their right to get from us what we have to sell, at the time when they want to buy."[65] Time and again, the particularly modern argument of public service provided a generic justification for issuing a seventh daily edition. After months of debates in its letters to the editor, the *Chicago Inter-Ocean,* for example, explained its new Sunday edition in 1883 as a "response to demands of a large proportion of patrons."[66] The new Sunday edition of the *Philadelphia Inquirer* in 1889 was "meeting the demands of progressive journalism," explaining how "Sunday editions of reputable, clean and honest newspapers have become a necessity."[67] Despite Sabbatarian concerns, the argument was repeated that the public simply demanded a newspaper every day of the week. A seventh-day edition was a marker of modernity, indicating that a newspaper embraced the ideals of progress. An important survey of the American press in 1880 for the U.S. Census Office noted that "the habit of printing a Sunday edition in connection with the six issues of the week is of comparatively recent date, and is rapidly increasing in the principal cities."[68] This trend recognized how "the American people are a nation of newspaper readers, and desire their regular pabulum from the press without reference to other interruptions in their habits of life."[69] In short, Sunday papers proliferated because there was a market for it.

In the 1870s those papers that had Sunday editions most often simply published seventh-day issues with little to distinguish them from weekday papers, although they were "generally made up of a lighter character of reading matter . . . especially prepared for acceptable reading in the family circle."[70] Even when a Sunday edition included an additional "supplement" sheet, it was not necessarily distinct in form or content from the rest of the paper. Similarly, material differences between Sunday and weekday editions cannot be simply linked to genre; serialized novels, editorial cartoons, and illustrations all predate the modern form of the Sunday paper and are hardly restricted to special sections in weekend editions. Nonetheless, the association of Sunday supplements with illustrated features, cartooning, and serial fiction became routine in the late 1880s, joined by specialized columns and pages providing reading material for women and for children, sometimes even addressed explicitly to "women and children." The introduction of the illustrated banner for such material was a significant formal development in the late 1880s. On the one hand, banners provided the continuity of a branded visual marker for periodical content and serial features that could be expected each Sunday. Banners visually and aesthetically demarcated leisure sections from serious news. Of more importance, banners delimited columns or pages address-ing the particular interests of specialized readers: household or fashion columns for the female reader; puzzle and story pages for juvenile readers; fun or humor for the reader seeking leisure; and "magazine" features for those seeking fiction or investigative human interest. Columns bannered with decorative illustrations denoting their intended readership grew into pages, and then sections, and in some cases were eventually bound and printed in color or on fine paper to make separate magazines. Why would newspapers turn to the magazine form to mark their modernity? Fending off competition from magazines is a starting point but hardly the end of the matter. We argue that the appearance of magazine formats in newspapers transformed the Sunday paper into a prototypical case of media convergence, in Henry Jenkins's sense.[71] The anachronisms inherent in such an argument constitute the contours of our history of the multi-sectioned Sunday paper. Overall, we propose that the Sunday paper must be understood as an inter-medial institution, a popular pastime for the masses that continually gestured to other media to stretch the limits of material circulation of print copies, thereby laying a foundation for America's new mass media society.

A WORD ABOUT METHOD

Our methodological scope was not prescribed selectively in advance, nor did we formally conduct a comprehensive review. There are interesting examples of newspaper supplements in the archives—others not even archived—that pre-date or complement those we have gathered. Some may even stand as counter-examples. Nonetheless, our survey offers a robust characterization of the field of Sunday newspaper publishing throughout the United States at the turn of the twentieth century.

Our methodology was aided by the great expense of producing multi-sectioned newspapers at the time, especially those that were illustrated and in color, for this almost entirely restricted the innovation and implementation of Sunday supple-ments to mass-circulation newspapers in just a handful of metropolitan cities until standardized forms later emerged at lower costs. Overall, the story traces the origins of continent-wide syndication following metropolitan innovation—but not just in New York. Indeed, we offer a corrective to the many histories of yellow journalism that rely only on the famous news publishers of Park Row. Although New York publishers had the deepest pockets and the largest circulations, inno-vations in Sunday supplements just as often emerged elsewhere, although not just anywhere. All of our earliest examples of illustrated women's and children's pages, color printing, tabloid inserts, and comic illustration emerge in a very small number of newspapers in the biggest cities on the continent: New York but also Philadelphia, Boston, Chicago, St. Louis, and San Francisco. We verified that newspapers in the next tier of large cities, less metropolitan in influence, did not invent or introduce the form and features of the Sunday paper. Although regional papers may have struck important chords of modern rhetoric in their prose and printed text, we found few examples of enduring, inventive forms or formats for supplements outside the major metropolises.[72]

In Detroit, Pittsburgh, Atlanta, Denver, Seattle, and cities of similar population, Sunday newspapers followed the norms created first in the six major metropolitan centers. With just a few exceptions, and often short-lived, Sunday papers in smaller cities did not contain weekly illustrated, color, or comic supplements until costs declined with the economies of scale afforded by syndication in the twentieth century. No project could aspire to survey all existing newspapers in all of their content and features. We inspected many dozens of newspapers to confirm the presence and absence of enduring design aspects and then searched methodically to trace the introduction of each trait, paying special attention to the reflexive publicity, self-serving justification, and instructions to readers accompanying the introduction of novelties.

In the years since we began this research in 2007, a plethora of digitized newspapers have become searchable and browsable online. These were rarely useful in finding innovative design aspects at the early end of our period in the 1880s, but they were incredibly helpful in assessing the extent of syndicated content and standardization in the later years under consideration in the 1910s. Browsing layouts in digital newspaper databases ironically foregrounded the form of the historical printed page in ways taken for granted when hoisting an unruly sheet of flimsy, inky newsprint was a daily habit of mass readerships.[73] In considering *The Nineteenth-Century Press in the Digital Age*, James Mussell argues that "we have always been users" as much as readers of newspapers, although that insight comes only with the anachronism of a digital file abstracting the form from its material basis.[74]

The Sunday Paper begins and ends with the paper itself—what it contained, the claims made on its pages, what it represented, and how it circulated. The papers themselves, their pieces and supplements, often become the subjects of our sentences in a way more traditional historians are careful to avoid. Our approach is strongly informed by Lisa Gitelman's argument, after Rick Altman, that "media represent and delimit representing."[75] For us, it follows that conducting media history is distinct from approaches to other histories because media are "socially realized structures of communication, where structures include both technological forms and their associated protocols."[76] Also, the technology of the Sunday paper form is inextricable from the reading protocols needed to decipher its meaning. To garner a robust understanding of the cultures surrounding the newspaper and its reading publics thus demands a unique methodological mind-set.

Accordingly, our study of the Sunday paper questions how the media form is constituted within certain historical conditions,[77] defining its cultural influence through its articulations to other media forms within circulatory networks. Insights from theories of articulation and actor-networks are helpful for building ways to conceptualize links and junctures where disparate and discrete entities connect. These networks bind objects, people, and processes into enduring connections and relations of power, which in turn become culturally meaningful, accepted ways of seeing the world.

Series of articulations produce networks through the deployment of power, and that power is not distributed equally throughout them. To conceptualize through articulation is to investigate the conditions under which relations come to be fixed as though inevitable, how they come to be a "structure in dominance."[78] In other words, "to understand how networks privilege some possibilities and preclude others, we have to foreground the work of power in forging and breaking the connections that constitute [them]."[79] In defining actor-network theory, Bruno Latour is less concerned with ideology but similarly understands the social to be a "circulating entity."[80] By pointing to the relations between artifacts, discourses, people, and institutions rather than the artifacts themselves, both theories are nondeterministic and invested in mapping the social field, which is seen as a landscape of articulated connections or networks between cultural objects, such as specific technologies and aesthetic forms, and the ideologies and creativity of cultural actors, such as publishers and journalists.

In practical terms, this allows us to bracket the largely unknowable question of actually experienced Sunday newspaper reading, and we seldom speculate about the intentions or motivations of editors, journalists, newsboys, or readers. We do speculate conceptually about the subjectivity subscribed to in the mass reading of Sunday papers, but without making an empirical claim about any specific reader's individual experience. Instead, the social position of Sunday news reading is a conceptual generalization about the multiplied pleasures of common pursuits in a mass society, the cumulative and social effects of ephemeral, passing amusement obtained at a minimal expense of a few pennies and requiring minimal attention of at most a few hours. Of course, a parallel subjectivity is found in the economic logic of the mass market more generally, with profits gained by exploiting maximal numbers of people each at a minimal cost. The exploitation is evident only at a social scale, but the subjectivity of Sunday paper subscriptions was an investment in a periodical that looked ahead to a future string of interested engagements with the paper, a secular Sabbath of faithful belief in public interest.

WHAT'S IN *THE SUNDAY PAPER?*

The Sunday paper came in parts *and* it came apart, but how did the Sunday paper come to be more than the sum of these parts? Consider the latest craze in Sunday supplements from 1922: Invisible Color Books from World Color Printing

Company, a St. Louis company that had been syndicating preprinted comic supplements for more than two decades already. Among the early adopters of the 1922 novelty was the *Boston Globe*, which promoted the new feature with a series of comics called "Scenes from a New England Home on a Sunday Morning." The first shows a tantrum under way as Mother asks, "What's all this racket about?" A little boy cries, "Daddy's coloring my *picher* book," and, sure enough, Father is on the floor surrounded by the pages of the paper, coloring the magic pictures himself.[81] The next day's comic promotional sketch shows a more pleasant scene at home on Sunday, with Mother this time curious why all six kids are so well-behaved (see fig. 5). Each is at work coloring—one at a desk, one on a chair, one at the table, and another with the pages strewn across the floor. The message is succinct: "Don't forget the kids—They're all asking for the Invisible Color Book."[82] The following week, a third comic scene depicts a lineup of hundreds of Boston parents outside a newsstand: "If I don't get a *Globe*—they won't let me in th' house," cries one man near the front of the line.[83] In this first year of commercial radio in 1922, Sunday papers like the *Globe* explicitly promoted their value as fun and leisure for the whole family—not just solitary readers, but the kids playing and making their toys from supplements as Mother and Father read their respective sections. In these cartoon scenes of Sunday mornings with the *Globe*, we see the problems

FIGURE 5. "Scenes from a New England Home on a Sunday Morning," *Boston Globe*, April 8, 1922, 10.

that provide our structure in the chapters that follow: how *subscription* defined the common interest of a mass public; how *circulation* was both facilitated and constrained by print; and how *syndication* permitted the commercial character of newspapers to simultaneously extend across an entire continent.

Part I of *The Sunday Paper* begins with two chapters that consider how the Sunday paper provided a uniquely reorganized form of news reading that went beyond news, and in doing so, we explore the concept of *subscription* in terms of committed readership. To subscribe to the paper guaranteed that it would be reserved at the nearest newsstand or delivered to the doorstep by newsboy, but a subscription also implied an adherence to the culture ascribed by the paper and thus entailed a way of life. Even before Sunday supplements brought additional features, newspapers strengthened their relationship with readers through fund-raising campaigns, where readers "subscribed" to worthy charitable or public campaigns by donating pennies and nickels in return for having their name published in the paper. Subscriptions donating to these special funds conflated subscriptions to the paper with commitments to the public interest. Later the charitable causes were eliminated, replaced with popularity votes and guessing contests, with prizes given to readers who came closest to predicting news outcomes such as election results or how long it would take *New York World* correspondent Nellie Bly to travel around the globe. We argue that such contests rewarded expert newspaper reading, albeit expertise reduced to a single dimension, such as estimating the number of words in a thirty-two-page *San Francisco Examiner* in 1896. Engagement with the form of the newspaper, becoming an expert in its textual composition and material shape, emphasized not just the heft of Sunday papers as they grew in size but also the new skills involved in navigating their pages. Clipping and collecting coupons rewarded readers by transforming a subscription to gain possession of the newspaper into some more durable prize.

In chapter 2 we explore how the logic of prizes and coupons was extended to collectible keepsakes. Some of the earliest Sunday supplements were "Art Supplement" posters inserted into the paper or given with its purchase, intended to be kept, framed, mounted, or compiled in souvenir portfolios. The popular arts—in serial form—were a constant presence in the Sunday edition. From serial fiction to columnists and cartoonists, to music supplements, rotogravure pictorial sections, and serial films, ongoing regular features reinforced the predictable but desirable pleasures that came from planning to receive the paper over many months, week in, week out. They placed the Sunday paper near the heart of an emerging promotional culture that offered increasingly extravagant prizes in exchange for committing to a subscription to the paper and, in extreme cases, for being the reader who coaxed the most neighbors to take out new subscriptions.

We then turn, in the two chapters of part II, to investigating the Sunday paper's *circulation* of modernity as a mediated audiovisual environment, as an extension of reading. Here we show how the printed form of the Sunday paper was constantly translated into visual and audiovisual experiences and forms and how the printing and circulation of the Sunday paper was transformed into a spectacle in itself. If the printing and delivery of the paper was animated into spectacles, Sunday news of all stripes embraced illustration and intermedial forms of reporting in pursuit of "perfect communication," by which we mean the constant espousal of a transparent and seamless mediated environment in which experience itself is transmitted without interference. Following John Durham Peters's review of the concept, we argue in chapter 3 that the incorporation of supplementary media forms into the voracious compendium of the Sunday paper was intended to connect each reader unproblematically to the totalizing communication network of all reader-citizens.[84] Such faith in the eventual eclipse of the need for media ironically foregrounded media technologies of the moment. We trace a continual emphasis on efforts to animate the news through illustrating and engaging with the static constraint of print on the page. This chapter also demonstrates the cross-promotional rationale of newspapers' forays into the work of moving picture newsreels and radio news broadcasting as idealistic endeavors approximating the totalizing mediation of modernity.

In chapter 4 we begin on the floor of the newspaper printing room, with its massive multi-cylinder presses. The printing floor was routinely depicted as a nexus of wonders among the animated, pictorial, and instantaneous transmission of information and story in newspapers and across other media in turn. Next comes the story of the immense efforts and monopolistic companies that controlled how the paper got delivered. Coordinated timetables in transportation networks worked through the night on Saturday to ensure that the multi-sectioned variety of the seventh-day edition arrived on the breakfast table Sunday morning, not just in the city but across the entire metropolitan region and beyond.

Finally, in the two chapters of part III, we turn to newspapers as profit-seeking corporations intent on the pursuit of mass popularity through Sunday supplementary features. This is not, however, a business history. Beyond the formal terms of corporate cooperation and consolidation, we organize chapter 5 around conceptualizing *syndication* beyond its surface connotations of commercial distribution. The chapter discusses the variety of ways the newspaper represented itself as a corporeal, personified entity, realized through its depictions of itself as comic characters and circulation figures—sensorial, tactile, textured, and in vivid color. Comic mascots transformed satirical cartooning into recurring characters and foreshadowed the syndicated commercialization of copyrighted features, including the characters in serial comic strips.

In chapter 6, we finally turn to the Sunday funnies as syndicated supplements whose comics entered national popular culture. Syndication provided an efficient exploitation of the mass market principle of marginal returns, allowing Sunday supplements to blanket the continent. They brought color printing and magazine inserts within the economic reach of smaller cities' weekend editions, although obviously also lining the deep pockets of metropolitan press magnates. The ideal of a networked syndicate of standardized popular content was already set by the time newspapers collaborated with the moving picture industry to create regional newsreels. As we also explore in chapter 6, newspaper-owned radio stations in the 1920s helped extend the broadcasting networks of the Radio Corporation of America to a national scale.

We conclude by briefly looking at the changing forms of newspapers today, where new intermedial forms of reader engagement have transformed print editions into online reading. No longer supplementing just one issue weekly for leisurely weekends, now every story is accompanied by continually updated streams of podcasts, video, and commentary while readers pay premium subscriptions for full access. The news remains inextricable from its media of circulation; even as the newspaper becomes digital, it remains intermedial, relying on older forms of media—like a return to print or physical meetings in cultural milieux around the city—to create social engagement.

Historically, Sunday newspapers were inextricable from the railways and telegraphs that comprised continental communications networks. In addition to the routines of urban delivery at newsstands and by newsboys, Sunday papers were uniquely distributed well beyond the urban marketplace of their department store advertisers. They were as likely to circulate in an interregional railway delivery network in a similar manner as subscribed magazines, becoming part of the transnational consumption of branded manufactured products. More importantly, the Sunday newspaper played a central role in the development of the public understanding of and esteem for technological progress. The Sunday paper's circulation did more than employ existing communicative infrastructure to engage with emerging markets; it constantly experimented with form in an attempt to find new ways that it might be delivered beyond the limited range dictated by its paper-and-ink materiality. This explains newspaper publishers' keen interest in perfecting simulations, instantaneity, and connectivity through photographic, phonographic, cinematographic, and wireless audio and televisual technologies. Newspapers continually profiled these techniques with utopian zeal long before such technologies were commercialized in entertainment industries and mass media. The crafty combination of information, entertainment, and promotion extended and transfigured the polyglot address of the multi-sectioned Sunday newspaper. In other words, the interrelationship of modern mass media was not merely a matter of convergence or mutual promotion but the very essence animating American modernity.

PART I

SUBSCRIPTION

Subscriptions were key to the success of the Sunday paper not only because they boosted the economic viability of the newspaper but also because they helped to produce expert reading subjects. The act of subscribing to the Sunday newspaper offered readers new opportunities for becoming citizens of modernity.

What did it mean to subscribe to a newspaper? The call from the paper to "subscribe" involved a series of actions beyond the literal act of requesting that it be delivered to readers: clipping, guessing, and collecting were some of the acts that interpellated readers into the rhythms and mediations of a modern world. If we think of the Sunday paper as a reading technology, how do we extend that logic to its puzzles, paper toys, and lithographed posters? Their status as *supplements* is key—discrete material objects inserted within the Sunday paper yet also part of it, perhaps even constitutive of it. But how do such objects function?

The various elements that came to supplement the Sunday paper and the newspaper proper transformed newspaper reading from an encounter with an apparently ephemeral object of passing leisure into a process of cultural import, not incidental to the ideals of journalism and the democratic public sphere but supplementary to them. As Jacques Derrida has argued (and as we explore further in chapter 1), the supplement is never simply an extra object that is merely added to the object proper. The technique of "reading" the Sunday paper was not only about looking at text; it involved all manner of operations. To read was to clip, fold, admire, and preserve—and, later, to listen or view (as we explore in subsequent chapters). From guessing contests to art supplements, magazine supplements, and folio novels, to later developments like newsreels and radio programs, these material and media objects all supplemented the Sunday paper. These objects not only transformed the experience of reading; they also changed the character of the paper into something no longer recognizable as a newspaper, as the U.S. Postal Commission found.

As discussed in the following two chapters, several theoretical concepts drawn from a range of traditions help us to make sense of what newspapers were doing and why it was important for contemporary society. For example, Bruno Latour's actor-network theory is helpful in describing how material objects can function as social actors in order to signify how social effect is applied "indifferently to both humans and non-humans."[1] Objects, like texts and speech, contain scripts for their use that prescribe repertoires of actions for people who interact with them and other objects related to them: "Materiality and sociality produce themselves together."[2] This theoretical foundation helps us to see how the newspaper functioned as a reading technology, connected to and influenced by other technologies in a manner that produced a changing cultural and social milieu.

As we will see in chapter 2, the supplement consisted of a range of paper objects and print formats inserted within the newspaper. We review how lithographed art supplements became more elaborate as they became common across the continent, taken up by small and regional city newspapers as a particularly effective way to entice female readers and influence their decision about which paper to receive by home delivery. In subsequent variations, women readers reached a true appreciation of the Sunday paper's value through operations like collecting an entire series of souvenir posters, playing sheet music on the household piano, constructing paper dolls from fashion plates, and creating dresses from the accompanying patterns.

Paper toys and games extended the repertoire of available operations to children as well. Rather than insert expensive posters, some newspapers simply printed their pages to create folded tabloid or quarto-size supplements, converting a page of the newspaper into sheet music, transforming a children's page into a junior journal, or formatting pages of fiction into a sixteen- or thirty-two-page novel in newsprint. Within these special children's sections, contests were mobilized in the name of art and literary education, and prizes were given for solutions to puzzles or for coloring within the lines, even as special inks introduced the novelty of "magic" hidden pictures. Children learned, too, that the paper was incomplete without them doing their part: to color it, solve it, cut it, and rearrange its pieces or to bring into sight pictures printed with special "magic" ink by operations like heating, rubbing, or wetting the page.

In the chapters that follow, we argue that the Sunday paper's supplements, in all of their varieties, were central to the transition from a black-and-white seventh-day edition in the mid-1880s to a read-all-over conduit of popular culture and mass society by the late 1890s. We offer a historical account of the Sunday supplement that also grapples with the gradual institution of color, illustration, humor, and distraction, which soon became routine with the comic supplement, rotogravure section, and the women's magazine. We reserve consideration of these standardized Sunday supplements for the final chapters on syndication, analyzed there in light of its character as the cornerstone of a continent-wide distribution of popular cultural forms. Before and alongside the emergence of those distinct sections came a flurry of more ephemeral and fleeting inserts and supplements—poster and paper-toy giveaways, puzzles, and prize contests of all sorts. Initially appended to the Sunday paper as extratextual practices, these temporary tactile supplements preceded changes in the material composition of the paper itself by first changing the relation between reading and reader. These material components of the Sunday paper required the development of reading techniques that produced new kinds of reading subjects, transforming the commitment of a subscription into the social relations of mass leisure. Sunday supplements linked self-interest to public interest by appending the sustained engagement of expert reading for entertainment value to the weekday paper's practical gleaning of information. In the first chapter, we develop further this idea of reading with the help of Michel Foucault's insights about techniques of the self.

The logic of leisure in newspaper supplements carries through the entire process of *subscribing* to the paper—often literally but always also subscribing to its inscribed repertoire, its prescribed subjectivity. As Latour observes of actors in networks, the proclivity for signing-up and opting-in defines *subscription* as the way agents "tend to . . . accept or happily acquiesce to their lot."[3] Our conceptual framework for subscription similarly takes the supplement as an inscribed subjectivity, and positions the Sunday paper as a technology for accepting and happily reading oneself into the collective public of mass culture at the turn of the twentieth century.

1

SUBSCRIBING TO THE SUNDAY NEWSPAPER

Immediately following the election of William McKinley as president of the United States in November 1896, Joseph Pulitzer's *St. Louis Post-Dispatch* announced a contest in its Sunday "magazine" section.[1] A hundred-dollar prize was offered to the first reader to submit a correct guess of all of McKinley's cabinet selections. Entries were accepted immediately, but the winner, of course, could not be known until the inauguration in March—four months away. In the meantime, the Sunday *Post-Dispatch* would each week feature "a cabinet possibility" and list the latest speculations of Washington gossip.[2]

The contest employed a material connection between the reader and the newspaper to institutionalize reading, rather overtly creating a weekly routine reason to subscribe to the Sunday edition for the next four months. For the contest to be any better than a lottery, readers would have had to weigh the news each Sunday and assess their own judgment in relation to an imagined mass public of other readers, each of them also balancing the pursuit of knowledge in the public interest but spiced with a dash of self-interest. All in good fun with a clear element of dumb luck, the contest was nonetheless a measure of a newspaper reader's expertise in reading the newspaper on a continual periodic basis, each Sunday, for the span of the contest.

This particular guessing contest was tied closely to news, as the "cabinet possibilities" animated presidential politics and transformed weekly news from Washington into a game. The form of the contest's rules, tactics, and strategies of even possibly winning the game were similar to dozens of other contests in metropolitan Sunday papers at the time. Some involved guessing, others skill;

many required following the news, others solving a puzzle; most required cutting out coupons printed only in the Sunday paper, thus ensuring long-term interest in the papers and boosted circulation. To win, news readers needed to commit themselves to a sustained, serial, and invested reading of the Sunday paper—a skilled extension of its leisure features and quality pastime on the day of rest.

In this chapter we first discuss the idea of subscription as the foundation of our conception of Sunday newspaper supplements producing a modern social subjectivity. We then trace the genealogy of Sunday supplements to new forms of New York journalism in the 1880s that embraced public fund-raising campaigns in which readers became "subscribers" to a fund supporting some public good. A small inflection twisted those charitable fund-raising efforts toward political or popular appeals, contributing votes instead of money—to reward the best policeman or streetcar driver. Then came contests for the smartest schoolgirl or the cutest baby, which soon devolved into elaborate guessing contests that came under scrutiny of laws banning lotteries in mailed publications. Other enticements to subscribe included entire series of keepsakes and premium giveaways, inserted in the Sunday paper or wrapped around it as a souvenir cover. Ultimately, all of the supplements to the newspaper considered in this chapter and the next encouraged readers to leave or collect material traces of their reading, evidence of their effort and commitment to participating in modernity's mass society as curated by the mass circulation of the Sunday paper. We begin by looking at an exemplary case of how that process works: newspaper contests.

Contests were emblematic of recent changes in the form, content, and conditions of reading newspapers in the mid-1890s—changes that became codified as "the Sunday paper" by the turn of the twentieth century. Prize contests were a cornerstone of Sunday editions from the late 1880s and lasted for a century. But the possibilities for interacting with the Sunday edition did not end with contests. All of the operations that participating in a newspaper's prize contest required—collecting, cutting, and counting—contributed to the production of an attentive expert reader familiar with a range of ways of engaging with the news, as well as the Sunday paper itself as a material object that prompted a range of potential interactions. Such interactions were also elicited by a panoply of forms of newspaper supplements whose inclusion in the Sunday edition transfigured both the material nature of the paper and what it meant to be a newspaper reader.

THE LOGIC OF THE NEWSPAPER SUPPLEMENT

Far from being extraneous to the Sunday paper, the ephemeral supplement defines it as a form of leisure built upon the slow-paced pleasures of interacting with light news, fiction, and illustrated features. Beyond reading for leisure, the appeal of supplements involved manipulating the material page itself: to color, cut, or fold in order to solve a puzzle, collect a coupon, or create a paper toy. As Laurel Brake has carefully considered for British periodicals, the "lost and found ... elusive aspect" of paratextual supplements is often reflexively promoted as a "generous" feature provided above and beyond the routine form of a publication.[3] To understand this surplus of usage and appreciation, we propose that the Sunday supplement is best understood through Jacques Derrida's concept of supplementarity.[4]

The contradictory character of the supplement's extraneous yet definitive relation to the paper—and the Sunday paper's superfluous yet definitive relation to daily newspapers—is akin to Derrida's observation that as an addition to speaking, writing both completes and complicates speech. The supplement adds to an original that once seemed complete but is now revealed as partial; it is an accessory that reinforces the realization of an initial incompleteness.[5] And yet it is always merely "compensatory and vicarious. . . . As substitute . . . its place is assigned in the structure by the mark of an emptiness."[6] That is, there is no end to supplementarity; other supplements can be substituted for ones that are already in place, or added onto them in endless chains, without ever "completing" the object to which they are attached. Moreover, the presence of supplements often reveals that the supposed original is, in and of itself, always a supplement to something else.

In considering—indeed defining—the Sunday paper as primarily providing leisure, we are similarly esteeming its supplements with a place of privilege in an imaginary *completion* of the daily newspaper, in making up for its incomplete provision of leisure. On Sunday, the serious journalism of the weekday edition is shown as lacking a sense of fun and games. The same relation defines the weekend as a supplement to the workaday routines of laborious weekdays. The Sunday supplement reinforces the incompleteness of the daily newspaper, opening space for new and other forms of supplements, including from other media. This conceptual framework explains the supplement in relation to the rest of the paper, and the Sunday paper to the news in general, and describes the role that the newspaper supplement played in the production of specific kinds of reading subjects.

Producing Expert Sunday Readers

Modern subjectivity allows individuals to imagine governed relations to entire populations of others as a matter of personal responsibility. Michel Foucault defines "techniques of the self" as procedures suggested or prescribed to individuals to determine their identity, maintain it, or transform it for certain ends through relations of self-mastery and self-knowledge.[7] Foucault cites in passing the Greek concept of *otium* (leisure) as time given over to reflection, free time one spends attending to oneself.[8] The pleasures of mass culture in modernity are an extension of this classical privilege of having time and means to attend to oneself, now accessible to the entire population through mass leisure as time away from serving others, time "for what we will."[9]

In considering the various supplements of the Sunday paper as techniques of the self, we are proposing that leisure reading provides a passing but periodic attention to ephemeral pastimes, largely divorced from the work of productive labor and its manipulation of things, the pursuit of learning and its manipulation of symbolic meaning, and the workings of power and its manipulation of others. Trivial as supplements may seem, the logic of supplementarity suggests that regular participation in those pastimes transformed what it meant to be a newspaper reader. The Sunday paper's supplements may have only minimal weight in the weekday concerns of work, economics, and politics, but they potentially cast long shadows over readers' sense of satisfaction and social embodiment. Technologies of Sunday reading emerge within a complex domain of regulated practices and procedures that are voluntary within a circumscribed domain of possibility, and thus means to habitually enact self-reflection about one's relation to the public and the population. This is the undercurrent behind theories of popular and vernacular news reading, familiar from the concepts of publics and imagined communities.[10] Although not explicitly describing weekend leisure reading, it is possible to extend the purview of these theories to reading the Sunday paper, at leisure at home on the day of rest. The specificity of *when* reading the Sunday paper occurs points to another overlooked aspect of newspaper supplements: their temporality.

SUPPLEMENT TEMPORALITY

Ephemera are curious temporal objects. Souvenirs and mementos are meant to be kept, at least for a while, but there is no prescribed way to collect them. Posters and clippings are meant to be appreciated again and again, but rules for keeping or displaying them abounded, following trends of the moment. Coupons need to be set aside but not filed away; a special edition or series insists on being compiled, but most collections miss intermittent issues; interest tapers off and availability is unpredictable. "The improbable survival of ephemera is therefore noteworthy in itself," according to Harry G. Cocks and Matthew Rubery. "Remnants seem to offer access to a kind of unguarded or vernacular version of the past."[11] The two coauthors note that the most expansive definition of ephemera includes "everything printed that is not actually a book," but we primarily want to distinguish Sunday supplements from the broadsheet sections of the newspaper.[12]

From our perspective, the distinction is not merely a dichotomy between the enduring and the ephemeral. Whereas the newspaper is quickly discarded and replaced with the next edition, supplements such as posters, paper toys, and magazines, and features of the Sunday paper such as coupons and contests were all designed to be kept and appreciated—often appreciating in value all the more by being collected as a series. A collectible series of any one type of supplement was finite, lasting no more than six months to a year at most, not coincidentally the duration of a prepaid subscription. By the 1890s Sunday papers had long been associated with syndicated serial fiction and literary columns.[13] A lengthy but finite series of special features acted similarly as motivation to subscribe for a prescribed period or to at least anticipate forthcoming issues within a given time frame. In contrast, the newspaper itself, day in and day out, year after year, could seem an intangible commitment beyond the horizon.

In defining the genre of miscellany that made up a weekday paper, James Mussell notes that each edition is "situated between all the issues that have preceded it and those yet to come. . . . What readers understand as 'the newspaper' extends beyond the printed object in their hands."[14] But Sunday supplements reorder the periodical rhythms of daily newspaper reading, with its newsworthy information tied so tightly to timeliness and swift circulation but just as quickly discarded and replaced with the next edition. James Guillory explains that news as information "demands to be transmitted because it has a shelf life, a momentary value that drives the development of our information technologies in their quest to speed up, economize, and maximize the effectiveness of transmission."[15] But the Sunday paper and, especially, its supplements demand to be committed to as objects—tangible and desirable commodities.

Just as its leisure reading required a day of rest, the Sunday paper's intermittent periodicity demanded patience but instilled anticipation, a fitting complement to the daily news, whose very newness was constructed by the pace of publication, driving the market for an increased frequency with evening or more frequent editions and extras during the day.[16] And yet, ironically, although special supplements were more enduring in the moment of reading, they were often rendered ephemeral, omitted from compiled numbers of archived editions of newspapers, bound into book form for safekeeping and future reference as the record of the day.[17] More often than not, in our experience, supplements were discarded from library editions, and it is especially from the perspective of historians using microfilmed and digitized newspapers that supplements become ephemeral, excluded from the revered domain of old newspapers as pages of the past. Sunday's limited series of supplements, puzzles, and contests exist in a mid-temporal zone between the throw-away quality of the daily paper and the preservation practices associated with library binding. We were more likely to find intact examples of Sunday supplements through online auctions of century-old memorabilia than in libraries and archives, where runs of entire Sunday editions are often missing.

Chapter 2 explores types of supplements in detail, but our argument here does not necessarily describe historical readers' intentions and experiences. Rather, we map the Sunday paper itself as a media object, an archived object, that had cultural importance at the time but has left only itself as a trace of that impact. We argue that entering a guess in a contest, trading in a coupon, and collecting a souvenir supplement enact more than simple self-interest, although for many there was such motivation. Rather, participating in an emergent reading public was equally in the public interest as an "act of citizenship," a particular form of cultural citizenship.[18] In this light, we start before such supplements proliferated and first consider an earlier ritual of the "new journalism" of the 1880s: the public subscription to a fund-raising campaign where the newspaper, as a public institution, overtly mediates the public interest by coordinating the actions of its mass of readers toward a collective effort in the public good.

The Contested Field of Sunday Readership

News value and entertainment value became entwined as weekend newspaper reading became a primary form of popular culture—one that was able to include commentary on and interpretation of all others. By the 1880s, newspaper reading explicitly began to address women and children through special sections. It is not incidental that the political contest we described at the opening of this chapter is a feature in the feminized magazine section, amid its mix of distracting features and leisure reading and despite the presumably masculine character of the political content. This particular contest transformed the vernacular six-day newspaper into a Sunday feature by introducing room for play.[19]

All contests provided a mechanism and a motivation to take personal interest in the newspapers' stewardship of public interest—not incidental for women and children as disenfranchised readers. Spurring more readers to read with more engagement, contests were explicitly designed to prompt the more committed step of a prepaid subscription for home delivery, which was especially important for the domesticated Sunday paper. The variety of contests was bewildering. All, however, turned reading the paper into a rule-based game, with a lottery payoff, an admixture combining some degree of talent and luck—except that the talent consistently involved reflective abstraction about the content of the Sunday paper itself. Contests entrenched readers' choice of paper among the local market of available papers, and against other media such as magazines, but they did much more too.

Contests were just one form of supplement used to boost subscriptions as the Sunday paper was taking its modern form. On any week in the 1890s, a metropolitan Sunday paper from New York, Philadelphia, or San Francisco could offer a hundred-dollar prize, a souvenir poster, an entire novel, a song sheet, a children's activity book, or a toy—all of which are reviewed in this section. These contests, activities, and keepsakes weren't just ephemeral supplements, however much they were treated as such by libraries and archives. (They are now more likely found through an online auction than the microfilmed or digital record of the paper.)

These supplements to news are all avenues through which the metropolitan press in America transformed the Sunday paper in the 1890s into a media form compiling and interpreting the entire popular culture of the day and, in principle, reaching the entire population (at least of normative readers in the bourgeois family). Unlike the weekday paper, the Sunday paper defined its readership *as* the mass public, while recognizing its various component parts (women, children) by including a range of forms that specifically addressed them. The contest to guess McKinley's cabinet members did not simply transform news and politics into the leisurely opinion and editorial features of Sunday journalism; it raised the stakes and made it fun.

"A NEW SCHOOL OF JOURNALISM FOUNDED UPON A MORAL IDEA"

The introduction of illustrated features, special supplements, and prize contests to the Sunday paper cannot be separated from the emergence of a new form of journalism in the late 1880s that built its influence and profits on a populist appeal to the broadest spectrum of readers.[20] The new sensational forms of investigative reporting for Joseph Pulitzer and W. R. Hearst were later castigated as "yellow journalism" and associated with fabricated muckraking paired with large and lurid illustrations of gruesome or licentious scenes—scantily clad showgirls and beach-going ladies were also a constant. By 1896 the phrase "new journalism" was routinely set inside ironic quotation marks, and Ervin Wardman, rival editor of the *New York Press*, coined the sneer "yellow journalism" early in 1897 after first toying with the snide twist of "nude" journalism—"nude because it has not even the veneer of decency."[21]

A decade earlier, however, when Hearst's and Pulitzer's newspapers were upstarts in their respective cities of San Francisco, St. Louis, and New York, their new forms of journalism initially aimed for populist reform in the public interest. To be sure, they relied on manufactured sensationalism in the form of undercover journalism and self-promotion of all sorts, but these journalistic tricks were at first aimed at routing out corruption and hypocrisy, often achieved by prominent women journalists. Pseudonymous "stunt girls" Nellie Bly and Annie Laurie, among others, built international reputations for their often daring feats of investigation at Pulitzer's *New York World* and Hearst's *San Francisco Examiner*, respectively.[22] "Behind Asylum Bars," Bly's pioneering 1887 exposé of abusive treatment of young, poor immigrants, made her the protagonist of her own reporting, front and center in the accompanying illustrations.[23] The first in the series of articles—on a Sunday—created such a stir that Bly's name appeared in the very headlines of subsequent reports.[24] Bly spawned a small but prominent number of imitators throughout the 1890s. Their stories were almost always Sunday features, profusely illustrated with the women themselves as central actors in the scenes portrayed, both object and instigator of the public's fascination with the evil deeds they upturned.

Bly's stunt reporting was quintessential to the new form of journalism, putting Pulitzer's editorial policies into practice by acting as a progressive agent in "the exposure of corruption, the apprehension and punishment of criminals, the defense of the innocent, the protection of the weak, the improvement of the law and the enforcement of justice," as the *World* itself recapped in a retrospective of its first four years of these journalistic pursuits.[25] On his first day as proprietor in May 1883, Pulitzer's inaugural editorial announced his foundational manifesto for the *World*: "different in purpose, policy and principle—different in objects and interests—different in sympathies and convictions... that will expose all fraud and sham, fight all public evils and abuses—that will serve and battle for the people with earnest sincerity."[26] These principles were reprinted and restated often, especially for annual May anniversaries of Pulitzer's proprietorship, such as the 1889 edition that proclaimed the *World* had begun a "new school of journalism founded upon a moral idea."[27] The same principles dedicated the cornerstone of the skyscraping Pulitzer Building on Park Row: "Let it ever be remembered that this edifice owes its existence to the public... that its every stone comes from the people and represents public approval for public services rendered."[28] This "new school" of progressive journalism was continually paired with publicity and fund-raising for various charities and civic projects, especially for New York's poorest. Sentiment and charity certainly cemented the public appeals, but the effort to secure donations from readers—public pledges were then called "subscriptions" to the collective effort—was nonetheless grounded in growing awareness of the experience of poverty among the crowded, immigrant-filled neighborhoods of New York. The fund-raising offered readers a way to act collectively in pursuit of the public interest.

Almost immediately after Pulitzer took ownership of the *World* in 1883, a heatwave brought news that tenement children were dying of exhaustion; the newspaper initiated a relief fund to send them on daily seaside excursions. Newsworthy political nepotism, and even police corruption, could be similarly combatted with the public outreach of fund-raising. In 1885 the *World* turned its attention to the plight of sixteen-year-old Maggie Morris, assaulted by a police officer but jailed while her assailant went free and uncharged for his crime. The *World* paid her bail through subscriptions from readers as its journalism doggedly pursued justice and called for the arrest of the man. These and a dozen other public funds were recalled in a special Sunday edition celebrating its tenth anniversary under Pulitzer's leadership: a "Sick Babies Fund" in 1887; a Christmas toy fund in 1889. Each summer, newsboys and other city children could escape the city's heat and dust on Sundays at the *World*'s playground in Shady Side, New Jersey, courtesy of a coupon printed in the Sunday edition for a free ferry ride across the river.

Despite the clear charitable purposes behind these public appeals, many other efforts admittedly verged on publicity stunts, such as an 1887 theater party in the Bowery for three thousand newsboys (and reportedly a few newsgirls, too) and an 1891 children's strawberry festival at Madison Square Garden.

One early fund-raising campaign organized by the *World* is still remembered even today. In March 1885, Pulitzer launched an appeal for the public to fund the completion of the pedestal for the Statue of Liberty, whose construction had reached an impasse. The statue itself was a gift from the people of France for the 1876 centenary of American independence. While the statue of "Liberty Enlightening the World" began construction in Paris, the United States needed only construct a suitable pedestal, at a cost of $250,000. Early fund-raising targeting the wealthy for large donations reached its limits early in 1885; a deficit of $100,000 remained. Pulitzer scripted a populist appeal to send subscriptions of any small amount directly to the newspaper in return for the recognition of having one's name printed in the paper:

> We must raise the money! *The World* is the people's paper, and it now appeals to the people to come forward and raise this money. . . . Take this appeal to yourself personally. It is meant for every reader of *The World*. Give something, however little. Send it to us. We will receive it and see that it is properly applied. We will also publish the name of every giver, however small the sum given. Let us hear from the people.[29]

The novelty wasn't having a newspaper steward the fund-raising; just days before, the *New York Herald* reported that its readers had sent in donations—but only for $19.25.[30] Nor was printing donors' names a new idea; the *New York Times*, for example, printed a list of recent subscriptions at the same time—at the top was John D. Rockefeller and five others for $1,000 each, and only one was less than $10.[31] Pulitzer's twist was appealing to the masses to each contribute according to their means, however modest. Unlike the previous years' worth of efforts, more than 90 percent of the funds subscribed through the *World* were less than $1 apiece. The populist appeal combining public recognition, patriotism, and an ounce of classic showman's ballyhoo did the trick. Even the smallest amounts added to the subscription list resulted, as promised, in the donor's name being printed in the paper.

One of the daily accounts on the editorial page recapped how "popular subscriptions to *The World*'s Pedestal Fund continue to roll in. Yesterday the pennies of 1,500 school children were received. The sum total was not large, but this tribute from the little people who are to have Liberty in their keeping for years to come is most gratifying."[32] And all of their names were printed on another page: "Clara Roth, 1 cent; Ida Taylor, 2 cents; Ina Taylor and Mary McShafery, 1 cent each."[33] It took less than 150 days to raise the required amount. On the day the

World topped the $100,000 mark, its front page offered a two-column editorial cartoon of the statue, its base freshly inscribed with a plaque of the newspaper's own design: "This pedestal to Liberty was provided by the voluntary contributions of 120,000 patriotic citizens of the American Union through *The New York World*" (see fig. 6).[34] Liberty was even inserted into the center of the logo in the *World*'s nameplate atop the front page.

FIGURE 6. "One Hundred Thousand Dollars!" *New York World*, August 11, 1885, 1; and "This Column, 400 Feet High," *New York World*, December 16, 1895, 3.

There's no denying how rallying the *New York World*'s influence behind a public subscription to a good cause doubled as publicity for its growing circulation. By the late 1880s, the *World* was the largest circulation newspaper in North America, more than twice any other paper in New York. Its circulation boasts had initially been questioned as competitors like the *Tribune* called for independent confirmations of the daily claims of superiority. In response, Pulitzer announced in 1887 that any advertiser, any competitor, any reader, could inspect both the pressroom and the subscription books. The spectacle of the paper's printing floor became a central metaphor for the extraordinary capacity of the newspaper as a public institution, a topic reviewed in more detail in chapter 4. The circulation figure itself was a daily spectacle too. The motto "Circulation Books Open to All" was added to its editorial page masthead in 1888 and then the front page in 1889 as daily circulation reached an average of 350,000 copies. Readers themselves were openly called upon to share the obsession with the circulation figure in the form of a series of guessing contests—some of the first and most prominent of many contests held by the *World*. Compared to how the "new school" of journalism of the 1880s corralled its readers in the public interest, the contests of the 1890s rarely called for collective action, but they still displayed the collective pursuit of reading. As with Liberty's pedestal fund, long lists of contestants' names were printed in the paper, a testament to each individual reader being uniquely positioned among the mass public.

Guessing Contests as a Technology of Reading Publics

The annual circulation of the *World* under Pulitzer's ownership increased tenfold between 1882 and 1887, from 22,331 to 228,465 copies per day—more than 83 million in total for the year. The *Sunday World* had grown even more dramatically, from only 14,727 copies to fully 257,267 copies, many dispatched far from New York. The addition of a one-cent *Evening World* late in 1887 meant the *World* was going to deliver more than one hundred million copies in 1888; one hundred dollars was offered to the reader lucky enough to estimate closest to the actual circulation for the year.

Conceptually, the contest was a brilliant, fun way to make the public of readers evident to itself, anticipating future issues, future increases in circulation, and future editions filled with other entertaining features. When the lucky winner was announced, fully 104,473,650 copies had been distributed in 1888. Contests didn't only involve guessing the progress of newspaper circulation. In October 1889 the *World* let loose the imaginations of its readers in an "Idea Contest" offering one thousand dollars to the best way to improve the conduct of the newspaper.[35] Over three hundred thousand serious and facetious suggestions poured in from across the United States and Canada concerning journalism practices, forms of advertising and publicity, and addressing the material qualities of the paper. The winning entry married the thousands of wildly divergent submissions to win the prize with the high-minded ideal of establishing a "World Bureau of Justice" as a "permanent public service" to investigate readers' claims of injustice and unfairness, wherever those crimes against the greater good occurred.[36]

Along the way, many more fanciful suggestions foretold of futuristic media technologies that would improve the newspaper's circulation or overcome the very need for circulating newsprint at all: nickel-slot newspaper dispensers at elevated stations; phonograph news speakers aboard ferries and streetcars; phonograph interviews to record and report the actual voice of newsmakers;[37] or, again, pneumatic-tube delivery of your paper; a telegraph linking all parts of the world to the *World*; even a suggestion, prescient of the syndicated supplements discussed in chapter 6, that "*The World* should establish in every principal city a daily edition," and again a "fac-simile edition with the necessary local changes . . . in San Francisco and St. Louis, and perhaps a Canadian city. It would not then be a New York newspaper, but an American newspaper."[38]

Newspapers had occasionally used guessing contests of various sorts to attract new readers, to appeal to different readerships, or at least to appeal differently to their existing readerships. Contests provided an incentive for readers to invest time and attention to reading with an element of luck masquerading under the veneer of skill or judgment of current events. Sometimes a contest provided a focus for fund-raising, such as when the *Philadelphia Item*'s newsboys' fund at Christmas 1887 offered two five-dollar gold pieces, one each to the girl and the boy raising the highest amount each week in December.[39] In this case the contest had the obvious intention of motivating middle-class children in the effort of charity in return for their name printed in the paper and a chance at the prize. Juvenile readers of the newspaper were a by-product of the newspaper providing a conduit for children molding themselves into good citizens. William R. Hearst's *San Francisco Examiner* had a contest in 1889 selecting May Ayers as a perfectly representative schoolgirl for having the highest final grades in all the city and rewarding her with a trip to Europe for being the *Examiner*'s prize pupil.[40] The prize was announced only after final grades were assigned, so May and all the other top students were "animated by no ambition other than the wish to make the use of privileges afforded by our educational system."[41]

Ayers's trip to Europe coincided with Nellie Bly's memorable journalistic trip around the world, assigned by Pulitzer's *World* to beat the mythical feat of Jules Verne's fictional circumnavigation in eighty days.[42] There was, of course, a guessing contest to get readers personally invested in the *World*'s regular reports of Bly's travels across the Atlantic, Europe, and by sea to Japan and back to America, with a final stretch on the transcontinental railroad from San Francisco to New York. The trip was initially promised to take seventy-five days; it wasn't supposed to be a race or include any contingency—quite the opposite, as Bly left New York with the tickets for the entire journey purchased in advance from Cook's Travel Agency: "With all the millions now invested in methods and modes of communication, interstate and international, the story of Miss Bly will give a valuable pointer in enabling the reader to appreciate these avenues of intercourse at their full value."[43]

This quickly gave way to such self-promoting hype as "Will she beat the record?" and "Jules Verne's pace is too slow for *The World!*" as the paper initiated a contest to guess exactly how many days and minutes the trip would actually take; the reader needed a coupon printed only in the *Sunday World* to submit a guess.[44] "Each copy of *The Sunday World* will contain a blank ballot. . . . By ordering extra copies of *The Sunday World* you can guess early and often. Free trip to Europe for the best guess."[45] Each Sunday in December, the *World* included its contest ballots alongside illustrated features of Bly's latest stage of travel, the better to estimate whether her itinerary had altered either in advance of schedule or whether she was delayed. The *World* was incredibly fortunate (or canny to somehow arrange) for Bly to arrive on a Saturday afternoon more than two days earlier than originally scheduled—just in time for an illustrated Sunday feature profiling the great journey's end and a full-page illustrated game that transformed her trip around the world into a children's pastime (see fig. 7). Reports of the homecoming in Monday's issue implicitly cast the guessing contest in light of the previous public effort of the pedestal fund when Bly was compared to Lady Liberty (or at least to the *World*'s logo), noting how "her face, tanned by the sun and wind of both hemispheres, has upon it the glow of health."[46] An equally newsworthy part of the story was how the *Sunday World* had entirely sold out all 290,000 copies printed the day before. The logic of a public subscription to a fund in the public interest had been upended; for this contest readers needed a personal subscription to the paper to pursue their personal interest in the guessing match.

Guessing contests often centered on predicting the outcomes of elections or sometimes census population counts. For the 1890 census figures, Hearst's *San Francisco Examiner* offered twenty guesses to all renewed subscribers for a chance to win one of more than seventy-five thousand dollars' worth of prizes and premiums. Election outcome contests, in fact, became such a fad among newspapers across the United States that the attorney general was asked to provide a formal ruling on whether or not they constituted a lottery and should therefore be banned under an updated amendment of the Anti-Lottery Act passed in 1890. The specific case was an election-guessing contest offered by the *Cincinnati Enquirer* for local and state-level offices that year. The attorney general's ruling needed to determine whether the cost of purchasing a paper to obtain a ballot or coupon constituted a payment for playing a raffle. On this point, the ruling decided the intended prize to readers outweighed the benefit of publicity to the newspaper and its advertisers; the small cost of the paper did indeed amount to a fee to play.

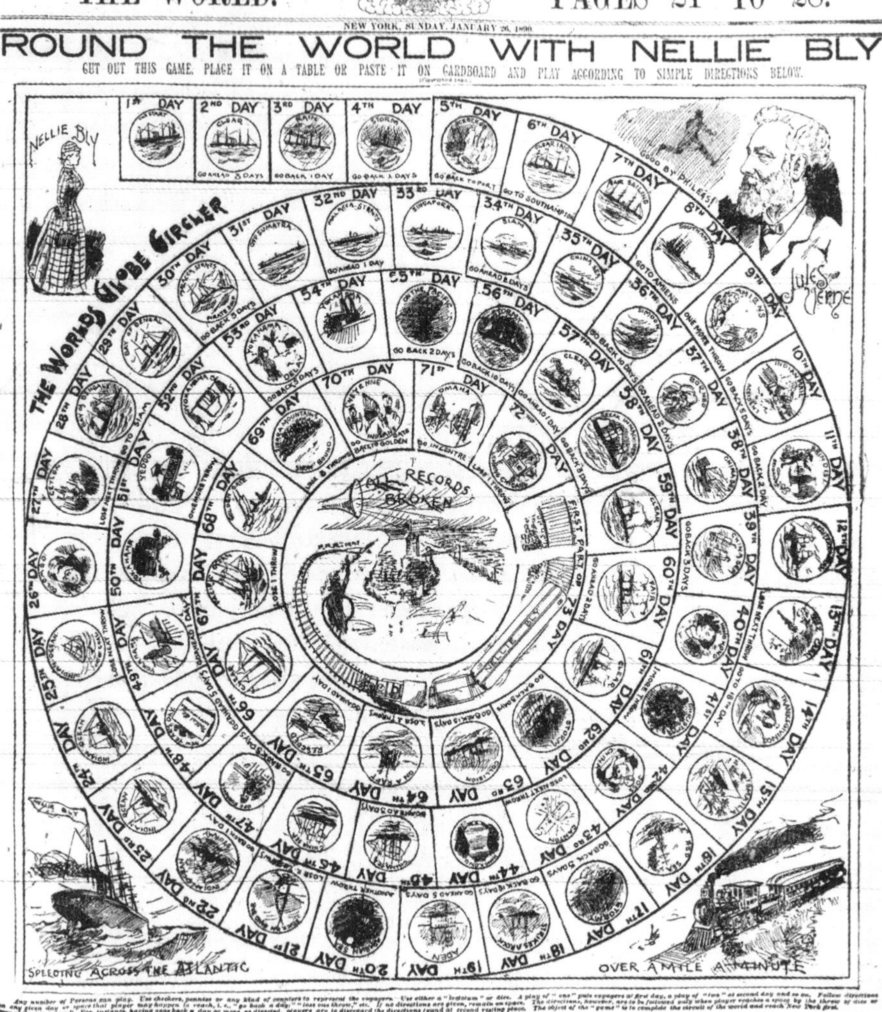

FIGURE 7. "Round the World with Nellie Bly," *New York World*, January 26, 1890, 21.

But a second aspect of the decision hinged on the balance of luck versus skill. On this point the specific device of an election outcome was sufficiently based on the informed judgment of contestants as politically invested news readers: "Estimates made upon the probable political action of the people in a given State in a pending election cannot be said to be dependent upon chance."[47] The decision stood for fifteen years and was used to determine that a contest guessing the

1900 census results was legal and that another guessing the size of the opening-day crowd at the 1901 Pan-American Exposition in Buffalo was likewise permissible. The tide turned in March 1905, however, when an Ohio Supreme Court decided to reverse the precedent, in a case lobbied against three newspapers, again from Cincinnati. For nearly twenty years up until that point, however, guessing contests in newspapers were a constant form of public involvement and investment in the collective pursuit of reading the paper.

In some rare but fascinating cases, the very structure and form of the Sunday paper was the subject of the contest. In 1895 Hearst's *Examiner* and its rival *San Francisco Chronicle*, both gave a prize for guessing how many words would be printed in an upcoming Sunday paper. The idea was first launched by the *Chronicle*. On the surface, the contest was cast as an opportunity to "secure a little sympathy for the hard-worked editors, reporters and proof-readers, and the mechanical force upon whom so much of the efficiency of a great newspaper depends."[48] The one-hundred-dollar prize to guess the number of words in a twenty-eight-page Sunday edition of the *Chronicle* depended on three chief matters of uncertainty: unpredictable amounts of advertising and classifieds, the volume of telegraphic news, and the number of local events covered by the city desk. Although the container of twenty-eight pages of broadside newsprint was known in advance, the number of words depended on the balance of those elements, each with its different-size type and varied use of space. Readers were invited to collect three coupons from consecutive Sundays, simultaneously learning more about the newspaper and the number of words each week, in order to submit a prediction in advance of the subsequent Sunday. The winner guessed just 14 words higher than the actual count of 202,457 words.[49]

Starting its own contest just weeks later, the *Examiner* mocked the mere one-hundred-dollar prize offered by its competitor and raised the stakes of its prize tenfold to one thousand dollars. It also mocked its competitor's mere twenty-eight pages by flouting the *Examiner*'s ballooning volume of advertising as the cause of its thirty-two Sunday pages. The Hearst paper shielded itself from mockery of its sensational journalism precisely through its quantifiable commercial success; tautologically, its journalists did not have to worry about profits because they worked for a profitable paper. Fifteen-year-old Lois Hatch guessed 213,167 words—over the actual fact by just two words. The *Examiner* made much of its winner having "the superior wisdom of a woman. . . . Miss Hatch's coupon was a model of neatness and extremely good to look upon."[50]

Similar contests had happened before, such as guessing the number of classified want ads in the *St. Louis Republic* in July 1895, and they would continue in various forms, such as the *Philadelphia Times* rewarding the best story composed from lines of Sunday advertising text in May 1899. The parallel contests to guess the number of words in a Sunday paper abstracted the device almost to a paradigm. The very size, heft, and material form of the voluminous Sunday paper was the object of fascination for readers, addressed as contestants and rewarded for their skillful handling of the paper. Contests encouraged readers to subscribe to being long-term, committed, and expert readers. In some cases, bad publicity resulted from readers' compulsive efforts to win the prize. Consider a parable of "Coupon Journalism" reported by the *Buffalo Courier* about a rival newspaper's coupon-collecting contest for a lucky reader to win a free trip to the Chicago Columbian Exposition and World's Fair. A young woman had saved $75 to attend the fair modestly, but the contest enticed her to use this money instead to buy newspapers to collect coupons to win the first-class trip to the fair; her friends reportedly spent another $325: "But this sum was not quite enough. The free trip went to somebody who had 20,500 coupons against her 20,000. . . . Would any honorable newspaper take money so procured?"[51] Detached from skill or merit, contests could indeed be dismissed as exploitative lotteries.

Given the centrality of contests in constituting habitual readers, it should come as no surprise that one of the earliest children's Sunday pages—perhaps the first—held a contest to inaugurate its novel features. The Sunday edition of the *Philadelphia Times*, "The Great Family Newspaper," launched a specially bannered page "Our Boys and Girls," on New Year's Day 1888. The banner signified how "Our Boys and Girls" addressed a new type of reader, delivering them into the fold of the paper's mass readership: "Two pages devoted expressly to the young people of the family. Short tales, household amusements, games, puzzles, and useful occupations, abundantly illustrated."[52] Central to the new feature was a one-hundred-dollar-prize contest for the girl and boy submitting the best stories "that show the most originality in construction and the most interest as a story."[53] The paper justified the contest as an educational pursuit, inviting every intelligent boy and girl to set aside the idea of winning and write their best short story irrespective of the contest: "It may not draw a prize; it may not be published, but it will be the best possible instruction to the writer even in failure."[54] The *Times* also proposed that the contest was in keeping with its boys and girls page being a new, modern form of amusement: "New occasions create new duties, and the wonderful progress of our civilization has made the Sunday newspaper of today one of the necessary agents of our social enjoyment and culture."[55]

Such prizes for the best writing or art were common on Sunday children's pages. The *St. Louis Post-Dispatch* also began a "Children's Corner" page in January 1888, including a "P. D. Puzzlers' Club" "open to every boy and girl who is anxious to devote some little time to studying out the puzzles and problems that will be published each week."[56] The first puzzle was a word-making contest to submit the highest number of words out of the letters THE POST-DISPATCH, "never mind that little hyphen." The winner, fifteen-year-old Elfrida H. Schaper, submitted a list of 1,290 different words to win a set of encyclopedias.[57] But puzzle prize contests were not limited to juvenile readers. The *New York Herald* held a prize drawing contest for illustrators and a prize waltz contest for musicians, both in 1890, then a prize play contest in 1891. The *Herald* then focused the efforts of its prize contests to women readers of its "Paris–New York" fashion page. Beginning early in 1893, and lasting for more than a year, editors of that Sunday page held a series of prize contests judging best submissions from readers. The first was the best drawing of a design for an Easter bonnet; others judged the best swimsuit, bicycle outfit, business dress, and doll's costume. Although clearly aligned with the fashion focus of the *Sunday Herald*'s women's page, some of the later contests asked for thoughts about more elevated pursuits, including best design for a six-room flat, best photography, and best plan for a summer vacation. Each monthly contest's winners provided a page of illustrations and built anticipation among readers.

"A Plot for a Million": Serial Novel Contests

Another type of contest attached prizes for guessing the final plot twists of serial mystery novels, which solved the problem of untalented readers being effectively disqualified. One of the first such stories began in the *New York World* in March 1895 and was coyly named "A Plot for a Million," although the prize was only one thousand dollars. The rules for this and subsequent prize novel contests were simple and similar to the many lottery-style guessing contests in the previous decade: "For the correct, most complete and first received advance explanation of the last chapter, *The World* will award a bag of 100 Gold Eagles, $1000 in Gold."[58] Of the 30,000 entries, no one was both complete and accurate, and the prize was divided among 35 best guesses. On the list of winners, half were from outside the city, as far as Vermont, Ohio, and Washington, DC.[59] The gimmick proliferated across the continent over the next year and more. The *Boston Post* offered only one-tenth the prize and limited the contest to its "feminine readers," but it received 9,321 entries, of which only 17 gave the proper motive and culprit.[60] The *Chicago Inter-Ocean* also clarified that guesses could come only from women and girls, but "they can receive help as to their guesses from any member of the family or from all the family."[61] While the form of the contest was widespread, in these early cases the stories themselves were not widely syndicated.

In contrast, the *Chicago Record* created a syndicated version of the mystery story contest by first holding a contest for *authors* to submit serial mystery stories. The resulting prizewinning stories were subsequently published in conjunction with a continent-wide series of contests in at least eight metropolitan newspapers. The first-prize winner, "Sons and Fathers" by Harry Stillwell, began in serial form in March 1896; the second-prize winner, "The Mill of Silence" by E. J. Capes, began in May, with the *San Francisco Examiner*, for example, plastering the town with mystery billboards showing a woman-sphinx reader of the *Examiner* imagining a one-thousand-dollar bag of money: "Will She Guess It?"[62] Although only two thousand dollars was open to women *Examiner* readers, the list of prizes in other cities' newspapers was included in the list to make it appear that over ten thousand dollars was being offered to the mystery guessers: *New York Journal*, three thousand dollars; *Chicago Record*, three thousand dollars; *Philadelphia Press*, one thousand dollars, and four other papers. This syndicated version of the prize story contest turned out to be the start of a rather abrupt end to the fad. The craze for mystery-guessing stories lasted less than two years. The gimmick did not reappear on any widespread scale until 1914, when the movie industry collaborated with Sunday papers to run serial stories to accompany serial films. One used a contest to whip up female moviegoers' fandom for the weekly cliff-hangers, offering ten thousand dollars for the prized privilege of writing the plot for the final install-ment of *The Million Dollar Mystery*.[63]

Another newspaper that embraced contests fully was the *New York Morning Journal*, which had an entire "Prize-Winner" section for most of 1893, running a variety of puzzles and contests simultaneously as a regular feature for several months in a row. The *Morning Journal* had earlier launched a spree of contests late in 1889—at that time to match the *World*'s turn to contests for guessing its circulation growth, the best idea, and Nellie Bly's arrival from her worldwide trip. The *Morning Journal* focused on voting in popularity contests, highlighting how the Sunday edition catered to readers' interest in New York's wealthy, powerful, and famous. Throughout 1890, for example, readers could cut out coupons in the Sunday edition to vote and guess the tally for the Most Popular Man in New York (it was Mayor Hugh Grant), the Most Popular Queen of the Stage, or the Most Popular Ball-Player. Such contests were a genuine fad around 1890 and worked to boost circulation of five-cent Sunday editions to obtain coupons.[64] At least one newspaper editor sarcastically warned that the disease of "guessing matches, voting contests and other catch-penny devices inaugurated by some New York papers to attract attention and swell circulation" was becoming an epi-demic adopted by small-city papers across the country.[65] But perhaps the most self-serving was surely the Most Popular Newsdealer contest, which instructed readers to cast judgment on how well their newsies handled the multi-sectioned Sunday edition: "The dealer who takes greatest care to have plenty of papers and neatly folded pictures on hand will be likely to get the greatest number of votes."[66] Sunday newspaper contests transformed the transaction of buying a paper into a serial renewal of interest in expertly reading the paper. To be sure, this process also served the corporate interests of publishers. The Sunday edition was a primary arena for a fierce battle for higher circulation whose tactics were often extravagant prizes, novelties in illustrated journalism, and elaborate supple-ments. In one important case, the competition was also grounded in intense sibling rivalry.

THE OTHER PULITZER: THE *MORNING JOURNAL* AND THE SUNDAY SUPPLEMENT

The *New York Morning Journal* deserves its own spotlight as a pioneering experimenter in Sunday newspaper formats and collectible supplements on top of its contests and coupons. Our focus on its Sunday supplements must follow a brief recap of this largely forgotten New York paper, which has become merely a footnote for being sold in 1895 to William Randolph Hearst, sparking the notorious legacies of yellow journalism.[67] The *Morning Journal* was started in November 1882 by Albert Pulitzer, Joseph's younger brother. Albert had worked in New York journalism for over a decade at that point, including many years as a reporter at the *New York Herald*.[68] At first, rumors were reported that Joseph was backing the venture, branching out from his ownership of the *St. Louis Post-Dispatch*.[69] Just six months later, with Joseph's takeover of the *New York World* in May 1883, presumptions of the brothers' cooperation were permanently replaced by tales of sibling rivalry, often at the expense of Albert's reputation.[70] *The Journalist*, a trade periodical, recalled how Joseph Pulitzer had "watched with concealed anger the establishment of the *Morning Journal*, and refused point-blank to put one dollar behind it, predicted its early ruin, ran down the men Albert employed on the paper and in various ways did what he could to discourage his brother from going on any further."[71] The older brother prevailed, and "within months, *The World* was the sensation of Park Row. Albert held his peace for a decade, rarely speaking to his brother."[72] Gossip from Gotham's newspaper row made light of the Pulitzer brothers' opposition, how "no one would know they were related to see them pass each other on the street."[73] More senior, more talented, more ambitious, and more successful, Joseph Pulitzer's political and editorial ambitions are well known in journalism and beyond, still commemorated in his eponymous prizes for the best annual journalism. Despite having established himself in New York first, Albert quickly became "the other Pulitzer."[74]

One of the reasons for the poor reputation of the *Morning Journal* was its cheap price and even cheaper tone. Launched as a one-cent paper, half the cost or less than other morning papers of the 1880s, Albert Pulitzer's paper adopted a simplified, sensational reporting style that catered to the interests of ordinary housewives as well as men and women who worked outside the home: "Albert made no pretence of being an intellectual leader or a political force. . . . He produced a bright, gossipy paper that sold for a penny to people who worked in factories and department stores."[75] The *Morning Journal* focused on hearsay of the wealthy "400," the latest tidbits about the Vanderbilts and Astors, with a hefty dose of sensational reporting about threats to women's and children's safety in the metropolis.[76] Advance promotion for a Sunday edition in 1889, for example, promised illustrated features asking "Can Baby-Barter be Suppressed as the Law

Stands?" and "New Jersey's piling-up Woman-Murder Mysteries."[77] Another single Sunday issue early in 1890 featured illustrated voyeuristic reporting on "The Dressing Rooms of Our Society Belles" and "Our Girl Athletes in Full Swing" alongside stirrings over "Chinese Wretches who abuse Little White Girls" and "Why the Pool-Rooms Must Be Closed."[78] One frank chronicle explained that this working-class appeal relied on a unique mix of innuendo and insinuation that verged on outright falsehoods: "The names in the stories might be fictitious, the addresses might be vacant lots. . . . And then there were authentic news stories that were a little too raw for the orthodox papers to be very explicit about."[79]

Albert Pulitzer's own explanation of his editorial approach was far from high-minded and idealistic. An overall lack of editorial ambition was deliberate, carving out a niche in the late 1880s as a woman's paper for home reading: "You want to know the secret of the success of the *Morning Journal*? . . . The great unexplored mine which I hit upon was the woman . . . short, crisp paragraphs . . . piquant, personal, and yet pleasant details about people in whom everyone is interested—these appeal to the woman's heart. . . . In America our sisters and daughters do nearly all the shopping. Advertisers therefore prefer a newspaper which women read to any other, a paper that is the favourite in the home circle."[80] The focus on women readers and the resulting financial boom was acknowledged in journalistic circles at the time: "Before Mr. Pulitzer started the *Journal*, no morning paper had been published which the ladies cared to read."[81] At this goal the *Morning Journal* was indisputably successful, to the begrudging respect of some of its contemporaries: "It is alive and vigorous, bright, good-natured and, if the advertising columns are any criterion, making money."[82] The mass appeal paid off in circulation and advertising revenues, which both matched or bettered more costly competitors (see fig. 8).[83]

A consequence of being motivated by popularity and commercial success was early innovation and an energetic embrace of costly Sunday features. Between 1889 and 1891, the *Morning Journal* launched a constant stream of special Sunday supplements. Illustrated and comic sections; art poster giveaways; entire novels in booklet format; sheet music and dressmaking pattern coupons: all of these appeared earlier and more elaborately in the *New York Morning Journal* than in any other Sunday edition (see plate 2). The timing of these novelty supplements may have been a response to match the growing popularity of brother Joseph's paper, which had made efforts to appeal to home readers in 1888, issuing entire novels as special summer reading supplements.[84] By the end of 1888, the *Sunday World* had also introduced a humor page under the illustrated banner "The World's Funny Side."[85] The *Morning Journal* matched these efforts, first by offering its own complete novel supplements as Sunday sections.[86]

Then came ever-more lavish illustrated features and special supplement sections. In April 1889 the *Morning Journal* issued an illustrated special Sunday section, ostensibly to celebrate the centenary of George Washington's inauguration

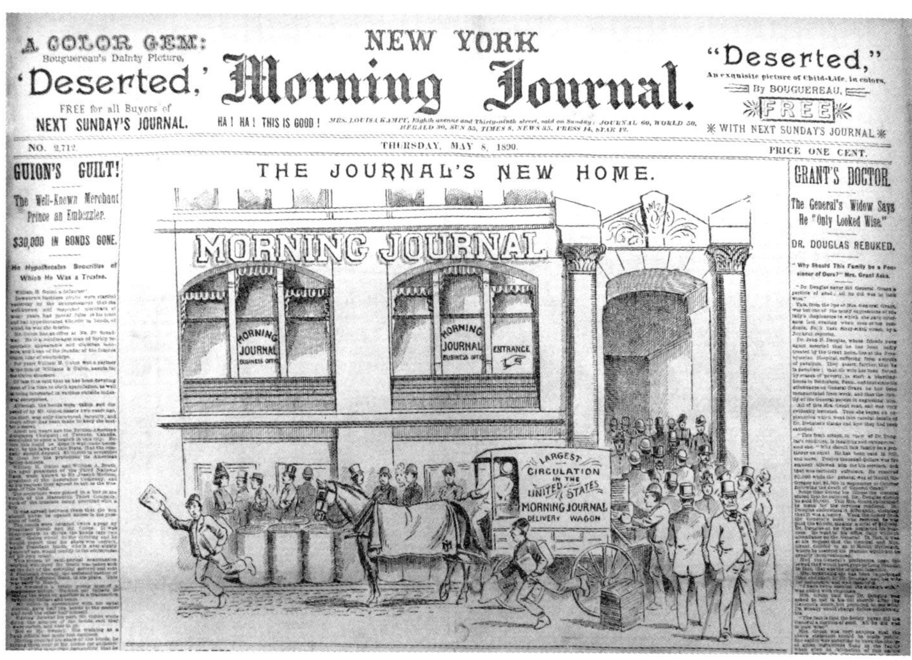

FIGURE 8. "The Journal's New Home," *New York Morning Journal*, May 8, 1890, 1.

as the first president of the United States. An early popularity voting contest, the entire illustrated section was filled with etchings of beautiful women, one from each of the forty-two states in the Union, selected from photographs submitted across the country.[87] The gimmick must have been a great success, because another beauty contest occurred in November, this time without the pretense of historical celebration, simply an excuse to fill two separate Sunday supplements with portraits of beautiful New York women.[88] The *Morning Journal* even followed this in January 1890 with a "King of Beauty" contest to pick the most handsome man in New York: "Modern Apollos! Thousands of Hearts will be set fluttering to-day."[89] Other illustrated features followed in 1890, including entire pages of reprinted comics from *Puck* and *Judge*, a "Flash-Light Panorama of New York," and "Snap-Shot Interviews" with actresses and prizefighters. And yet the *Morning Journal* was still often simply imitating the *Sunday World*, such as following suit with bannered children's and women's pages after they began in the *World* in September 1889. A truly unprecedented effort soon followed.

THE ART SUPPLEMENT

In November 1889 the *Morning Journal* began offering free posters with the Sunday edition. The first series were reproductions of sentimental favorite paintings, etchings rather than color lithographs, but still printed on relatively fine, heavy paper, 16" by 23" in size, larger than the broadsheet newspaper. The first poster in the months-long weekly series was *The Angelus*, by Jean-François Millet, an immediate success that required a second run a week later: "No reproduction of a great work of art has ever had such a wide circulation as that accorded latterly to *The Journal*'s etching."[90] The logistics of distributing the posters were not trivial, even within the existing mechanisms for delivering the Sunday paper across metropolitan New York. Initially the posters required a coupon, which needed to be presented within a few days at a designated newsstand.[91] The posters were popular enough to require the instruction "Don't forget to tell your dealer to lay by for you a *Sunday Journal*" (see fig. 9).[92] In January line-drawing reduced-size previews of the etchings were printed ahead of each Sunday's poster, "destined to be one of the most popular numbers in *The Journal*'s varied and entertaining Picture Gallery."[93] Number thirteen in the "Picture Gallery" was an 18" by 24" copy of *The Grand Canal, Venice*, by J.M.W. Turner, "the Grandest Yet ... a pure line engraving, clear, luminous."[94]

A second series began in February 1890, portraits of American national heroes, starting with "A hero for our homes! John Faed's superb picture, 'Washington Receiving a Salute at the Battle of Trenton.'"[95] From this point, the posters were included as inserts and delivered with the Sunday paper itself: "No coupon will be needed; every newsdealer, every newsboy from whom you purchase the Sunday *Journal* will deliver you the engraving. ... Be sure and secure the picture, and remember that in securing it you get with it that pearl of Sunday papers, the ubiquitous, fascinating, amusing and instructive *Journal*."[96] In April and May 1890, a third series of numbered "Art Gems" were issued with Sunday editions—this time "aquarelle" posters, smaller but printed in vibrant colors. With the turn to color art supplements, the *Morning Journal* began to emphasize the educational value of its pictures: "Free to all with every copy ... of the fascinating and instructive

FIGURE 9. Promoting the Art Supplement. "To-Morrow's Picture Free," *New York Morning Journal*, December 14, 1889, 1.

*Sunday Journal.... * Hundreds of thousands of readers in town and country appreciate none of its excellences more than this bringing of good arts to their very doors."[97]

Damaged and missing posters were two obvious logistical problems. Coupons were reintroduced, with an explanation of the difficulty of getting the pictures into the hands of subscribers "in an entirely perfect and unrumpled condition ... without creases or fold-marks and ready for framing."[98] Clearly some posters were arriving damaged in the action of inserting them into the paper or, in other cases, were entirely missing. The *Morning Journal* ended this pioneering Sunday art supplement series in June 1890, turning instead to a novel supplement for summer months. This time the *Morning Journal*'s "Library" section was issued in a booklet format to mimic a bound book better than it had done with previous broadsheet novel sections—another innovation in Sunday supplements.[99]

The experiments with supplements must have been costly, on top of logistical issues of circulation, and the *Morning Journal* halted them for a few months before bringing back poster art supplements in November 1890 for a much longer term and then adding booklet-style novel supplements again in November 1891, offering both types of supplements concurrently for over a year until financial and circulation issues must have started to mount. As part of the background for the 1895 sale to Hearst, journalism historians have noted how Albert Pulitzer acted in folly or desperation in 1895 by raising the price of the daily *Morning Journal* to two cents, precipitating a drastic loss of circulation and the brief interim sale to John McLean of the *Cincinnati Enquirer*. That nutshell summary masks how hints of the financial precarity of the *Morning Journal* can be traced to its early lavish turn to special Sunday poster and novel supplements starting back in 1889. Sunday competition among New York newspapers escalated, and other papers began to include weekend art and novel supplements.[100] The *Morning Journal* clung to its innovative permutations of added premium supplements throughout the early 1890s.

As has been well chronicled, the *Morning Journal* raised its daily price to two cents in April 1895, a few weeks before the sale to McLean in May. Despite admiring compliments about his changes, McLean failed to quickly resuscitate the paper and chose to return to a one-cent price early in September 1895, just weeks before the sale to Hearst. This end of the story elides the even more drastic efforts and changes that had been taken with the *Sunday Morning Journal* in the previous year while still under Albert Pulitzer's ownership. In March 1894 the price of the *Sunday Journal* was reduced to four cents, while special children's and women's supplements were added to the one-cent Saturday edition. Even more extravagantly, in September 1894, buyers of the still one-cent morning edition were offered daily art supplements, while the price of the Sunday edition was further reduced to three cents even though it still offered novel supplements and color posters. Offering ever-more art supplements for free as a bonus for buying an ever-lower-costing paper, the desperation to find new circulation for the *Morning Journal* is evident earlier and in an entirely opposite direction than what is portrayed by the end of the story in 1895. Indeed, putting art supplements at the center of the story traces the crucial moment back to 1891, when a new morning paper was launched in New York by a set of new actors on the stage of Gotham journalism, including the predominant American poster printer of the day, the American Lithographic Company. Albert Pulitzer's *Morning Journal* had begun offering art supplements in 1889 as a tactic to gain a circulation advantage over his brother's looming shadow. The new competition in 1891 put lithographed art supplements at the core of its circulation-building business plan from the start.

Following the *New York Morning Journal*, another early adopter of the art supplement as a serial bonus in Sunday papers was the *New York Recorder*; lithographed posters were given away with every *Sunday Recorder* from its first edition on March 22, 1891, a month after the first daily edition. Although the *Journal* had them first, the *Recorder*'s art supplements spurred a fad that spread far beyond New York. Before 1891, newspapers from any location might offer an occasional illustrated extra or special edition; typically, souvenir supplements were posters of a new president, illustrated covers for Christmas or Easter, or commemorations of important anniversaries. Magazines, too, especially art magazines, had been including special color or lithographed supplements or centerfolds throughout the 1880s. This is where the term "Art Supplement" was established to promote a keepsake, separate or detachable from the periodical itself.

There was also a specialized cottage industry to provide even small-town newspapers with special women's editions or town booster editions.[101] The *Morning Journal*'s and the *Recorder*'s interventions were not the specific idea or option of a souvenir or a supplement but rather the serial, periodic character as a predictable weekly feature of the Sunday edition. When the *Recorder* was started with millions of dollars from W. Duke, Sons & Co.'s American Tobacco Company, another partner was Joseph P. Knapp, whose dominant lithographing company provided lavish color posters as premiums to new subscribers when the paper started up in February 1891.[102] With the launch of the *Sunday Recorder* a month later, lithographed posters became a weekly supplement, on top of a fully illustrated front page (see fig. 10). Knapp had made his fortune in lithographed posters, but also printing trade cards, slipped into packages of Duke brand cigarettes, as well as packets of coffee and tea. Blank cards had initially been inserted with cigarettes to stiffen the package, but by the 1880s they were printed in color lithograph collectors' series to ensure brand loyalty. The *Recorder*'s inserting souvenir art supplements in Sunday editions brought the logic of 1880s loyalty marketing from trade cards in branded packaged goods to newspaper publishing. Although the *Morning Journal* had done this earlier, the *Recorder* built its entire appeal to subscribers upon these supplements as much as the paper.

A PICTURE THAT RETAILS FOR 10 CENTS IS PRESENTED FREE WITH THIS ISSUE.

NEW YORK
JULY 19, 1891.

Sunday Recorder.

"IN NATURE'S MIRROR."
A Solargraph in Colors of a Salon Prize Painting is the Art Supplement Presented with To-Day's Recorder.

PRICE 5 CENTS.

PRICE 5 CENTS.

FIGURE 10. "News of the Week Illustrated," *New York Recorder*, July 19, 1891, 1.

In addition to reproductions of paintings, the *Recorder* also issued photographic lithographs in series with themes such as ships, bridges, and buildings of New York, stage actresses, theatrical managers, and professional athletes. These lower-quality supplements were numbered to double as a lottery for prizes each week, and one perforated edge doubled as a coupon to submit a classified ad. Newsdealers across the metropolis were addressed collectively to take the lead in promoting the special art supplements by displaying advance copies at their newsstands. They were instructed to explain, and display, how the poster was a bonus gift offered free of charge as a novel reason to buy the fledgling Sunday paper: "The cost of production of the pictorial art supplement exceeds considerably the retail price of the paper, but as it is the aim of The Recorder Company to popularize the Sunday edition and make it a welcome visitor in every home, no expense will be spared to attain that end."[103] The *Sunday Recorder*—almost entirely because of its art supplement—found subscribers well beyond New York. Advertising appeared in Boston newspapers, with special mention of the art supplement, even taking pains to explain how several thousand copies of the *Recorder* arrived on a special train every Sunday morning, "arriving in Boston at Boston and Albany depot at about 8 a.m. from which point they are delivered by special wagons to all newsdealers, and are on sale at 9 a.m. Be sure to buy *The Sunday Recorder* with the handsome painting as supplement."[104] A North Carolina newspaper took notice that "Every Sunday edition of *The New York Recorder* has an art supplement which is worth many times more than the paper."[105] And in York, Pennsylvania, a local newsdealer took out an advertisement especially to promote its local availability: "The Art Supplement presented to every purchaser of *The Sunday Recorder*."[106]

As a souvenir poster inserted without extra cost or commitment with a Sunday paper, the art supplement brought the logic of a contest and the form of a subscription premium into the actual material folds of the Sunday paper. Art supplements were primarily intended to facilitate brand loyalty as a rationale for consumer behavior, a technology shaping readers into consumers. The technique was explicitly borrowed from trade-card advertising that had been exploited thoroughly in the 1880s by disposable, optional, and addictive consumer products—cigarettes, tea, and coffee, although most familiar to Americans of later decades for being packaged with chewing gum.

The problem for the *Recorder* in particular was that many readers were drawn to subscribe *only* for the art supplements, which were promoted continually for their value—a value that was said to surpass the nickel cost of the paper itself. Early Sunday editions boldly stated across the top of the nameplate: "A picture that retails for 10 cents is presented *free* with this issue."[107] Readers taking the paper primarily for the art supplements would, of course, fall quickly away once the premium value ended. The *Recorder* was roped into the expense of providing the supplements every week for years, a problem that was first cited by its inaugural editor in chief, Harold Carroll. After leaving the paper, he dismissed the *Recorder*'s "tea store plan" for building circulation, because "you are left with the problem [of] how to keep it up when you pull out from under the newspaper the props and extraneous aids of the gift system."[108] He may have been correct; the *Recorder* was a relatively short-lived venture that closed in 1896 after just five years of operation. Although it briefly rivaled the *World* in circulation, it never paid back dividends to Duke, Knapp, and its other financiers. It nonetheless transformed the Sunday paper by entrenching art supplement inserts and, in 1893, introducing the first color printing to New York—on a daily basis—an aspect of its history covered in chapter 5. If the art supplements were the primary cause of lost revenue, they were not abandoned; indeed, they were soon widely imitated enough to briefly become central to the very definition of a metropolitan Sunday paper.

Supplementing the Arts

Other papers followed suit with their own art supplements. Another New York newspaper introduced its own variation of Sunday art supplements in 1891 to meet the upstart competition from the *Recorder*. In April the *New York Press* began a short-lived but entirely innovative two-month series of halftone photographic section art supplements. The first four were broadsheet magazines of miscellany: portraits of political candidates, baseball players, actors and actresses, as well as historical etchings and cartoons, all supported by a back page of large illustrated advertisements. Most prominent were reproductions of winning submissions from the *Press*'s amateur photography contest. These impressive four-page halftone art supplements were promoted in advance as "a new idea in newspapers! The most important step in journalism for a decade. The standard of newspaper illustration raised."[109] The short-lived novelty certainly gave readers a reason to stick with the *Press* rather than switch to the *Recorder*.

Faced with the new competition's more systematic approach to providing Sunday art supplements, the *New York Morning Journal* escalated its prior efforts. More than any other New York paper, the *Morning Journal* met the challenge of the *Recorder*'s supplements and raised the stakes by adding new supplements late in 1891: turning to color lithographs for its art supplements, now joined by a revival of its literary novel supplements, while sponsoring a series of free musical concerts featuring the greatest artists of the day in the special setting of Castle Garden. Promoting the concerts, the *Morning Journal* published an elite list of donors' "subscriptions," headed by the paper's publisher, Albert Pulitzer, as well as financiers Jay Gould and J. Pierpont Morgan, each donating one hundred dollars.[110] The large concert hall had been one of the main amusement sites of New York in the 1840s before becoming an immigration landing station in 1855 (later the city aquarium in 1896). The site was returned to the city parks department in 1890 when the federal government took charge of immigration and opened a temporary station on the Battery before Ellis Island was ready in 1892. To celebrate Castle Garden's legacy, the *Morning Journal* offered a series of special performances featuring top talent visiting from around the world: Anton Seidl, the Scharwenkas, and singers such as Anna Louise Tanner (whose success in New York was noted, for example, in North Dakota, where she had performed earlier in the year): "Thousands of souls listen nightly to the sweet singers and many hearts are made glad. *The Morning Journal* prints a coupon for the poor and they go and listen to the very best music obtainable. It is a charitable act and one which will bring *The Journal* everlasting gratitude."[111] Here are all the elements of reading as a technique for production of the self in mass society: coupons for mass leisure, the dissemination of high arts to a wide readership, the celebration of liberty and freedom, and the pursuit of a collective public good through a newspaper's institutional organization of subscriptions to a public fund for a good cause.

As the Castle Garden concerts ended, the *Morning Journal* conjoined its art and novel supplements as twin features in its Sunday edition that extended the concerts' provision of popular art education. In November, the *Morning Journal* introduced its own chromo-lithographed art supplements, replacing etchings that had not been colored. It also returned to story paper supplements, "*The Morning Journal*'s Library," in the then-unique form of a broadsheet printed so that the reader could fold it into quarters and cut the edges to form a small booklet "novel" as a keepsake. On November 15, for example, the library supplement was the entire story "The House of Shadows" by Oswald Crawfurd, while other supplements in the "library" were biographies of famous figures or melodramas especially of interest to New York's new immigrants.[112] Such fold-and-cut and tabloid supplements were a crucial development in using Sunday sections as a form of popular education in music and literature.

As with the *Recorder*'s subscription premiums, the *Morning Journal*'s art supplements were full-color lithographed reproductions of European artworks, with a distinct emphasis on melodramatic and sentimental pictures suitable for the home or personal scrapbook. Selected pictures dwelled especially on motherhood, young romance, and female-centered biblical subjects such as "Delilah" with the artist's signature reproduced, too, as if a genuine copy.[113] Sentimental art reproductions became standard as art supplements became widespread. The *Philadelphia Inquirer*, for example, began modestly by inserting a special portrait of President Grover Cleveland's wife, Frances, early in March 1893 to celebrate the inauguration, identical to one issued the same day in the *Recorder*. (The *New York World* had portrayed her as Santa Claus in December, just after the election.)

In April the *Inquirer* began the "new and novel feature" of a weekly art supplement; for the first, titled "Resting Before the Ball," a line-drawn version was published in the paper in advance, encouraging readers to imagine the larger color version and how much more attractive it would be.[114] The same device previewed the art supplements issued with the very first Sunday editions of the *Boston Post*: "A faint hint" was coyly noted above a small etching replica of the picture. "This masterpiece of art, which would cost 50 cents at the art store, given with every copy of *The Sunday Post*. An equally fine art supplement each Sunday";[115] and again, a black-and-white etching gave "a faint idea" of the first art supplement to be given away with the *Washington Times* (see plate 3).[116] The same lithographs appeared in multiple newspapers. Series of pictures could be contracted from Knapp's American Lithographic Company or another printer, such as Wood and Parker of New York, which had supplied the *Chicago Times* with some of the same pictures used in Boston and Washington months earlier. Even small-city newspapers could afford to include lithographs in their small-circulation Sunday papers; some of the earliest newspapers to offer art supplements were the *Richmond (VA) Times* and the *St. Paul Globe* in the fall of 1892.

In metropolitan cities the art supplement became a staple of Sunday papers. Competing newspapers in Chicago, Philadelphia, and Boston routinely included poster giveaways from 1893 to 1896. The Sunday art supplement was, if anything, more standard in those cities than in New York, where establishment papers like the *New York Times* and the *New York Tribune* steered clear of the populist fray. At least four Chicago Sunday papers began concurrently circulating art supplements during the Columbian Exposition and continued long after the fair. The *Tribune* began weekly art supplements in March 1893, reproductions of watercolor scenes at the world's fair painted by Charles Graham exclusively for the paper. In Chicago, both the *News-Record* and the *Times* offered color poster inserts, while the *Inter-Ocean* issued a twice-weekly eight-page "illustrated supplement" on its new color fast printing press. A similar color newspaper press provided the *New York World* with the same alternative to inserted lithographs; its only foray into a series of art poster supplements was a series of politicians' portraits leading up to the 1892 election.

We will discuss halftone magazine sections and color sections fully in chapter 6, but there was certainly a degree of overlap between them and the various forms and types of art supplement souvenirs. The term "Art Supplement" was used for early halftone sections introduced in 1891 in the *Toronto Mail* and the *Toronto Globe*; for early color sections at the *Chicago Inter-Ocean* in 1892 and the *New York Herald* in 1894; and the *Boston Journal*'s photographic section in 1894. The *Louisville Courier-Journal* called its new halftone section an "Art Supplement" in 1896, despite having used the term already for its lithograph giveaways in 1895. There was even a variety of art supplement that sat exactly in between a color poster and a color section: the *New York Press* briefly began wrapping its Sunday editions in color souvenir covers on fine magazine paper in 1893, doubling as a souvenir poster despite the newspaper's name and date being prominent. As color printing became more routine, full-page color pictures—even on ordinary newsprint—were often described as artworks worth keeping or framing and, of course, needing to be sought out with an advance order or subscription.

Potentially dismissed as commercial fluff and derivative distraction, these interactive supplements to the paper "subscribed" people into the public sphere—not least women and children—as subjects of artistic, literary, fashionable, playful, and puzzling features. People opted in to publics through techniques of newspaper reading that extended well beyond the literal reading of words to all forms of appreciating a variety of texts and supplemental objects. The Sunday paper's supplements conflated news-reading publics with advertising markets, as readers appreciated the domestic and public value of their committed engagement with the paper. The subjectivity of mass participation in the public sphere was all the more potent when interiorized as amusement, as aesthetically pleasing moments of leisure, as a collection of souvenirs, as intellectually gratifying games or puzzles, in the play of a toy or the hope of entering a contest.

2

APPRECIATING THE ART OF THE SUPPLEMENT

Art supplements were marketed to women in particular, since they were the moral leaders of the home. As an affordable, popular gift that doubled as a form of education, art supplements provided news publishers a hint of public service for the middle and lower classes of the readership. Giveaways in the Sunday paper appealed to the domestic woman reader through a mixture of sentiments surrounding monetary value and saving, collecting and savoring of material goods, good parenting and education, and aesthetic decoration of the home. Lithographed posters in particular begged to be framed and mounted to gain a semblance of aura, despite their status as reproductions.[1] Ephemeral evidence from today's online auctions and collectors' fairs demonstrates that many readers did indeed savor and cherish their art supplements by pasting them into scrapbooks or framing them. When originally circulated with the paper, some local stores began to advertise frames sized to fit supplements exactly. Sometimes the newspaper itself gave away the frame as a subscription premium: "'Where can I get a nice frame for this picture?' This question has been asked by thousands of people who are anxious to keep *The Tribune* Art Supplements as ornaments for their homes. . . . On receipt of 52 cents for one month's subscription . . . The Tribune Company will send a frame to any address in Chicago free of charge."[2] Readers were instructed on how to decorate the walls of their homes with art supplements, especially children's nurseries: "The walls are hung with pictures selected from those given away with *The Sunday Recorder* in subjects most likely to please the eye and taste of children. . . . Do not forget that early impressions cut marvellously deep and are very hard to rub out."[3] In some cases, specialized albums allowed readers to collect specific series of supplements as a bound portfolio. For these higher-quality series, sometimes of real photographs, publishers effectively partnered with newspapers, using their circulation offices as their distributors and promoters.

Chapter 1 explored how contests helped establish practices of seeking, collecting, clipping, and otherwise performing operations on the paper's contents. Chapter 2 turns to a habitual, though distinct, practice of interacting with the astonishing supplements that routinely appeared in Sunday papers at the end of the nineteenth century. As discussed in the book's introduction, the supplement, though apparently an afterthought outside of the proper "newspaper," came to define the Sunday paper, distinguishing it from its daily counterpart through the leisurely paced habits it invited readers to adopt for Sunday reading.

We continue to explore in this chapter how readers were "subscribed"—that is, interpellated—as subjects of a new kind of differently mediated and networked newspaper that imbricated readers in an emergent mediated culture. The redefined temporality of the newspaper, with Sunday features like contests, coupon clipping, and art supplement collecting, linked weekend to weekend, making a subscription all the more logical. Art and photographic supplements appealed to a public through technologies of reading that involved decidedly more than reading. While the weekday paper was tied to the rhythms and bustle of the workweek and engagement with the world of work, weekend papers established a different kind of readership, tied to the rhythms of the weekend and engagement with the home.

In this chapter we review how the Sunday newspaper made a space for itself via the cultural aesthetic of the home. Unlike some other inserts given away for free, readers enticed to collect and preserve a more refined and costly treasure often had to clip a coupon to mail to the paper's headquarters with a dime, or a series of coupons to mail with a dollar. One of the first such portfolio schemes was initiated by the often-pioneering *Chicago Inter-Ocean* as it repurposed its existing color-illustrated Sunday supplement in May 1893 for the Columbian Exposition and World's Fair and added a second weekly color supplement on Wednesdays. For each of the twenty-six weeks the fair was open, readers could collect their supplements, simple enough. But they could also cut out and save up a total of fifty-two coupons, one for each supplement beginning in May, and in November trade them in for a free binder to create a formal portfolio. If that seemed entirely daunting and unrealistic to anyone but the idle, there was an alternative: with a six-month subscription, paid in advance to any newsdealer or by mail to the paper, a reader would receive the binder immediately as a premium.[4]

The impetus behind taking out a subscription often included an incentive beyond simply wanting to receive future issues of the daily newspaper. Special premiums and giveaways were crucial catalysts for convincing readers to opt into a commitment for future issues delivered to their homes or reserved at a newsstand.

Considered one issue at a time, the feature stories and serial fiction of the routine Sunday paper perhaps justified its higher cost, typically five cents, compared to a two-cent daily paper around 1890. But it often took gifts of special souvenirs and a series of supplements to instead provide enough bonus or surplus value to begin a subscription or switch from one Sunday paper to another. As we discussed in chapter 1, beginning in 1891 and becoming a pervasive fad across the continent by 1895, art supplements of all shapes, sizes, and interactive content established a new expectation for Sunday newspapers: collectible souvenirs in colored, lithographed, or halftoned illustration. Some art supplements were posters of artworks to savor sentimentally or patriotically; others provided a printed activity to cut out and construct. Sometimes art supplements included a coupon or numbered code for a possible prize. Most were issued in a collectible series to encourage a long-term subscription to the paper, but in all cases, special print supplements merited aesthetic appreciation atop appreciation of their value relative to the low cost of the newspaper.

The fad waned after 1896 as newspapers turned to color sections, comic supplements, and magazine inserts, as we will discuss in detail in the final chapters on syndication. Nonetheless, the logic of the art supplement was a crucial link between the "new" journalism's public fund-raising efforts and gimmicky guessing contests of the 1880s and the syndicated continent-wide popular culture affixed to comics and magazine supplements in the early 1900s. The mechanism for the subtle shift from regional populist politics to continental popular culture was a concerted focus on providing women readers with material for aesthetic appreciation and juvenile readers with material for aesthetic play. The Sunday paper became a conduit of popular education explicitly including all members of the family as reading subjects invested in the subscription to the newspaper and, specifically, the Sunday paper.

SUPPLEMENTS AS ART, MUSIC,
AND EDUCATION FOR THE HOME

By September 1893, even before the Chicago World's Fair closed, there were already other art portfolios than the one that involved collecting the *Inter-Ocean*'s biweekly color sections. Especially prominent was "Trip Around the World," an album of photographs with detailed descriptions by renowned travel lecturer John L. Stoddard. Published by the R. S. Peale Company of Chicago, Stoddard's portfolio had, in fact, already been available for eighteen months through traveling salesmen across the country. Now in 1893 it was discounted through coupons in Sunday newspapers across the continent, from the *Boston Journal* to the *San Francisco Chronicle* and at least ten other prominent papers, including the *New York Recorder*. The first coupon was printed within a standardized full-page advertisement that showed the peoples of the world in ethnic costume congregating around a bust of Stoddard himself, reversing the structure of his lectures, where he appeared in person and the foreign peoples were frozen in lantern slide pictures.[5] Other portfolios collected depictions of picturesque America, historical events, or encyclopedic catalogs of wild animals or exotic flowers. One widely available item was *The Century War Book*, a history of the American Civil War.

Newspapers reported crowds aplenty clamoring for portfolios at newspaper offices: "Before 7 o'clock hundreds of men and women were in line with seven coupons and four 2-cent stamps waiting. . . . At 1 o'clock the entire supply of 5000 was exhausted."[6] One advertisement, widely used in second-tier city newspapers, printed an illustration of an unruly "clamoring multitude" at the doors of a newspaper office, with people on lampposts and electric poles fishing for a way to jump the queue.[7] An account in St. Louis noted how turnstiles were used to get an accurate count of the crowd, who "came in throngs—thousands call for *The Post-Dispatch* portfolios."[8] The *St. Louis Post-Dispatch* depicted art portfolios analogously as a couple at the altar, "the golden wedding of education and art."[9] In more of a pun than a metaphor, the *Philadelphia Inquirer* depicted an elevator car jam-packed with people reading their art supplements: "the elevation of the masses."[10] Art education was consistently proffered as a benefit of art supplements, such as with a set of reproductions from the Paris Salon of 1895, flashed by ocean cable to make them available the same day as the art exhibition opened.[11] And yet there's an unintended irony in the *Boston Post* showing "The Whole World Awakened" to the educational pursuits of their art portfolios: a crowd cheek by jowl, each head down in their albums rather than learning together.[12] More amusing and less overtly uplifting were albums of popular music and songs, such as "Harmonized Melodies," including four hundred songs and ballads, which the *Boston Globe* offered at Christmas 1893 for one Sunday and two daily, or five daily coupons, plus twenty cents.[13] Altogether the attraction was visual entertainment and aesthetic appreciation, provided cheaply for the masses.

Music supplements were some of the first keepsakes offered with newspapers because they could be printed on the same paper and printing press as the newspaper itself. Even in the 1880s, many newspapers typeset a musical song sheet as part of a larger page of text; the reader could use scissors to cut it out. The front and back of a four-page music sheet could easily be printed on either side of the top half of a newspaper page. By the mid-1890s, more elaborate forms of music sheets on fine paper, often with color picture covers, came hand in hand with the beginnings of color comic supplements. Fine paper music supplements had, in fact, appeared over a decade earlier, as perhaps the very first special supplements, issued with the *Chicago Inter-Ocean* every Wednesday from December 1881 until July 1885. Not mimicked for a decade until art supplements were standard fare, the *Inter-Ocean* returned to the vanguard of music supplements in 1894 with a brief series of tabloid-size color song sheets with poster cover portraits of the composers: "The Portrait, the Biography, the Song complete, 4 full pages in all."[14] This same supplement was concurrently provided to readers of the *Indianapolis News* and the *St. Louis Republic*, which emphasized the combination of entertainment, education, and attractive illustrations: "Tone! Color! Poetry! Portraiture! Not pictures merely, but pictures with a use attached to them."[15]

Another form of music supplement derived from printing a newspaper page in such a way that the reader could fold it in quarters and carefully cut the folded edges to produce an eight-page song sheet—a quarto-fold supplement. The *Boston Sunday Post* tripled the effect for several months late in 1895, using three broadsheet pages to offer a twenty-four-page music booklet. In 1896 Hearst's *New York Journal* was redesigned to add multiple color sections, and one of the features was a color-covered song sheet. One of the first was "The Yellow Kid Song," celebrating how the comic mascot had moved from the pages of Pulitzer's *Sunday World* to the rival *Journal*. Hearst newspapers in San Francisco and New York offered Sunday song supplements well into the new century, joined by sister sheets in Chicago, Boston, and Los Angeles as the chain expanded, often connected to Hearst's famous syndicated comics, as we shall see in chapter 6. More than lithographed artworks, song sheets could appeal to readers' desire for amusement but without entirely tipping all the way over into fun and games. The subsequent phase in the art supplement craze turned to fashion, play, and games more explicitly, with dress patterns, paper dolls, and cutout theaters and toys each having their day in the spotlight between 1895 and 1896.

Clothes patterns were another print industry paired with Sunday newspapers. Long part of women's magazines, coupons for cut-paper dress patterns began appearing in Sunday papers late in 1893 alongside offers for art portfolios. One of the first newspapers to adopt these offers, the *Boston Globe*, printed two fashion plates each Sunday, soon also on Wednesdays; patterns for the pictured outfits could be obtained directly from the newspaper office for ten cents and the accompanying coupon.[16] The idea was quickly copied and franchised to newspapers across the continent by the long-standing Bazar Glove-Fitting Pattern Company. Since the 1870s the company had been supplying catalogs for dry goods stores to act as exclusive local dealers for its patterns. Many of these stores' newspaper ads mentioned the connection, but now the newspaper itself would act as both the catalog and the salesperson. In the *St. Louis Republic* the new feature was launched with fanfare, offering patterns for two basque coats with rippled cape sleeves, No. 4021 and 4023 in the company's catalog: "No scheme ever inaugurated by a newspaper so fully meets the wants of the ladies."[17] The same series of patterns ran in Sunday editions of the *Boston Post*, the *Louisville Courier-Journal*, and even in small-town papers and in Canada—except in these cases, readers had to send the coupons directly to the pattern company in Manhattan.

THE SUNDAY PAPER AS PLAYTHING:
PAPER DOLLS AND CUTOUT TOYS

Soon the art supplement itself turned to fashion, in the form of cutout paper dolls. One of the first sets of Sunday supplement paper dolls began in the *New York Herald* in December 1894, printed right onto the relatively thick paper stock of its color section (see plate 4). Not quite fashion figures, its dolls tended to be miniature effigies of real people in the news, perhaps because they were printed within the newspaper proper, albeit the color Sunday section. The first set portrayed three opera singers, including the famous soprano Melba, dressed as she appeared in the opera *Il Pagliacci*.[18] The second set depicted President Cleveland dressed in a fine tuxedo and New York's mayor-elect William L. Strong dressed in a formal overcoat.[19] While the *New York Herald* aimed to inscribe children in contemporary affairs, another early series of cutout doll supplements was presented more as children's play toys than fashion figures. The series began in the *Chicago Herald* in December 1894: "Delight the children . . . four figures representing Grandpa, Grandma, a Milkmaid, a Farmer, which are intended to be cut out and fitted."[20] The *Herald* explained their value in the classic terms "supply is limited and the demand great," and readers were prodded to take out or renew their subscription to ensure home delivery of the entire series. Otherwise, back numbers of the doll supplements could be purchased for five cents each—the cost of the entire paper![21] The *Detroit Free Press* invoked parents' guilt when it introduced the same sets of paper dolls a few weeks later, predicting that "children who do not get it will make life miserable for parents. . . . If you wish to keep peace at home be sure to have your newsdealer or newsboy reserve you a copy. Better yet, have the paper delivered or mailed to you regularly so that the little ones may be sure to get this wonderful colored paper doll supplement each week."[22] Even as the series concluded, the drive to boost circulation and secure committed subscriptions became transparent in a final reminder that "if you want one be sure and have your newsdealer or newsboy reserve you a copy, or send in your subscription at once."[23]

The direct link to women's fashion came with a paper doll supplement begun in February 1895 at a second Chicago paper, the *Record* (not yet the merged *Record-Herald*). Widely syndicated, the lithograph company was a familiar force under a new name: the G. H. Buek Company, a subsidiary of J. P. Knapp's American Lithographic Company. Unlike other lithographed supplements, these fashion plates were syndicated concurrently, each Sunday paper joining the series at the current edition but with its own nameplate and numbering starting from number one. At the end of March, the *Philadelphia Press* and the *Boston Herald* inaugurated the series by circulating the underclothed figure that would wear the coming weeks' cutout clothes. Although paper dolls had long existed, clear instructions explained how collecting the series depended on carefully keeping the initial figure: "Issued to-day [is] what is called the model figure. All costumes, cloaks and other fashionable garments are so made that they may be fitted over this figure, and the effect thus easily studied."[24] While young girls especially would know exactly what to do with these dolls, their decontextualized place within the newspaper as an object to keep would require instructions, with the promise of future pieces to further animate the model figure.

These paper dolls were clearly cast as women's "fashion plates" and as an extension of the Sunday paper's women's page and fashion column. Three potential types of women would appreciate the fashion dolls: "Your Little Girl" would be pleased with the new feature, which was also "Of Interest to Every Lady," as well as a special draw for "Dressmakers and Milliners," because they would be "revelations" of their art.[25] The series followed in the *St. Louis Republic*, in Cleveland, Cincinnati, and Washington, D.C. The *San Francisco Chronicle* did not adopt the syndicated fashion dolls until November 1895, but the appeal was the same as months earlier in other cities: "It will be a rare pleasure to sit in one's own home and study the effects of coloring in the very latest styles of costumes and wraps, and that, too, with an element of certainty hitherto unknown in fashion plates. . . . To have the latest Paris fashions placed before one every Sunday, with the colors perfect and the patterns ready for instant use, will be the happy lot of every lady in the land who subscribes for *The Sunday Chronicle*."[26] Emphasis also fell on the color lithography; the cutout doll doubled as a fashion plate to provide a vivid and realistic vision of the latest Parisian creations, to assist "lady subscribers" in their imaginations—or even in reality; many newspapers also offered coupons to redeem for patterns of the outfits.[27] The *San Francisco Chronicle*, for example, offered the dress patterns at the newspaper office for ten or fifteen cents—with a coupon—allowing readers to make for themselves the very gown, bonnet, and cloak depicted in the art supplement.

Paper dolls proliferated as Sunday supplements throughout the summer of 1895. Starting several months after the *Boston Herald*'s syndicated doll series, the *Boston Globe* offered high-quality figures from the Boston-based Forbes Lithograph Manufacturing Company. "Forbes Dolls" were already well known as cutout trade cards and advertising souvenirs for products such as Ivory soap and Pillsbury flour; the company's specialty was adding game elements and connective piecework. The cut pieces of a Forbes doll had to be intricately folded and combined to give them moving parts, a third dimension, or to make a stand so that the dolls stood upright on their own. The series began with an abundant set of four dolls, each with two fitting costumes, doubling what was offered in other Sunday doll supplements: "Whenever *The Globe* does anything it aims to do it on a broad and generous scale, regardless of cost and beyond comparison. . . . *The Sunday Globe* will give its readers more dolls and more costumes, superior in every respect, in the single month of June, than any other newspaper attempted to issue in a whole year."[28] In signifying cultural currency and appreciation for aesthetic form, fashion plates, pattern coupons, and paper dolls all showed that the paper matched the fashionable taste of its women readers.

Paper doll supplements were immediately appreciated as inexpensive toys, as if the Sunday paper was providing a public service to the poor. One *New York Herald* reader wrote "in praise and encouragement of your weekly editions of paper dolls. I know of several families of poor children to whom these dolls are giving regular weekly pleasure, and some friends of mine—readers of *The Herald*—cut out each Sunday the doll sheet and forward it to poor children whom we know about."[29] As they had latched onto trade cards a decade earlier, children and young women certainly collected art supplements as the special lithographed sheets in Sunday newspapers became more collectible and interactive in order to appeal more directly as a form of play.

In choosing the Forbes company as partner, the *Boston Globe* signaled that its paper dolls had a more complex charm than other papers' static fashion plates: "They will delight the hearts of all young people, girls and boys alike, with their originality and beauty, and be highly instructive to every woman of taste. Even the men will enjoy these striking pictures of pretty girls."[30] To stoke this broad appeal, the Forbes supplements soon turned to topical and historic themes, beginning with a paper doll of its comic mascot, "a handsome picture of The Globe Man, which can be cut out and will be a unique addition to *The Globe* collection of dolls that our readers have received and preserved."[31] We discuss such mascots more in chapter 5 in the final section on syndication; suffice at present to note how this overtly reflexive supplement—the Sunday paper depicting itself—marked a transition to a wider variety of cutout toys. "Something New!" hollered the promotion for a diorama of a farm: "the cow, the horse, the sheep, the dog, the cat, the pig, the rooster, the farmer, the milkmaid, the stable, the fence and the whole barnyard . . . Free with next Sunday's *Globe*."[32] A miniature replica of *Defender*, the winning yacht from the America's Cup, was the "most unique of all in the popular series of *Sunday Globe* paper toys. . . . Here is a chance to get a yacht and become a yachtsman free of cost."[33] Such claims of startling realism and unprecedented novelty were typical. Famous cyclist Arthur Augustus Zimmerman became a paper toy atop his wheel; other cutout toys pieced together a diorama of a family at Thanksgiving dinner, a Roman chariot race, or one of a series of tableaux of historic American battles. Firefighters were captured "Going to the Fire! . . . Cut it out and set it up and you will have a true and fascinating picture of the most stirring scene in city life."[34] Working locally with Forbes allowed the *Globe* to issue locally themed supplements such as a scene of Boston Common or a parade on the Bunker Hill monument with the Globe Man as marshal.

Other Sunday papers soon adopted the Forbes or competing lithographers' supplements. Some newspapers switched from one lithographer to another and back again—even the *Boston Globe* later had some supplements from Boston's Anderson & Company, part of local book publishers Houghton, Mifflin and Co., others from New York's Donaldson Brothers Company, yet another subsidiary of Knapp's American Lithographic conglomerate. Each Sunday paper's circulation manager seems to have selected from catalogs, since no two newspapers have the same cutout toys in the same order. Although produced in Boston for the *Globe*, some of the Forbes dolls and dioramas appeared first in the *Philadelphia Press*, while others showed up there but never in Boston; those in the *New York Journal* came weeks after Boston, sometimes months. Forbes adapted its designs for local inflections—not just a local paper's name and date, but actually redesigning figures with a local spin. The USS *Philadelphia* was different from the USS *Boston*, although they sailed in identical waters; a circus tableau had the Globe Man in its box office in Boston, while in Philadelphia it was cast as a scene of Barnum & Bailey's Greatest Show on Earth. All of these efforts to connect with readers were designed, of course, to connect locally, as citizens of a city and of the home.

"No Dull Sundays": Paper Theaters

Paper toys gave way to paper theaters. A series of dioramas designed by American Lithographic's Donaldson Brothers subsidiary appeared simultaneously in December 1895 in the *New York Recorder* and the *Boston Globe*. Even more than the dolls and toys, parents were encouraged to help construct the theaters and act as audience. The first play was Palmer Cox's *Brownies*, bug-eyed elves whose illustrated books were a constant of children's commercial culture at the time: "A whole theatre free . . . with a stage, curtain, scenery, a company of actors, 'The Brownies,' all handsome in finish, beautiful in color."[35] This first play came with a stage and proscenium arch to use with subsequent weeks' scenery, just like the initial underclothed model for paper dolls. Priming public interest for the second theater, *Little Red Riding Hood*, the theater was puffed in the *Globe* as "the grandest gift ever made to its readers by any newspaper in the world."[36] Sunday papers routinely made such claims of unprecedented generosity, but the boasts seem especially superlative for paper theaters. The *Philadelphia Inquirer* issued one of the Donaldson Brothers theaters, showing the story of Rip Van Winkle, which, it vouched, was "The Most Expensive Art Supplement ever issued by any newspaper . . . an ornament worth many times the price of *The Inquirer*."[37] On Monday the paper printed a fictionalized story recounting a newsdealer's telephone call begging for additional copies of the unfathomably popular supplements: "Ting-a-ling-aling. 'Hello! Yes, this is *The Inquirer* office. What can I do for you? Send more *Inquirers*? My dear sir, I would do almost anything else, but that is an impossibility.' . . . Why Everybody Wanted It. . . . 'My customers are beginning to realize that they can get a hundred times the worth of their investment.'"[38] When the *Washington Times* later issued the same theaters, it boasted how "the Joy of the Children will overflow all bounds when next Sunday's *Times* is opened. . . . These historic and popular characters are brilliantly colored and costumed and are sure to make the popular paper more popular!"[39] A few weeks later, the *Times*'s claim was even more pointed: "No Dull Sundays Now! . . . Keeping the children amused on Sunday is a thing of the past."[40] The "investment" of the Sunday paper was not only a relative bargain against other entertainments like magazines; it provided other unexpected returns as well. That children were also being subscribed to the practices of the paper—the anticipation of the next edition, the habit of collecting, the desire to sit with its rich, colorful pages—was not only important for making a case for a "family paper," but it also ensured the paper endured within the space of the home.

Competing newspapers adopted alternative paper theaters, sometimes with more mature, elaborate, or exotic plays and scenes. The "Boston Herald Opera House" debuted with a revival of Gilbert and Sullivan's *Mikado*: "the newsdealers of New England will act as ushers."[41] A set of Forbes paper theaters delivered that company's unique brand of intricacy and durability. Advance promotion showed the stage assembled and children playing with the figures: "This theater is different from any other ever given out before by any newspaper. . . . Preserve It. The whole structure interlocks in such a way as to make a very substantial toy."[42] An even more impressive "Souvenir Fairy Theatre" came with the *Philadelphia Inquirer*: "the largest, most artistic, most elaborate, most perfect and most complete souvenir ever given away by any newspaper."[43] In this case the *Inquirer* claimed no equivalent could be purchased at a store for less than four dollars; readers failing to obtain the initial stage with their five-cent Sunday paper had to pay a quarter to buy one from the newspaper office.

Paper Flowers, Zoetropes, and Other Diversions

Perhaps it was the fuss of so many intricate parts, but the toy theater craze passed even more quickly than the series of fashion dolls and cutout toys. The Donaldson Brothers Company developed a series of "real" flowers in pots made from curling the paper into a cylindrical base; they could supposedly be placed on the mantel and mistaken for actual tulips, carnations, or roses. With the start of summer 1896 came several versions of paper-toy baseball games—most valuable of all as collectors' items today. "Base Ball at Home. A New Invention, for playing nine complete innings of our National Game in all kinds of weather."[44] In April 1896, the same month Thomas Edison's Vitascope debuted, several Sunday papers offered zoetrope "moving picture" supplements: "An Unending Wonder. The Newspaper Novelty of Novelties . . . Inanimate figures endowed with life. The crowning triumph of newspaper supplements. Amusement blended with scientific instruction. A child's delight. An adult's wonder."[45] In this case the link to Edison's scientific invention conflated the wonder of play with popular education.

To end its series of paper-toy art supplements, the *Boston Globe* had the Forbes Company create a miniature version of its own fast printing press: "It will be like a visit to the busy pressroom itself! See how *The Globe* is printed, paged and folded by this magnificent machine."[46] Allowing readers to play with the very machine that produced the Sunday paper was a fitting conclusion to the paper-toy fad; in their place the *Sunday Globe* doubled its color section to eight pages. By the fall of 1896, only the *New York Recorder* was still issuing weekly art supplements and it soon stopped, too, when the newspaper itself finally folded; its five-year lifespan of losses and deficits had derived primarily from exactly this reliance on supplements.

The craze had escalated dramatically since the *New York Morning Journal*'s first Picture Gallery etchings in 1889 and the *Recorder*'s first color lithograph poster giveaways in 1891. There was even a brief period in 1895 when art supplements were included on a daily basis in the *Recorder* and the *Chicago Tribune*, but their prevalence gave way to color comics and magazine inserts. Special supplements of cutout toys, paper masks, uncut jigsaw puzzles, sheets of postcards, and the perennial paper dolls were still occasionally given away in the twentieth century but never again for such extended periods or across so many Sunday papers at once. In retrospect the art supplement was an expensive transition between the plain Sunday supplement of the 1880s (simply extra pages of leisure reading) and the color-illustrated, multi-sectioned metropolitan Sunday paper of the late 1890s. In the first decade of the twentieth century, those metropolitan features gained a continental reach through syndicated color comic funny pages and real lithographed magazines. The souvenir art supplement was the precedent for that mature form of Sunday paper even as it continued as an occasional special feature within it. More than anything, however, it lent its logic of serial investment to a more general appreciation of Sunday news reading as a collective pursuit of the artful, playful, fashionable pleasures of modern popular culture. Above all else, the art supplement incorporated women readers into the Sunday paper's mass public, and the paper-toy supplement brought children and juvenile readers to encounter the Sunday edition with great anticipation and appreciation.

THE LIVING PAGE OF SUNDAY SUPPLEMENTS

Art supplements provided the Sunday paper with a strong sense of collectible seriality, but they were inserts, not actually integrated into the paper. Many Sunday sections also had a supplemental relation to the paper, marked apart from the main news section by special format or layout. Children's sections often came in a diminutive form; fiction sections often mimicked the layout of a small book; women's sections were fashionably patterned and dramatized with sentimental pictures; comic sections were colored and, of course, illustrated. The printed form of these Sunday sections reflected how their contents addressed a special class of readers. Simply put, a specialized size and layout often reinforced the specialized address of a Sunday supplement, sharpening its effect with a distinctive shape and design. In its mature form in the twentieth century, each of these supplements to the Sunday paper was often a separate section or inserted magazine of its own.

Consider Pulitzer's *New York World* in the early 1910s. To add an element of variety with little additional cost, the *World* reformatted its Sunday features into a new color section alongside its long-standing "Funny Side" broadsheet comics. First it corralled the "junior page" material into a new quarto section, "Fun": "a 16-page Joke Book, fairly bubbling over with puzzles, jests, stories to tell, tricks to try, &c."[47] This miniature joke book continued for many years, notably introducing Sunday crossword puzzles in December 1913. The *World* then took its fiction serial stories and material from its women's pages and created "The World's Magazine" in 1912, a tabloid "24-page volume of handy size, crowded with articles and stories of unusual interest."[48] None of these weekly supplements were particularly innovative by 1912, but now there were three full-color sections, each with its own distinct size, form, and function—broadsheet comics, tabloid fiction magazine, and quarto joke book—signaling the different moods readers could entertain through the single object of the paper. A "mood" more conducive to Sunday leisure was precisely behind the *Boston Herald*'s own 1912 small-size section: "Is the Sunday newspaper of the future to be a series of tabloid sections? . . . The truth is that the modern newspaper is a bit cumbersome. It does not invite the mood of the book or the magazine."[49] The tabloid form parlayed a more private and intimate relation to reading for smaller hands, for reading at length, and for putting down and returning to repeatedly.

Fashioning the Supplement for Little Hands

Tabloid and quarto supplements first distinguished weekend papers from their weekday counterparts in the early 1890s. In chapter 1 we noted the 1890 introduction of quarto-size "Library" novel supplements in the *New York Morning Journal*. Another small-size pictorial insert came with the *Chicago Inter-Ocean*'s "Illustrated Supplement," considered the first color-printed section in any American newspaper when it began in June 1892. The *Inter-Ocean*'s special supplements were tabloid-size but appeared a full decade before the term "tabloid" was coined for the "condensed" small-form of the "busy-man's paper."[50] The same advances in printing technology that allowed the flourishing of illustration and advertising lay at the root of this other primary trait of folded small-size Sunday supplements. Pages could be laid out in various sizes and turned sideways or upside down so that a single full sheet of newsprint (32" by 22", give or take) could be folded just once to provide the typical four back-and-front broadsheet newspaper pages (16" by 22"). Another fold and cut along the original folded edge created eight tabloid pages (each 11″ by 16″). Folding and cutting again made sixteen quarto pages (each 8″ by 11″). Sometimes folding and cutting the specially sized sections happened at home as the first step of reading. Opening the paper (or now the occasional reel of microfilm or digital image), the special section's pages would appear as something of a jumble in their opposing directions and sizes, rectified with a letter opener slicing along a couple of fresh folds.

As noted above, *the New York Morning Journal* may have been the first to experiment with this kind of miniature booklet pages in fold-and-cut fiction supplements. The *Morning Journal's* "Library" began as a Sunday section in 1890; a special page or two could be folded and transformed into a quarto-size book containing a complete story. By 1894 the *Morning Journal* also offered the tabloid-size "Little Journal" on Saturdays. The *Boston Post* started a tabloid "fiction supplement" for Christmas 1893, just a few months after launching its first Sunday edition. The *Post* let the supplement's literary merit blur into juvenilia by rechristening it the "Children's Sunday Post" after a few months, adding features like puzzles and comics but still with the emphasis on stories. Children's tabloid sections were even introduced to weekend papers in surprisingly small cities. Both major Atlanta papers had tabloid children's supplements surprisingly early. The "Constitution Junior" began on Saturdays in March 1894 before shifting to the Sunday paper; on its heels came the "Juvenile Journal" on Saturdays in September 1895—before the *Atlanta Journal* even had a Sunday edition. Other six-day papers also took up the tabloid-size children's paper—the "Boston Standard Junior" began in March 1895 and the "Minneapolis Junior Journal" in February 1898—a testament to the low technical bar and small cost needed to produce them.

To be sure, the quarto-size section was initially a common way to create "junior" journals or children's heralds, such as two early initiatives that began concurrently in December 1893. The *St. Louis Post-Dispatch* used the insensitive term "Midget" as the name of its small-size children's paper, "a nickname for the Little Paper for Little People."[51] While no copies of this supplement remain to fully judge the content, much was made in promotion of how "Your Little Paper" was a special, almost magical, prize that resulted from searching for it on Sunday mornings: "Get up early tomorrow and be the first to find 'Midget' hidden away in the folds of the big *Sunday Post-Dispatch*."[52] Starting at the same time, the 1893 Christmas edition of the *Chicago Inter-Ocean* changed the format of its eighteen-month-old "Illustrated Supplement," transforming it from a world's fair souvenir into the platform for its youth department and color comics by in-house illustrator Charles W. Saalburg. Advance promotion boasted how "this unique feature in Sunday journalism—this Children's *Inter-Ocean*—with its three little columns to a page—will be the newspaper accomplishment of the year."[53] The novelty was introduced at a moment when the *Inter-Ocean* was employing nearly every gimmick, premium, and special supplement mentioned above: poster art supplements, coupons for special portfolios of photographs and sheet music, more coupons for ornamental binders to collect those souvenir supplements, and yet more coupons and premiums for the new subscription year offering almanacs, cookbooks, and dictionaries. Soon named the "Inter-Ocean Jr.," the children's supplement was delivered as the covering broadsheet pages of the Sunday paper, a quarter-size keepsake made by readers themselves by folding and cutting the special Sunday color covers.

Within a few weeks, the "Inter-Ocean Jr." featured recurring comic characters by Saalburg. He began by simply copying Palmer Cox's Brownies (see plate 5). Saalburg soon introduced his own creation, the Ting Lings—an orientalist cast of crass stereotypes and cheap jokes. Not surprisingly, the first continuing color comic characters in newspaper supplements epitomized the casual racism of the time. Another notable feature of the color pages of the "Inter-Ocean Jr." was a weekly prize picture puzzle. Picture puzzles became a cornerstone of children's sections of all shapes and sizes, especially in early color comic sections. Saalburg's version of the picture puzzle mixed a newspaper contest with his color illustrations, inviting readers to take up their scissors and destroy the very supplement they had coveted with anticipation all week—snip, snip, paste, paste—in order to recreate the pieces of the page as a valuable solution to enter the contest and win the prize. The prize picture puzzle was partly a game like paper dolls and cutout toy supplements but, with a cash prize and one's name published in the following week's paper, the ante was significantly increased for the paper's youngest readers. Like some of the other contests at the time, the prize picture puzzle also doubled as a way to perceive and fully recognize the work behind the composition of the Sunday paper as a material object and, in this case, the famed cartoonists' talent. Picture puzzles played with printing technologies in and of themselves, encouraging appreciation for Saalburg's illustrations and the technology behind printing the illustrated section.

Other versions of prize picture puzzles were geared toward adult readers and more typically offered a challenging contest for them. Consider a special contest run by the *Philadelphia Inquirer* in Sunday editions during the presidential primaries in March and April 1896. For the first contest, eleven portraits of "Presidential Possibilities" were printed around a composite superimposing three of them; the winner had to correctly guess which of the men's drawings were combined to make the apparently moving, unfocused puzzle portrait. The contest complemented the *Inquirer*'s Sunday prize puzzles in its illustrated women's magazine section. Features built around visual or literary puns and riddles were common in Sunday papers, but solutions to earlier versions typically required a depth of knowledge of current events, history, literature, or the arts.

After the creation of its color section in May 1898, the *Inquirer*'s picture puzzles were directed more toward young readers. Similar features were common in early comic supplements, such as the weekly "Great Prize Picture Puzzle" in T. C. McClure's early syndicated funny pages (see fig. 27 in chapter 6).[54] A few versions of the puzzles were custom-made for Sunday papers, such as the *St. Louis Republic*, which combined the picture contest with "magic transformation pictures," a widespread fad in 1902. The *Republic's* first "Prize Color Page," drawn by in-house comic illustrator H. F. Thode, provided readers with a palate of color ink daubs. Not a puzzle at all, in this case prizes went to the best-painted pictures.[55] An early first-prize winner, Malvyn Hunter, came from an artistic house: "Her father, who is dead, was a painter and her mother has devoted some study to the art. . . . Nevertheless, her mother declares that the child received her artistic training from the color pages of the Sunday newspapers."[56] Third-place winner Genevieve Lewry also supposedly "procured her knowledge of painting from the newspapers."[57] The feature provided children with fun, the *Republic* claimed, but "the secondary purpose [is] developing any latent skill with the brush they might possess and assisting in the cultivation of the artistic temperament by educating them in the harmonious arrangement of colors."[58] If the claim of art education seems incredulous, there is a kernel of truth to it: like many of the technologies of reading reviewed in this section, appreciation of the form and features of the Sunday paper are combined with a prize and the possibility of being named an expert reader of the Sunday paper. The weekly coloring contest continued for four months; each week up to a dozen photographs of winners were printed in the paper—rewarded for coloring the comics of the Sunday supplement themselves. By the early twentieth century, the new journalism's 1880s gimmick of printing names of subscribers to a public fund had become illustrated collages of photographs of prizewinners—the *San Francisco Sunday Call* even made a puzzle out of this collage, printing a jumble of faces of "puzzle workers," asking, "Is your picture here?"[59]

Magic Ink and Trick Pictures

With "hidden pictures," Sunday comics used "magic" inks that required some type of manipulation. In certain versions, as those used in the *St. Louis Republic*, you dipped a brush into a "paint pot" on the page, transferring color to another part of the page; in others, you wet the page with a paintbrush to reveal part of the comic that wasn't apparent before; still others had "invisible" ink that had to be rubbed with a coin, gently shaded with a pencil, or heated with an iron to make the image appear. In 1902 most every newspaper with a color printing press exploited one or more of the novelty color inks. Hearst's *New York Journal* even advertised its new "magic for the little ones" with small notices on the front pages of competing newspapers: "Nothing you can buy for your children will interest them more."[60] Sometimes the veneer of art education was entirely discarded, such as for the *Philadelphia Press's* "Watergraphs": "You touch them with water, and in a second they become beautiful water color paintings. No skill is needed."[61] The *Cleveland Plain Dealer* had a series of "Mother Goose Magic Pictures," one picture for each letter of the alphabet. Readers were told to "take a brush or sponge dipped in water and go over the pictures carefully as if you were painting them. . . . Don't rub the paper!"[62] In those other "rubbed" versions, blank space was magically illustrated with just a little pressure.

There was even a syndicated "transformation magazine" supplement titled the "New Era." When launched in December 1901, the *Indianapolis Journal* explained how "the wonderful transformation effects are either highly instructive or amusing and at all times undeniably entertaining. . . . Things that children should know are made to rise up from the blank pages and lifelike object lessons will impress them far more than arduous study."[63] The "transformation supplement" also included fiction, women's features, and children's games. The *Buffalo Times* called it "a household necessity . . . a beautifully printed bound magazine with clean, refined literary features."[64] Preprinted syndication made the supplement affordable for smaller-city Sunday editions and even some small-town Saturday papers.[65] Another early version was the "transformation pictures" in the bound magazine supplement to the *Boston Journal*'s Christmas edition—"an idea covered by patent, surprising and most unusual."[66] The teasing promotion for a subsequent edition makes it clear the picture emerged from rubbing a pencil lightly across the apparently blank spaces to make "the most interesting pictures mysteriously appear."[67] Rechristened "magic pictures" in February, the *Journal*'s instructions changed to indicate that you could rub them with a coin instead of a pencil lead. This must have relieved some parents, since it was relatively clean, especially compared to spreading daubs of color all over the page.

Never to be outdone, the *New York World* introduced "magic paint-box pictures" and puzzle "wonder pictures" in March 1902, drawn by Charles Saalburg. As with his work years earlier for the *Chicago Inter-Ocean*, these pictures had to be cut out and folded, the paper reformed in shape to reveal a hidden meaning or scene by aligning pieces of the pictures. The *Pittsburg Press* told its readers to rub the page's blank spaces with "the bowl of a spoon upon a hard surface" to discover the hidden pictures, in a twist on the nuisance of newspaper ink rubbing off on readers' fingers.[68] In another gimmick, children had to carefully heat or moisten the paper to "develop the negative" of the "Hidden Pictures" in the *Boston Post*—a cheeky introduction to the magical processes of photography.[69] In some cases the microfilmed and digitized pages are preserved and we can see the "hidden" part of the picture—sometimes clearly, sometimes only faintly, or sometimes not at all (see fig. 11). In any case, we can't "develop" the preserved pictures ourselves. Indeed, the impossibility of digitizing these particular types of art supplements shows how the pleasures of print culture in the Sunday paper were material: taking hold of the page to skillfully rub, cut, wet, fold, and tear the

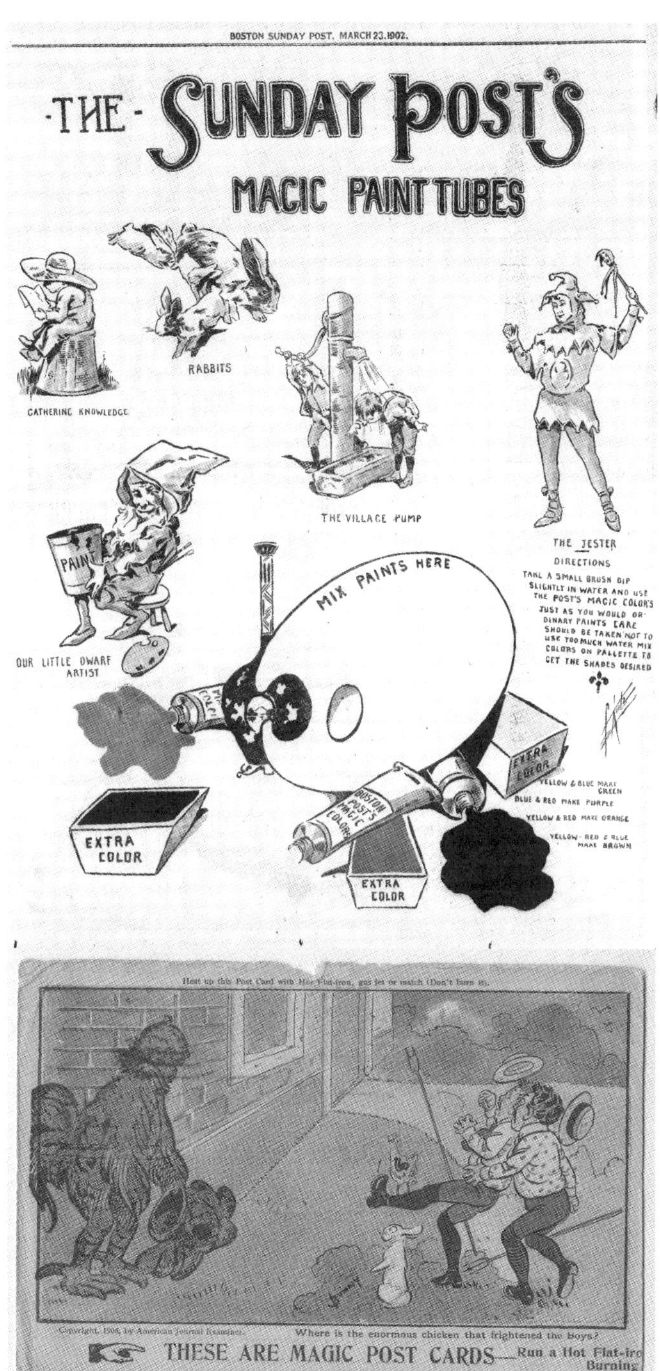

FIGURE 11. "The Sunday Post's Magic Paint Tubes," *Boston Post*, March 23, 1902; and "These Are Magic Post Cards," Sunday supplement, Hearst *American-Journal-Examiner*, June 1906. (Authors' collection.)

paper. The paper needed to be possessed and then processed—used correctly, the paper had to be used up.

Sunday "magic pictures" were not the only novelty going by that name in 1902: the "trick" genre of moving pictures was also then known as "magic pictures," and the coincidence affords an opportunity to consider the Sunday supplement's technologies of reading as an actual media technology in direct relation to early cinema—two competing players in an emerging media culture. Key among cinema's early genres were trick films, a specialty of French producer Georges Méliès, in which various types of stop-motion and superimposed layers allowed the illusion of disappearing acts or impossible juxtapositions. One famous example, "Man with the Rubber Head," had Méliès's own head inflate like a balloon, filling up more of the cinematic frame until it appeared to explode in a poof of smoke.[70] At the turn of the century, trick films were a primary attraction of moving picture programs. By 1899 the most prominent traveling film exhibitor, Lyman H. Howe, was calling them "magic pictures," as did other film exhibitors.[71] At least associatively, the Sunday paper's turn to newsprint "magic pictures" tapped into the concurrent magical novelty of cinema.

For Christmas 1904, Hearst's *Los Angeles Examiner* and other papers in the chain gave away free "Wizard Glasses" in order to view the Sunday supplement's special, colored "wonder pictures, or the plastograph and anaglyph as they are scientifically termed."[72] These stereoscopic, three-dimensional "anaglyph" pictures were, at first glance, a blur of multicolored dots, but the two-toned "plastograph" glasses brought the realistic image into relief, exactly as 3-D cinema would work in later decades. The *Philadelphia Record* introduced them with the explanation that "this novelty, so baffling to science, consists of an apparently blurred picture and a plastograph or 'Magic Spectacles.' . . . Looking at the picture at the proper focus, a result, entertaining and interesting, will be at once produced."[73] Other newspapers soon followed suit. The *Syracuse Herald* offered an anaglyph portfolio of a "Tour of the World" for a coupon and ten cents;[74] the *Buffalo Enquirer* and the *Detroit Free Press*, for example, offered a book of "plastic stereoscopical views of the world" for a coupon and ten cents, while the *Boston Herald* offered the same free to all who purchased a classified ad in a particular Sunday edition.[75]

By 1922, with the advent of commercial broadcast radio and everyday movies, such printed and written descriptions of fantastic accounts of reality were augmented by audio and visual practices. Within this multimedia environment, it is notable that the play of cutting, painting, and folding newspaper pages again became the basis for children's Sunday supplements. The resuscitation of the "magic pictures" fad can be traced to two national syndicate publishers of Sunday color comics: Hearst and World Color Printing. For two decades by then, both companies had long pioneered strategies for popularizing color comics in major metropolitan newspapers and even small-town weekend editions. But late in 1921,

Hearst Sunday papers began including an eight-page tabloid-size "Book of Magic." When the *San Francisco Examiner* and the *Washington Times* began including the "special children's section" in December, the supplement compiled so many different choices for fun, games, and activities that juvenile readers were warned to "not wet or cut any of the pages until you survey the entire book and make your choice."[76] On the cover was a magic ink picture by well-known illustrator Nell Brinkley, needing to be wet to see the colors. Two more "magic picture" pages inside transformed illustrations of flowers into colored pictures and brought a rainbow fantasy scene to life in full color. On the back cover was a paint-box feature—wet the daubs to create a palette of colors to create your own episode of *Bringing Up Father*, one of Hearst's famous comic strips. Inside was a paper doll to cut out and dress as a toy; another page had the pieces to construct a kicking donkey, Maud, to knock over Si, more then-famous characters from Hearst Sunday funnies; on the inside fold was a pirate's mask and hat to cut out and wear as a costume.

The panoply of Sunday supplement tricks and treats continued for the months the section lasted. World Color Printing's "Invisible Color Book" began in March 1922 as direct competition, another eight-page children's supplement with magic paint pictures that was nationally syndicated to at least a dozen Sunday papers and, curiously, with different titles: the *Des Moines Register* had it as their "Magic Picture Book," while the *Louisville Courier-Journal* had it as their "Magic Ink Section," and the *Cleveland Plain Dealer* named it their "Fairy Color Section." In addition to four "invisible ink" sketches, World Color's special supplement relied more on riddles and games, since they did not have the draw of famous comic characters.[77]

REGULATING SUPPLEMENTS

Taken collectively, the ability of Sunday papers to include novelty forms of print innovation as special supplements is remarkable. It did not go without notice by authorities. In 1905 such Sunday supplements were deemed "manifestly illegal" by Edwin C. Madden, a doctrinaire assistant postmaster general who would dog the newspaper publishing industry for more than a year. At issue was the legal definition of newspapers as second-class mail, which was subsidized for rural delivery to distant subscribers. Newspapers were especially vulnerable to such rulings of the postal commission because all newspapers—especially Sunday papers—traveled in the mail well beyond their local areas of circulation. Madden insisted that a newspaper must contain news, pure and simple, and that a supplement had to be clearly "germane" to the news: "matter supplied in order to complete what is left incomplete in the paper itself."[78] This opinion rested upon 1879 legislation that permitted publishers to "fold within their regular issues a supplement; but in all cases the added matter must be germane to the publication which it supplements, that is to say . . . omitted from the regular issue for want of space, time, or greater convenience."[79] Was an enfolded comic, music, or art supplement left out of the main sections of the paper only for lack of space or time? Only for convenience? In Derrida's sense, as noted in chapter 1, these supplements mark a material surplus that newsprint normally neglects. Their color, durability, and collectability offer all the more evidence they were not necessarily germane to the news. They do not complete the news; they offer something *other than* the news. Even the fate of comic funny pages and magazine sections became uncertain and the clear-cut case of toy and poster supplements was effectively shut down. In Madden's official opinion, the Sunday newspaper had strayed too far from its mandate of public service in delivering the news. Madden's circular instructing his army of local postmasters was quoted at length in newspaper reports about the decision. It offered a good summary of the previous fifteen years' development of the Sunday paper:

> These alleged supplements consist of calendars, sheet music, patterns, blocks of post cards, series of cut-out animal pictures, animal masks, plastographs, cut-out dolls, soldiers, naval vessels, circulars, hand bills, special detached advertisements, cardboard spectacles, sheets containing disks of soluble paint to be used in coloring outline drawings, &c. . . . The practice of adding things like those above enumerated to newspapers under the guise of "supplements" is the outgrowth of modern competition and no doubt the result of a desire to add to the attractiveness of the papers by such extraneous matter. That consideration, however, cannot justify the department accepting them at the privileged second-class rates provided by law only for the newspapers themselves. . . . The utmost good faith must be observed by publishers availing themselves of the benefit of these privileged rates. Those rates cannot be employed for the transmission of matter manifestly illegal to the detriment of the revenues.[80]

Although Madden acknowledged that there was no intent to defraud the government, he nonetheless stridently insisted that publishers had to observe "the utmost good faith" to receive the subsidy; special supplements were "manifestly illegal to the detriment of the revenues" of the postal commission.[81]

One indication of how the new directive was implemented can be found in a complaint lodged by a Maryland paper, the *Frederick News*, ridiculing Postmaster Madden for hypocrisy in allowing Baltimore papers to issue a New Year's calendar as a "part or section" of their voluminous Sunday papers while insisting the small city paper could not issue a calendar as a gift supplement.[82] Even though both calendars served the same purpose, the one needing to be torn apart from the paper was legal, while the one inserted in the folds was not permitted. Recall our discussion in chapter 1 of another 1905 ruling that deemed circulation-boosting guessing contests to be lotteries, resulting in the strict adherence to talent and skill as the basis for contests such as prize puzzles. Sunday papers now also needed to include their games, puzzles, dolls, souvenirs, and storybooks *within* sections that were self-evidently part of the paper, not supplements to it.

The complaint that supplements were not germane to the paper, in fact, dates back to the very first special supplements, more than twenty-five years earlier. In reference to the *Chicago Inter-Ocean's* collectible musical supplements from 1881—perhaps the first series of supplements in any paper in North America— an editor from St. Louis immediately grasped the crux of the matter and pithily noted, "If this thing continues, a daily newspaper will come to be something like the candy and pop-corn packages which train boys peddle on the railways; every sheet will be expected to contain some sort of a prize, from a pinchback breast-pin up to a hand-organ and a trick monkey."[83] Funny enough, one of the Forbes company paper dolls for the *Boston Globe* in 1896 allowed readers to make their own cutout toy of an organ grinder with his monkey sidekick, flanked by a little boy and girl, thrilled with their cheap entertainment.

In the twentieth century, Sunday papers' reliance on inserted novelty supplements began to wane. As we discuss fully in chapter 6, special souvenir art supplements became replaced by standardized, nationally syndicated comic sections and magazine supplements. As we review in chapter 3, news publishers began to collaborate with wireless companies and film producers to supplement the paper with entirely other media, heard and viewed in other spaces and times. Here, in the final section of this chapter, we turn to the newspaper's adoption and promotion of another mediated technology in the 1920s with the opening of newspaper-owned radio stations and other uses of radio that extended the supplement even further and into new material states. Radio augmented and expanded upon many newspapers' commitment to public service by sponsoring civic engagements, public education, and popular entertainment, all initially following the logic charted by earlier supplements to the paper.

THE BROADCAST SUPPLEMENT
OF NEWSPAPER RADIO

Histories of early radio frequently remark that newspaper publishers owned a significant number of the earliest radio stations in the United States and Canada. Operating many of the most powerful and influential early broadcasting stations, newspaper-owned radio licenses made up a relatively small proportion of U.S. broadcast stations but among the most prominent stations in their respective cities.[84] Newspapers and their newly formed radio stations in 1922 had more than a mere commercial relationship; the radio stations were, effectively, another form of newspaper supplement. Newspapers understood radio as enabling a fulfillment

of their mandate of public service, including (but not limited to) providing popular entertainment, also serving as a school for readers "learning to listen."[85] By
1924 *Editor and Publisher* claimed that nearly one thousand newspapers in North
America were printing daily radio columns, and at least two dozen printed weekly
radio tabloid magazine supplements, including the *New York Herald* and the *New
York World*, the *Chicago Daily News*, and the *Los Angeles Times*.[86] For Judith Walker,
who ran the *Chicago Daily News* station, WMAQ, the connection was explicit. Following the logic of the magazine and newsreel in earlier years, the station's radio
programming reflected the structure of the newspaper. As Walker later said in an
interview, "When I thought of a women's program, I would think of it emanating
from the women's department of the paper, or a children's program coming from
the children's department. . . . We tried to tie the paper and the station together."[87]

Explanations of the early adoption of radio by publishers generally build upon
contemporary rationales provided by newspaper editors themselves. First is the
instrumental explanation of cross-promotion in the face of competition from
other newspapers.[88] Owning a radio station meant broadcasting the newspaper's
name as a form of advertising to encourage buying the paper itself. "Aided by its
ability to publicize its program schedule," the *Detroit News* forged the way on an
amateur license 8MK in 1920 (later WWJ on a commercial license) and "wasted
no opportunity to capitalize on each nuance of this fortuitous synergy from day
one."[89] A second explanation is that newspapers were keen to take up fads and
novelties or, phrased more charitably, to adopt new technologies in order to fulfill
their established place in the cultural vanguard: "Newspapers are always 'the first
by whom the new is tried,' never 'the last to lay the old aside,'" as one editor put it in
a speech to his peers about "The Relation of Radio to Newspapers."[90] Newspaper
publishers were likely to espouse a principle of public service as their social function, albeit a sentiment that could be self-serving. Newspapers' established public
service and professionalism extended to radio for the manager of the *Kansas City
Star*'s WDAF: "In terms of management, public service, and program quality, the
newspaper was simply the best kind of owner."[91] Newspapers perceived an affinity with radio as the latest fad to secure publicity, and therefore sales, but also
the more principled stance of serving "as a natural extension of and supplement
to their role as media of communication."[92] On the most basic level, this meant
offering the same variety of news and other features as the newspaper.

The *Detroit News* was the earliest newspaper to extend its circulation with
broadcasting, using its experimental station 8MK to announce state primary
election results in August 1920: "This is the first time in the history of radio development that a newspaper will use the radiophone in the transmission of news.
. . . A hundred years from now, perhaps, all news will be transmitted by wireless
telephone; who knows?"[93] In October 1921 the paper later received one of the
very first commercial broadcast licenses. One early program featured visiting

vaudeville star Fanny Brice, who "treated *The News* radio audience to a rehearsal of 'Second-Hand Rose,' used by her as an entrance song for her appearance in Ziegfeld's Follies. There are many stars in Detroit's theatrical heavens this week."[94] The newspaper also installed one of the first powerful long-distance transmitters in February 1922, giving its radio news circulation nearly continent-wide reach: "Detroit touches hands each night with places far and near, great and small, some of them 2,000 miles distant, talks and sings to the man of affairs, sitting with his family in the snug comfort of his living room, gives the latest news of land and sea, to those far off in lonely places, to whom even the convenience of a daily newspaper is frequently denied."[95]

Hearst and Pulitzer stayed clear of New York radio airwaves, dominated by anchor stations operated by American Telephone & Telegraph (AT&T) and the Radio Corporation of America (RCA).[96] The Sunday paper moguls' sister originating publications in San Francisco and St. Louis, however, were early broadcasters in those cities, and among the more prominent newspaper-owned stations nationally. "Hello, hello, hello. This is *The San Francisco Examiner*'s broadcasting station, K.U.O.—K.U.O.," began Hearst radio's first test of its new transmitter in March 1922. The paper explained the basis for expanding its mission into the ether: "Broadcast from *The Examiner*'s high-powered station on the Hearst building ... Unlike other means of communication there is no cost for service. Like opening the window and inhaling the air this new means of entertainment fits any pocketbook and popularizes the family fireside."[97] Reporting on early broadcasts verged on hyperbole, describing radio as "a chapter from some prophet's dream-book ... a ceremony simple and unique in character yet uncanny in its weird manifestations."[98] On the other hand, the craze for radio in 1922 was real, despite newspapers puffing their own stations: "Never was there such a degree of enthusiasm over any fad, if it can be classed as such, until *The Examiner* announced its plan of serving the public by this means of modern scientific wonders."[99]

Inland at St. Louis, Pulitzer's *Post-Dispatch* launched station KSD in similar terms, with a spotlight shining on the company's New York headquarters. The station's inaugural broadcast spoke of a sample of "'news possibilities' lying at that moment before the managing editor of the *New York World* ... to appear a few hours later in that newspaper, and be read at the Sunday breakfast table by New Yorkers."[100] Another early program, "Selling St. Louis," featured the president of a realty company praising the city for the paper and its famous publisher: "'*The Post-Dispatch* is something more than a news disseminator. It is an institution founded 44 years ago by Joseph Pulitzer and developed by him and his successors as an expression of an old ideal—an ideal of service in the public good.'" After listing the annual acts of charity sponsored by the paper, the speaker continued: "'This broadcasting of news, music and talks is another service given to the public by *The Post-Dispatch* from which it derives no direct profit—a fine example of this newspaper's enterprise.'"[101] Other early newspaper-owned stations were opened in the Midwest, along the Pacific Coast, and in cities across the South. In chapter 6 we explore how these newspaper-owned stations were crucial to expanding the radio network outside its anchor in New York. Suffice it to note how newspaper publishers in the Northeast kept clear of the airwaves. There were no newspaper-owned stations in New York, Philadelphia, Boston, or Washington, leaving AT&T and RCA stations free rein to develop the medium without competition.

Wireless Pages and Radio Columns

Although New York newspapers had no direct involvement in broadcasting, most began reporting radio news or providing radio features or supplements to readers. The *Sunday World* began a modest weekly column and program listing in January 1922, with the *Sunday Herald* following in February. The *Tribune* took the lead among New York Sunday papers with an illustrated feature written by a leading personality of the new wireless medium.[102] For the most part, however, New York's six-day evening papers were left to cater to the nightly rituals of the growing numbers of radio fans. The *Evening World* began a daily "radio phone service column" in January 1922.[103] Publicity for the *New York Globe and Commercial Advertiser*'s new radio magazine in February claimed to be "the leader of all others."[104] In March the *New York Evening Mail* launched a Saturday "16-page illustrated radio magazine," encouraging the novice, "If you don't know radio, read this magazine and learn."[105] In Boston, old rivals the *Herald* and the *Globe* took hold of the radio reins with more energy, each launching Sunday radio pages in February 1922. The *Globe* page edited by Lloyd C. Greene began a week earlier but stuck to technical advice.[106] The *Herald* page edited by Joe Toye, on the other hand, addressed the reader as a potential radio fan: "At last! A feature that will interest EVERYBODY—men, women, boys and girls, old and young. Radio! 'Wireless,' you may call it."[107] But even in Boston, the *Traveler*, a six-day evening paper, took the real lead with radio news, publishing a daily "Citizen Wireless" column to match its broadcast bulletins for a local station.[108]

Unsurprisingly, contests were part of newspapers' strategies for engaging radio fans as habitual readers of the new pastime's feature page. The *San Francisco Examiner* printed a picture of a "happy family with its radio phone and receiving set gathered to enjoy the thrill of radio concert music" and gave a ten-dollar prize for reader-listeners to snap the "best photo of a radio family," posing at home listening in to KUO.[109] The *Boston Traveler* gave a weekly prize of a dollar to radio-fan readers "for the best article submitted on the subject named for that week. . . . The subject for this week: 'The cheapest receiving set.' Get busy!"[110] The most elaborate prizes were not for contests. Some newspapers dangled premiums of free radio sets for young radio-fan readers in return for selling the paper itself by wrangling new subscribers to the paper. In San Francisco, again, the *Examiner* offered a cure for "*radioitis* . . . solacing the sufferers from the malady through its offer of a complete $65 Cosco Radiophone Receiving Set to each person, child or adult, who will devote a little spare time to interesting new readers in the 'Monarch of the Dailies.'"[111] St. Louis saw "1000 Radio Receiving Sets Offered FREE to Boys by *The Post-Dispatch*" if they could secure ten new home delivery subscriptions.[112] How much spare time was needed to secure twenty new six-month subscribers to the paper? Only "a little of your time," according to a similar offer from the *San Francisco Chronicle*, under a cartoon of "everyone" in an extended family listening on their own headsets (see fig. 12).[113]

FIGURE 12. "Everyone Can Win a Radio Receiving Set Free," *San Francisco Chronicle*, April 12, 1922, 6.

Some newspaper-owned stations tested novel ways to get readers to engage with the paper through radio. The *Kansas City Star*'s WDAF, for example, put windows in their broadcast studio walls to allow small public audiences to watch the announcers and musicians live as they were listening, reminiscent of viewing galleries and tours of printing presses, discussed in chapter 4.[114] Early WDAF broadcast concerts could also be enjoyed in a group of local movie theaters across Kansas City: "Choose Your Neighborhood Theater. . . . They offer this entertainment in addition to a program of high standard pictures."[115] WDAF also began to broadcast a regular fashion chat by the *Star*'s women's page editor, who promised to "give style hints and coffee recipe tonight . . . the fall forecast of fashions from the style centers of the world. New lines, new colors and the latest accessories of dress."[116] Indeed, this idea had begun in February 1922, in a New York collaboration, when Pulitzer's Press Publishing syndicated columnist Margery Wells began a "Fashion Talk" on WJZ, accompanied by illustrated features in the *New York Evening World*: "Hear these talks over the radio every Saturday evening—Read them in *The Evening World* the following Monday."[117]

Westinghouse-owned WJZ was initially located in Newark, New Jersey, and soon was RCA's key early radio station for New York. Because WJZ was not co-owned by a single newspaper, it solicited several publications to contribute daily or weekly features. In March 1922 alone, the *New York Evening Mail* began a nightly bedtime story, the *New York Telegram* a series of "Animal Stories," and the *Newark Evening Call* a serialized version of "The Man in the Moon." Hearst International Features syndicated cartoonist George McManus even began a spoken version of his hit comic strip, *Bringing Up Father*.[118] The Westinghouse station in Chicago, KYW, began broadcasting nightly programs from the *Chicago Tribune* even earlier, in January 1922, which combined several features into a single variety sampling of spoken elements from the paper. One early program in "*The Tribune*–Westinghouse Radio News Service" began with "The Teenie Weenies," a bedtime story from the paper's syndicated comic section, then "A Line o' Type or Two," a spoken version of its humor column. Financial and market summaries led into news bulletins, live from the wire, and then a musical program, tied up with more "bulletins from *Tribune* correspondents all over the world."[119]

As an important aside, until we delve further into national syndication in chapter 6, the *Chicago Tribune* later launched what became *Amos 'n' Andy*, a few years after it started its own radio station, WGN ("World's Greatest Newspaper" was its long-standing motto). The newspaper wanted comedians Charles J. Correll and Freeman F. Gosden to develop a radio version of its own comic strip, *The Gumps*, but the blackface minstrel performers instead created original characters to create a "radio comic strip."[120] "Meet 'Sam 'n' Henry' tonight! The funniest ten minutes ever are in store for radio fans this evening with the first appearance over WGN, *The Chicago Tribune* station."[121] Still in 1926, the immense success of *Sam 'n' Henry* seemed like a novelty needing explanation rooted in the long-standing ideas of serial newspaper features: "The idea of the aerial comic strip is good in itself—daily doings of a few funny people, in a continued story for those who can hear it every night, and with each evening's episode an entity in itself for the benefit of the irregular listeners."[122] The *Chicago Tribune* and many other newspapers, of course, had long been contributing spoken versions of their leisure and humor features, as well as news, from the very start of commercial radio.

Newspaper illustrators and cartoonists were called upon to narrate and provide talk accompaniments to their printed pictures. In 1926 *Chicago Tribune* radio WGN broadcast a series of "adventure talks" by "John T. McCutcheon, cartoonist, author and traveler, whose cartoons have appeared on the front page of *The Tribune* for years."[123] In 1924 a long-running series of "radio-photologues" began on *Chicago Daily News's* own station, WMAQ, tied to a page of pictures in its rotogravure section. Adding voice and sound to images only otherwise created in the mind via words on a page, radio-photologues combined sensory experiences in ways seen earlier in other spectacular mediated experiences, like the Parisian panoramas of the nineteenth century that provided a multisensorial presentation of reality:[124] "It's all aboard for a fireside trip around the world, by photogravure and radio. . . . The traveler, with his 'photo' before him and his set tuned in for WMAQ will hear the pictures brought to life by travelers skilled in story-telling."[125] Since the first months of radio broadcasting, sports news was a key feature of newspaper radio. The *Wisconsin State Journal's* own station, WGAY in Madison, gave live returns of a college football match against Minnesota, with the radio editor announcing live on air while "several thousand football fans stood in front of *The Wisconsin State Journal* building to receive returns of the game."[126] The joint radio station of the *Dallas News* and *Dallas Journal*, WFAA, played sports reports in August 1922 live outside its offices for "baseball fans who were unable to gain entrance to Gardner Park."[127] The *News-Journal* radio truck, the paper explained, would also be "stationed at various principal street intersections at different times during the day to enable the people near those intersections to hear concerts, addresses, market reports and news bulletins as they are broadcast from WFAA."[128] Also in Texas, the 1922 World Series baseball games were heard live on loudspeakers of the *San Antonio Evening News* radio car outside the newspaper office.[129]

Supplementing news circulation through loudspeakers on automobiles and trucks was a surprisingly common pursuit of smaller-city newspaper-owned radio stations. In San Antonio, for example, the *Evening News's* radio car gave neighborhood concerts across the city "for the benefit of those who have not yet installed radio receiving sets in their homes."[130] In Rochester, New York, the *Democrat and Chronicle* sent its radio car to county fairs to give rural listeners their first taste of the new broadcasting fad. In Livonia, New York, "The truck stopped in the center of the main street . . . and several hundred people turned out to enjoy the music."[131] With radio, newspapers extended the circulation of their variety for thousands of miles and expanded the logic of subscription to include the simultaneity of mass listening in combination with reading. Like all the contests and premium offers, broadcasting was not a distraction from newspapers providing print news, but was instead a supplement to the modern variety that the Sunday paper had specialized in for more than three decades. Upon the launch of its own radio station, WGN, the *Chicago Tribune* turned to the metaphor of a variety of tastes on a restaurant menu to explain the mandate it embraced with radio: "*The Tribune* will endeavor to make one of the most entertaining, instructive and diversified programs broadcast anywhere in the country . . . a record breaking menu with radio morsels to suit every taste."[132] This had exactly been the implicit mandate and explicit promise of the Sunday paper.

In 1922 William Randolph Hearst's *Chicago American* reported a news story about a newsreel film of an Easter Sunday radio broadcast. The film was produced by Hearst International Newsreel Service, and the broadcast was sponsored by the *American* to celebrate a new arrangement providing daily radio news bulletins to Westinghouse broadcasting station KYW. The article, printed on the *American*'s upstart daily radio department page, explained, "The picture was designed to give the radio public which heard that great *Chicago Evening American* concert a graphic impression of what was happening at the other end of the ether lane, while it was sitting at ease at their receivers."[133] The intricate network confluent here is curious for its confusion of forms and overlapping media technologies; it has newspaper readers imagining theater audiences watching silent movies of a radio broadcast, with each mediated public inextricable from the others.[134] The twinned ideals of reproduced sensation and mass circulation had now been combined in an intermedial conflation of broadcast, print, and moving pictures, where reporting, newsreels, and entertainment were combined in public service. These premises were made explicit by the newspaper article itself, which ascribed such interplay to a natural extension of the routine function of the newspaper as an institution of public service: "Another instance of this newspaper being in radio First With The Latest, as well as in all other departments."[135] Radio, the newest medium in this assemblage, was presented as merely another department of the newspaper, a supplement alongside the magazine, color comics, and departments for fashion, sports, and entertainment. This alchemical mixture of media publics was at the heart of American newspapers' pursuit of expanded cultural circulation through their Sunday edition supplements. The adoption of new media technologies pursued a more descriptive journalism, a more imbricated readership, and a wider circulation through the multisensory technological reproduction of the newspaper itself.

In the two chapters of this section on subscription, we charted how the variety of special features in Sunday editions called for more investment on the part of readers: their time, their attention, and their money. In pursuit of increased circulation, wider readership, and greater cultural influence, newspapers expanded the form of the newspaper. Postmaster Madden was exactly right on one point: supplements were an attraction to readers; but they were not necessarily a distraction from the news. As we noted in introducing the chapter, a supplement completes a paper precisely by refusing to be germane to the function of news. The effect is only heightened by refusing to adhere to the form of the newspaper. Ornament is meaningless without structure, but an accessory doesn't devalue what it adorns. Similarly, the pleasure of supplements accentuated the leisure of Sunday papers, and in turn the Sunday paper contributed to journalism's standing as a public institution.

We defined a subscription as all at once a technology of reading, an act of citizenship, and an adoption of the subjectivity of mass popular culture. Subscription, then, is one of the ways news reading becomes culturally structured through participation in mass society, in popular culture and consumption, and in the democratic public sphere. Defining a contest, coupon, or keepsake as a technology of reading allowed us to demonstrate how different supplements of the Sunday paper subtly but continually shifted which reading public was the imagined community at play. From Joseph Pulitzer opening up to view the spectacle of the *New York World*'s pressroom to the *Chicago Tribune*'s radio comic strip and other papers' radio cars with their public concerts and newscasts, newspaper publishers have continually emphasized their circulation as a social relation to their readers, one mediated through technologies. The Sunday paper made modern subjects of its readers and syndicated regional publishers into a continental media network.

Preliminary versions of such endeavors can be seen in early experiments with telegraphed and wireless news in the late 1890s. With the foundation of the printing press as a technology exceeding the capacity of human labor, the Sunday paper's efforts to overcome the constraints of circulating newsprint in material form embraced circulation as a modern ideal and transformed journalism from pen pictures to moving picture newsreels and radio broadcasting. Intermedial relations between reading, seeing, and listening, and intermedial forms such as newspaper-sponsored newsreels and newspaper-owned radio stations demonstrate the long-standing aim of the Sunday paper to address all media publics as a single public; newspaper readership was defined as the mass public.

As we wrote earlier, it is easy to imagine that listening to a radio program could be so enhanced by features and articles printed in a newspaper's radio page that a listener might feel the experience was incomplete without having read the newspaper. Conversely, the newspaper reader interested in listening to the radio without being able to hear the nightly broadcast might feel knowledgeable about the novelty, but the experience of reading was likewise incomplete. This promise of a complete experience was precisely the point of publicity and promotion supporting newspapers' supplementary contents, from the earliest art supplements, music sheets, toy theaters, and paper dolls that animated society and fashion pages, theater reviews and listings, and feature stories about contemporary culture. The mass broadcast of the radio program was likewise designed to be accompanied by the mass reading of the newspaper and supplemented in turn by seeing the newsreel at a theater, as we review in the next chapter. Taking newspaper reading beyond the page and transforming knowledge gleaned from reading into social activities was an organizing principle for the Sunday newspaper. As we have suggested throughout our first two chapters, extratextual practices that were initially appended to the Sunday paper as temporary, tactile supplements changed the material composition of news reading well beyond the paper itself and in turn changed the relation between "reading" and reader. These supplements were material instances that conditioned a unique subjectivity for reading the Sunday paper, transforming the commitment of a subscription into the social relation of mass leisure.

PART II

CIRCULATION

The first section of this book described how the newspaper's various supplements required learning new reading practices that produced new kinds of readers through their very form and design, even as the Sunday paper's form shifted in response to readers' demands and changes in the industry. The combination of the Sunday paper's serial continuity and its segmented construction oriented the reader to an ongoing, long-term commitment to sustained interest in active techniques of "reading." We paid particular attention to the use of contests, coupons, and premium giveaways as modes of organizing reading in terms of a continually renewed commitment to being a reader who responded as well as consumed. Subscription and home delivery are metonyms for the commitment of readers to the paper as a material thing, but the specific materiality of the Sunday paper meant that its cultural circulation depended on its print form getting delivered. If the expanded features of the Sunday paper and subscriptions were to pay off for readers, newspapers had to actually reach their hands on Sundays.

This section turns to the material agents that made wider circulation possible: newsboys, fast trains, fast presses, and the continental distribution system of the American News Company. Meeting demand for an expanded mass readership meant establishing new (or altered) networks made up of technologies, people, discourses, and systems of transportation. This network of disparate components stabilized into the infrastructure that supported the growth of the Sunday paper. The discourses of marvel and wonder that emerged around it posited the Sunday paper as a spectacle of modern society that was connected to all the important advances of the day. Further, it positioned its readers as modern subjects, participating in public culture through the simple act of purchasing a paper. In this articulation of people, technologies, practices, and networks of distribution, the Sunday newspaper acted as a central agent in mass society.

What was happening in this deeply modern moment was not only the establishment of mass media but also the emergence of *mass participation*. Certainly circulation figures were essential for establishing the political economy that would dominate the news industry for over a century to come. The story is a familiar one and still characterizes some aspects of the media today: audiences became the commodities that were sold to advertisers who, in turn, provided the needed revenue to fuel further growth in circulation. Circulation numbers, as we explore further in chapter 4, became a critical element in how the very market of mass media would be established. With the exception of public broadcasting initiatives, American radio and television would likewise follow the same economic model, leading to a generation of critical media scholars devoted to exploring the political economy of media, particularly the foundation of audiences as commodities sold alongside the content of the paper.[1] But the well-documented interest of modern citizens in mass participation—in feeling and acting as part of modernity, especially, to use Lisa Gitelman's phrase, through "the enormous, framing tide of newsprint"—requires that we think about circulation as more than just numbers.[2]

As is the case with any other medium, thinking about newspapers as media involves paying particular attention to their structures and networks of circulation. Work by media historians such as Gitelman has considered the cultural circulation of media as "always already new," part of what Will Straw terms "the circulatory turn"—self-evidently important in times of global media and online social networking.[3] In common usage, a newspaper's "circulation" is a quantified sales figure that serves as a sort of shorthand for the entire process of mediated communication. The circulation figure encompasses not only the work of journalism and publishing (production), and not only the practice of buying the paper and reading it (consumption), but also how news circulates through the world in material form, affecting culture around it and metamorphosing in the process (distribution). Circulation figures helped active readers to conceive of themselves as participating in the mass audience of hundreds of thousands of readers of metropolitan newspapers, a matter of "partial non-identity" crucial to the formation of modern media publics.[4] But from this theoretical perspective, circulation covers the entire process of an object's movement through culture and the various interactions that occur as a result. David Henkin could not have said it more succinctly: "Media history, at core, is a study of the forms of circulation."[5]

In addition to looking "inside" the newspaper page, we are concerned with the wide scope of the newspaper's various regimes of flow, exchange, and distribution. Theories of cultural circulation chart movements across various trajectories, tracing how objects transform culture and are transformed in turn as they encounter new practices, technologies, national spaces, and other cultural forces. In this respect, theories of circulation generalize from the moment of connection and articulation, a hallmark methodology of cultural studies.[6] The concept of circulation has a long and varied history of use in cultural scholarship, emphasizing shifting representations within an ideological field.[7] As a complement to the insights of actor-network theory and the rhizomatic theory of Gilles Deleuze and Félix Guattari, theories of circulation trace assemblages of movements and trajectories.[8] Benjamin Lee and Edward LiPuma employ the concept of circulation to insist that the study of the interactions between cultural objects as they circulate entails a move away from focusing on interpretation and meaning.[9] What all of this scholarship shares is a concern with understanding how cultural artifacts exert effects on and extend influence over the cultural field, particularly at the moments when they cross paths with other cultural forms. This attention to the intersection of cultural artifacts, in conjunction with the mixing and remixing of forms, media, and formats, is particularly well suited to theorizing the constantly changing intermedial forms of the late nineteenth- and early twentieth-century newspaper.

A key insight from this body of theoretical literature is that networks do not preexist circulation; they come into existence through acts of circulation. That is, networks are an effect of the regularization of circulation practices. It is not surprising, then, that at moments when the paper is growing and expanding its circulation, new networks would be formed. The innovation and experimentation we see in this period—fast presses, hot air balloons, intermedial connection with radio and film, telepictures, and so on—demonstrates the networks that were produced, however temporary some may have been. As we will see in the final chapters of the book, on syndication, sedimentation and innovation often worked together as successes in circulation brought about efforts to solidify and firm up connections.

Both chapters in this section on circulation highlight the ongoing articulation of Sunday newspapers to the latest technological advancements to heighten and extend the sensory experiences of newspaper reading. If the chapters in the previous section on subscription focused on things readers were asked to *do* with their newspapers, this section on circulation consolidates a whole series of sensory experiences readers were asked to *feel* by dint of receiving and consuming their newspapers every Sunday. In chapter 3 we turn to how circulation relied on other media, expanding the newspaper's reach further than could ever be accomplished through its network of distribution channels, however marvelous, spectacular, or advanced they were. Newspapers drew heavily on intermedial forms, like the newsreel, to do more: to reach audiences in different ways, to titillate different senses, and to remain at the center of a mediated cultural experience that was rapidly changing. As much as newspapers were circulating across the country through syndicates, newsagents, newsboys, and delivery vans, the affective experiences of Sunday newspaper reading were also circulating. Chapter 4 lays out the material and discursive construction of the networks that supported the distribution and making of the Sunday newspaper. Continually spotlighting the spectacle of its own production and delivery, we conclude that the Sunday paper's excessive circulation of its own reproduction and distribution is central to the formation of a modern saturated media environment.

3

THE INTERMEDIAL IDEALS OF THE SUNDAY EDITION

Sunday newspaper publishers were brilliant at many things, and perhaps self-promotion was the area in which they excelled the most. The period we describe in this book saw countless experimentations and additions to the paper alongside bombastic descriptions of the marvels the modern age promised. As this chapter explores in more detail, publishers described in self-congratulatory words, pictures, and other media the wondrous production that was at the heart of circulation. Papers in this period also routinely captured their excesses in lists:

> Next Sunday's Journal. Every Page a Marvel of Interest, and There Will be Many Pages. Four Separate Papers in One Issue. The Woman's Home Journal. 8 Pages . . . The American Magazine. 16 Pages. Every feature striking, Every Feature Clean, Splendidly Illustrated, Well Written . . . The American Humorist. 8 Pages . . . A Great Newspaper. 28 Pages . . . Order it Early—Price Five Cents.[1]

The *Philadelphia Press* took a full page out of its Saturday edition to entice readers with the pleasures of the next day's edition. Presented as series of clipped mastheads, the paper itself is the star of ad:

> The New Sunday Press—To-Morrow. 7 Big Sections—Greatest of All Sunday Papers. 1–General News. 2–Anne Rittenhouse's New Woman's Magazine in Colors. 3–Local News. 4–Playroom Chatterbox Book in Bright Colors for the Children. 5–Special Illustrated Magazine in Colors. 6–The Great Section of 5000 Want Ads. 7–The Only Special Sporting News Section in Philadelphia. Same Price—5 cents—Don't Miss It.[2]

However loudly proclaimed in weekday or Saturday editions, their true excesses were best displayed on the pages of the Sunday paper itself, often in color and always accompanied by breathless wonder.

The early 1890s was an age of great advances in the audiovisual production of moving images in sound, color, and three-dimensionality—what André Bazin called "the myth of total cinema."[3] Photographic technicians in the Lumière factories in France and in the Edison laboratories in the United States (two prominent spaces of invention among many others) were building apparatuses to record and recreate scenes in lifelike motion, striving to link the image to sound, to reproduce or to transmit it electronically. Edison's phonograph and various other devices for sound recording were finally realizing a market for preserving popular performances of music and speech.[4] Telephone systems had become commonplace, using telegraph lines to reproduce the voice at a distance.[5] Halftone printing, often in color, transformed the photograph into an everyday experience in magazines and some newspaper supplements.[6]

Self-referential technological explanation was no less important for news publishers when introducing color printing than it was when installing a new press or arranging express circulation by railway. Hearst's *San Francisco Examiner* installed a new color press in 1897 to allow its Sunday edition to match the qualities of the company's still-recent venture in the *New York Journal*.[7] Although the written substance of the article emphasized the inhuman speed and monstrous capacity of the press machinery, which we discuss fully in chapter 4, the illustration that accompanied the *Examiner* piece attends to a very different aspect of media technology. The three-color and black ink process was explained visually, through a series of one- and two-color picture fragments, allowing readers to both understand and appreciate the "Wonders of the Newspaper Color Press."[8]

Despite being primarily associated with caricatures and comic strips, color printing foregrounded other aspects of aesthetic appreciation, including an approximation of a realistic simulation of the sense of vision. The Sunday color supplement was one of many visual agents that contributed to the production of new techniques of observation (in Jonathan Crary's sense), aiming to take pleasure and command in understanding the rational deconstruction and technological reconstruction of the sense of vision.[9] The experience of seeing could be reproduced scientifically through the print interplay of primary colors. With the installation of a new four-color fast press in 1898, the *New York World* explained that its color printing improved upon the variety expected, for "there is no cloying monotony in the unparalleled New Sunday Magazine . . . Numerous tints that can be produced by mingling and shading . . . Brilliant flashing hues are succeeded by cool translucent tints in agreeable variety."[10] The variety of the sensory aspect of the color supplement was a foundation, then, for sustaining sensationalism for readers through constant novelty in illustrations and feature story subject matter.

In sum, in the late nineteenth century, the rapid-fire emergence of new media technologies and a corresponding public interest in their ability to convey sensation and information quickly and accurately were often fueled by hyperbolic discourse from the inventors of those technologies. These cultural conditions set the stage for the enthusiastic uptake of intermedial forms by the Sunday paper as part of its quest for greater circulation. Intermedial forms are transitory and temporary—that is, they are how media operates when it is in the process of becoming something else. But circulation is also fundamentally about change; as Dilip Gaonkar and Elizabeth Povinelli observe in "Technologies of Public Forms: Circulation, Transfiguration, Recognition," cultural forms not only change culture as they move through it; they are also transfigured themselves as they circulate.[11] As each new technology became a supplement to the Sunday paper, it helped the paper circulate to new subscribers, elicited new techniques of reading, and produced new kinds of reading subjects. But in the process, the addition of each supplemental form transfigured the general sense of what the newspaper was—or what it could be. At least before syndication, when some element of standardization was enforced, "the Sunday edition" was not so much a stable object as a roiling assemblage of forms—supplements all the way down. Accordingly, this chapter tracks some of the major intermedial forms of the Sunday edition, with particular attention to their role in newspaper circulation.

"PEN PICTURES": INTERMEDIAL WRITING

Printing had been called "the art preservative of all arts" by typographical societies for its role in documenting, disseminating, and archiving the culture of the age in popular form.[12] We extend this sentiment to engraving and illustration in the 1890s because the mass circulation of newspapers was central to the overall development of "the myth of total mediation," to adapt Bazin's phrase. Positioned within the media matrix of sound, color, movement, simultaneity, and circulation, newspaper illustration compensated for its shortcomings in detail, sound, and movement with its ability to *circulate*, for the ultimate goal was the immediate, realistic transmission of audiovisual experience. Precision, sound, and movement could be built atop newspapers' strengths in mass address, especially upon the long-standing realm of descriptive writing, the domain of the correspondent.

The evocative writing of journalism had often presented itself discursively as a form of visualization and illustration. In that sense, the medium of newsprint, well before its turn to illustration, photographic halftones, and color printing, had a firmly entrenched purpose of conveying experience—that is, helping the reader imagine "being there" with the eyewitness reporter. John Nerone's work on the history of journalism professionals cites the distinction between the reporter and the correspondent before the 1890s. The former worked locally to write a faithful reproduction of the novelty within everyday life, whereas the latter provided political intelligence at a distance through colorful observation and personal insight: "Unlike the reporter, whose work and work routines inclined toward voicelessness, the correspondent was supposed to be the readers' eyes and ears at the centers of power."[13] While Nerone is concerned with technology's role in reshaping a distinction between editing and reporting in the workplace, his observations are applicable to the wider changing relation between newspapers and other media technologies as the printed word became supplemented with other forms of visualization. A key concern was the eclipse of distance, which required a more descriptive and embodied perspective, even as that personal vision depended on technologies to transmit and circulate the correspondent's writing as a replacement of experience. The report about modern novelties nearby—often reports about emerging technologies—could be depicted with strict empiricism as a supplement to everyday experience. Of course, this distinction between distanced detail and nearby brevity could be upended with a column of "telegraph briefs" or "pastepot and scissors," both of which foregrounded techniques of editorial selection in order to reprint decontextualized items from afar for the sake of mere curiosity with hardly any attention to description. The function of reportage as correspondence, in that sense, did not merely span distance; it also needed to sustain disbelief across space and time theatrically, the story becoming immediate in the sense of its mediation falling away through the idealized conflation of the here and now of the reader with the "there and then" of the news.

Description and depiction were journalistic twins. Particularly descriptive columns were routinely labeled "pen pictures," a phrase used by the popular writer Henry Ward Beecher in the 1850s to denote how he provided "A book that talks!" written in animated and accessible language.[14] The term was taken up by popular novelists and journalists, especially foreign correspondents, as an appropriate moniker for their vividly descriptive writing. In this light the very model and motivation behind reportage can be taken as a form of intermedial montage, and it should be no surprise to see, or rather read, that newspaper publishers in North America were routinely involved in adopting each novel media technology that appeared at the turn of the twentieth century.

But first, in a more elementary form, newspapers routinely used other media as models and labels for inventive forms of leisure writing. The *Philadelphia Item*, for example, introduced a Sunday column called "*The Item* Telephone" in 1887, in which the "distinguished citizens" at the centers of the "sensations of the week" were supposedly interviewed by telephone, providing invariably humorous and pithy responses.[15] To offer another example, just months after the public debut of moving pictures in 1896, the *Washington Post* ran a Sunday column called "Vitascope Pictures," which gave vivid written descriptions of urban vignettes.[16] The realism and eyewitness origins of the column were redoubled under the label of moving pictures as the latest means of improved technological sensory reproduction. The last of the series makes the rationale explicit: The Sunday feature is an observer at a mediated distance. It depicts a woman on a wet and windy sidewalk, beleaguered with her bundles after shopping, who grows weary and frustrated as she receives no assistance from passersby. "*The Post*'s Vitascope is the only thing watching her, and being inanimate, it cannot come to her rescue."[17] By positioning both the newspaper and its readers as present in sensation but helplessly absent in reality, this article is unusual in that it lays bare the social failings of newspaper reading, even with the literal and metaphorical aid of new media technologies. Such examples use technology metaphorically to convey the style of witness in columns, accompanying an expanded role for technologies in journalism.[18]

INSTANTANEOUS PHOTOGRAPHY AND THE VISUAL INTERVIEW

Realistic newspaper illustration served the purpose of vivid visual description, as opposed to bringing out political connotations through cartooning. The art of etching was recontextualized as a transmediation of photography in the late 1880s, when the eyewitness of reporting was more often supplemented with the camera lens, especially for natural disasters, sporting action, and the speeches of politicians or performances of celebrities. When newspapers wished to provide readers with an immediate sense of seeing something as if "actually being there," the illustration was likely to be captioned with the phrase "from an instantaneous photograph."[19] Those images so labeled are ironically frozen in their realism compared with the more animated narrative style allowed with the creative license of illustrations.

Magazines had an edge over newspapers for realistic illustrations because of their higher print quality and earlier adoption of halftone reproduction. Magazines were first to promote their pictures in terms of photorealism; advertisements for *Scribner's* in 1887 promote the use of multiple images of an athlete in motion and the aftereffects of a tornado. As illustration became more routine in Sunday newspapers, feature articles picked up the same routines of labeling depictions of movement as being "from an instantaneous photograph," such as an article in the *Boston Sunday Herald* on the science of cyclones by the very same professor who had contributed the article to *Scribner's* two years before.[20] It is vital to recognize the cinematic connotation in the adjective "instantaneous," for it evokes Eadweard Muybridge's well-known work on picturing time and movement and was thus entirely distinct from the posed immobility of portrait photography.[21] Illustrations "from an instantaneous photograph" captured more than just an image; they claimed to capture an event as it happened. Thus, newspapers added the element of reportage atop the science of instantaneous documentation. The phrase accompanies all seven etchings in a Sunday feature story recounting how *San Francisco Examiner* reporters and artists in 1889 were sent on the newspaper's own boat to report dramatic flooding on the Sacramento River.[22]

Pulitzer's *New York World* took the animated logic of the instantaneous photograph illustration to another level by adding the element of publicity with a pair of "photographic interviews" in 1890.[23] Although Frank Luther Mott's *American Journalism* mentions that the move was in response to the *New York Herald*, which had aimed to outdo its rival in 1889 through its own increased illustration, it is also worth noting that the experiment of the photographic interviews happened just as the *World* concluded its stunt of sending Nellie Bly around the world.[24] Bly's correspondence was combined with commercial cross-promotions in contests and games, and her reports were compiled in books. The *World* was primed for intermedial play as it turned to animated photography for its next major "novelty in American journalism," devoting two four-page Sunday supplements to extensive interviews with prominent public figures noted for their animated oratory style: straight-talking Kansas senator John J. Ingalls and the Rev. Dr. Thomas De Witt Talmage of the Brooklyn Tabernacle, whose sermons were one of the most popular religious experiences of the day.[25] "Novel in conception and execution," advance publicity for the first Sunday "Photographic Interview" supplement specifically noted its printing on "fine paper" and proposed that the public should "read it and preserve it for your children's children."[26] "Full of wit and sarcasm, Senator Ingalls is the most unique figure in American politics [and] every newspaper in the country will talk about this great interview," not entirely a false claim, as the *World*'s photographic interview was indeed widely commented upon and excerpts from it were reprinted in many other papers.[27]

The first interview with Senator Ingalls printed thirty photorealistic etchings of the speaker in animated poses; the second, with Reverend Talmage, added even more (see fig. 13). After the introductory framing device of typical *World*-style self-important explanation of the significance of the supplement, the feature writing accompanying the interviews was a verbatim transcript rather than a summary and interpretation, furthering the impression of live coverage as if prescient of newsreel actuality footage. The *New Haven (CT) Register*, for one, took the stunt as an opportunity to generally lament the illustrated turn in news publishing among its metropolitan rivals for readership. Laced with sarcasm, the *Register*'s editorial dismissed the technological imperative as a matter of fad populism in journalism: "'The photographic interview' is no longer a dream. The camera is mightier than the phonograph, just as the pen is mightier than the sword. We have lived to see newspaper illustrations develop into this. There is no longer any sense imagining its future."[28] The thirty etchings of instantaneous photographs accompanying the senator's interview resembled pages in an animated flipbook more than news illustrations. Ingalls was shown sitting down, standing up, leaning on a table,

FIGURE 13. "A Photographic Interview," *New York World*, April 13, 1890, 19.

lounging in a chair, and with arms theatrically uplifted, with his body language matching the rhetoric of his "biting epigrams."[29] The *Register* wryly noted that "if the interviewer followed him all about the room, as the illustrations otherwise suggest, it wasn't an interview at all, it was a footrace."[30] The *World* itself would hardly have disagreed.

The full rationale and advantage of the innovation introduced the second interview with Reverend Talmage: "[With] *The World*'s new device for giving the weight and effect of personal presence to the utterances of distinguished men . . . the reader is permitted to see the speaker interviewed as he appeared in the very act of uttering the words recorded."[31] The technique, then, proposed to better

record and transmit the oratory of a great public speech into print by supplementing the interview text with photorealistic pictures. The *World* claimed, indeed, that
the value of the instantaneous photograph in "presenting thought" was precisely
to overcome the limitations of popular address "imposed by the impossibility of
making the voice heard by more than a few thousands of persons at once. To entertain a photographic interview in *The World* gives the opportunity of addressing
millions, almost as if with the actual voice and in personal presence."[32] A prototype
of broadcasting combining oratory and visual description, this representational
experiment was tested at a moment when Edison's phonograph was about to be
revitalized to achieve precisely this aim of mechanical reproduction of spoken and
musical performativity. Several years before Edison would succeed in unveiling
commercial moving photographs, the *Sunday World* briefly took center stage in
the history of cinema through its photographic interviews. They also have their
place in the history of American politics too, because the unedited, decontextualized "liveness" of the gimmick ended Senator Ingalls's career. A full decade later,
after Ingalls had died, the interview was still cited as leading to his defeat in the
election of 1890, because he had been grossly impolitic in his frank replies to the
World's questions about political reform and partisan infighting in Congress.[33]

The idea was almost immediately mimicked by Albert Pulitzer's *New York
Morning Journal* in Sunday editions late in May 1890, continuing occasionally
for several months. The *Morning Journal* turned the gimmick toward illustrated
spotlights of celebrity actors and athletes. The first "Snap-Shot Interview" was
with the actress Della Fox, who recounted her early career on the stage: "A big
camera and a *Journal* reporter went up to her home on Thirty-first Street and Fifth
Avenue the other day. The camera snapped at opportune moments and caught
the little lady in characteristic poses while she talked in her charming, innocent
way."[34] Fox was pictured in ten poses, gesticulating with her arms and posturing
to melodramatic effect. The next week came another "Snap-Shot Interview" with
the "King of Pugilists," John L. Sullivan. The champion heavyweight-prizefighter-
turned-actor, "the latest celebrity to experience the delight of being interviewed
by the *Journal*'s spontaneous camera," was interviewed in his dressing room at the
People's Theatre after appearing on stage.[35] Quotations were annotated by stages
of undressing and changing into evening clothes as he was pictured in thirteen
poses reenacting his boxing moves.

Ultimately the faddish character of Sunday photographic interview features
overshadowed its technological aspirations. The very same day as the *World*'s
profile of Reverend Talmage appeared, a humorous page in the *Boston Sunday
Globe* depicted a futuristic page from the year 2000, denoted "Bellamy's Boston,"
in reference to the famous author of the utopian science fiction novel *Looking
Backward* and promising a "photographic interview" with the man in the moon.[36]
After halftoned photographic reproduction began appearing in newspapers, the
phrase "from an instantaneous photograph" continued to be employed for realistic

eyewitness and caught-in-action snapshots, often enough to be used sometimes by cartoonists as a joke when showing an obviously comical *lack* of realism.

The photographic interview, however, was continually reanimated by successive newspapers, always claiming a technological innovation merely by the association of a series of otherwise unremarkable newspaper illustrations with latent forms of cinema to supposedly create a more realistic reading experience "as if" reporters and readers had been present in person.[37] Photographic journalism in various forms was certainly standard for weekend editions by the turn of the century. Shortly after starting its color halftoned magazine section early in 1897, within a single week the *New York World*, for example, printed "the last and first" photograph of President McKinley and his cabinet working *in camera*, taken by "*The Sunday World*'s own photographer"; published a series of etchings from pictures extracted from the official Veriscope moving pictures of the heavyweight prizefight between James J. Corbett and Bob Fitzsimmons; and had dancer Loie Fuller "define" pantomime, photographed in "illustrative poses" of human emotion, again "from photographs taken especially by *The Sunday World*'s photographer."[38] These features were modest compared to the double-page "exact reproduction" of the presidential review of a memorial parade for General Grant passing in front of Grant's Tomb—"the largest picture of a news event ever printed since the art of illustration was invented."[39] The illustration was, in fact, the second of its size in just a few days, as a bird's-eye view was also imagined before the event and "drawn especially for *The Sunday World*" by artist Charles Graham, but the claim of photorealism did not apply to the illustration drawn in advance.[40]

Moving Picture Interviews

In the context of actual moving pictures having finally reached a mass public, the *Chicago Inter-Ocean* revamped the photographic interview in the election year of 1900, adding a twist this time by describing the subjects—that year's Democratic nominee, William Jennings Bryan, and the Republican vice presidential candidate, Theodore Roosevelt—as actually having posed for the newspaper's own moving picture machine. The Democratic nominee posed for the *Sunday Inter-Ocean*'s moving picture machine at his home in Lincoln, Nebraska. Appearing to have learned a lesson from the *World*'s obviously staged experiment with the photographic interview a decade earlier, the *Inter-Ocean* took pains to show the ordinary downtime of the politician, depicted performing the banal preparations behind the scenes of his political campaign, as if the moving picture camera's special gift was to give access to the private, normally hidden moments of public figures: "Mr. Bryan was so busy thinking over his speech that he was reluctant to pose for the representative of W. N. Selig's Polyscope Company, sent to Lincoln to procure pictures for *The Sunday Inter-Ocean*."[41] The posed and feigned naturalism of the election-year scene can be confirmed in light of an almost identical encounter between Bryan and a moving picture camera two years earlier, with

Bryan stating reluctance, having the mechanism explained to him, and negotiating a suitably naturalistic scene to be photographed before allowing the filming to proceed.[42] In 1900 the Sunday illustrated article and moving pictures again reinforced the ordinary, plain doings of this populist politician, but the final paragraphs emphasized how the technologically enhanced novelty of moving picture journalism maintained an emphasis on speed and urgency: "Lightning time was made with the exposed films after they reached Chicago" to prepare prints to exhibit in theaters.[43] However, before they were distributed to viewing audiences, the *Inter-Ocean* was on the mark to circulate etched frames from the films as a special feature in its Sunday edition.

Equally interesting, but for entirely different reasons, was the *Inter-Ocean*'s follow-up the next week, when it promised similar "moving pictures of Gov. Roosevelt" within its half-page advance promotion for the *Sunday Inter-Ocean*.[44] Public figures such as Queen Victoria and Pope Leo XIII had been "biographed" already by the turn of the century, but Roosevelt reportedly refused to pose for the cinematograph. The solution, so obvious to our sensibilities today, was to film him in public. Thus, during a parade of Republican clubs, the driver of Roosevelt's carriage was reportedly bribed to move slowly when passing a moving picture machine on the street. Three panels in series showed the moment, and the *Inter-Ocean* acceded the disappointment of merely reproducing his passing in a parade: "They are interesting chiefly as showing what may be done in the way of securing a picture when the principal subject refuses to pose before the camera."[45] The underhanded stunt made the news in a widely reprinted report from rival paper, the *Chicago Tribune*, that quoted the "elated" cameraman.[46]

The incident demonstrated a point the *Tribune* had already advocated about the role of moving picture technology conveying unmediated images of public figures. In an editorial from the week before that circulated widely in boilerplate for months, the "Biograph Fiend" was positioned as "a terror to public men." It opined that the technology was best kept out the hands of the general public because "the aim of the fiends naturally would be to secure statesmen in the most undignified attitudes possible."[47] Like the instantaneous photographic interview beforehand, it was hotly debated whether moving pictures were an advancement in the field of journalism and should be embraced as a supplement to newspapers. Since Edison first publicized his efforts to animate moving pictures in 1891, Sunday newspaper features had repeatedly reproduced etchings (later colored halftoned photographs) of filmstrips and projection devices to explain how cinema worked. In many ways the weekend edition was a full-fledged partner in creating the mass viewing public by circulating illustrated features about early cinema to its mass reading public. The newspaper did more than simply reproduce depictions to explain other media; it also took interest in the public adoption and circulation of novel media technologies.

FROM THE BIRD'S-EYE VIEW TO
THE WIRELESS NEWS NETWORK

Newspapers routinely espoused ideologies of technological progress to announce the latest approximation of immediate sight-and-sound communications—what would be called broadcasting, once successful. Newspapers' quest to provide a sort of God's-eye omniscient daily overview through media technology, simultaneously and pervasively covering the entire national public, can be traced back to the development of the telegraph and its adaptation for newswire services—the first customers of Western Union to purchase dedicated transcontinental wires. Although the imperative to illustrate events at a distance retained a distinct pictorial function for the Sunday newspaper, new technologies adapting the telegraph for pictures were also embraced by newspapers' weekend editions as well as Guglielmo Marconi's wireless telegraph. Illustrated Sunday newspapers had long employed strategies to achieve totalizing mediation. Technology's role supporting journalism is hardly corralled to the newsroom. To be sure, reporters and correspondents were routinely among the vanguard experimenting with novel means to achieve ever-greater immediacy in their pursuit of timeliness. But their stories at these moments of experimentation often reflexively spotlight and illustrate the more abiding concern of trying to realize an all-encompassing journalistic sensorium. In a sense, new media technologies were just a means to that end.[48]

Perhaps none took the ideal of the God's-eye perspective so literally as Pulitzer's repeated turns to the bird's-eye location of hot air ballooning as an amusing and spectacular way of animating the *Sunday World*. In 1887 the *World* sent a reporter in a balloon from St. Louis to just outside New York, "searching the firmament," to bind Pulitzer's two sister papers in a national network of observation and spectacle over the very landscape itself.[49] Accompanying the navigators and scientists was John G. Doughty, a photographer who was "ready to catch views of the wonderful panorama which will be spread out below the lofty observers," and correspondent Edward Duffy, "a trained writer, who will present in word picture to the readers of *The World* what he has caught with eye and ear far up in the untraveled area of the upper skies."[50] At this point, although photography was also in use, the pen pictures of written journalism remained the primary technique for reproducing hearing and vision for the newspaper's readership: "Why does *The World* organize the balloon trip? . . . There is news above the cloud line, and *The World* wishes to secure it."[51] Ostensibly in the scientific interest of meteorology, the trip was equally meant to demonstrate that the newspaper—an illustrated Sunday newspaper especially—could bring fantastic fiction to life, could awaken to reality the dreams of modern life: "It will enable *The World* correspondent . . . to give to our readers a story which shall be after the manner of Verne, wonderful and entrancing except only with the difference that every word of *The World* narrative will be truth from an experienced eye-witness."[52] When the balloon was launched in June, telegraphed dispatches "began to pour into *The World* office from all the towns and villages within twenty-five miles of St. Louis." The newspaper took pains to list all the towns across Illinois and Ohio that could simultaneously see the balloon, like a materialization of the kind of vast national readership Pulitzer was aiming to build.[53]

It is no surprise that, even in these early years of newspaper illustration, etchings of the balloon accompanied the article, rather than leave readers' imaginations at the mercy of the pen picture. The *New York Graphic* could not help but protest that, in fact, these were not the early days of newspaper illustration nor of using a balloon for that purpose: "Imitation is the sincerest flattery," it captioned juxtaposed illustrations of its similarly sponsored balloon expedition in 1873.[54] The *New York World* would repeat such aerial expeditions in 1895, aboard "a real flying-machine at last!"[55] This time the contraption was smaller, with a bicycle-pedaled rotary motor and wings for steering, allowing an agility of movement. Named *The World* and emblazoned with that label, the flying machine was sent out to entertain the summertime crowds of New York City. Once more the comparison was to science fiction but made real through illustrated journalism. "The performances of *The World* read like the dream of a novelist, but they are absolutely sober facts, as the people of New York will soon have a chance to see with their own eye."[56] The *World*'s "Sky-cycle" flying machine returned on several occasions, such as at the Tennessee Centennial Exhibition in 1897.[57] This relaunching of the Sky-cycle coincided with yet another balloon ascent in pursuit of a novel form of sensorial, sensational journalism. This time the balloon was imprinted with the moniker *The Sunday World* to capture "a superb panorama of the nation's metropolis photographed from 1,000 feet over Grant's Tomb" (see fig. 14).[58]

Well into the era of moving pictures and mechanized photographic vision, the article jarringly notes—so different from the balloon ride of a decade earlier—that the technique was *constrained by* the bodily limitations of eyewitness reporting: "The view from that height was magnificent. The field of vision was limited only by the power of the eye."[59] With the imminent availability of a technological replacement for eyewitness testimony, even resorting to the skies in search of instantaneous communication seems wanting. A month later a double-page spread appeared, labeled the "first bird's-eye map of Greater New York from photographs taken in *The Sunday World*'s studio balloon."[60] As if photographed from high above the Hudson River, the bottom half of the map ran from Westchester County across the Bronx and Manhattan to the Statue of Liberty. The map tapered off in perspective toward Brooklyn so that the very top horizon of the map showed the city limits from Hollis, Queens, and to Far Rockaway on the Atlantic Ocean (see fig. 15). Large illustrations of cityscapes as if photographed from a God's-eye perspective were not unique to Pulitzer's *World*.

FIGURE 14. "The Sunday World's Balloon," *New York World*, May 2, 1897, 31.

FIGURE 15. "Greater New York Photographed," *New York World*, May 23, 1897, 34–35.

Telegraphing News Pictures

Beyond the balloon and the flying machine, illustrated newspaper reporting adopted and experimented with novel technologies and intermedial relations that we would still recognize as precedents for twenty-first-century new media. On the heels of cinema's public debut, in October 1896 came a series of articles about transmitting pictures a thousand miles by telegraph. Hearst's *New York Journal*, which that very month had poached R. F. Outcault and his Yellow Kid along with much of the staff that had built the popularity of Pulitzer's *World*, scored a coup by collaborating with the Edison laboratories. The *Journal*'s exclusive test of "exact reproductions by wire" printed telegraphed pictures of Edison, presidential candidate Bryan, dancing girls, and the ubiquitous Yellow Kid, now mascot for the *Sunday Journal*:[61] "The seemingly impossible has again been achieved."[62] Unsurprisingly, the new technology went hand in hand with treating images as an improvement upon words in descriptive journalism, as if the illustrated trend in Sunday papers was scientifically linked to the progress of modern communications: "In the near future it will be quite as easy for a newspaper to send pictures of an event occurring in Chicago or Washington as it will be to send written descriptions."[63] As with moving pictures (let alone hot air balloons), the basis of the breakthrough was the capacity of yet another machine to exceed the limits of human perception—in this case the appearance of unbroken line drawings reproduced mechanically as minuscule dots transmitted by telegraph.

Other newspapers reimagined the future of "visual telegraphy" through illustrations depicting scenes prescient of live television broadcasting or video-linked teleconferencing. Thus, the capacity to telegraph pictures was immediately transformed into media futures where audiovisual transmissions would occur between two individuals or a live image of an event reproduced for a theater audience simultaneously at a great distance. Pulitzer's *World* actually scooped Hearst's *Journal* by illustrating, one Sunday edition earlier, "how pictures may be transmitted a thousand miles" with an etching across the top of two adjacent pages showing an audience in a Chicago theater as if looking onto a panorama of Madison Square in New York, linked through telegraph wires.[64] The *World*'s version of the story also imagined one-on-one uses as a visual telephone so that the same technology would one day have "distant friends brought face to face."[65] The only limitation was patience for the imagined possibilities to progress through technical invention into public use: "This device for seeing at a distance is perfect in theory, and those who have given it the most thought believe that it can be made equally perfect in practice."[66]

On the Pacific Coast, Hearst's *San Francisco Examiner* also dedicated half a page of a Sunday edition to an idealized illustration of the possibilities of sending pictures by telegraph, but now giving the invention a name, the "telephote,"

invented by Elias Ries of Baltimore: "When the telephone was invented, somebody called it a long-distance ear. Now a long-distance eye has been found to
work in conjunction with it. . . . Nothing will be left to the imagination. You will
look into a broad transmitter and see . . . in plain and actual vision."[67] The article
ends with a utopian manifesto, claiming that the telephote "will bring the peoples
of the earth nearer together by one half. . . . It will multiply a thousand fold the
possibilities of newspaper illustration," but, oddly, not by replacing the printed
newspaper itself (see fig. 16).[68] The telephote could assist its professional composition with color photographs from distant newsworthy events sent to newspaper
offices to publish on newsprint.

Just months later, a practical application was introduced and put to use in newsrooms in order to improve the illustrated articles of Sunday editions. In 1899 the
New York and Boston *Heralds, Chicago Times-Herald, Philadelphia Inquirer*, and
St. Louis Republic all simultaneously installed a "telediagraph" for their halftone
illustrated Sunday supplements, allowing them to share illustrations in a telegraph
network just as the newswire had long allowed stories to be instantly transmitted. As Noah Arceneaux has noted, the effort was first of a string of moments
when the *New York Herald* went beyond the page to provide "news on the air."[69]
In New York, the *Herald* printed images sent from all four of the other newspapers, demonstrating the capacity of the technology to link illustrated news in a
national network.[70] Two of the first pictures printed by this means were images of
the Boston and New York *Herald* buildings, transmitted by wire to appear in the
Sunday edition.[71] The rudimentary system still allowed only etchings rather than
halftones, such as an image of a train wreck on the Reading Railroad "received by

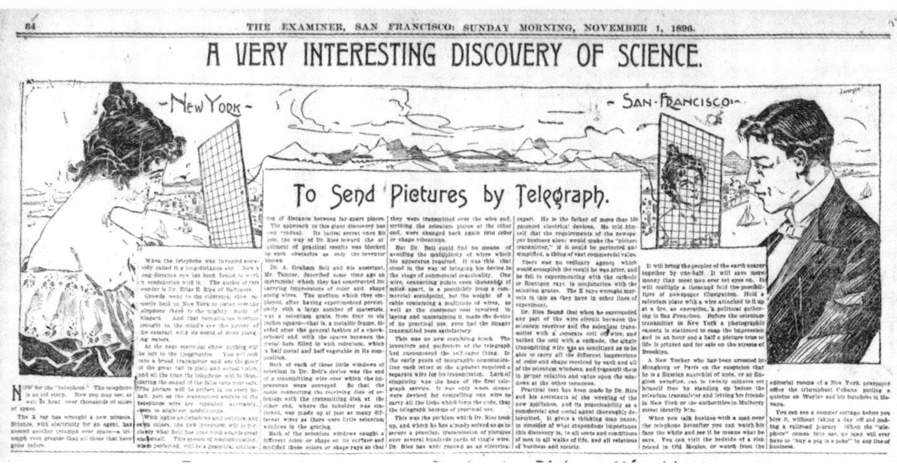

FIGURE 16. "A Very Interesting Discovery of Science," *San Francisco Examiner*,
November 1, 1896, 34.

telegraph from Philadelphia."[72] Nonetheless, the capacity for "newspaper illustrations sent by wire" was reality by the end of the century, with the *New York Herald* running tests of its new equipment that were "so severe that there is no possible doubt now but that the problem of sending pictures by wire, the same as messages, is at last successfully solved."[73]

The new device was reportedly of such interest to the public that the day after being featured in the *Boston Sunday Herald*, it drew a large number of visitors to the paper's illustration department to see it in action, including the city's police commissioner, interested in its possibilities for the distant instant sharing of suspects' pictures.[74] Transmitting images faster than the fastest express train, no criminal's flight could outpace it. The capacity for visual telegraphy, "flashing pictures around the world," sustained repeated illustrations in Sunday newspaper features for several more years.[75] A widely syndicated feature showed how the "magical mirrors" of Jan Szczepanik's "telectroscope" could turn "colors into electric currents" and reproduce "not only transmit[ted] pictures by wire, but . . . moving images in all of their natural colors."[76] While the *New York Times* concurrently reported its own Sunday feature story about the telectroscope and the promise to bring live scenes from the forthcoming 1900 Paris Exposition to North America, it left the story without illustration, as was its practice outside of its high-class halftone illustrated magazine. In contrast, the *San Francisco Call* used a full page to depict how the telectroscope would use the Atlantic undersea cable to send pictures of the Eiffel Tower to audiences in a New York theater, and from there linked by telegraph to Buffalo, St. Louis, Denver, and San Francisco, as if the newswire service had already become a continental television network.[77] In fact, something similar would happen just the following year before the end of the nineteenth century.

In October 1899, promoted for months in advance, Marconi arranged to transmit the progress of the America's Cup yacht race as it occurred by wireless to the *New York Herald*, which then telegraphed the updates in real time via newswire service across the country. This was not the first time that wireless experiments had been held in conjunction with newspaper publicity. Two years earlier, the *New York Sunday World* illustrated Marconi's new media technology, depicting the very atmosphere between the Eiffel Tower and St. Paul's Cathedral in London as electrified and animated with "*The New York World*'s motto, Publicity! Publicity! Publicity!" pulsating through the air between the two capitals (see fig. 17).[78] London correspondent Edward Marshall had arranged for Marconi to conduct a first transmission of wireless telegraphy from London to Paris as a public demonstration in collaboration with the newspaper.[79] Of course, famously in pursuit of commercial public adoption of his technology, Marconi accepted the offer of "*The World*'s great experiment," which Marshall promised would occur as soon as possible.

FIGURE 17. "A Boy Wizard to Flash the World's Motto," *New York World*, August 8, 1897, 29.

In the meantime, Pulitzer's flagship paper conducted a wireless demonstration of underwater transmissions between Staten Island and New Jersey as inventors and journalists from electrical and engineering magazines listened in to the signals aboard "*The World*'s Tugboat."[80] Proffered as a vital defense technology during these months of the Spanish-American War, an illustration showed how the underwater wireless could allow the American fleet off the Florida Keys to be simultaneously in communication with commands.

The novelty of wireless news transmission was even caught up in the craze of magic and spiritualism of the day. While wireless has obvious resonances with ghostly appearances, connections to the afterlife, and communication from beyond the material realm, at least once the object of spiritualism was meant quite explicitly to be a Sunday newspaper. In an attempt "to whisk *The World* from here to India in a day by unseen hands," Prof. R. M. Jhingan, an artist of the occult, accepted the challenge of making a copy of the *New York World* "materialize in Lahore, India, within a day of its publication in New York City."[81] While this supposed feat was not done at the urging of the *World*, the newspaper took great pleasure in illustrating a Sunday article about the accepted challenge, which arose as a result of the musing of W. T. Stead's *Borderland* magazine about the imminent possibility of transporting a copy of a newspaper from New York to England in a single day. Within just a couple of years, wireless was actually being used for news reporting, although hardly at the globe-encircling scale initially imagined.

Returning to Marconi's great success in wireless journalism for the 1899 America's Cup races, dozens of newspapers across the country concurrently claimed to be offering the public news by wireless, posting updates at their offices as crowds gathered to witness reports of the live events. The *San Francisco Call* used a full page with extensive illustrations showing the wireless signals being sent from the steamer fifteen miles off the New Jersey receiving stations and from there "flashed across the continent by special wire to *The Call* Office, 3000 miles away. . . . The efficacy of wireless telegraphy as an aid to modern journalism has again been demonstrated."[82] In Philadelphia "crowds in front of *The Inquirer* building" were depicted listening to the bulletin announcer on the street.[83] Over the next few years, such use of wireless for instantaneous news reporting became more localized—for example, used for the first time by a Canadian newspaper in 1903 when the *Toronto Star* covered a yacht race in Lake Ontario as it happened.[84] At the start of 1904, the *San Francisco Call* claimed to be "foremost among American newspapers in advancing the causes of experimenters with wireless telegraphy" when it received a message from the U.S. Weather Bureau's new transmitter on the Farallon Islands off San Francisco Bay, graphically depicted as if being sent straight to the *Call* office.[85] Newspapers and their weekend illustrated supplements were already partners with Marconi and government institutions in exploiting the public applications of the new media technology, and, as we shall see in chapter 6, newspapers were a central part of commercial radio broadcasting when it began two decades later.

Sporadic collaborations with moving pictures and wireless remained common intermedial supplements of Sunday newspaper reading. There was a strong affinity between newspapers and early cinema, whose aims were to create a "visual newspaper" for its ability to bring newsworthy and popular scenarios to life.[86]

With cinema's turn to narrative storytelling around 1903, however, came a decade of relative antagonism between the movies and newspapers. The problem was the loss of respectability in the new century of both popular cinema as it turned toward entertainment and, concurrently, the demonization of Hearst's and Pulitzer's brand of sensational yellow journalism. In short, both became associated with the urban working class, rendered ethnic and prone to persuasion, sensationalism, and distraction. As middlebrow values of objectivity and political neutrality took hold of journalism, modeled in the upsurge of the *New York Times* against the *World* and the *Journal*, many newspapers began to partner with moral reformers and social uplift movements and devoted attention to the crass influence of moving picture melodramas and comic strips on children of all classes, even as the color comic supplement spread to prominence through syndication. Specific to cartoonist R. F. Outcault, for example, out went the ethnic urban street of the Yellow Kid's *Hogan's Alley* and in came the bourgeois antics of *Buster Brown*.[87]

THE NEWSREEL AS NEWSPAPER SUPPLEMENT

Publishers did not ultimately pioneer news films to supplement routines of print journalism. Instead, newsreels emerged from within the film industry shortly after 1910 as a rationalized miscellany of actuality footage. French film producers Pathé Frères, which had dominated the film industry even in America in the decade before 1910, introduced the *Pathé Fait Divers* newsreel to France in 1908, and it arrived in North America as the *Pathé Weekly* in August 1911. For the debut of the "film newspaper" to Portland, the *Oregonian* printed a brief item on a page of news—not the theater page—about the "greatest novelty of the motion picture world, a newspaper in films."[88] The specter of transforming the field of journalism through film technology made the news pictorial notable "not so much for what it is in its present shape, as for the tremendous possibilities contained in the idea."[89] By the end of 1913, every key film producer had begun issuing weekly moving picture compilations of their actualities. For its first decade after 1896, cinema had modeled its variety on emulating a "visual newspaper," but by 1911 the moviegoing habit was firmly entrenched and the "movies" were undeniably a big business and a cornerstone of mass leisure after a tempestuous period of moral concern about "socially combustible" audiences at makeshift firetrap picture shows.[90]

Newspapers became fulsome partners in movie publicity in 1913, and especially in 1914, with the national standardization of serial and daily moving picture stories in newspapers to supplement viewing.[91] With the solidified allegiance of the two media, newspaper publishers finally moved to produce and coproduce national, regional, and local newsreels to supplement their readerships' print news consumption. Hearst was the first prominent newspaper publisher to directly collaborate in producing a weekly moving picture newsreel, initially released in

March 1914 in conjunction with Selig Polyscope Co.[92] It was the first in a series of collaborations between the Hearst Corporation and film studios—*Hearst-Vitagraph News* followed in 1916, then *Hearst-Pathé News* superseded the *Pathé Weekly* in 1917—ultimately leading to the establishment of Hearst International Newsreel Service as an enduring, dominant film-news producer and an extension of Hearst International's established syndicate for news photography.[93]

Hearst's involvement in the film business extended well beyond newsreels, well known for the publicity afforded Cosmopolitan Corporation film productions, not least those later starring his mistress, Marion Davies.[94] However, there was little publicity for the launch of the moving picture news weekly in 1914 in Hearst newspapers or beyond. The explanation of this unusual lack of hype is not difficult to speculate about, as Hearst had just begun collaborating to print daily moving picture stories with Pathé—of all studios the originator of the news weekly—with several double-page ads in the film trade press puffing the collaboration under collages of Hearst mastheads.[95]

Further, the main publicity focus for moving pictures in Hearst papers at this time was *The Perils of Pauline* serial, about to begin in March 1914 as the first of many newspaper-film serials to follow Selig's pioneering *Adventures of Kathlyn* in the *Chicago Tribune* and other papers.[96] Pathé's *Pauline* was clearly the commercial priority, and it received lavish multiple pages of publicity, leaving the *Hearst-Selig News Pictorial* all but orphaned until late in the year after the war began, when much publicity accompanied the rebranding of the *Hearst-Selig Weekly* as pictorial wartime news. In the film trade press, however, the rhetoric for the Hearst newsreel was as sharp as ever to entice showmen to book the new option for their programs: "No such combination of the best trained newspaper men in the world, working hand in hand with a matchless producing company, has ever before been known."[97] While the Hearst entry intro newsreel production is well known, it is actually unique for its international scope and long-standing prominence. In its day, the closer connection was between serial films and Sunday supplements, which involved the movies completing a story that began with reading the paper. More overtly than newsreels, publicity for serial movie episodes claimed to animate the illustrated story versions in Sunday papers, exceeding the capacity of print. This point was sometimes explicitly depicted, as in a trade ad for Pathé's *The Romance of Elaine*, serialized in the Hearst chain and other papers, which showed a realistic photograph of the heroine bursting through a fading reproduction of the printed story page.[98]

It is surprising, in hindsight, that a moving picture equivalent of a syndicated Sunday newspaper magazine supplement only briefly emerged in isolated cases, as it would have been easy enough to replace the titles and intertitles of a newsreel with a series of names of regional newspapers. Simply put, editors presumed a magazine supplement would boost sales of the print editions of Sunday papers, while a newspaper-sponsored newsreel, they worried, could discourage buying and reading the paper at all. The exceptions are telling, as in 1915, when several regional "stringers" supplying local footage to the national *Universal Animated Weekly* were briefly sponsored by newspapers to create, for example, the *Omaha Bee-Universal Animated Weekly*, the *Milwaukee Wisconsin-Universal Animated Weekly*, and the *Indianapolis Star-Universal Animated Weekly*. The effort lasted only a few months. Equally briefly, but better established on a regional scale, in 1915 a team of Chicago news photographers formed a film company and created the *Northwest Weekly* in collaboration with dozens of local newspapers in Minnesota, Wisconsin, and the Dakotas. Local footage was included in each participating town and city in order to allow a "reel of real news . . . a 'reel' newspaper" supplement to the *Minneapolis Tribune*, the *Grand Forks (ND) Herald*, and smaller-town papers such as the *Bemidji (MN) Pioneer*.[99] The logic was to animate the newspaper with moving pictures of regional and local events, supplementing the situated, localized character of the newspaper by replacing the international, corporate package of established newsreels. As the *Duluth News-Tribune* explained, "The story of the printed page will be amplified and enlivened by the motion picture, and the sole aim of the organization will be the sincere application of the slogan, 'See the Northwest First.'"[100]

Despite the rarity of syndicated newspaper-sponsored newsreels, on a more autonomous and individuated basis, many newspapers did participate in the production, or at least promotion, of local and regional newsreels, lending their names to a moving picture newspaper to supplement their print editions. Local newsreels, frequent if not routine, transformed many newspapers' film pages into films and provided moviegoing readers a way to extend the habit of news reading at home into the evening hours at the theater. They are thus closely aligned with the emergence of the daily moving picture story in February 1914 as a brief fad. Both were presented as ways to read the news and then see it, on a daily basis for the fictional stories or on a weekly basis for the nonfiction newsreels. Given the relatively capital-intensive, technological, and material requirements needed to distribute films, even on a local or regional basis, and the existing competition of established alternatives like the *Pathé Weekly*, the efforts of some newspapers to create film supplements to their print editions is remarkable.

Nonetheless, these small-scale local and regional efforts by newspapers to establish newsreel parallels to their print editions is important, in hindsight, for presaging how dozens of newspapers across the continent would become owners of radio broadcasting licenses in 1921 and 1922, as we shall see in chapter 6. Local and regional newsreels appeared on the heels of the success of the *Pathé Weekly*, although not at first in conjunction with newspapers. Two of the more prominently promoted were the *Golden Gate Weekly* late in 1913 and the *New York Weekly* early in 1914. As metropolitan news films aiming for a broad appeal, these were advertised for sale to independent showmen across the continent in the film trade press.[101] The international reach of the newsreel genre was clearly opening a space for a more localized approach, more akin to the metropolitan coverage of an actual newspaper rather than providing only newswire syndicate material of general appeal. Eventually newsreel companies themselves closed this gap by issuing regional versions with a modest amount of film from local events, but for a brief period there was an opportunity for other companies to create metropolitan and regional film news. Many newspapers were enticed to grab the chance.

"Here are the Herald Movies*"*

Perhaps the first newspaper-run newsreel debuted when the *New Orleans Item Animated Weekly* began in March 1914, for several months compiling a regular magazine of local events. The *Item Animated Weekly* claimed to have been the first to film Mardi Gras festivities in 1914; warships on the Mississippi River heading to fight in Mexico; suffragettes giving speeches; and the chief of police posing with his "family" in a city park inundated with dozens of children wanting to pose for the moving picture camera with him.[102] By its third weekly issue, a moving picture "comic section" was added to make the "*Item* pictures alive with news."[103] "*The Item*'s News to be Shown in Movies" was the headline announcing the venture into animated news: "To go the world one better in the marvels of the motion picture, *The Item*—greatest paper [in the] South—has advanced the industry into journalism. Every day this great paper has given in written accounts the best that brains can offer, and . . . '*The Item Animated Weekly*' will show in cinematograph accounts all that skill and co-operation can offer."[104] The *New Orleans Item*'s weekly newsreel specialized in local sports footage, following the Pelicans pro-baseball team on the road and gaining much publicity when visiting athletes like Ty Cobb arrived in town to play against the home team. Remarkably, it was produced entirely in-house, although incorporated separately with ten-thousand-dollar investments from local businessmen. The *Item Weekly*'s laboratory for developing and reproducing film prints was located on the top floors of the *Item*'s annex building, and the public was instructed to telephone the *Item* operator to connect to the animated weekly.

Shortly afterward came an even higher-profile newspaper-run newsreel with the *Chicago Herald Movies*, a regional weekly composed entirely of filmed events in the Second City and its environs. The *Herald* had originated the idea of a daily picture story and a daily movie theater directory, both in collaboration with Universal Film Manufacturing in February 1914. In July it launched a new venture, reframing Chicago itself as a celebrity worthy of spotlights: "Here are the '*Herald Movies*.' Chicago has become a 'movie' star. You and the other 2,388,490 residents of the city make up the supporting company of the most remarkable film producing concern in the world."[105] The novelty of a newspaper-run newsreel was the special attraction of depicting the local public itself on screen, drawing upon the unique ability of a newspaper's familiarity with the city beat to do so. "It will be the city's debut as a film star and, possibly—just possibly—it will be yours," explained the *Herald*, making explicit how a local newsreel would portray locations and events from everyday life and thus show the local viewing audience onscreen, possibly the viewer herself.[106] The newspaper's long-standing dedication to public service was invoked too in explaining how the "miniature army" of moving picture reporters would bring the city's news to the city's people, interchangeable with the newspaper's readership.[107]

Even more than the *New Orleans Item Weekly* a few months earlier, the *Herald Movies* explicitly drew a direct parallel between the newspaper publishing and newsreel production. The joint effort paired perfect supplements following the same logic and professional techniques: "Just now the 'movie' news editor is working out departments just like those in the great dailies. . . . In *The Herald Movies* will be found a complete pictorial supplement to *The Chicago Herald* such as no newspaper ever before has been able to offer to its readers."[108] The *Herald Movies* even signified its supplementary relationship to the printed paper by adapting the *Herald*'s motto for the medium of moving pictures: "Whereas *The Chicago Herald* is 'Easy to Read and Worth Reading,' *Herald Movies* will be 'Easy to See and Worth Seeing.'"[109] One local theater manager playing *Herald Movies* was quoted predicting a future "when each newspaper will have its own theater, named for itself, where it will show the news from day to day in pictures."[110]

The *Chicago Tribune* was spurred by this competition to create its own newsreel, at first produced in-house by its own team of news photographers. It was not the *Tribune*'s first venture into news films, as it had sponsored moving pictures taken by Edwin F. Weigle on the outbreak of World War I.[111] The *Tribune Animated Weekly* began in June 1915. Each newsreel had a special featured moving picture version of the *Tribune*'s key comic strip, *The Adventures of Old Doc Yak*, which had been distributed for several years on film already but had now been brought under the direct umbrella of a filmed version of the newspaper to anchor its newsreel. The *Tribune*'s regional weekly was a widespread success, able to include footage from national and European wartime events, and was soon transformed into a national newsreel by joining forces with Chicago's Selig Polyscope Co., after that film production company severed its relationship with Hearst. The hook was the *Tribune*'s reputation as a serious and authoritative provider of news compared to Hearst's notoriety for sensationalism: "When William N. Selig, President of the Selig Polyscope Co., decided to issue a news reel superior to the *Hearst-Selig News Pictorial*, he . . . [took] steps to select a news gathering organization having both the prestige and facilities to cooperate with 100% efficiency . . . *The Selig-Tribune*, a combination of cinema reels and newspaper columns into a reel newspaper."[112] Again, as the *Chicago Herald* had done the year before and as the *Tribune* would bring forward when it later entered radio broadcasting under the call WGN, the newspaper's existing motto, "The World's Greatest Newspaper," was transformed for the medium of movies: "*Selig-Tribune*—'The World's Greatest News Film'—Shows All Reel News First."[113] In the long term, the *Tribune*'s usurping Hearst as Selig's newsreel partner seems only to have spurred the *Hearst International News Weekly* to become the dominant player in the field. The company's newsreel service began operating parallel to its syndicated news photo and wire services. Indeed, Hearst International soon consolidated several competing newsreel titles in a takeover process similar to later newspaper buyouts, first combining with the pioneering *Pathé Weekly* and then the *Universal Weekly* and *Mutual Screen Telegram*.[114]

One alternative to Hearst's creation of a newsreel with national reach was trying to affiliate existing newspapers in supporting a syndicated newsreel, an idea tested briefly in 1915 by Lewis J. Selznick's World Film Corporation. The "World Weekly" syndicated newsreel service involved the direct, on-the-beat "cooperation of cameramen with reporters of metropolitan papers [which] assures timeliness and guarantees interest for up-to-the-minute photographic review of news-happenings."[115] Each regional World Film exchange across the country released the "Weekly" with a slightly different title adopting the moniker of its local partnering publishers, such as the *Dallas News World Weekly* or the *Cincinnati Enquirer World Weekly* (see fig. 18). Including local content in national newsreel service was lauded as an innovation paralleling the long-standing national newswire services and syndicated amusement features: "*The Buffalo Enquirer*, at

FIGURE 18. "25 Great News Journals Combine with World Film," *Moving Picture World*, August 7, 1915, 952–53.

all times on the lookout for something new, once more shows its enterprise by affiliating with the national News Weekly. . . . It will assist in placing the news of Buffalo and of the nation on the screen. Residents of this city will now be able to read of local events in this paper and see them in moving pictures in their neighborhood theatre."[116] The idea had begun in Chicago with the *Herald Movies*, but the syndicated venture aimed to "make this service nation-wide—to establish, in other words, an associated newspaper film . . . a most comprehensive review of national events—a bird's eye view, so to speak."[117] The venture folded after just a few months, after briefly changing distributors to Metro Pictures.[118] Its imagined pairing of local journalists and newsreel photographers, supposedly working together, clearly failed to recognize the distinct spatial and temporal patterns each type of news needed to witness and report events.

Rather than news reporting, the starker link between newspapers and filmmaking lay in advertising, which provided a more enduring model in some scattered cases. Perhaps the longest-lasting local-newspaper-linked newsreel was the *Cleveland Plain Dealer's Motion Picture Magazine*, begun in June 1917 in conjunction with that city's Argus Film Company as a way for regional filmmakers to get established as reliable producers of industrial and advertising films.[119] Previous efforts to combine newspaper and newsreel followed established conventions for journalism, collaborating to provide news in a more vivid, photographic realistic form. But Argus Film instead focused on the local attraction of possibly being in the pictures or knowing someone in them. Resolutely local, the *Plain Dealer* explained the attraction precisely as the possibility to "See yourself in the movies! If you have been on Cleveland's down town streets lately, it's pretty near certain you have been caught by *The Plain Dealer's* movie cameras."[120] Movies could still improve upon the technological realism of journalism by providing "the latest news in picture form [to] tell the story more vividly than the ablest writer."[121] Local color and local nuance were precisely the point. As had happened decades earlier with Pulitzer's *New York World*, bird's-eye-view movies of downtown Cleveland and the city's lakefront were taken from a hot air balloon, "only one of the snappy features of *The Plain Dealer* weekly movies."[122] The idea of a local and regional hybrid of film and newspaper was occasionally brought to life by various papers joining with small, regional film producers, as the *New Orleans Item* and the *Chicago Herald* had first done. While each effort was only briefly successful, the continual draw of the idea between 1914 and 1922 was clearly setting the stage for the more concerted and enduring intermedial forays of newspaper publishers into radio station ownership.[123]

PUBLICITY!

In the next chapter of this section on circulation, we connect the drive to increase the newspaper's reach beyond mass readership and massive sales figures into the spectacle of circulation—that is, its delivery and the monopoly business behind its regional distribution. The drive for total circulation was also an ideological mandate for novelty and simultaneity that embraced intermedial technologies that allowed news to extend itself into forms other than print. As we have described in the previous section on subscription, while newspaper publishers' primary identity and business model remained rooted in print sales of newspapers, many newspapers' weekend supplements had long been experimenting with intermedial forms—paper toys, glossy magazines, and then collaborating to produce newsreels and eventually radio programming.

In the final chapters on syndication, we aim to animate these supplements and recount their histories, continuing to redefine newspaper circulation from a position other than an accounting of its profitability, moving into an account of its cultural reach. Mass readership is not merely an instrument to reap profits in a mass market; the people, newspapers, and money involved in networks of news reading are mutually constituted in our media history of the structures of Sunday news reading. In esteeming circulation and making it central to the history of the Sunday paper, we avoid reducing people and their practices to mass markets and profits. Public interest? Popular interest? Consumer self-interest? Always also exploited for the profit of advertisers and newspaper corporations—our conceptual definition of "circulation" as a social relation between newspapers, readers, and technologies of reading has allowed us to mediate the balance among those possibilities.

By 1922 newspapers were practiced in adopting intermedial strategies for expanding circulation, and newspaper reading had already come to include other activities. As we saw in chapter 2, the paper itself now included cutout toys, puzzles, and collectible inserts; its amusement and sporting columns helped schedule leisure time as its advertising helped schedule consumption. Further, newspapers frequently sponsored community events from trade shows to charity concerts to election night gatherings that turned voting results into popular festivals. While this is clearly a matter of commercialization, the emergence of Sunday supplements as a central part of popular culture and a significant part of newspaper publishing should be taken as an extension of publicity. Publicity, in the sense of making public or constituting a public, transforms the pursuit of increased circulation into a complex relation of public service and popular appeal, not reducible to maximizing advertising and profits. Recall how "Publicity!" was the motto of the *New York World*, transmitted via wireless by Marconi to announce his new communication technology that would transform reading into listening and writing into speaking. This is not to deny the importance of circulation as a matter of sales but rather to attenuate that aspect as only part of the social relations of publicity. Newspaper readers were addressed as a social and civic public, not just a market.

As we will see in chapter 4, the spectacles that produced and delivered the Sunday paper, the fast press and the fast train, fascinated the reading public with their speed and coordination in networked systematicity, part of what David Nye has termed the "American technological sublime," linking technology to a faith in "new beginnings."[124] In this chapter, we first recounted how newspapers collaborated with moving picture producers, wireless experimenters, and even with hot air balloon pilots. This drive to collaborate and experiment with intermedial, audiovisual forms of news is not simply explained through this ideological fascination with technology. We framed the string of attempts to go beyond "pen pictures" as a quest to find technologies that better approximated the immediacy that written news had long promised. The reporting and correspondence of journalism had long held the goal of vivid, realistic depiction.

4

THE SPECTACLE OF SUNDAY DELIVERY

The variety of the Sunday paper escapes even the most expansive definitions of news. Consider "The Anatomy of a Kiss," an article by Kate McGuirk reviewing Edison's production of a moving picture for the *New York Sunday World*, appearing the very same week Edison's Vitascope debuted to the public in 1896.[1] The feature celebrated the novel wonder of lifelike moving picture filmstrips depicting in life-size close-up a key scene from the play *The Widow Jones*. Its celebrity stars, May Irwin and John Rice, "posed before Edison's Kinetoscope . . . at the request of *The Sunday World*."[2] The film contained "42 feet of kiss in 600 pictures. . . . Here are forty camera winks of kiss," reproduced on the page as nearly identical etchings of still frames from the film:[3] "What the camera did not see in the kiss did not exist."[4] Here the Sunday newspaper was glad to be part of the uncanny development of voyeurism through technology in one of early cinema's most famous scenes. Reproducing sensation was a constant concern of Sunday illustrated features about technological progress, such as another scientific study of a kiss in 1897; this time it was the human subjects put to a physiological test in a ten-hour kissing marathon.[5] The illustration combined an anatomical diagram of the nerves and muscles of the face underneath a heart-shaped reproduction of the sentimental painting *The Kiss* by Eduard Lebiedzki.[6]

In the same *Sunday World* in 1897 was the latest article by McGuirk, aboard a locomotive hired as *The World's* Special to set a new speed record.[7] Her reporting conveyed the experience as much as the facts: "Now I have travelled faster than any other mortal alive except the three men who were necessary for the achievement of the unparalleled record! . . . The fairy tales of the age are coming true."[8] The illustration, "from a photograph," showed the *World's* locomotive in deep perspective, as if coming through the printed page—or, rather, as if coming through the cinema screen, mirroring the novelty of early moving pictures of oncoming express trains (see fig. 19).[9] With such achievements of technological reproduction and propulsion, scientific progress had exceeded the capacities of human beings, but the sensationalism emphasized in the weekend edition's journalistic features demonstrated that the superhuman capacities of technology were subject to the enjoyment of newspaper readerships.[10] The production of such features by the fast printing press and the millionfold mass distribution of

FIGURE 19. "Rides a Mile in Thirty-Two Seconds," *New York World*, October 24, 1897, 33.

newspapers to readers across vast metropolitan regions was, in turn, a continual topic of illustrated features in Sunday editions.[11] The networked production and circulation of the very paper held by the reader was cast among the greatest spectacles and technological wonders of the age.

The two ideals of mass circulation and reproduced sensation were combined in such illustrated Sunday features as another "exciting ride on the fast newspaper train," under the byline of "*The World* Woman."[12] Her eyewitness report of active participation to help deliver "myriads of *Sunday Worlds* distributed through the state at hurricane speed" combined the twin concerns of this chapter: How was Sunday newspaper circulation a product of communication technologies?[13] And how did Sunday newspapers themselves facilitate an appreciation for the effort behind those same technologies? Our answers depend on careful attention to self-referential illustrated articles and supplements that foregrounded the production and circulation of the newspaper itself, all within the wider context of progress toward the modern ideals of mass communication.[14]

Typical of the reflexive viewpoint of such articles, *The World* Woman reporter aboard the train in 1896, "which leaves this city every Sunday morning loaded with tons of *Sunday Worlds*," asserted that "few of the vast numbers of readers of *The Sunday World* in New York City know that thousands of people in every other county" read their newspaper on the same day: "The system by means of which a great army of readers is supplied with the greatest Sunday paper published is a triumph of modern ingenuity and skill."[15] Although other media technologies (like instantaneous photography and the wireless telegraph) were achieving similar feats and inspiring dreams of progress, the Sunday paper was the medium for their initial exposure to the public, as we saw in chapter 3. Self-reflexively, the newspaper's technologies of mass printing and circulation were also subject to exposure and animation in illustrated articles and other forms of display. The mixing and blending of technologies within the form of the Sunday newspaper, its built intermediality not only changed the Sunday newspaper by extending the cultural reach of the newspaper literally and discursively, it further allowed the Sunday newspaper to "borrow" from the newness and wonder of those technologies in keeping this older medium of printing at the forefront of technological change.

We argue that despite the popularity and suasive power of Henry Jenkins's arguments about media industries, the phenomenon of intermediality that had the Sunday paper as nexus cannot be reduced to cross-programming and "corporate convergence."[16] Newspapers thoroughly entwined their own circulation and production with intermedial supplements—print illustrations, photographic reproductions, and, later, moving picture newsreel and wireless radio broadcast supplements. New and old media technologies were often deeply entwined in print in Sunday supplements, confounding any precept of progress that each medium's designers, audiences, or interface might espouse for linear, chronological influence.[17]

The expanded size of the Sunday paper's multiple sections is inextricable from the drive to grow circulation, which determined advertising prices, which in turn translated into revenues and profits. Premium content helped boost circulation and balance larger amounts of increasingly elaborate advertising. Yet the drive to sell more copies of the paper fails to fully explain the special efforts and extraordinary material forms added to the Sunday edition, because the obsession with circulation itself goes beyond simply delivering more papers. The expanded form of the Sunday paper gestured to faith in the limitless capacity of communication technologies to achieve boundless circulation, an ethos expressed widely at the time as first the telegraph and then wireless, broke the connection of the spread of information from the speed of movement.[18] The fascination with regional delivery aboard the fast train reminded readers that getting physical copies of the paper into their homes insisted upon conquering the limits of time and space, even if the paper could never achieve instantaneous circulation like the telegraph and wireless.

In all of these ways, we define *circulation* as more than simply the quantities of newspapers sold and readers addressed. We also mean the cultural reach of the newspaper, and of the illustrated weekend edition in particular, which reflexively transformed its own printing and production into a spectacle of mass communication. While "the lure of illustration" and "the mass image" have been the subjects of scholarly analyses,[19] we propose that the Sunday paper's continual circulation of its own mass reproduction is central to the formation of a saturated modern media environment, typified in networked broadcasting in the twentieth century, which we address in chapter 6. Here we take newspaper readers' ability to witness, understand, and take pleasure in the mass circulation of their own experience as central to the Sunday paper's cultural function. As discussed in chapter 3, newspaper publishers' interest in supplementing their pages with other media was an extension of a more generalized espousal of technological progress within the promise of perfectly mediated communication. However, as much as it was their means of communication, the material constraint of circulating newsprint was also a problem for publishers. Maximizing print circulation through speeding up delivery and expanding geographic distribution was a process that remained anchored in the delivery of a material object. To achieve its own image of itself, to overcome the limitations of its own print form, the newspaper had to exploit intermedial networks with other technologies and cultural relations.

NETWORKS, ARTICULATIONS, AND ASSEMBLAGES

Approaching the material and technological bases of print culture in Sunday papers requires tracing the extent of their cultural reach beyond the printed page. This is a matter of networks and assemblages. As Elizabeth Eisenstein has suggested, the difficulty of grappling with print culture is that we are shrouded in a "veil of print" and it is well-nigh impossible to apprehend the whole from within it.[20]

This chapter explores how the deeply ideological ways technology is often discussed are linked to modern notions of progress through mediated communication. While particular media connections and articulated elements have varying degrees of effect and prominence, ideals such as perfectly mediated communication can maintain a degree of tenacity that shapes possibilities, practices, and configurations: "Some lines of force are so firmly held in place by a host of social forces that they seem, for all practical purposes, to be permanent, fixed, necessary and natural."[21] As discussed introducing the section on circulation, theories of articulation have been primarily concerned with how ideology, power, and identity work to constitute the cultural field.[22] The turn to theories of actor-networks has focused on material relations and how agency is built into the design of material things. If a focus on articulation exposes the radical contextualization of objects, peoples, and relations within culture, the turn to actor-networks concentrates attention on the relations between material objects and agents. As John Law and John Hassard suggest, "Entities achieve their form as a consequence of the relations in which they are located. But this means . . . they are *performed* in, by, and through those relations."[23] Each association between elements acts as a mediator "and no longer as a mere compliant intermediary."[24] Following this insight, our consideration of circulation in this chapter takes mediation as achieved not only by humans but also by objects: "Actors are not conceived as fixed entities but as flows, as circulating objects, undergoing trials."[25] From this perspective, communicative action is severed from intentionality, and objects become capable of conveying ideas. As a result, the cultural impact of a class of material objects, such as Sunday supplements, can be conceptualized through its articulated networks of circulation. We can therefore consider the cultural relevance of the Sunday paper through its design and circulation without privileging the intentions of journalists and publishers—indeed proceeding even without an archive of those intentions (which would have to be interpreted as an archive of material documents, regardless, rather than a window into the minds of historically influential people). Further, by mobilizing this theoretical apparatus, we can displace the crude accounting of circulation as simply how many papers sold, even as we recognize how these numbers, as unreliable as they are, tell us something about the history of the paper at the time.

This theoretical ground centers on how relations between humans and objects become more or less standardized through a network (like "the newspaper") of aesthetic, professional, and social practices and discourses over time. In our reconsideration of what a Sunday newspaper is, the explanation is not somehow held within the page itself, waiting to be uncovered. Rather, the cultural meaning of the Sunday paper is mapped in the relations within which it is embedded and those it helps to produce as well as new techniques of reading and ways of interacting with the printed paper itself. Through this lens, the newspaper is rendered a complex assemblage of materially diverse networks of technologies, peoples, words, images, practices, and more that cohere to produce "the Sunday paper" as a bounded object with a definable audience and a public role. In such a formulation, printing presses, delivery trains, newsstands, and newsboys matter as much as the daily rag that carried the news, because they are also part of the assemblage, with specific kinds of agencies. The discussion of circulation that follows maps out how the cultural reach of the Sunday newspaper, in its expanded understanding, came alive in illustrated feature articles that aimed to resonate in the lives of its readers. It's clear that the Sunday paper did reach more readers and thus expanded its purview. But it also expanded its mediating function as a connection point between an emergent modern mass readership and the world around it.

MAKING CIRCULATION VISIBLE

Below the buzz of newsroom and business office activity, the pressroom was the literal and metaphorical ground floor for the production of a mediated public and a media society. The Sunday paper's continual spotlighting of technological marvels begins, accordingly, with publicity featuring newspaper printing presses. Press technologies were routinely profiled by publishers when purchased—not surprising given the great expense and capital outlay needed to replace or expand their capacity for circulation. One survey of the *New York Tribune*'s printing presses in 1878 noted with satisfaction how "the spectacle of a newspaper press-room was one that never failed to impress the imagination."[26] The press itself was central to journalism's business and, in turn, its cultural authority. Within publishers' headquarters, printing facilities had symbolic predominance as the corporeal heart and means of mass production of newspapers by the tens of thousands per hour. Rather than simply announce the purchase of a new infrastructure of production, newspapers regularly provided the means for the reading public to imaginatively take pleasure in understanding and seeing newspaper technology at work. A sublime spectacle derived from the massive fast press machinery churning out newspapers—more than sixty newspaper sections printed every second—a process described in articles detailing the mechanics, illustrations of the apparatuses, and even a cut-and-paste cardboard toy of a printing press, given away free as a Sunday edition art supplement.

The *Boston Globe* began printing color cover pages for its Sunday editions in 1894. The following June, it also began giving away color lithographed cardboard inserts primarily for paper cutout toys. As Sunday papers turned to color print supplements in the early 1890s, such lithographed "art supplements" were common—whether collectible posters or cutout toys—but their production was usually subcontracted to specialized lithograph printers. A color newsprint supplement, however, required the *Globe* and other publishers to buy new color-ink fast printing presses of their own. Having installed a color press at great expense, the *Globe* was nonetheless pushed into adopting cutout toy art supplements by the competing *Boston Herald*'s later inclusion of them, which was no doubt a response to the *Globe*'s color supplement. Weekend after weekend for more than a year, the *Sunday Globe* gave away paper dolls, then theater dioramas with miniature stage sets and cardboard actors, as well as other cutout playthings, until along came a specially made paper toy in August 1896. "See *The Globe*'s Biggest Press at Work!" lauded the promotion a few days in advance.[27] That week's toy was a miniature version of the *Globe*'s own mammoth color printing machinery. Readers were encouraged to imagine the labor of producing the paper as an entertainment for their own amusement: "Cut it out and set it up! It will be like a visit to the busy pressroom itself! See how *The Globe* is printed, paged, and folded by this magnificent machine" (see plate 6).[28] Whereas all such art supplements turned buying and reading the paper into a leisure activity, this particular insert made a game out of the technology producing the paper itself. Perhaps more surprisingly, the supplement was meant to recreate an in-person visit to see the *Globe*'s technology in action, something that had actually become a popular tourist attraction in Boston: "So great has been the public interest shown in *The Globe*'s pressroom that the management have erected a gallery from which visitors may watch the presses at work."[29] Such efforts were, indeed, routine in metropolitan cities across the continent for several decades at the turn of the twentieth century.

Although the cutout toy press may be truly unique, the *Globe*'s reprinting an illustration of its press and pressroom in a Sunday feature story is hardly exceptional, nor is its setting up a visitors' gallery to see the sublime mechanical reproduction of newspaper printing under way. This was not even the first time the *Boston Globe* had self-referentially profiled its color press on the same color supplement pages that were printed by it. An early cover illustration of its color supplement in January 1895 had shown the "*Globe* Wonders" of the then-new color press. A detailed article explained the work behind the scenes, or rather underneath the sidewalks of downtown Boston, and a narrative of human progress accompanied the color reproduction of the deus ex machina that produced the very page held by the reader. The vast quantities of newsprint were first presented as food for the voracious appetite of the personified color printing press: "Think of a Saturday night supper weighing 55½ tons! Think of devouring 111,000 pounds of paper in a single night!"[30] The newsprint was "transformed into the delightful literary dish which will be served up for mental refreshment on the morrow," so that the ultimate appetite was readers' cravings for leisure on their day of rest: "Public demand has served to make such an undertaking imperative."[31]

After an accounting of the past decade's increase in pages in each Sunday paper and its overall circulation, the article then shifts to explain the printing technology mediating the process: "It would be difficult to conceive that it could respond to even the slightest touch as promptly as if it was possessed of a human spirit. . . . The word is given, the lever is pressed, and the ponderous machine moves, slowly at first, but gradually increasing to lightning speed, making the varied colors flit before the eyes until neither space nor size has any meaning to the bewildered looker-on. Dear reader, it is your *Sunday Globe* that is being printed."[32] The mystique of modernity's ephemeral conflation of spiritual and material processes is invoked as part of the parallel conflation of worship and leisure on the Sabbath actualized by the Sunday paper: "The gigantic task of printing almost 200,000 papers of 36 pages each . . . must be completed, and the messengers with the news of the world be on their way to their widely separated destinations before the bells chime out for early church service on the morrow."[33]

The Fast Printing Press

Bearing witness to the technological sublime came to include the process of modern newspaper printing.[34] In combination with the color image of the press itself, the *Boston Globe* crystallizes an internal logic of self-replication and self-referentiality that would apply to mediated communication in the age of "technological reproducibility," to borrow Walter Benjamin's famous term. The promotional rhetoric for newspaper printing's own technologies was routine in this period, thoroughly embedded in what Susan Buck-Morss, in her synthesis of Benjamin's "Arcades Project," has termed the "display value" or "exhibition value" of modernity, which is extended here well beyond department store windows to envelope mediated communication in its essence.[35] In a functional sense, the public witness of press technology stood as a simple matter of documentation to secure the boosterist claims of circulation figures, part of what Alfred D. Chandler has termed the "visible hand" of modernity's "managerial revolution."[36] A widely syndicated article in June 1899, written by Richard March Hoe, inventor of the web-perfecting high-speed printing press, expressed the point succinctly, proposing that his company's efforts deserved to rank alongside Edison's in importance: "The modern newspaper, with its wonderful service in spreading information and molding opinion, is perhaps the greatest civilizing and controlling force of the time. The rapid printing press, by making the newspaper possible, deserves to rank as one of the great achievements in an age of mechanical invention."[37] If the high-speed cylinder printing press was, in a sense, the assembly line for the mass reproduction of the image and word, it is rarely left as a mere matter of banal mechanics by newspaper publishers themselves, who continually presented illustrated articles depicting their presses to stoke public awe for the technological basis of the newspaper readers were holding. The ideological overstatements and transformation into play and display are extras seeking to reanimate and make lifelike the process of mass reproduction of newspaper pages, and to animate the involvement of the reader too into an admiring onlooker taking pleasure in the spectacle of industry (see plate 7).

Admiration for the pressroom soon extended into admiration of the newspaper's headquarters. "Using architecture as a delivery mechanism for notions of patriotism, nation building, individual aspiration, education and moral uplift," the newspaper office staked a claim for the paper's institutional legitimacy and cultural centrality.[38] A new skyscraper headquarters for the *Philadelphia North American* coincided with its inaugural Sunday edition in 1901, which included a special sixteen-page color supplement, "The Process of Producing Philadelphia's Great Daily Newspaper," depicting and explaining every aspect of work at the newspaper office.[39] "Better than a personal tour of the building," the print tour of the *North American* began with photographs of the editorial council and reporters in the city room.[40] It depicted the complex network of humans and nonhumans busily working to produce the paper in the readers' hands: copy editors; telegraph wire copy transcribers; the illustrators, photographers, and cartoonists studio; the composing room; engravers; stereotypers; a special profile of the pressroom technology; and the building itself. No detail was insignificant. The subscription and mail department, the library and filing archive, the advertising and classified offices were not neglected, nor were the workers in the boiler room and managers of the electric generators. The supplement showed two tons of newspapers being loaded onto special trains that would circulate more than two hundred thousand copies across four states by Sunday breakfast. With a final intermedial nod to the panoramas of the previous century, the last page of this special section shows the "cyclorama" view from the roof of the *North American*'s new office building, overlooking a vast region where "a million and a half people earn a livelihood and have their home."[41] Placing the Sunday paper in those homes was precisely what transformed weekday labor into livelihoods by reciprocally providing weekend leisure for the whole family.

Well before the focus turned to the specialized production of tabloid and color supplements in Sunday editions, advances in printing machinery had often been depicted with pictorial illustrations, or "cuts," when newspapers installed new presses. A simple announcement of the *Chicago Inter-Ocean*'s purchase of two of William Bullock's perfecting presses in 1876 reportedly only stoked curiosity to see what they looked like. "In response to a desire expressed by many of our readers," a cut illustration was reprinted from a catalog.[42] When one of Walter Scott & Co.'s "lightning folders" was attached to the press a year later, the *Inter-Ocean* took the chance to print a modified cut illustration and offer "a word about ourselves," because "there are few readers of any paper who are at all aware of the complicated and expensive machinery required to transform the webs of white paper, as they are sent to the office, to the neatly printed and folded sheets for which the reader pays."[43] While provincial newspapers printed similar overviews of improved technology to print tens of thousands of papers weekly, the heft and circulation of Pulitzer's *New York World* allowed for a series of illustrated articles about the production of its millions of papers. Opening the *World*'s pressroom to public view in an early example from 1885 was connected to the novel publicity stunt—soon made into an enduring slogan—of turning its "circulation books open to all."[44] Since the *World* had taken the public "into its confidence, and opening its books freely . . . it continues its autobiography to-day by telling the story of the production of a great newspaper."[45]

Such stories tie capital investment, efficiency, and expanded capacity to public service in a theme that would stand as publishers pursued new intermedial ventures over the following four decades. Illustrated with no fewer than fifteen cuts from one to three columns wide, the feature showed the composing, stereotyping, telegraph, postal, and delivery rooms, with the largest picture devoted to the *World*'s pressroom and its ten perfecting presses. But Pulitzer went one step further than simply illustrating the process; in parallel with opening his circulation books for inspection by competitors and readers alike, he "Cordially Invited! The Editors, Proprietors and Publishers of all New York Newspapers" to visit the pressroom to "witness *The World*'s Circulation of Over a Million a Week."[46] Several hundred advertisers were specially invited to see the spectacle of the *Sunday World* being printed, a "glimpse into a real magician's workshop."[47] Similarly illustrated features accompanied every milestone Pulitzer reached in the rest of the century as technological improvements matched expanding circulation, all in tandem with the growth of the heft of the *Sunday World*. New presses in 1887 were proffered as "the mastodon of printing machines, the largest, fastest, costliest and most perfect printing press ever constructed for any newspaper."[48]

The opening of the Pulitzer Building on Park Row in 1890, briefly the tallest skyscraper in New York, afforded another opportunity to illustrate the labor of production normally hidden from view with a four-page souvenir supplement on fine paper.[49] Opening that scene to the public was built into the very design of the new building, which included a viewing gallery over the pressroom: "A Cavern of Wonders . . . The public is welcome here. A special gallery, running midway between the lanes of monster machines, has been especially provided for the public's free admission."[50] Installing four new "gigantic" quadruple presses in 1892, the *World* printed another behind-the-scenes exposé, with a full-page illustration showing the viewing gallery occupied by well-dressed ladies and men in top hats (see fig. 20).[51] The workers are shown almost at ease, contrasted with an accompanying cut showing anxious faces in Johannes Gutenberg's press room. The mythologizing continued: "Mr. Gutenberg's press capacity was thirty printed pages an hour. *The World*'s press capacity is 6,524,000 an hour. People used to go

FIGURE 20. "'The World's' Gigantic Presses," *New York World*, November 6, 1892, 32.

see Gutenberg's pressroom because there was nothing like it anywhere else—and people visit *The World*'s pressroom nowadays for precisely the same reason."[52] Many metropolitan newspapers wanting claim to the adjective "modern" followed suit in building viewing galleries overlooking newly built pressrooms.[53] You could watch the *New York Herald* being printed from the sidewalk outside the building through plate glass windows.[54]

A sense of the attraction is best explained in the retrospective offered by R. M. Hoe at the turn of the twentieth century. Printing technology was superhuman, and its achievement derived from superseding the abilities of human talent and human senses: "The machine weighs over sixty tons and is massive in its proportions. Yet its touch is as deft as that of human fingers. . . . Human hands could not work fast enough to keep up with the requirements of the modern newspaper. . . . This press for the first time did away completely with hand labor in the process of printing."[55] But the printing process was still subject to the leisure of the reading public when transformed into spectacle. Newspaper publishers' self-interest in foregrounding their own modern printing technologies was at the center of a wider intermedial engagement providing public knowledge of all advances in science and technology, especially media technologies. In tandem with the development of the Sunday supplement as a cornerstone of its cultural work, newspaper publishing embraced a mandate well beyond public information and circulation of the news, let alone the printed newspaper. This is first apparent in the printing technologies required to produce millions of Sunday supplements. The ideology undergirding the entire intermedial mix, however, was a deterministic embrace of immediacy; the momentary attention on mediated communication promised to give way to a pervasive, instantaneous connectivity. Promoting the marvel of mass print production was only the start of the networked process of circulation; mass delivery was thus likewise profiled with equally sensational self-promotion.

The entertainment of pressroom tours aside, American newspaper publishing was characterized by cutthroat competition. A special visit to the Pulitzer Building's pressroom was arranged in March 1894 for a remarkably powerful group of the most prominent businessmen in New York. To verify its latest circulation figures, the *New York World* gathered an elite panel consisting of J. Edward Simmons, president of Fourth National Bank and ex-president of the New York Stock Exchange; Thomas L. James, president of Lincoln National Bank and former postmaster general of the United States; A. B. Hepburn, president of Third National Bank and ex-comptroller of the United States Currency; E. W. Bloomingdale of the great department store; financier Henry Clews; and Charles W. Dayton, prosecutor for the City of New York. Although the men "observed with interest *The World*'s color press, which was running off the colored covers for *The Sunday World*, printing the five colors at once," their main task for the day was an independent examination to verify the paper's "circulation books, pressroom reports, mail-room reports, paper companies' bills for amount of paper furnished, receipts of said bills, orders from news companies and such other records as might be found necessary for an accurate investigation of *The World*'s circulation."[56] The publicity stunt put into action Joseph Pulitzer's motto, "Circulation Books Open to All," an embodied visit of what had become a daily published certification of recent circulation figures. Not yet competing directly on the same newsstands and street corners, both Joseph Pulitzer and William R. Hearst had just goaded their respective state legislatures in New York and California to create new laws against publishing dishonest circulation figures. In 1893 boasting about circulation was no longer a simple matter of publishers' posturing against competitors; as described in the coming pages, exaggerating and manipulating circulation soon became an actual crime.

"CIRCULATION BOOKS OPEN TO ALL"

Higher and higher circulation figures were meaningless until sales numbers were transformed into a publicity campaign taking direct aim at the eclipsed figures of the front-running competitor. Joseph Pulitzer's invitation to examine the *World*'s circulation books was more than a motto on top of tours of the pressroom printing floor. The gesture only worked—and was only initiated—after the *World* had reached the apex of circulation in America, dethroning a brief reign at the top by the *New York Morning Journal*, published by his brother, Albert Pulitzer. In chapter 1, we reviewed in detail how "the other Pulitzer's" *Morning Journal* began introducing novel features and forms of Sunday supplements in a quest for increased subscriptions to fight its declining stature in the face of competition from the *World*. In chapter 6, we review how Hearst's later takeover of the *Morning Journal* began his development of a directly owned chain that leveraged syndication to gain truly nationwide reach, eclipsing the levels of circulation that either Pulitzer achieved on his own. For our present purposes, let us isolate the role of circulation figures in these twinned fights, a decade apart, between the *Journal* and the *World* (see table 1).

Albert Pulitzer's *New York Morning Journal* was claiming its 238,800 copies daily average in October 1889 as the "greatest circulation in America" at a time when the *World* was claiming 342,206 copies as a daily average for the past six months, a "circulation guaranteed greater than that of any two other American newspapers combined."[57] In the fight between the two Pulitzer brothers, the desperate swings of Albert seemed to be flailing as his paper's energy faded. Judged from today's perspective, more than thirteen decades later, the still-famous Pulitzer, Joseph, seems clearly ascendant, if not already victorious. The next month, in November 1889, in an apparently last-ditch publicity test of its circulation, the *Morning Journal* compiled sales figures from twelve "representative" independent wholesale dealers across the city.[58] In this tabulation, *the Morning Journal* outsold the *World* at

TABLE 1. A Sample of Sunday Circulation, 1884 to 1904

	1884	1886	1888	1893	1896	1898	1904
Boston Globe	60,000	93,365	126,033	170,738	229,708	244,500	283,753
Boston Herald	81,440	83,744	97,616	112,591	144,404	144,404	100,000
Chicago (Times- / Record-) Herald	23,237	30,000	65,000	125,000	127,349	110,000	201,078
Chicago Tribune	58,976	59,119	62,189	128,500	128,500	185,000	175,000
New York Herald	135,000		110,000	100,000	100,000	245,000	245,000
New York (Morning / American and) Journal	100,000	150,000	225,000	75,000	75,000	425,000	800,000
New York Recorder				96,244	150,000		
New York Sun	152,106	124,025	120,000	150,000	150,000	150,000	150,000
New York World	60,324	209,998	257,267	282,686	324,904	500,000	450,000
Philadelphia Inquirer				93,742	95,500	117,224	156,898

Source: Selected N. W. Ayer and Sons, *American Newspaper Annuals* (changing titles indicated by parentheses).

eight out of twelve borough news outlets. The circulation publicity claimed, "No competitor, not even *The World*, approaches its local sales. . . . Other papers may claim larger sales in distant places, but in New York and its vicinity, *The Journal* easily leads them ALL!"[59] Based on this, the *Morning Journal* continued to claim "the largest circulation in New York and vicinity of any paper published" as its front-page motto for the first months of 1890.[60]

In March 1890, as if to protect this particular type of top circulation claim, the *Morning Journal* launched a contest for readers to vote for the "most popular newsdealer" in New York, Brooklyn, New Jersey, Staten Island, and Connecticut: "The dealer who takes greatest care to have plenty of papers and neatly folded pictures on hand will be likely to get the greatest number of votes."[61] The following week, an enthusiastic report of boosted sales appeared on the ear of the front-page nameplate: "Sold 208 copies last Sunday. 'Do it again!' Keep on doing it, never stop, yours truly, Thos. E. Parr, newsdealer."[62] The next day, under the paper's name came the tagline "Journal, 50; Herald, 30; World, 30. Sunday sales at the Coleman House."[63] This would certainly have been the strangest temporary motto to ever run on a front page, except it was followed by ever more detailed versions, such as "And still we boom! Frank Manessy, 117th Street and 3rd Avenue, writes: 'On Sunday, I sold: *Journal* 130, *World* 80, *Sun* 56, *Herald* 40, *News* 55, *Star* 11, *Press* 10."[64] This odd attempt to boom the circulation hardly quelled the tide toward Joseph Pulitzer's *World*, which gained ground on the *Morning Journal* only further and more definitively as it added color comic supplements and other novel features in the early 1890s. In 1885 newspaper directories, the *Morning Journal* had the highest-circulation Sunday newspaper in America, but by 1893 it was ranked eighteenth in the country, ninth out of the eleven Sunday papers in New York.

The emphasis on circulation was not unique to New York. Hearst's *San Francisco Examiner* front-page banner began listing its daily "known circulation" in 1891, beside question marks for its competitors, the *Chronicle* and the *Call*.[65] The impetus for an actual law enforcing "newspaper honesty" was articulated, for example, in an editorial supporting an early effort.[66] Turning to comparison with pure food laws, the *Examiner* asked, "Why should newspapers with known circulation be compelled to stand on the same footing with journals that defraud their patrons with adulterated and watered claims?"[67] Putting talk into action, the *Examiner* began printing its circulation figures in the form of sworn and notarized legal documents, "always ready to open its books and pressrooms to interested parties in confirmation of its statements."[68] On New Year's Day 1893, a full chart of every day's circulation for the previous year was printed, along with a facsimile of a year-end summary statement from its supplier, the Willamette Pulp and Paper Company, that more than 5 million pounds of newsprint had been delivered.[69] In the next weeks, special reports from Sacramento tracked the introduction and passage of Section 538 amending the Penal Code of California: "Every proprietor or publisher of any newspaper or periodical who shall willfully and knowingly misrepresent the circulation of such newspaper or periodical for the purpose of securing advertising or other patronage shall be guilty of a misdemeanor."[70] The full wording of the act was added to the masthead next to the daily notarized circulation figures.[71]

Seeing a perfect alignment of politics, publicity, and editorial rhetoric, Joseph Pulitzer wasted no time advocating for an identical bill in New York. Just days after the new law's effect in California came news, datelined Albany, about Section 717a, "a bill to put an end to lies about circulation. . . . If the bill becomes a law it will do away with 'the circulation fiend.'"[72] On the editorial page, the bill was positioned as arising "at the request of *The World* . . . intended to prevent gross deception amounting to cheating."[73] Curiously, on the day of the bill's passing, the *World* included in its masthead a signed testimonial from prominent retailers vouching for the accuracy of the paper's circulation.[74] It was somewhat similar to Hearst's notarized letter, with the twist that the signatories were accountants and superintendents of the most prominent advertisers in the paper, including Bloomingdale's and Macy's: "The undersigned advertisers . . . have traced the circulation in various periods from the contracts for the supply of paper to the bank deposits for the sales of the paper. They have verified the published statements of circulation, and are satisfied of their accuracy."[75]

The twinned circulation strategies of Hearst and Pulitzer came into direct competition just a few years later. Early in November 1896, for the first anniversary of Hearst's ownership of the *New York Journal*, another special panel of businessmen gathered to verify a booming circulation growth. In what was almost a satire of the same gimmick Pulitzer had used in 1894, Hearst gathered "the largest purchasers of advertising space in the world, and probably the best judges of its value . . . to judge and to get at the truth" of how the *Journal* had gained the largest circulation in America in a single year, "its growth the most rapid in the history of newspapers."[76] Just as the bankers and Bloomingdale had verified the accounting for Pulitzer in 1894, this later panel examined all of Hearst's circulation books and advertising contracts. Yet this time, as if it were part of an elaborate in-joke about snake-oil peddlers, the panel was a selection of "world-famed advertisers"—all presidents of companies manufacturing patent medicines: Castoria, Sapolio, Hood's Sarsaparilla, Scott's Emulsion, and Carter's Little Pills. The possible in-joke does not mean we should presume the numbers were false; these brand names were as familiar to any reader (or researcher) of American newspapers of the 1890s as Coca-Cola, Ford, or Kodak would be in later decades.[77] The gesture to include advertisers was not only rhetorical in validating the value and veracity of a newspaper's reach. As much as this gathering of prominent advertisers was a public display of growth and power, it was equally a business strategy signaling to other potential advertisers. As Lincoln Steffens observed in 1897, "Most people buy a newspaper for a sensation, and the reward for gratifying this demand is advertisement which increases circulation."[78] It's little wonder that almost 120 years later, Tim Wu would label newspaper publishers "the first attention merchants."[79]

Timed for perfect effect, the publicity stunt coincided with the launch of Hearst's new color comic and magazine supplements, in which famous artists and journalists from the staff of the *World* were recruited to work for the *Journal*. Under Hearst's hand, the daily morning edition had grown more than 500 percent from 77,206 copies in November 1895 to more than 417,821 copies per day in October 1896. Even without the impact of the color supplements that had just begun, the *Sunday Journal* had grown more than 600 percent in a year, from 54,308 up to 351,751 copies each weekend. In the weeks after the launch of the color supplements, Sunday circulation grew another 125,370 in a single month, from just 321,046 on October 11, up to 437,636 by November 1.

NETWORKS OF MOVEMENT: THE "NEWSBOY GIANT" AND NEWSPAPER TRAINS

Beyond the spectacle of presses and boasts of massive circulation growth lay technologies and humans networked into systems that amplified the work of journalists, columnists, illustrators, and editors, among other newspaper workers. Thus far this chapter has focused on situating how the cultural reach of the newspaper was sustained through its reliance on spectacle and bombastic discourse. As the newspaper office published more and bigger newspapers, the challenge of circulating them remained. The remainder of this chapter turns toward exploring how newspapers materially circulated and how new routes and assemblages were forged as the reach of the newspaper grew more pronounced in the homes of citizens around the country, especially in the cities and their suburbs.

Controlling Circulation: The American News Company

The bulk of circulation in the final instance relied on a mass of human labor in teams and squads of newsboys—the domain of orphans and street urchins and the subject of endless efforts at labor reform and child poverty advocacy. Even then the ideal of technologies for circulation was central. Consider how Philadelphia "*Item* Wagons" were lauded by newsagents when introduced in 1887, eliminating the need to travel to the central delivery office, because they efficiently administered neighborhood delivery of morning papers.[80] Or consider the variety of "automatic newsboys"—news boxes based on nickel-slot devices—which are reviewed in detail later in this chapter.[81] Such attempts to make circulation more efficient reflect the centralized coordination behind systems of delivery (including even the humble newsboy). For all the fury of competition and choice at newsstands, the supply side of the business was tightly controlled by the monopolies that were characteristic of the Gilded Age. During this period, newsprint and ink production gradually became consolidated.[82] In addition to the regulated monopoly of the Western Union telegraph network, newswire services like the Associated Press and the United Press throttled the supply of European and metropolitan news across the continent.[83] In the newspaper industry, the semblance of local competition over circulation masked tight monopoly control in regional distribution of periodicals, especially in the largest metropolitan cities.

In his account *The Daily Newspaper in America*, Alfred McClung Lee explains how selling the penny press necessitated a shift to new "aggressive circulation methods," since each individual paper could pay the newsagent only a fraction of the one-cent price.[84] Before the 1830s, newspaper carriers had been selling papers for six cents and, at first, would not handle sales of Benjamin Day's *New York Sun* at one cent each because the profit margin seemed too low. Instead, Day "rounded up six or eight boys and gave each 125 sheets and a district. He paid the boys $2 a week for selling these and allowed them additional papers at nine cents a dozen. When men learned that boys earned as much as $5 a week with Day's plan, they organized routes and hired carriers to deliver sheets."[85]

These early "boys" are not the same as "newsboys" in later decades and especially the newsboys of the twentieth century, who achieved some improvements in their working conditions and could be treated as employees of newspapers rather than as "little merchants."[86] The penny press system's exclusive carrier routes contain the origins of the later monopoly on distribution by the American News Company by creating licensed carriers with territories protected from competition. The routes became valuable commodities owned by professional newsagents, increasing in value more than tenfold in just a few years. Carrier routes were created in surrounding towns, instigating an emphasis on regional and interregional delivery networks. McClung Lee identified in the penny press carrier-route system two principles of modern newspaper circulation, introduced as "ready expedients to the mass-distribution problems created by cheap mass-production."[87] News publishers first took control of the terms of circulation by setting retail prices, but then gave up control by contracting out distribution to independent newsdealers who owned their own routes. For more than a century, attempts to regain control of delivery routes (by Horace Greeley's *New York Tribune* and by James Gordon Bennett's *New York Herald*) proved ineffective and only reinforced the system that would eventually lead to a single corporation controlling nearly all regional and intercity circulation. For metropolitan daily newspapers, publishers directly managed only a small proportion of their circulation through newsboys working in city centers close to their printing room floors. Almost anything requiring farther than local transportation relied on wholesale distribution, which was almost entirely controlled by the American News Company, which McClung Lee termed the "newsboy giant."[88]

The sprawling conglomerate of branches of the American News Company became a crucial throttle on newspaper circulation that has rarely received more than passing mention in histories of American journalism. Its New York origins combined the effects of corporate control of carrier routes with important, specialized wholesale distributors handling out-of-town weekly papers and magazines: "Philadelphia with its first-class publications was a center of literary activity . . . and agencies were established in New York for this purpose. Boston sent others. . . . As travel increased, it began to pay the newsdealers near the hotels and railway stations to keep papers of other cities. . . . Its system has grown and been perfected, till to-day . . . in any city of the United States, any book, magazine or newspaper may be ordered from the nearest newsdealer."[89]

By the mid-1870s the American News Company was a nationwide intermediary between all types of publishers and almost any newsstand across the country—a regime that lasted for nearly a century. In the largest metropolitan cities, the company also handled most wholesale newspaper distribution to newsagents any distance from the pressroom. Although its distribution work lay only in the background of newspaper publishers' publicity and appeals to readerships, the American News Company's monopoly on the metropolitan and interregional distribution of all forms of print culture set the conditions for the development of the Sunday paper as a viable alternative to weekly magazines, dime novels, and lithographs. Without the American News Company's national reach, newspapers probably would not have become a conduit for mass-circulated popular culture.

The rare contemporary journalist who turned attention to its work often spoke in hushed terms; as "the keeper of a thousand secrets involving the fortunes of publishers and authors, . . . the American News Company surrounds its vast and intricate system with an atmosphere of mystery, so that few persons have any idea of its really astounding proportions."[90] The company was created early in 1864 when three prominent New York news agencies joined formally to incorporate: Sinclair Tousey was the first president. His son John was secretary, and their existing location at 121 Nassau Street near Park Row served as the first headquarters.[91] Henry Dexter was vice president, surrendering his competing distribution company located nearby on Nassau Street. Dexter had recently partnered with John Hamilton and S. W. Johnson and Company; Hamilton and Johnson became the superintendent and treasurer, respectively.[92] Finally, Dexter-Hamilton & Company's clever manager, Patrick Farrelly, also became a superintendent and managed all accounts with far-flung newsagents.

As separate distributing news agencies, Tousey and Dexter-Hamilton had gained significant success during the Civil War, with its increased demand for interregional news distribution. Their combined venture was well timed; railroads and telegraph networks were proliferating and making communication and transportation easier and cheaper. The precipitating factor was perhaps a threatened stamp tax on mail delivery, amounting to a severe disincentive for publishers to use the postal network to manage their own wholesale distribution: "The time had come for a central jobbing agency that would remove from the office of the publisher the problems of distributing his wares."[93]

In 1866, just two years into their conglomeration, the amassed weekly volume handled by the American News Company was listed as 41,000 daily papers and 650,000 weekly papers, as well as 295,000 magazines and 225,000 dime novels monthly. At this point the company's focus was still primarily in New York, but they already handled a substantial proportion of sales in Boston and Philadelphia.[94] With more than four million publications distributed monthly, their millions of dollars of annual revenue, gained from just a fraction-of-a-cent markup on each delivery, mapped a continent-wide trajectory that followed. Regional agencies were created as subsidiaries. For example, the Western News Company in Chicago bought out that city's key wholesaler, J. R. Walsh & Company, in 1866.[95] By 1869 Western News was already called a "veritable monopoly . . . the kings of the paper business. . . . Every town in the United States, of any size, has a box of its own and into this are thrown copies of everything published. The 'packers' come along and send off most promptly the packages for each news agent."[96]

Throttling Libel, Justifying Monopoly

By the 1880s the enormous conglomerate of the American News Company had established a network of thirty-two subsidiaries across the continent. One contemporary overview contrasted the American situation with that of the United Kingdom, where W. H. Smith & Company also held tight control but with direct ownership of retail newsstands so that the company could effectively dictate its own terms in dealing directly with publishers. In North America, however, the apparently robust competitive market of local retail newsdealers almost all relied on the American News Company's monopoly for wholesale distribution: "Every time there has been any opposition to it, the American Company has either bought out the people who started to fight it, or has driven them from the field defeated."[97] By 1887 it controlled or outright owned more than twenty thousand newspaper agencies across North America, with revenues of $17 million a year.[98] A primary subsidiary with a significant retail side was the Union News Company, which sold news and books to captive passengers aboard nearly half of the continent's railcars and at hundreds of railway stations.

The power and profitability of the American News Company derived from the cash basis of its accounts with newsdealers, reinforced by the commodification of novelty built into the periodical form: "The concern has the bulge on news dealers, who are obliged to pay one week's bill before they can get any of the papers for the next week."[99] With its origins in penny newspaper sales, the cash basis remained in place even as American News became a multimillion-dollar company. Daily and weekly periodical supply was simply cut off to retailers in arrears by even a brief period. Given the staggering continental distances across the United States and Canada, the company's wholesale distribution became the throttle point where strong-armed buyouts or cooperative consolidation among competitors most benefited from economies of scale.

This draconian control over periodical distribution led to the formation of a National Association of Newsdealers to establish cooperative and coordinated protection against unfair and abusive treatment. The association's 1887 meeting in Boston included extensive discussion "denouncing monopolies" and strategizing ways to coordinate alternative supplies (and, of course, a fraternal tour of the *Boston Globe* building and "the novel sight" of its printing presses at work).[100] When the time came for formal resolutions, newsdealers began by decrying the American News Company for "terrorism and intimidation . . . and the great injustice it inflicts," and resolved "that all publishers that are manly and courageous enough to stand aloof from this monopoly deserve the patronage and good will of all the trade."[101]

The American News Company's control over periodical distribution also made it the target of libel lawsuits, as the courts had always been fairly consistent in holding conveyors of libelous literature as equal conspirators with authors and publishers. Complainants against authors and small-time publishers of stage gossip and political screed could sue to hold American News "responsible as circulators" and go after their deep pockets for brow-raising damage claims.[102] Later state-level measures to protect newsagents against spurious libel claims could not protect the company's continent-wide business from lawsuits filed in other jurisdictions. At one point, lawyers for Standard Oil and John D. Rockefeller visited the headquarters of the American News Company to preempt a muckraking magazine feature, pressuring the company to stop distribution even before the article was published, based on promotional publicity alone.[103] The result was well known at the time; for decades, the American News Company acted as an unofficial American national censor. At least one commentator expressed appreciation for this "startling advantage" of the company's power, saying it "puts the entire population of the country under an obligation . . . and justifies any feature of monopoly. . . . The American News Company stands between the community and blackmail. It throttles libel on its threshold. Circumstances which are an inherent part of its business have forced it to assume the role of a censor of the press— obliged it to perform a duty that in other countries is recognized and attended to by the government. And this is accomplished without any hardship to anybody except scoundrels."[104] Indeed, Samuel Merrill's 1888 handbook on newspaper libel makes the point searingly clear: "Every newsdealer is legally presumed to know the contents of every publication which he handles, even if the interval between the time when he receives the paper from the office of publication and the time of his delivery of it to the purchaser is so short as to negative conclusively the possibility of actual knowledge of the contents."[105] Merrill then quotes a writer in *The Journalist* who had lamented failed laws protecting newsdealers for distributing libel in their publications, concluding with the observation that "as the law stands at present, the American News Company are compelled to be censors of the press in their own defence."[106]

On a more positive note, the American News Company's sprawling system of distribution provided a single periodicals market across the country, achieving a semblance of simultaneous coast-to-coast publication. By the 1890s an extensive profile in the *New York Herald* noted how more than a hundred periodicals used their networks to release issues on the same day and hour across the country: "To make this possible involves the necessity of shipping those publications from New York eight or ten days in advance."[107] This semblance of national-scale simultaneity had its daily equivalent on a metropolitan scale for newspapers, since the company handled wholesale distribution in most major cities, bundling competing newspapers for concurrent delivery to newsdealers dozens of miles away from newspapers' printing press floors. *The Herald* goes on:

> Although the methods of the American News Company astonishes one by its scientific smoothness and surety of method, the vortex of energy is in the daily newspaper department. Here fractions of seconds are important. The company distributes over seven hundred thousand daily papers and not far from one million Sunday papers. . . . The system of handling and delivering these papers to dealers has become a science. . . . Everyone connected with the delivery seems to understand distinctly the part of the work that he is expected to perform and to appreciate the fact that the seconds are golden."[108]

For the American News Company to achieve this incredible feat of movement, it needed to tap into a network of transportation routes that would allow it to move newspapers quickly around the country. This was essential for papers to reach beyond their immediate environs, a capacity now so routine in a cyber-networked world. The regional train system was crucial in this venture.

THE REGIONAL FAST TRAIN AND BEYOND

An essential part of the spectacle of Sunday paper circulation was the complex system of delivery across vast metropolitan regions and beyond. A series of illustrated features stoked curiosity with the effort it took to provide readers with the papers they held. For example, the *New York Herald* in 1899 went behind the scenes to animate the workforce that was responsible for local delivery. Urban circulation required systematic coordination, as the various newsdealers began lining Herald Square early Saturday evening: "The supplements are by this time printed and away they go to the distributing points of the agencies."[109] With the early morning printing of the main news sheet, the newsagents took their last bundles away to be sorted with the color and illustrated supplements: "A stranger watching the proceedings might think a wholesale theft was being perpetrated, so quickly, so almost savage, is the attack made upon the pile by the newsmen."[110] City delivery relied on a network of relatively modest modes of communication and transport, but the scale of horsepower in fleets of wagons and trucks was no less impressive. The power behind delivering Sunday papers beyond city limits, however, rested in the fast train—like the one Kate McGuirk rode as "*The World* Woman" reporter—an endless subject of illustrated fascination.

As previously described, in November 1885 Pulitzer opened his circulation books to public scrutiny, offered competitors tours of his pressroom, and published illustrated features behind the scenes reviewing the technologies producing the Sunday paper. The next step in connecting circulation and publicity was expanding the reach of the Sunday edition beyond New York. On the first Sunday morning of December 1885, the *World* hired a "Wildcat Special" locomotive and railcars to express copies for breakfast delivery to Philadelphia, Baltimore, and Washington.[111] With further connections to regional railway routes, the *Sunday World* would now be delivered on Sunday across almost all northeastern states: "The feat of carrying *The Sunday World* to those places is an event in the history of journalistic enterprise and its successful accomplishment is a matter of public congratulation." Of course, readers accompanied "*The World*'s steam messenger" on its pursuit of speedy circulation of the printed paper. As with the earlier profile of the pressroom, a prominent, heavily illustrated article reported the adventure in pursuit of circulation, transforming the network logistics into a thrilling chase against time and across land. The scenario is simply explained: The regularly scheduled Washington express train left the depot in Jersey City shortly after midnight, about two hours before the *Sunday World* was finished printing. Pulitzer hired his own train to catch the Capital Express by Philadelphia and to make connections to westward regional routes from there. The race against time began with the now-familiar scenes of the pressroom action, with its "120 compositors and printers" setting type into matrices and metal, "turning out the plates with lightning-like rapidity . . . speedily put on the battery of mammoth perfecting presses . . . turning out thousands of papers, printed, cut and folded and ready for delivery" just as the clock struck 2:00 Sunday morning. But that is only the background in this story, which is focused on the next steps in the relay race, now turning to describe in detail how mass circulation is achieved.

The printed papers were bundled in packages of five hundred copies, placed on the *World*'s delivery wagons, and run from Park Row down lower Broadway to an awaiting ferry for Jersey City. Only a few Sunday morning stragglers witnessed the horse-drawn wagon, but "sparks flew from beneath the flying iron shod hoofs and the rumble of the wagon-wheels reverberated through the dark and silent graveyard of St. Paul's." Onto the ferry and then to the depot, "thousands of twenty-four page papers were soon in place" on the *World*'s Wildcat Special, which pulled out of the depot at 2:26 a.m. Even as the train sped down the rails with "goblin-like progress," the bundles of five hundred were packaged for rapid transfer as the train reached each place along the line. When the *World*'s special train pulled into Philadelphia alongside the Capital Express, thousands of Sunday papers were transferred. Dozens of towns between Philadelphia and Washington are listed on the route, as well as those places along the "news express" route west through Pennsylvania and the Maryland towns connected through Baltimore: "At all those places dealers had assembled to get their papers, which were thrown to them from the speeding train." As the express pulled into Washington, "a small army of dealers" cheered as their bundles were thrown off, hustled into wagons, and raced to newsstands for delivery across the city: "It was a remarkable run, and everybody felt proud when the regular edition of a New York Sunday paper, crisp and fresh, was placed on the breakfast tables of Washingtonians."

The early Sunday morning "newspaper train" dated at least to 1860, making "the country for 500 miles, North and West, a mere suburb of New York."[112] Related to the U.S. Post Office's management of daily "fast mail" trains, the Sunday trains received special care in scheduling for early morning newspaper delivery.[113] A Sunday "special lightning newspaper train" on the New York Central Railroad began July 4, 1875, leaving Grand Central at 2:30 in the morning to arrive in Buffalo by 1:00 in the afternoon, allowing New York Sunday papers to reach Toronto and Detroit the same evening and Chicago early Monday morning, with just a day of delay in delivery.[114] New York did not monopolize the idea for long, and soon Boston and Chicago Sunday newspaper trains also fanned out regionally.[115]

In later years, dedicated Sunday newspaper trains started beyond major metropolitan cities. The *Kansas City Times*'s "fast train" began Sunday delivery across Kansas in 1889 to undercut St. Louis newspapers' later arrival on the regular postal express.[116] In the early 1890s, the *St. Paul Pioneer Press* began a special train to Duluth, and a new Sunday passenger train from Columbia, South Carolina, doubled as a newspaper train to deliver *The State* up-country. "A new era in the history of Los Angeles journalism" came with a special train in 1892 to deliver the *Los Angeles Times* to San Bernardino and beyond.[117] The *Times Flyer* was depicted in cartoons as the modern, express replacement of the old-fashioned "oxpress" wagon, outpaced by a snail.[118] Despite these regional efforts to expand Sunday news-reading markets, the operation of a collective New York Sunday newspaper train was paying off by spreading their circulatory reach farther across the continent.

Indeed, by 1893 New York publishers deemed their Sunday newspaper train so essential a national public service that they called for the U.S. government to take it over and run it under the "fast mail" system.[119] The rampant growth of Sunday circulation had "reached a point where it is impossible for any private system of trains to reach promptly more than a small part of the people who want the Sunday papers. . . . The prejudice against Sunday newspapers has practically disappeared, . . . [they] have become a necessity with the reading public."[120] The *Philadelphia Times* even added a satirical illustrated story mocking the hyperbolic genre of stories about New York newspapers' "scattering Sunday *Suns*" across New England, to seaside towns by steamboat, by pony express to upstate villages, and joking how "Pennsylvanians also were made happy yesterday by the appearance of a fast New York newspaper train among them."[121]

Even the famous competition between the yellow journalism of Pulitzer and Hearst extended to the realm of the newspaper train. The rivals raced to beat each other in speed and geographic reach of circulation each Sunday morning, too. Just days before Hearst's *New York Journal* sensationally reported the sinking of the U.S.S. *Maine* early in 1898, a new route to Buffalo for Hearst's *Journal* on the Erie Railroad managed to beat Pulitzer's *World* on the New York Central by ninety minutes.[122] A few weeks later, even as tensions mounted toward the Spanish-American War, the newspaper speed race was reversed in a small way when the *World* arranged its own special train from Scranton to arrive in Wilkes-Barre ten minutes earlier than the rival *Journal*.[123] The competition even extended to papers in other markets; as the *New York World* advertised in the Quaker City: "You can have it delivered at your home as early Sunday morning as any Philadelphia paper."[124] The push to use transportation systems to gain precious minutes in circulation time eventually included automobiles by 1901, when the *Philadelphia Inquirer* began motoring its Sunday editions to Atlantic City in record time.[125]

The appearance of a first Sunday edition of the *Boston Post* is similar in detail to many of the accounts above, but it adds a glimpse into the network of technologies that secured subscriptions and orders in advance of circulation. The key limitation to the circulation of the *Post*'s first compilation of supplements was that the inserted poster "art supplements" were already printed and the number available could not be increased. Thus, precisely 61,295 copies were circulated: "More than 40,000 were called for that could not be delivered [as] the management was averse to circulating incomplete papers."[126] This estimate of tens of thousands in lost potential circulation from unmet demand was established from orders "that kept swelling the total," so the *Post* could have "passed the 100,000 mark. Does this read like an extravagant boast? The orders contain the hard, cold, indisputable facts. By telegraph and telephone, by letter and postal card and by messenger, orders continued to arrive [till] Sunday noon."[127] An entire communication network again centered on the production of the newspaper but run through the subscription office rather than the newsroom, all to allow the circulation of a new Sunday paper throughout New England. *Sunday Posts* were aboard a morning train for Albany leaving at 3:00 a.m., throwing off in Springfield papers bound for Vermont. Another train to Maine left at 3:30, to Fitchburg at 4:00, to New Hampshire at 4:15, and to Newport at 4:40, while those for Providence went aboard the regular passenger train. Also at 4:00, the bulk of papers for local delivery were handled by sixteen wagons and thirty-two men of the Hotel and Railroad News Company. Reminiscent of the *Boston Globe*'s nearby viewing gallery overlooking its pressroom, now the *Post* drew gawkers to the spectacle of Sunday morning livery vans being loaded: "Sightseers, too curious to go home, stood about on the sidewalk watching *The Post*'s antheap swarming with activity."[128]

By the turn of the twentieth century, as ordinary modes of transport failed to supply the far-flung demand for early Sunday editions, systems for distributing Sunday papers out of New York had developed into a significant branch of

FIGURE 21. "How Sunday Newspapers Reach Thousands of Readers," *New York Herald*, October 8, 1899, 12.

the industry. An 1899 story in the *New York Herald* animated the scene at Grand Central Depot, furiously organizing the newspaper train to Boston filled with Sunday papers for New England, "like a many-sectioned snake . . . two city blocks of newspapers," just one of four trains headed out of New York "on its errand of enlightenment" (see fig. 21).[129] "The man who sits at breakfast in his home in Boston or Washington or at luncheon at his Bar Harbor hotel, wants his *Herald* on the day of publication. And he gets it." In smaller places along the route, "ton after ton of *Heralds* are disposed of in the 'throw-off.' . . . A dozen or so bundles flit through the air and strike the platform while the train whizzes by at hair-raising speed." The *Herald* claimed to have organized the "great system of distribution" in the 1880s, recognizing that "the country wants its *Heralds* and the country must have them. Have them, too, in accordance with the most approved rules of systematization." The multi-sectioned form of the Sunday newspaper allowed careful coordination, as the newspaper train took time to prepare, with the "sups" (the color sections, the halftone parts, the literary sheets) printed and loaded in advance, awaiting the last-minute arrival of the current news in the "mains" to leave at exactly 3:00 each Sunday morning: "If the last bundles aren't on board on the dot, the last bundles stay in New York, that's all."

THE LABOR OF DELIVERY AND
THE AUTOMATED NEWSBOY

But what about newsboys? This chapter on newspaper circulation has focused on the modern spectacles of the fast printing press and the fast train, which gained the attention of Sunday feature journalists, transforming the multi-sectioned, multicolored Sunday paper into a spectacle of its own creation, presented as a type of modern miracle. Trains were essential to the delivery of papers into regions beyond the city core and to the expansion into a national public, but local delivery and sales provided a crucial connection between the newspaper office and the urban public.

In myth and reality, "street urchins" selling newspapers on every corner were emblematic of modern city life, a daily interface between wealthy Gilded Age businessmen and the crowded tenements of the urban poor.[130] Often characterized across the board as orphans, newsboys provided an essential service, despite their exaggerated cries and the likely scams of their sob-story pleas. Newsboys earned admiration as striving, climbing entrepreneurs—and, thus, future businessmen. They were the very essence of canny American salesmanship: utility and entertainment wrapped in promotion, the labor behind continental networks of circulation. The newsboy emerged in the 1830s alongside the new penny presses of New York, Philadelphia, and Boston. By the 1880s nearly every working journalist, writer, editor, and newsagent alike—and not too few Gilded Age tycoons—recounted their first position in the business as hawking papers as a lowly newsboy.[131] Even the leaders of the American News Company started as "train boys," the lowest-level employees of the Union News Company, who would solicit rail passengers to buy a paper or a dime novel, albeit a far cry from the dirty-faced "urchins" selling papers on city street corners.

Despite their popularity in our urban mythology, city center newsboys hawking papers on downtown street corners only made a fraction of newspaper sales. In the newspaper distribution system dominated by the American News Company, home delivery and newsstands mattered far more, especially for morning and Sunday editions. For example, newsboys' street sales accounted for only 5 percent of an 1870 edition of 70,000 copies of the *Philadelphia Public Ledger*, compared to 80 percent in routes handled by carriers.[132] In New York in 1880, newsboys' sales of the *New York Sun* represented less than 10 percent of its 134,000 circulation, compared to three-quarters handled by the agents through the American News Company's subsidiaries.[133]

Into the 1890s the business of delivering papers in New York had "drifted more and more into the hands of those who, under the titles of news companies or as individual dealers, have practically divided up the city [of New York] among themselves."[134] These newsdealers hired news carriers to handle home delivery, dividing the city into districts of thirty to forty blocks for the several hundred dealers in the city. These carriers were paid a salary rather than being paid through a cut of the sale of each paper. This was especially the case for the morning papers, such that "the majority of people who read morning papers get them at their houses before breakfast." Those in charge of their districts picked up the papers from the newspaper offices and then handled distribution to the boys: "This system requires more capital and credit, more time, better attention, and an older head than the old way. It is driving out the boys." Coupled with the expected reselling "graft" of the various individuals who appeared along the multiple nodes of the route from newspaper office to home—gatemen on the elevated road, conductors on trains who could collect as many as a dozen left-behind copies on Sunday mornings, janitors and hall boys of the various rooming houses—"the drain" on the profits for a newsboy was too substantial to support previous enterprising ways.

Newsboys frequently worked directly with newspapers' own circulation managers, picking up papers at the home office to sell directly to downtown businessmen. Newsboys had among the highest public profiles of any anonymous person encountered in modern city streets. Even the American News Company honored the humble newsboy at the apex of its headquarters: "On the dizzy height of its cornice stands the statue of a newsboy, emblematic of the inspiration and the beginning of this great corporation, and the signet of its trade-mark."[135] Circulation managers were often cautioned in the trade press to treat their newsboys well, especially as the sale of afternoon papers grew in importance in the twentieth century.[136] As Vincent DiGirolamo notes, with the rise of the professionalization of circulation management, conventions and newsletters for circulation managers continually discussed how to grow and secure the numbers, loyalty, and productivity of their newsboy workforce.[137]

Newsboy Strikes

The early image of newsboys in the nineteenth century as urban waifs and orphans was buoyed by later social surveys and documentary investigations, notably Lewis Hine's photography of child labor, including dozens of pictures of newsboys on city streets.[138] Yet the sentimental impression of the newsboy was already evident in the sympathetic and amused descriptions of their antics during occasional, but exceptional, moments of striking and boycotting evening newspaper publishers. Seemingly every attempt by evening daily papers to increase the rate newsboys paid for papers resulted in a newsboys' strike, and reporting about these newsboys' strikes became a genre of journalism in itself. The *St. Louis Dispatch* experienced an early boycott in 1876, more than two years before Joseph Pulitzer would purchase the paper at auction to create the *Post-Dispatch*. At the first sign of trouble, the *Dispatch* advertised on its front page that "fifty men can find employment by applying immediately at this office. The carriers will deliver the paper to subscribers as usual."[139] The competing *St. Louis Globe-Democrat* covered the "*Dispatch* Difficulties" with rapt attention.[140] As police officers tried to keep the peace, striking newsboys attacked and destroyed the papers of African American boys who showed up for the chance of work. The journalistic description was clearly charmed and admiring, if patronizing: "Three or four long-legged policemen are of little use in managing a horde of newsboys. The young ones are as active as monkeys and as fleet on the foot as deer and moreover possess the faculty of fleas in not being there when the pursuer just thinks he has caught them."[141] Already in 1876, even in St. Louis, a vaudevillian treatment of the newsboys' own street slang and lower-class dialect crept into the prose, turning the boys into comic caricatures: "Keen-eyed, bare-legged, and boiling over with boyish pluck; up to every possible trick, and with a mouth brimful of ready blasphemy, which he is not old enough to understand . . . 'Wal, neow, we not gwine to be put upon. . . . If we stick for a week, we'll bust that old Dispatch.'"[142]

Perhaps the best-known New York newsboys' strike occurred against the *Evening World* and the *Evening Journal* in 1899. Taking hold three years into the "Yellow Journal War" between Hearst and Pulitzer, which had reached a nadir with their 1898 Spanish-American War coverage, contemporary accounts of the July 1899 strike describe heated protests, fighting "scab" newsboys, and tussles with police: "Crowds of angry boys armed with sticks filled the street in Printing House Square, Manhattan, this morning, and woe to the lad who was detected with either of the boycotted sheets."[143] By this point at the turn of the century, however, these plot points in the newsboys' strike genre had already been circulating for two decades. This was not even the first newsboys' strike against Hearst's and Pulitzer's yellow journals in New York. Only a year earlier, Manhattan newsboys had boycotted the same papers when they first raised the cost by one cent for each ten papers. At that time the coverage in Brooklyn papers was just as colorful: "As a result of the strike there have been several scraps between the newsboys who have the temerity to sell the papers and those who are on strike. It is a sort of guerilla warfare."[144] And, again, street dialect was key to painting a more colorful picture of the conflict: "'Shut up, or I'll kill you, you sneakin' little scab,' . . . The Journal an' World want everything to themselves and we newsboys have no chance.'"[145] Their placards even gestured to the famous Yellow Kid's own street ruffian catchphrases: "'Hully Gee, Don't Buy them *New York Worlds* or *Journals*, they is fake papers, signed Newsboys.'"[146]

This disruption was one of a string of remarkably similar boycotts in the previous decade, both in New York and other metropolitan cities. In August 1889, cries of "Boycott the *Evening World!*" and "Boycott the *Evening Sun!*" followed a raise in the cost to newsboys from five to six cents for ten one-cent evening editions. Brooklyn papers reported how the lads organized and "marched in large bodies between both offices, headed by a few improvised bannerettes and picketed . . . to the amusement of passers by."[147] On-the-scene eyewitnesses were again sure to quote their street slang for comic effect, despite an attack on another boy who dared pick up a pile of papers to sell: "'Kill der scab,' shouted one of the tiny strikers. 'Drown der rat. Trow 'im inter the sewer,' suggested another. 'Smash him in de lug. Belt the life out ov'm,' and with a wild howl the mob of urchins closed in on its victim."[148]

Notably, the American News Company's city trucks were also singled out for harassment: "Delivery wagons on the up-town routes had a serious time of it. All the way up Broadway and on the west side they were followed by a howling mob of half-grown men and boys, who showered them with volleys of stones and brickbats at every opportunity."[149] The bemused observation about the "junior" strike tactics accompanied reports about a similar fracas over ending returns of unsold copies of evening papers in San Francisco in October 1896. As a morning paper, Hearst's *San Francisco Examiner* was not affected, but it nevertheless reported the rousing calls from the newsboys' leader, nicknamed Gabby Jim: "'Are youse wit me or agin me?' 'We're wit youse,' replied the assembled newsboys in chorus. 'Dat's good!' yelled Gabby with a smile of confidence illuminating his freckle embossed features. . . . 'It's fight if dey don't, an' de gang is too many fer em.' 'All right. Let 'er go. De strike is on,' . . . 'We'll soon fetch dese poipers to time.'"[150] Another morning paper, the *Call*, noted a remarkably organized effort to compel advertising merchants to boycott the evening papers and getting the city's labor council to mediate a compromise to end the strike.[151]

Despite the sentimentality and charity extended to newsboys, even while on strike, relying on children's labor for newspaper circulation was a problem that drew the attention of tinkerers and inventors, with a string of efforts as early as 1886 to unveil coin-operated news boxes, piggybacking on fairground penny-in-the-slot devices: "The automatic weigher, cigarette-seller, stamp-seller, etc., is becoming a familiar object in public places, and now we hear of what may be called the automatic newsboy."[152] Actual inventions were reported soon enough, reportedly manufactured in Chicago in 1888 and on display for inspection in Boston in 1890.[153] Claims that the device would manage newsboy labor were met with skepticism, indicating that the real utility of newsboys went far beyond simply giving you the paper in and of itself:

> The inventor claims that much money will be saved to publishers by the use of his device, as the sale, being direct to the consumer, will be at no cost of commission allowed to the newsboys. It will not be popular with the boys. It will not make change, or run across the street when a gentleman says "Hi," or catch on to a street car in motion, or make a neighborhood lively and sociable-like on Sunday mornings, or do anything that makes a newsboy the sweet boon that he is in every American community.[154]

On the Pacific Coast, a company in Seattle announced that its "silent newsboy" had overcome the obstacle of handling a variety of newspapers of different sizes, weights, and prices: "Newspapers abhor uniformity and will not come down to any arbitrary size, thickness and price, but vary according to the taste of the publishers and their patrons, and the occasion on which they are issued."[155] The silent newsboy "can be put where newsboys can't go. It can stand on trains and street cars, in hotels, restaurants and big office buildings. It will sell newspapers in remote suburbs, where a newsstand does not pay and which the ubiquitous newsboy does not penetrate."[156] Just a few weeks later, a working device was installed outside the San Francisco Chronicle Building and announced with great fanfare for offering a Sunday paper: "Drop a nickel in the slot and get a *Chronicle*. . . . The first machine of this kind ever put in practical operation in the world will be exhibited to sell *The Chronicle* in front of *The Chronicle* office this morning, and it will undoubtedly attract much attention by its novelty."[157] Now named the Silent Newsboy Company of California, the company's announcement doubled as an investment prospectus and sketched a business plan to "give employment to about 200 machines to commence with. . . . *The Chronicle* expects to put these machines all over the city and especially at the more remote points."[158]

The *San Francisco Call* wasted no time in its opposition, attacking its competitor for its plan to unleash "machine newsboys" that threatened the livelihoods of "those of flesh and blood" and that would "take the bread away from the poor widow" mother of hardworking newsboys across the city: "No really thoughtful person will ever buy a newspaper by means of one of these machines. Buy from the live, flesh-and-blood, loud-voiced, cheery-toned and always poor and needy newsboy. Who objects to newsboys? . . . That man—that excuse for a man, we might say—would patronize a 'machine newsboy,' even though a poor, starving, flesh and blood newsboy were standing by its side and offering him a paper."[159] Furthering its attempt to embarrass its competitor, the *Call* spurred on an outraged newsboy protest and reported the scene in detail: "It took three policemen to keep the crowd moving in front of *The Chronicle* building last evening. . . . Soon after 8 o'clock about a dozen of the boys gathered at Market and Kearny streets, and forming in line marched up and down in front of *The Chronicle* building calling loudly upon the people to boycott that sheet and its proprietor. . . . They were cheered again and again by the crowds that thronged the sidewalk on either side of the street."[160] By the time of the protest, the device was already removed. By the end of the week, the *Chronicle* forced the Silent Newsboy Company to issue a statement to "completely exonerate the proprietor of *The Chronicle* or anyone connected with the paper from any concern in the machine whatever."[161]

The silent newsboy incident in San Francisco drew nationwide attention from newspaper editors and publishers: "Thank God his scheme did not work. The machines had not been outside more than an hour when it created much of a stir. Honorable men and women stepped into the business office and stopped their subscriptions."[162] Other commentators shook their fists at the relentless, heartless drive of modern automation: "The invention Juggernaut grinds rapidly and it grinds exceedingly small. The next victims to fall under its remorseless wheels will be the newsboys. . . . Instead of the strident cries of 'All about the murder in Tenement Row!' we have only the hard, metallic soulless rattle of coins dropping into slots."[163] And yet out of Chicago the very next month came reports that Seattle's Automatic Newspaper Distributing Company had been incorporated with stock of two hundred thousand dollars and was reportedly receiving a license to install news boxes at the 1893 world's fair.[164] Again, real-life newsboys had their defenders, who argued, "This is an infringement on the rights of the American newsboys, which should be promptly resented by the public, and probably will be. Some of the brightest men in the country started in life as newsboys, and there is a national sentiment in favor of the little fellows who fight their way through life by their pluck and shrewdness."[165]

Still, the quest to perfect and proliferate an automated newsboy continued. Another contraption was offered in 1896 by the Automatic News Company of New York. The *Fourth Estate* reported that "invention has done so many things for the newspaper publisher that it is not so surprising after all that an automatic newsboy should say good morning to the newspaper press. . . . It enables the public to secure copies of papers at all hours of the day without regard to weather or other conditions. The publisher is enabled to maintain an exact control of his circulation and revenue from sales of copies. . . . The automatic newsboy, it is claimed,

PLATE 1. Richard F. Outcault, "Sunday Magazine and Woman's World," *New York World*, March 13, 1898, S-1. (Duke University Libraries.)

PLATE 2. A sample of *Morning Journal* supplements. *Clockwise from top left:* "The Morning Journal's Statesman's Gallery No. 1," March 23, 1890 (broadsheet etching art supplement); "Morning Journal Library," June 22, 1890 (quarto supplement); "Delilah," November 29, 1891 (quarto lithograph art supplement); "The Boys and Girls Sunday Journal," November 26, 1893 (tabloid supplement). (Bound copies, Library of Congress.)

PLATE 3. "A Faint Idea," *Washington Times*, November 8, 1894, 2; and "Two Bites to a Cherry," *Chicago Times*, January 6, 1895, art supplement. (Authors' collection.)

PLATE 4. Early paper dolls were printed in the color supplement to cut out of the newspaper entirely. Later fashion plate dolls came as lithographed poster inserts. *Top,* "Actors and Actresses as Children's Dolls," *New York Herald,* April 14, 1895, S5-8; *bottom,* "Fashion Figure," *Chicago Record,* August 1895; *Boston Herald,* June 9, 1895. (Authors' collection.)

PLATE 5. Charles W. Saalburg, "The Brownies' Prize Puzzle No. 6," *Chicago Inter-Ocean*, February 11, 1894, Junior supplement. (Authors' collection.)

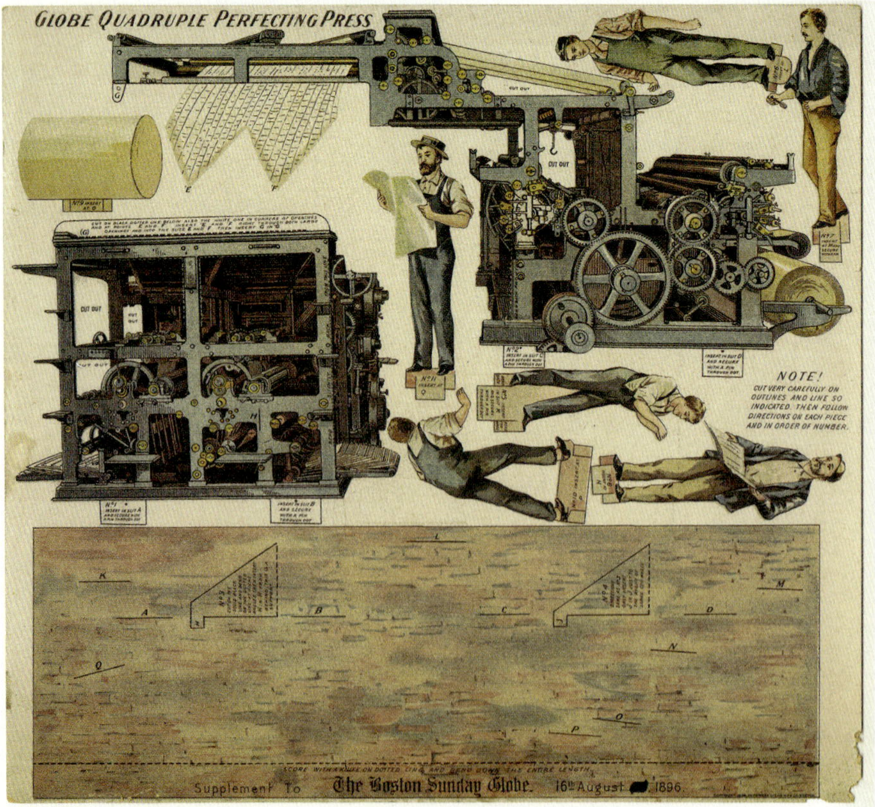

PLATE 6. "Globe Quadruple Perfecting Press," *Boston Globe*, August 16, 1896, art supplement. (Authors' collection.)

PLATE 7. "The Biggest Press in the World," *New York American and Journal,* May 10, 1903, *American Magazine.* (Authors' collection.)

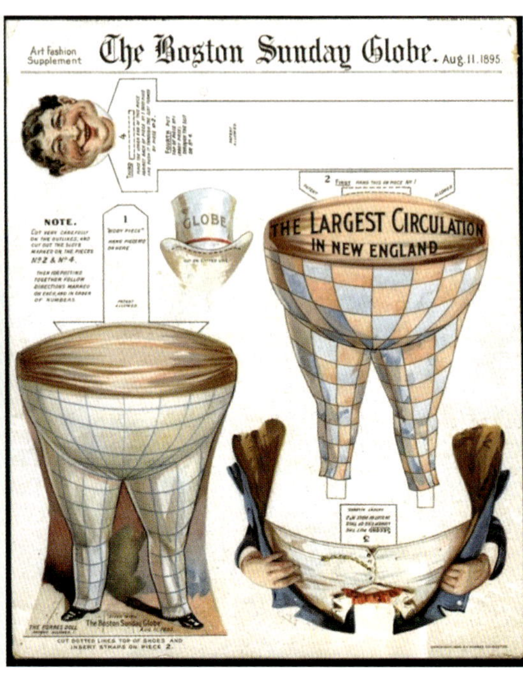

PLATE 8. Forbes Lithograph, "Boston Globe Man," *Boston Globe*,
August 11, 1895, art supplement. (Authors' collection.)

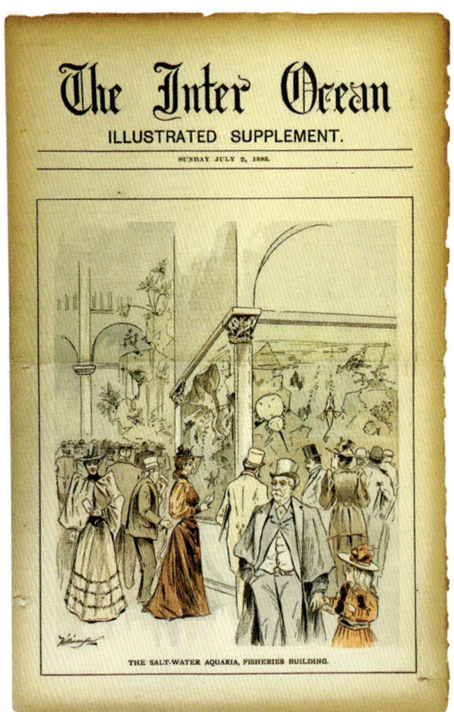

PLATE 9. Leading up to the 1893 Columbian Exposition, the *Chicago Inter-Ocean* launched
a tabloid color-illustrated supplement. Begun in 1892, it is considered the first of its kind.
"The Salt-Water Aquaria," *Chicago Inter-Ocean*, July 2, 1893; and "Our Uncle Grover,"
Chicago Inter-Ocean, November 19, 1893. (Authors' collection.)

PLATE 10. Early Sunday comic supplements were launched well beyond the yellow journals of Hearst and Pulitzer. "Sunday Press Jester," *Philadelphia Press*, February 14, 1897; and "Twinkles Serio-Comic Supplement," *New York Tribune*, November 15, 1896. (Authors' collection.)

PLATE 11. This color comic was the first Hearst strip syndicated widely in at least six different newspapers in December 1900 and, here, in January. "The Katzenjammer Kids Dig a Tunnel in the Snow," *San Francisco Examiner*, January 6, 1901. (Authors' collection.)

PLATE 12. Comic characters were often self-referential and interacted with each other. Richard F. Outcault's new character, white middle-class Buster Brown, greets his predecessor, African American Pore Lil Mose. *New York Herald*, July 20, 1902. Herr Spiegleburger, protagonist of Otis Wood's recurring T. C. McClure syndicated comic, imitates the antics of Simon Simple after reading the other character's latest comic. *San Francisco Chronicle*, July 17, 1904. (Authors' collection.)

PLATE 13. Early *Associated Sunday Magazines* covers of the *St. Louis Republic* gradually transitioned from art supplement lithograph to magazine. *Left*, January 31, 1904; *right*, March 13, 1904. (Authors' collection.)

opens many new channels for circulation. . . . There is scarcely any labor required, and the box also acts as a cash register and money box."[166] A sample machine was installed at the Astor House, and a classified ad in *Publishers' Weekly* promised it "requires no caretaker."[167]

The *New York Sun* defended the "automatic newspaper selling and advertising cabinet" from arguments about putting newsboys out of work: "As the cabinet is not intended to run in opposition to the newsboys, it will not be used to a great extent in this city or other large cities. It will be put in hotels, barber shops, restaurants, and railway stations."[168] This particular contraption also had a desk, pen and ink, a letter box, bulletin board, and spaces for twenty advertisements, illuminated by electric lights—a total hawking machine, connecting travelers to locales in an intricately networked mechanism for extending a variety of circulatory regimes. The promise of automation fulfilling an unlimited reach in time and space was abundantly evident in decades of coverage about the automatic newsboy. Newspapers were as likely to advocate for the utility of the machines as defend the labor of the lowly newsboy. The *Philadelphia Inquirer* in 1919 explained that its "slot machines are not competing with newsboys or newsstands. They are mainly to fill in gaps. Where there are no newsboys or newsstands they supply the need."[169] The boxes improved service for voracious readers, letting them buy a paper after newsboys had gone home and newsstands had closed for the night.

The arguments for the advantages of coin-box dispensers signify a general faith in technological progress, but they also expose and spotlight the particular concerns behind a new profession in the newspaper realm: the circulation manager. Early specialists from across the country gathered to create the National Association of Circulation Managers in 1898. Until the 1890s, planning and overseeing circulation had fallen under the umbrella of publishers' advertising departments, pairing the twin sources of revenue. Developments in the late 1880s and 1890s— not least the introduction of the metropolitan Sunday edition—had made it clear that a single person "could no longer act as both advertising and circulation manager."[170] Rather than focus on automating delivery, however, the national association "undertook to standardize circulation methods and accounting forms, to promote newsboy welfare, and to exchange new ideas."[171]

These disputes and newsboys' labor disruption focused especially on evening papers, which relied much more heavily on newsboys' street sales than morning or Sunday papers' suburban subscription deliveries. As we saw in chapter 3, the fascination with technologies of circulation and the drive to invent automated newsboys stemmed, at least in part, from an understanding of journalism itself as an audiovisual medium, despite its being anchored in print form. The eyewitness of journalism too was continually partnered with new technologies for reporting and new ways of seeing, but the humble labor of newsboys' delivery was the more enduring of all aspects of newspaper circulation.

BEYOND CIRCULATION

This chapter has illustrated how the act of reading the newspaper encompassed bearing witness to its production and circulation, sometimes explicitly. In the self-reflexive promotional narratives that we recounted here, the very same Sunday paper that the reader held and read was transformed into a protagonist in a thrilling narrative that was the epitome of modern spectacles. In these and other illustrated feature stories, the Sunday paper's form and content became the medium for transmitting meaning and understanding of other technologies, starting with the fast printing press that produced it. Sunday papers, of course, circulated well beyond the cities named in their mastheads, especially when that city was New York. Sunday papers with the largest circulation had a national reach that approximated a continental scale. As discussed earlier, Joseph Pulitzer's *New York Sunday World* printed a map of its continental circulation for a special edition in 1893 to honor the tenth anniversary of Pulitzer's ownership: there were subscribers in all forty-eight states, albeit only three lonely readers in Nevada, as well as readers in Canada and Mexico.[172]

Circulation figures came to life in the routine and seemingly endless displays of the effort behind making and delivering the paper: crowds watching fast presses in galleries or outside newspaper buildings, faster trains delivering newspapers earlier each Sunday, and the curiosity of technologies like the automatic newsboy. Circulation numbers took bodies, practices, technologies, and networks to achieve—all deeply imbricated in a thoroughly modern sensibility of progress. Above all, these features communicated newspapers' and readers' participation in modernity. Growth, expansion, speed—all central elements of circulation and modernity—were the hallmark signals of how the newspaper would utterly change the North American cultural landscape.

In this chapter we argued that the material, temporal-spatial, and cultural elements of circulation transformed the place of the newspaper in American culture, not merely by achieving greater reach into the average household but also by forging an imagined and imaginary relationship to readers through mass participation via the newspaper. Readers themselves became part of modern spectacles of technological advancement by reading how the Sunday newspaper was a product of that advancement. The paper allowed readers to participate actively in modernity and to imagine themselves, as Lisa Gitelman writes about other historical media at the time, "as part of a modern, educated, tasteful and recordable community, an 'us' (as opposed to 'them'), formed with similarly modern, educated, tasteful, and recordable people."[173] Through circulation, readers came to expect their paper to arrive at a certain time, in more and more places, in increasingly diverse and intermedial forms, offering every member of the family something to read (and later a preview of something to watch and listen to), while encouraging them to participate actively in the paper's own further growth.

PART III

SYNDICATION

For the entire twentieth century, syndicated comics and magazines were the key features that distinguished most Sunday papers from their weekday namesakes. When first introduced, syndicated supplements were openly promoted as making national popular culture available regionally through the Sunday edition of the local paper. In a limited sense, syndication is an economical means to achieve wider circulation of popular material, but it transforms the basis of circulation from an individual's or family's subscription into the newspaper's adoption of a standardized service. Syndication connects a local newspaper to the network of popular culture, interpolating local metropolitan news and features into a common national yet still regional package.

In this final section, we propose that the drive to syndication on the part of newspapers and readers alike was linked to the imagined overcoming of the limited range of print circulation. Rather than reduce our analysis of syndicated color comics and illustrated magazine features to a mere matter of cultural homogeneity and concentrated profits, we emphasize how syndication produced a national network for print versions of popular culture that facilitated metropolitanism on a mass scale, providing a sense of currency and connectivity, of being "in the swim" of modernity. This laid a foundation for the subsequent popular commercial programming of network radio broadcasting, which at times specifically adopted the model of newspaper syndication by linking newspaper-owned radio stations. Newspaper publishing is rarely considered as a mass medium with networked content. Most accounts treat newswire and syndicate services as separate services in the formation of mass culture that the news publishing assemblage helped create. Simply put, syndicated features came to define the Sunday paper and made it a cornerstone of popular culture in the twentieth century.

Syndication articulated newspapers to each other, explicitly displaying how a group of metropolitan media outlets could cooperate to create a national media network for the near-simultaneous circulation of leisure reading every weekend, across the entire country and beyond. In terms of technology and ideology, then, the cultural effects of syndication are similar to those of the telegraph—obviously kin to newswire services—in forging standardized, interregional markets.[1] In this sense, syndication is the "visible hand" in the "managerial revolution" of modern newspaper publishing in North America,[2] allowing regional and local publishers to ascribe to modern business practices and act as if they were managers in a conglomerated media industry. Such discussions were commonplace at Newspaper Publishers Association annual meetings, whose creation along with similar associations signaled how the news industry was seeking modern standards for management. Yet syndication began when newspapers were still formally independent, before the emergence of vertically integrated chains. As a business strategy, publishers would have dropped syndicated features if readers were disinterested or if the expense of licensing copyrighted material did not increase circulation and revenues.

Syndication was not just a management tactic; subscribers were clearly drawn to nationally syndicated features as popular culture. Many readers were enthusiastic fans of the most popular comic strip characters and syndicated columnists, who had followings just like the fandoms of sports, stage, and movie stars. Well-known critical theories of popular culture and mass society began to develop later, in the 1930s, in light of emerging fascism, but are still useful for defining the draw of public interest. For our purposes, Walter Benjamin's pinpointing of the "loss of aura" in the age of technological reproducibility is key to casting the attraction to mass syndication as a matter of networked metropolitanism and cultural currency.[3] Unlike his German contemporaries who focused on amusement and entertainment as a "cult of distraction" for the "deceived masses,"[4] Benjamin focused squarely on the potential of photographic and film technology to work against the "aura" of traditional institutionalized art and culture by making it available to all. Implicitly, the withering of the aura of unique art objects opens an alternative through simultaneous mass access to popular works.

Public and critical discourse in the late nineteenth century paid little attention to the all-consuming draw of commercial leisure as it was emerging on an unprecedented continental scale. As a turn of phrase, "popular culture" was initially cast as a public good—the result of informal education through public lectures, museums and reading rooms, newspapers and magazines. In a sense, the term meant the opposite of cultivated taste and connoisseurship, which was prone to elitism and moralistic concerns that severed self-improvement from amusement. An editor's decision to have a Sunday edition chock-full of syndicated features—illustrated fiction, humorists' columns, cartoons, and comics—positioned readers within a continental sphere of popular culture that was distinguished from local institutions of education and uplift, which were often traditional and parochial, sometimes exclusionary and patrician. In this context, the turn to popular syndicated material positioned a more modern, more metropolitan newspaper against its hidebound competitors. In the twentieth century, to be sure, popular culture became inextricable from mass-distributed and -broadcast networks of commercial entertainment, but the process began with the print syndication of Sunday newspaper features.

5

THE CORPOREAL CHARACTER OF CIRCULATION

Cartoon depictions of newspapers' milestones often personified circulation growth. One year into the fray of competition against Joseph Pulitzer's *World*, William Randolph Hearst's *New York Journal* animated "How *The Journal* Has Grown in Twelve Months" in comic cartoon form.[1] The newspaper was shown as a beautiful young woman who had been a mere toddler a year earlier. As she grows, she does not simply become larger; she takes interest in herself and learns to create herself. Her circulation growth is represented as the emergence of complexity but also of maturity. At the end of 1895, when Hearst first adopts her, she holds a pen and paper, but only in the next months does she learn to read herself, and write herself, as her own dress (made of *New York Journals*) becomes more attractive and decorative. Then she learns to paint herself in colors, studies herself closely, and finally is able to present herself in public (see fig. 22).[2] The cartoon specifically celebrated the fact that the *Journal* distributed more than a million and a half copies the day after the 1896 presidential election. But it also marked how central women readers of the Sunday features had become to the success of the paper. That is, this cartoon stands as a figure not only for the growth of the paper but also for the techniques that the Sunday edition mobilized in order to produce new kinds of reading subjects—women and young people. Those new reading subjects are not peripheral to the interests of the paper, but, as in this figure, they come to stand for the paper itself. Hearst had just introduced "The American Humorist" as a color comic supplement and "The American Magazine" as a color feature section. Soon came a third color section in "The American Woman's Home Journal." Attractive, young female figures were strewn throughout

FIGURE 22. "How the Journal Has Grown in Twelve Months,"
New York Journal, November 8, 1896, 15.

the *Journal*, appealing to men and women readers alike. The cartoon of the *Journal* as a woman reading, writing, coloring, and presenting herself is a surprisingly apt figuration of the moment when the Sunday paper became a standardized compilation of comic strips and magazine features.

In this chapter we recount the origins of the Sunday comic supplement by considering early innovations and permutations in the nineteenth century before the later syndicated, standardized form. For many readers in the twentieth century, the Sunday funnies distinguished the weekend edition from the daily newspaper more than any other section. In later decades, Charlie Brown of *Peanuts*, and the eponymous characters Blondie and Garfield, among many others, were as much a part of American popular culture as the fictional personalities from any novel, movie, or radio or television show. Some of the earliest comic strips were just as prominent in their day: Buster Brown, the Katzenjammer Kids, and the Happy Hooligan were as famous as any celebrity in the first decade of the twentieth century.[3] Their weekly adventures were followed by millions of readers across the country, just as the latest film from a movie star, record by a musician, or episode from a broadcast star would be in later decades. But if color comic supplements are perhaps the most important and distinctive feature of the Sunday paper, how did Sunday comic strips come to be so widely available in such a standard form? How did nearly every weekend paper in North America come to include a comic supplement with more or less equivalent content? One simple answer is that mass syndication of copyrighted materials permitted the commercial exploitation of popular features. Alternatives to the prized copyrighted characters of New York Sunday papers could be imitated by other papers, but popularity could not be reproduced by imitation.

By the 1890s syndication was already the primary mechanism to release the most popular novels and stories. Newspaper syndicates like those run by S. S. McClure and Irving Bacheller provided a prepackaged product of popular material by famous authors. While newswire and exchange services adequately circulated daily news items, syndicates were the primary means for circulating copyrighted leisure reading on a continental scale, especially the serialized novels and entertaining features that were the staple of Sunday supplements. Syndicates were crucial in providing an affordable means for smaller newspapers to include leisure supplements in their Sunday editions and to fill those additional pages with the literary, amusing, or informative content of stories by well-known authors or about modern world culture. In short, syndicates circulated popular culture on a continental scale in a widespread, commercial distribution network.

Although paying for a newswire service instantly provided outlying newspapers with metropolitan stories, long-standing news exchange practices tolerated reprinting of published articles.[4] To protect an individual article, newspapers had to register copyright under its headline as the title of a "book." The U.S. Copyright Office began listing periodicals as a separate category in 1891, but at first only magazines took advantage of the option. Newspapers and syndicate companies continued to register only selected feature articles separately under their headlines. In 1892, however, the *New York Sun* began to protect its daily editions whole, and other newspapers followed suit.[5] Surprisingly, Pulitzer was not quick to copyright entire issues of the *New York World*, waiting until December

1895 to go beyond lists of headlined stories and initially only listing "The World's Sunday Magazine" for protection.[6] By the new century, most metropolitan newspaper publishers consistently registered the copyright of individual editions and volumes to prevent news exchanges from reprinting without license. This was the start of national illustrated Sunday feature syndication, and comic strips were its bricks and mortar.

But rather than start with Sunday comic strips and illustrated features, we start the story of syndication with the curious way newspapers often used cartoon characters to personify themselves and their drive for circulation. Our reconceptualization of syndication as a cultural relation—not just a business proposal—focuses on the reciprocities between popular culture and circulation growth. We begin with newspapers' own presentation of themselves as comic characters not because they were somehow direct precedents for later comic strip characters; instead we present a conceptual relationship rather than claiming a causal link. We tie syndicated comics to corporate mascots in order to consider how the drive for circulation growth was linked to the popularity of the paper with a mass public. Comic strips eventually became a cornerstone of that popular culture, but the story began by animating circulation figures into comic figures.

The propensity to use comics and cartoons to embody the work of the newspaper was, of course, extended to the work of journalists themselves, most notably in the "stunt girl" reporting that Joseph Pulitzer honed through the work of Nellie Bly in the late 1880s. The connection to commercialization was apparent at the time. As Bly circled around the world for Pulitzer, the prospect of her return to New York was depicted in a cartoon in the *World* as a commodified frenzy of opportunism. "Will it come to this?" was the caption for an editorial cartoon showing a greeting party of "enterprising friends" of all ages and genders, offering the returning Bly not just good wishes but also sponsorships of consumer goods of all sorts—soap, hairpins, typewriters, sewing machines, chewing gum, corsets, cigars, tooth powders, cameras, and more—as if the *World* itself was not enterprising toward commercial ends in sending her off in the first place.[7]

As chapter 1 noted, Bly was the prototypical subject of periodical appeal, and her adventures became a series of games, contents, and circulation boosters spurring subscription orders. The spotlight on Bly's popularity—which can be taken as satirical criticism of Bly's commercialization—exposes the *World*'s own drive for circulation as inseparable from the popular appeal of sensational journalism personified in Bly's own adventures. Sunday journalism was linked to popular entertainment years before color comic supplements and collectible leisure magazines became standard fare. Beyond syndicated color comic supplements, this chapter also considers nationally syndicated magazine supplements, which used a chain-store strategy to link readers of noncompeting Sunday papers—one in each metropolitan city—into a single continent-wide mass public. As the nascent movie industry organized film distribution through a similar network of regional exchanges, Sunday newspaper publicity became central to movies' achieving a single mass audience, coast-to-coast. We end the chapter by considering how the meaning of syndication shifted when newspapers began to collectively rely on Bacheller, McClure, and other companies to provide popular features for early Sunday supplements. This bridges to chapter 6 and the role of newspaper-owned radio stations in establishing network radio broadcasting. Long before Hollywood chains and network radio, syndicated strategies for increasing circulation already had been central to the cultural address of the Sunday paper.

CIRCULATION FIGURES

Spearheaded by the development of profusely illustrated leisure features in their Sunday editions, mass-circulation metropolitan newspapers dramatically pursued increased readerships and cultural reach in the late 1880s. Publicity focusing on circulation figures became commonplace. The typical approach was to present ledgers of audited tallies, juxtaposing increases over time on an annual, monthly, or weekly basis, sometimes contrasted against their primary competitors, especially if circulation managed to eclipse an opposing paper in the past month or year. Audited accurate circulation is not a simple measure of the quality or commitment of a newspaper's readership, but the figures sufficed as a way to assess the relative popularity of a paper over time or compared to other papers. Circulation was, in effect, what advertisers purchased when contracting display space in the paper.

By the 1880s two annual newspaper directories compiled information and circulation figures for all of North America's periodicals. Rather than a cooperative effort to collaborate among publishers, both annuals were produced by advertising agencies: Boston's George P. Rowell first issued its *American Newspaper Directory* in 1869, and Philadelphia's N. W. Ayer and Son first issued its *American Newspaper Annual* in 1880. The primary target for their compiled directories of circulation figures was advertisers. The science of circulation wed journalism's public sphere to advertising's marketplace and transformed newspapers into the medium for a continental consumer culture. Sunday newspapers' secular, popular amusement gave shape and substance to the link between circulation and consumption. Introducing their inaugural annual of 1880, listing details for every periodical in North America, N. W. Ayer and Son noted that "one of the most unsatisfactory portions of a work of this kind, and one that occasions the greatest amount of anxiety, is that which treats of circulation."[8] In this early period, they explain, they merely provided the opportunity for publishers to furnish truthful statements for readers' careful consideration. A few newspapers featured testimonies from notaries in their advertisements in the 1880 annual, but there was not yet a centralized standard for auditing figures. By 1888 N. W. Ayer's annual began instead

by noting that "circulations for which affidavits have been furnished are printed
in bold-face figures; those furnished by publishers, but not sworn to, are designated by a double dagger (‡)."[9] One such sworn affidavit for Joseph Pulitzer's
New York World was given by Messrs. Camp, Baldwin, and James, three leading
bankers who made the investigation at the request of prominent advertisers. The
affidavit certified that 10,709,520 copies of the *World* were printed during March,
and its Sunday edition circulation was over a quarter million each week during
1888—by then more than double the *Sunday Herald* or *Sun*.[10] Pulitzer offered to
refund all monies paid for advertising if his circulation figures were found to be
false.

While sworn audited circulation figures in trade publications like Ayer's annual
signified the reliability and security of newspapers' contracts with advertisers,
circulation figures printed in newspapers themselves addressed readers as con-
tributors to that success. The circulation figure was evidence to a reader that they
were one of the many others (in New York, millions) making up the mass reading public. Beginning in the mid-1880s, as Pulitzer began making the *World* more
illustrated and sensational in its form and content, the top right-hand corner of
nearly every front-page nameplate contained a self-promotional blurb of some
recent circulation figure. Pulitzer wrote these himself, his most direct contribu-
tion to the paper, working via telegraph from his estate in Maine or wherever
his travels had taken him.[11] For New Year's Day 1889, that top-right box on the
front page summed the total for the entire previous year: "104,473,650 *Worlds*
Printed Last Year. This Is More Than the Circulation of Any Other Two American
Newspapers."[12] But this special occasion wasn't simply quantified in the routine
daily circulation puff. To introduce this New Year achievement, the remarkable
expansion of the *World's* circulation was personified as a cartoon character climbing "The Ladder of Prosperity."[13] Sitting atop the ladder was a jauntily dressed,
top-hatted, globe-faced character smiling with pride at having grown to maturity.
At the bottom, "starting with courage and grit" in 1883, when Pulitzer became
publisher, the top hat rests fully on his shoulders as the annual circulation of the
World sits at only twelve million.[14] As the figures rise along with his position on
the annual ladder—fifty-one million in 1885, eighty-three million in 1887—the
World man's globe-shaped head gradually grows to support his hat, until at the
present accomplishment he turns to face the reader. "Plucky as ever," he is not
afraid of looking back or looking down from the top of the circulation ladder but
offers his neighbors "a cordial New Year's greeting and cheerfully calls down to
them: Come On!"[15] Although in one sense, the *World* man literally looks down
upon his competitors from the top rung, the cartoon character is actually looking
out straight at those people who helped him achieve this success, imploring them
to "Come On!" because the top of the circulation ladder can be higher still.[16]

This "pleasing pictorial history of the unparalleled growth of '*The World*'" personifies not just the newspaper but also its popularity and its success in reaching a public and gaining circulation.[17] The cartoon plays straight into modern tropes linking success and popularity with progress and growth, so easily gained in those years of expanding transportation, urbanization, and population in North America. Yet the numbers alone would have told that story as they routinely were called upon to do. Here instead the circulation figure of the newspaper became a comic cartoon caricature, carrying the weight of signifying the *World*'s circulation as a combination of popularity, commercial value, and material geographic reach. The *New York World* would again, occasionally, depict itself as an animated globe over the years, but this comic creation did not become a recurring character. For a few other innovative Sunday papers, however, similar cartoon creations did become enduring mascots, overt links that foreshadowed how color comics would eventually constitute the cornerstone of the Sunday paper. These depictions of the paper as a cartoon are partly a matter of data visualization, depicting statistics and circulation growth through personified figures animated in comic scenarios.[18] Yet their recurring periodic usage transforms these cartoon figures into team mascots and turns the newspaper's readership into a committed popular fandom rooting for success.

Newspaper Comic Mascots

Following the conventions of editorial cartooning, newspapers occasionally personified themselves as comic characters in order to allegorize a theme or event. The consolidation of the *Chicago Times-Herald* was depicted as a courtly marriage of journalistic royalty, with the *Herald* as a lovestruck handsome prince and the *Times* as an endearing princess decorated with a fantasy of flowers.[19] In New York longtime Pulitzer cartoonist Walt McDougall used the 1897 anniversary of Pulitzer's ownership to depict the *World* as a youthful Statue of Liberty astride a bicycle, "scorching" breezily down a path marked by milestones of annual circulation numbers. The *World*'s path was strewn by other New York papers, caricatured as suffering animals: the *Times* was depicted as a squawking chicken; the *Sun* as a screeching cat; and Hearst's upstart *Journal* as a squealing pig; while the comic weekly magazines, *Puck, Life, Judge,* and *Truth,* hovered overhead as parrots. Some of the animals were lying dead down the path in order to depict papers such as the *New York Recorder*, which had just folded.[20]

In contrast to simple allegory, some newspapers introduced recurring cartoon characters as mascots to personify the paper's constancy and reliability but also its popularity and commercial value. Pioneers in color newspaper supplements in particular created reflexive cartoon figures of themselves to pose as active participants in the news and to embody their stewardship over readers. For its first Sunday editions in 1891, the *New York Recorder* briefly included a comic figure of itself as a precocious young messenger boy, framing and hosting its full-page editorial cartoon Sunday cover, "The News of the Week Illustrated."[21] As the global spotlight turned to Chicago's approaching Columbian Exposition, the *Inter-Ocean* conducted a contest soliciting a graphic depiction of "Typical Chicago" to act as a mascot and motif for the newspaper's own patronage of its readers' interest in the world's fair.[22] The winning depiction was created by hometown artist Charles Holloway, who inked a majestic helmeted goddess whose breastplate proclaimed her forbearance: "I Will."[23] She was immediately called into action to fight, alongside the *Inter-Ocean*, the corruption of municipal machine politics.[24] Her qualities were metonymic for the paper itself: "Strength, dignity, importance, resolution and conscious superiority are stamped upon the figure as a whole."[25] While the majority of these early efforts were brief or occasional, one Sunday paper built a continual relation to readers through a comic mascot.

The *Boston Globe* published its first color section for Thanksgiving 1894. The supplement would be "Printed on its own color press!" offering a whole page "in striking colors" of the Harvard and Yale football teams and a whole page "in beautiful colors of the Seven Ages of a man you all know!"[26] The football souvenir was an obvious feature timed to coincide with an important annual varsity match. But the full-page feature about the unnamed man turned out to be someone every *Globe* reader indeed knew: a profile of the *Globe* itself, personified as the cartoon figure of the "Globe Man": a corpulent capitalist whose torso was a perfect globe and whose waistband proudly stated, "The Largest Circulation in New England" (see fig. 23).[27] Although he went without being named in the advance publicity, he was no mysterious figure to regular readers; the Globe Man dated back to the 1880s and had been the *Sunday Globe*'s mascot in its weekly advance publicity for the entire year leading up to the launch of the color section in 1894, as discussed in chapter 2. The *Globe* clearly imagined that readers not only identified the comic mascot strongly with the paper itself but actually found the weekly recurring character entertaining. The Globe Man wasn't merely branding a logo or signifying a corporate identity; this feature was a souvenir celebrating readers' growing attachment to the *Sunday Globe* as a patron of their weekly leisure and a provider of fun and amusement, now provided in color.

The Globe Man originated in a humorous feature, "At the Telephone," in 1883.[28] The series initially caricatured politicians supposedly telephoned by a reporter, who was gradually personified as a cartoon figure and given the moniker "The Globe Telephone Man."[29] This character later introduced a new comic mascot for the paper, first called "Uncle Globe" before taking the rotund shape and name that lasted for decades.[30] Rather than speaking on the telephone to politicians, he became a voracious listener to the entire global network of phone lines: "The Globe Man gets all the news from everywhere."[31] A full decade later, for the presidential election of 1896, the Globe Man again personified the national network of

FIGURE 23. "The Seven Ages of the Globe," *Boston Globe*, November 25, 1894, 1.

telephones sending returns to the newsroom, personally gathering results across the entire nation to produce piles of election night extras.[32]

One of the Globe Man's early achievements came in 1887 when the *Globe* overtook the *Herald* as the leader in Boston circulation. A promotional cartoon showed "The Way the Great Journalistic Race in Boston Now Looks" as a marathon of runners passing a grandstand with "The Dear Public" cheering and the Globe Man handily leading the field.[33] The depths of memory expected of the reader is striking, as the cartoon updated an earlier version from 1883, at that time showing the *Globe* second but effortlessly gaining the lead as the *Herald* strains to keep pace.[34] Whereas the earlier footrace showed generic businessmen holding banners to represent their respective newspapers, the updated competition with the *Globe* taking the lead in 1887 used caricatures representing each of the papers in the race, employing the same characters over the course of the next decade for the *Globe*'s ongoing comic sniping over circulation battles. The *Herald* was a little brother, the *Journal* was a dandy, the *Post* a young messenger boy, and the *Advertiser* was an old granny.

The Globe Man was called into action to narrate the growing circulation of the Sunday paper many times. Just before he launched the color supplement, still in black-and-white, he was shown sitting comfortably atop the ladder of circulation, calling out, "There's plenty of room at the top," as competing Sunday papers scramble and battle to reach the middle: "The great struggle among Boston newspapers is for second place, and The Globe Man calmly leaves them to fight it out among themselves."[35] The *Herald* is depicted as a scrappy "little brother," while the *Journal*, in top hat, tries to pull him down and the *Post*, in uniform, manages to thrust up a rung.[36] None affect the Globe Man's secure position as Boston's patron of newspaper circulation and advertising.

Starting in 1893, another promotional item on the masthead said "Circulation Talks," and, predictably, it spoke through the character of the Globe Man.[37] Readers were even given their own toy version as a keepsake; shortly after the *Sunday Globe* began including color cardboard art supplement souvenirs, one of its first paper dolls was a cutout toy of the Globe Man himself—"A Man You All Know Becomes A Doll"—so that readers could make him stand on his own, at home (see plate 8).[38] At least twice he was explicitly used to sponsor particular products' *Globe* advertising: in April 1890 his copyrighted name and figure became its own brand of cigars, and in May 1893, for over a week on the front page, he shilled Metcalf's Water White Vanilla, "the largest circulation among good housekeepers."[39] When the *Sunday Globe* introduced everyday recipes, he was shown as a cook, chef's hat replacing his top hat, surrounded by homemakers, leaving "the women delighted."[40] Soon after, in the new color supplement, a full-page cartoon showed how *Globe* recipes transformed one family's dinners from "the same old thing" to "Eureka!"[41] In the final panel, the entire family goes on an outing, stomachs full and palates pleased, to visit the Globe Man in person to say "Thanks!"[42] By this point he was a weekly fixture within the advance promotion for the Sunday edition in addition to a constant personification of circulation gains. He acted as the *Globe*'s mascot for many more years, but in hindsight the Globe Man's primary role was to promote the Sunday edition as it became routine and took shape in the 1890s. It is no accident that he heralded the color supplement's arrival in 1894.

THE FUNNY PAGES OF EARLY COMIC SECTIONS

Comic mascots straddled the traditional satire of editorial cartooning and the emerging popularity of funny-page comic antics. As such, the Globe Man and other sporadic uses of mascots provided a reflexive frame for illustrated Sunday color sections that had to straddle several functions when they were first introduced. Early color supplements had to serve multiple purposes—decorative, humorous, and satirical—at once, and their illustrated front and back covers depicted two main types of scenes. The *Chicago Inter-Ocean* pioneered color newsprint sections in the United States with tabloid-size art supplements. Its color covers were often official portraits of political and newsworthy figures, such as the debut of the section in June 1892 commemorating the selection of Grover Cleveland as the Democratic presidential nominee. Its back cover was often comic at first, but when it began issuing a color supplement twice weekly as a souvenir throughout the Columbian Exposition, both covers were primarily picturesque souvenirs of scenes at the fair (see plate 9). When the *New York Recorder* began printing a daily cover illustration in color—an exceptional effort for April 1893—the paper pictured newsworthy current events in a serious tone, although its full-page Sunday covers skewed toward comic satire. Similarly, when Joseph Pulitzer launched the *New York World*'s color supplement in May 1893, its covers initially alternated between a serious illustration and a large-form editorial cartoon by renowned staff cartoonist Walt McDougall.[43] In June 1894 the *New York Herald* also introduced a color section that combined picturesque covers and comic panels.

These first color newsprint supplements were printed in color inks on only one side of one broadsheet page, producing color front and back covers for a single section. Although color covers often acted as art supplements—providing large collectible posters of pastoral scenes or portraits of famous faces—color supplements were also a forum, from their start, for an expanded role for editorial cartoons.[44] Color supplements are where we find the Globe Man and the *Inter-Ocean*'s "Typical Chicago," as well as famous cartoonists' signatures. These figures all provide a degree of personification for the newspaper itself, working as a framing device to understand the Sunday paper as massively popular. In this sense, newspapers' own comic mascots and cartoons of growing circulation are a key part of the genealogy of the "funny pages," years before popular syndication of comic strips began.[45]

Recurring cartoon characters sedimented the commercial value of the serio-comic format of color comic supplements long before the notorious rivalry between Hearst and Pulitzer over the little Yellow Kid. That battle ended with both publishers cast as culprits of yellow journalism and color comics vilified along with them. "The 'new journalism' should make an effort to keep the Yellow

Kid off its editorial page," quipped the *New York Press,* but the conflation between popular comic characters and the paper itself was now cemented.[46] In the early years of color supplements, Richard F. Outcault was an illustrator for Pulitzer whose specialty was the street urchins of *Hogan's Alley,* including the long-shirted hanger-on who became known as the Yellow Kid. Outcault had first inked the character in sketches for *Truth* magazine, some of which were reprinted in the *World* early in 1895 as Outcault began drawing original sketches for the paper. Throughout the course of the next year, Outcault's *Hogan's Alley* became squarely identified with the *Sunday World's* color supplement. At this point, the littlest urchin was named Mickey Dugan, but a brush of yellow was licked across his shirt when *Hogan's Alley* was first printed in color, and the unofficial name "Yellow Kid" stuck.[47]

Concurrently, Hearst became a direct competitor by purchasing the *New York Journal.* He had built the *San Francisco Examiner* to notorious fame using many of the same direct, active promotional schemes and illustrated journalistic techniques that Pulitzer had employed in New York. The story is a mainspring of American journalism history; Hearst transformed the *Journal* and the field of New York journalism by matching Pulitzer, often by poaching the most famous of the *World's* own staff of journalists, managers, and artists. Hearst's hiring of Outcault and the movement of the Yellow Kid to the *World* was the coup de grâce, resulting in a court case that determined while Pulitzer's *World* held the rights to the name *Hogan's Alley,* Outcault (and, thus, Hearst's *Journal*) could continue to draw the character. Now officially called the "Yellow Kid" but relocated to *McFadden's Row of Flats,* starting in October 1896, Outcault's cartoon character became a mascot for the new color section of Hearst's *Sunday Journal.*[48]

As central as the rivalry between Pulitzer and Hearst is to our history of the comic strip supplement, it has been mined in so many other histories of yellow journalism that we will simply state its significance without recounting further details. We have one novel observation, drawing primarily from the advance promotion for the two Sunday papers. In February 1896 the *Sunday World* doubled its color section and began lavishing advance promotion of its "eight funny pages" of color comics in large block advertisements in its Friday or Saturday editions, which had just been reduced in price to only one cent for weekday papers. In one promotion, Charles W. Saalburg's comic animals laugh at an advance copy of their own Sunday color comic section (see fig. 24). Hearst had taken over the *Journal* just a few months before but was still months away from launching an expanded Sunday paper with color magazine sections. The *World* singled out comic magazines, rather than other newspapers' color supplements, to target for comparison in their promotional ads.

In one of the earliest ads for the new funny pages, the *World* was depicted as an animated globe, just as in the circulation cartoon from 1889, but this time playing

FIGURE 24. Charles W. Saalburg, "Greatest of All Sunday Newspapers!" *New York World,* February 15, 1896, 16.

pied piper to Lilliputian figures representing *Puck, Judge,* and *Punch*: "More Humor than All the Comic Papers Combined."[49] A month later, in a two-week serial promotion, the *World*'s color supplement was again depicted as gigantic but this time as a baby being cautiously approached by the comic magazines, depicted as diminutive old folks.[50] In part one, the "would-be rivals" are warned, "Poor Old Chaps!" for the following week shows the giant baby whooshing them away with a blow (or a scream, perhaps, as the comic pages were called "screamingly funny").[51] Just as competition mounted against Hearst, the *World* instead showed increased hostility toward the long-standing old-time comic weekly magazines. Staking its claim to their territory, the funny pages of the *Sunday World* became a separate supplement in January 1896, soon named "The Comic Weekly." Hearst would copy this form by the end of the year, labeling his comic section "The American Humorist." However, whereas Pulitzer's *World* had been promoting its "Comic Weekly" as the primary draw for the Sunday paper, and had even used its own cartoon characters to symbolize the comic supplement, Hearst's *Journal* isolated the Yellow Kid and turned him into a mascot for the paper in general rather than just a feature of "The American Humorist." Like the Globe Man in Boston, continually used as a logo and personification of circulation, the *New York Journal* used the Yellow Kid to symbolize the Sunday edition; directly addressing readers, he sold the paper. The comic supplement came to characterize the Sunday paper altogether.

Once the Yellow Kid was Hearst's to use, he became center stage—fully a mascot in every sense—in a barrage of publicity: "Look out for 'The Yellow Kid.'"[52]

He was given his own color song supplement, "The Latest and the Greatest," to "fill a popular demand."[53] The lyrics began "Who doesn't know the 'Dugan Kid'? He is the very latest." This moment marks the transfiguration of circulation from promotion into embodied characters. This is the corporealization of the Sunday supplement, significant less for the corporate rivalry than for the incorporation of recurring comic characters into public awareness and promotion of the very form of the Sunday comic strip supplement.

Other newspapers immediately copied the technique. In September 1896, the *Boston Globe* briefly introduced *The Kittikat Klub*, a panel cartoon in which little kittens worked at a political campaign.[54] The final weeks of operation for the *New York Recorder* launched the paper's own daily color street urchin characters in *The Rag-Tags*, featuring a racially mixed (and racially caricatured) team of little kids up to no good.[55] In 1897, when the *San Francisco Call* began a more humorous children's page, one of its own illustrators, G. A. Bronstrup, created a weekly comic called *The Bumpkins*. Indeed, one of the things the Yellow Kid and his successors did was to turn the overt audience for the color comic sections into a juvenile readership.[56] Unlike their satirical magazine precedents, and unlike the scenic posters and editorial cartoons of the earliest Sunday color supplements, the weekly comic pages were aimed at kids but accessible to people of all ages. Rather than *Puck* and *Judge*, their precedents were amusing children's sketchbooks, the most popular of which were Phil May's *Gutter Snipes* (the immediate predecessor to those that depicted little urban ruffians, like *Hogan's Alley*), Palmer Cox's *Brownies* (a model for those depicting little fairy figures, like *The Bumpkins*), and W. W. Carew's *Circus*. The constant turn to animated animals was a staple comic style borrowed from children's literature. In newspapers an early use of animals came with Hearst illustrator Jimmy Swinnerton's *Little Bears*, which had been a long-standing item in the *San Francisco Examiner* years before Hearst's "American Humorist" introduced them to New York and other cities in its color comics.[57] The overlap with children's books went both directions, as one of the first by-products of popular comic strips was books compiling past installments of weekly comic series.[58] Overall, the periodical character of comic strip caricatures largely took its model from the cartoonists of children's book series, diametrically opposed to the topical, timely satire of editorial cartooning and adult humor in the comic papers.

SYNDICATED HUMOR
FOR SUNDAY'S FUNNY SIDE

Like other aspects of the fully-fledged Sunday paper of the early 1900s, the color comic supplement had previous modest iterations in black-and-white features.

Pulitzer was again a pioneer in introducing a bannered humor page late in 1888. "The World's Funny Side" was a page of original comic material, edited by Eugene S. Bisbee, mixing two-column cartoons with illustrated stories and other humorous items. Writers and illustrators were encouraged to submit articles to "the funny page" and sternly advised that rejected manuscripts would not be returned unless sent with a stamped self-addressed envelope.[59] The original content of the page was hardly the innovation, as newspapers had routinely included jokes and short stories in a lighter vein, especially for weekend editions. As a step toward the comic supplement, the innovation here is the illustrated banner that marked the page as a new, distinct feature apart from the rest of the *New York Sunday World* but available only as part of it. This use of banners to mark entire pages as sections was still rare until the 1890s (an exceptional precedent was the *Philadelphia Times*'s "Our Boys and Girls" page, begun in January 1888, which we discussed in chapter 1). The *World*'s Saturday edition promised the next day's paper would contain "whole pages of miscellany, humor and current news." The "Funny Side" in particular was called "a page of original humor" and "another page of fun," with the emphasis on the form as much as the content. The funny page was worth waiting for, worth seeking out, and worth keeping precisely because it was an entire page unto itself. As 1889 progressed, the page was reduced to a half page, but the illustrated banner proclaiming its autonomy was a constant, even as the name changed to "*The World*'s Funny Zone," "*The World*'s Comedy," and "*The World*'s Laughing Gas."

The original content for the *World*'s funny page lasted only a few months. By May 1889 the page was reprinting other newspapers' humorous stories and cartoons from the same comic weekly magazines (*Puck, Judge,* and *Life*) that the color supplement later boasted of surpassing. The page continued under a newly illustrated banner now showing paste pot and scissors, common parlance for material gleaned from exchange copies of other newspapers and magazines. Pulitzer's star illustrator, Walt McDougall, had inked front-page editorial cartoons since 1884, but in the early 1890s his cartoons became larger and more intricate in layout and design. For New Year's 1890, as Nellie Bly neared the end of her world-encircling stunt, a full-page cartoon provided an illustrated retrospective titled "Looking Backwards on 1889," in which McDougall depicted the *World* itself providing the pictorial tour, again turned into a globe-headed man, this time with spectacles and pointer, acting as a professor (see fig. 25).[60] Bly's globe-trotting spanned the top of the page, as the Pulitzer Building neared completion next to the Eiffel Tower, the Johnstown Flood, New York's fight with Chicago to bid for the world's fair, and four new states in the Northwest. All were shown in comic tones, as were wars and political intrigue. It was the high point of an early gesture to include comics as a focus for the Sunday paper.

FIGURE 25. Walt McDougall, "Looking Backwards on 1889," *New York World*, December 29, 1889, 17.

Bill Nye and M. Quad

Instead of full-page cartoons or compiled reprinted sketches from comic weeklies, most newspapers relied on syndicated humorists to provide mirth for Sunday editions. The written humor of two syndicated columnists, Edgar Wilson "Bill" Nye and "M. Quad" (pseudonym of Charles Bertrand Lewis), became the central humorous features in the *World* and other Sunday papers across the continent. These two comic journalists played vital roles in creating a national syndicated American brand of Sunday humor in the early 1880s, worth a short diversion from our emphasis at present on illustrated comic pages.[61] Early in their careers, both worked for newspapers without metropolitan influence and gained reputations initially from the extensive nationwide network of exchange copies sent without charge by post and rail to dozens of other newspaper editors. Both transformed their comic journalism into celebrity through lecture circuits, and their early columns contributed to the expansion of formal news syndication at the American Press Association. Eventually, both became writers for the *New York World* after Pulitzer offered wages that could not be refused. Only syndication would eventually trump that lucrative offer.

Bill Nye was founding editor and publisher of the *Laramie Boomerang* in Wyoming and by 1881 had gained a wide enough reputation for his wit and humorous columns that other newspapers gushingly announced when they began receiving the *Boomerang* at their exchange desks. Throughout the western territories (not yet states), editors profusely reprinted his columns, giving him and his prairie paper credit. By 1883 Nye had already authored two books collecting his writing and soon signed a deal with the American Press Association, giving him national circulation. His profile was so prominent as the singular writer of leisurely, humorous journalism that only a metropolitan publisher with the deep pockets of Pulitzer could afford to hire him. In December 1886 he became a New Yorker and an exclusive contributor to the *Sunday World*, where his column was peppered with illustrations. McDougall's caricature of Nye as a lanky, bald, bespectacled gentleman became the central character of Nye's own recurring comic column. Exclusivity then became syndication, with Nye's humor simultaneously appearing in Pulitzer's sister paper, the *St. Louis Post-Dispatch*, but also in the *Boston Globe*, the *Chicago Daily News*, and dozens of other papers. Nye died young in 1896, but his decade as a syndicated humorist was as important a part of the emergence of the Sunday comics as Outcault's Yellow Kid a decade later. It's easy to imagine that he might have transformed his column into a comic strip if he had lived just a few more years.

Charles Bertrand Lewis was nearly as prominent, lived decades longer than Nye (into the 1920s), and did indeed transform his persona as a humor columnist into a series of illustrated Sunday comics produced by a creative team of writers and illustrators. His pseudonym, M. Quad, derived from being a typesetter for a small weekly paper in Michigan, where he supposedly was compelled into writing just to fill space left blank by a negligent editor prone to drink. His regional reputation as a humorist led to work for the *Detroit Free Press*, where he wrote prolific amounts of material that raised the circulation and profile of the paper (and himself). When his contract with the *Free Press* expired in 1891, it became national news that New York publishers were offering to double his annual wage. Pulitzer reportedly nabbed him for the *Sunday World* for an astronomical fifteen thousand dollars per year. M. Quad and some of his comic creations would go on to later become profusely illustrated color pages of comic fun, but in the early 1890s, before color printing began, the pairing of Bill Nye and M. Quad gave the *World* a funny page of a distinctly verbose character, only lightly illustrated to accompany the stories of celebrity comic columnists. Unlike editorial cartooning satirizing current events, their syndicated columns provided a more popular brand of humor that could retain its humor for weeks or longer, which allowed columns to be compiled and recirculated as books. Their prominence confirmed the popularity of timeless humor—as opposed to newsworthy editorial cartooning—as the anchor of a modern Sunday supplement.

The Comic Sketch Club

While metropolitan papers experimented with full-page cartoons or compiled reprinted panels from the comic weeklies, syndicated cartoons arrived in 1893 but not at one of the established syndicates. Exclusively focused on cartoons, the Comic Sketch Club was a new company that employed dozens of illustrators to create panels for mass reproduction in Sunday papers. Working out of Baltimore, H. L. Cassard recruited Eugene "Zim" Zimmerman and Henry "Hy" Mayer, among other illustrators who had made their names as the cover comic illustrators for *Judge* and *Life* in the late 1880s. Interviewed in 1895, Cassard claimed, "Many of these gentlemen now give the Sketch Club their entire time in preference to the weekly journals."[62] By then its star artist was Claude E. Toles, "regarded by all art connoisseurs as one of the best comic artists of the day."[63]

The club's material was used—sometimes selectively, sometimes in its entirety—even by newspapers with their own art and illustration departments and even those already producing color comic supplements of their own. The *New York World*, for example, used these syndicated sketches for the black-and-white inside pages of its colored supplement. The earliest Comic Sketch Club set of cartoons included "Paderewski and the Camel" by A. S. Daggy and lampooning the famed concert pianist's distinctive, shaggy hairstyle. The comic was published simultaneously on August 6, 1893, in newspapers such as the *St. Paul Globe* and the *Cleveland Plain Dealer* as well as the *New York World*, all of which used a special decorative banner of a jester holding open a sketchbook, drawn by

W. M. Goodes. The *World* even promoted the feature as a highlight of the Sunday paper, naming the most famous artists: "The Comic Sketch Club . . . There is only one Zim and his sketches are always amusing and up to date. There are as many cartoons in *The World* as in any comic weekly, and the price is only one-half that of the weeklies."[64] The very first Sunday edition of the *Boston Post* featured a full-page compilation bannered "The Comic Sketch Club," with ten or more of the syndicated cartoons collected as a novel reason to seek out this new Sunday paper—"This page is where the laugh comes in . . . published exclusively by *The Post* in this section of the country"—and listing twelve of the illustrators by last name only as "the corps of artists."[65] The *Sunday Post* then briefly provided a full-page canvas to its in-house cartoonist, Norman Ritchie, to produce color covers in April and May 1894 but returned to syndicated comics, later among the first to adopt syndicated Hearst comics in December 1900.

Although it is clear that some newspapers, especially in smaller cities, used the Comic Sketch Club material only sparingly when space allowed, many Sunday papers in cities across the country began printing entire pages of cartoons, thanks to the profusion of weekly material made available through syndication. The *Philadelphia Inquirer* began using the syndicated material on its existing "With the Wits" humor page, which had previously used items from *Truth*, *Puck*, and *Judge*.[66] In 1894, Sunday editions of the *Detroit Free Press*, the *Chicago Tribune*, and the *San Francisco Chronicle* initiated comic pages drawing prominently from Cassard's cartoons. The *Cincinnati Enquirer* transformed its Sunday magazine pages into a self-described "Comic Supplement" in July 1895, with multiple pages of humor and cartoons and full-page sketches drawn in-house.[67] Starting in July 1896, the *Philadelphia Times* began a four-page color section, enclosing its women's fashion page and its compiled comics page between poster-size scenic or cartoon covers—often featuring *Huckleberry Court* by J. S. Moyer, its own response to the Yellow Kid's *Hogan's Alley*.[68]

The *Washington Times* began using the Comic Sketch Club material for a page first bannered "A Little Humor Now and Then, etc."[69] The curious addition of "etc." signifies how the humor page was not yet a juvenile comic supplement as color cartoons would soon become. The more or less random compilation of comic sketches, jokes, short humorous stories and songs, "etc.," did not yet distinguish mature satire from kids' fun. Even as cartoons came to predominate these early comic pages, the range of styles and subjects was still varied enough to include feminine, masculine, and juvenile readers all under the one umbrella. The initial common thread was illustration, in and of itself, as many of the sketches were still fairly detailed in line and etching, and even the cartooning still ranged widely from visual puns in silhouette to densely drawn scenarios. The point of the comic page was appealing to all readers, a little something for all senses of humor. As the *Washington Times* noted in promoting its Sunday edition, now that it included a

page of humor, the weekend paper in particular provided "something for everyone
. . . a paper for everybody. *The Sunday Times* is not a paper for any one class, sect,
section, set, condition, color, cult, age, or social standing."[70] Few of the Comic
Sketch Club illustrators made the transition to color comic strips, and their cartoons do not feature recurring characters, but they are often drawn in multiple-
panel strips, and their work is key to the later emergence of syndicated funny
pages simply because this syndicate allowed the early bannered humor pages in
Sunday papers to become a standard feature in dozens of different newspapers,
well beyond New York.

Comic pages in the 1890s did not yet have a standard form and were still
designed in-house at each Sunday paper. Some were unusually elaborate in their
layout and design. The *New York Herald* worked with five of the Comic Sketch
Club's artists to create a color page of "Christmas Fun" with the familiar styles of
the cartoonists, now in bright hues.[71] The page was framed by a ribbon of twenty
clowns and jesters, which C. E. Toles effectively made the main feature of the page,
despite acting as the margin for his colleagues' relatively traditional cartoons. The
New York World briefly had a full page of reprinted editorial comics from other
newspapers across the country. In one case, the panels were arranged as if fired
from a cannon; in another they appeared as a poster held aloft by giant hands
and gazed upon by a half-dozen people, as if the reader were standing behind
them, looking at the backs of their hats.[72] For six weeks leading up to Christmas
1896, the *St. Paul Globe* hired one of the Comic Sketch Club's illustrators, E. O.
Brooks, to create a limited but extravagant series of illuminated color covers.[73]
Even newspapers still working in black-and-white used striking designs to distinguish their comic pages. The *Philadelphia Inquirer*'s "With the Wits" page became
a forum for the skills of the paper's typesetters, freed to have fun themselves.
When "Funny Fancies" became its moniker, the letters of that label were made
of pages of comics, supposedly drawn by a mischievous boy's pen.[74] The "Funny
Fancies" banner was played with, moving to the middle of the page and a few
times placed diagonally. Sometimes the entire page was printed on an angle, with
a liberal amount of wasted white space, making the compilation of cartoons and
comic items strikingly distinct from the rest of the Sunday paper (see fig. 26).[75]
Remarkably experimental, these funny pages had to be handled, turned, and
held—played with in physical form just to be read. When the *Inquirer* introduced
a color section in April 1898, it continued to include old-style black-and-white
sketches on the inside pages even as it adopted the new style of color multipanel
comic strips on its covers.

The "Comic Weekly" and Other Jesters

Separate sections and distinct styles for editorial cartooning, comic sketching,
and recurring character strips required experimentation with layout and design,
but for comics to have their own supplement, the Sunday paper simply needed

FIGURE 26. "Funny Fancies," *Philadelphia Inquirer*, April 5, 1896, 40.

more pages in general and more color pages in particular. When the *New York World* expanded its color printing capacity enough to create two color supplements early in January 1896, one became the "Sunday Magazine" of illustrated feature stories, and the other became the "Comic Weekly." All previous color supplements combined sentimental features with editorial and comic cartoons.

Hearst's expanded *New York Journal* followed with a color "American Humorist" section in October 1896, a separate "American Magazine" in November, and a color supplement "American Woman's Home Journal" in December. The *New York Recorder* tried to compete by racing a tabloid-fold comic supplement into circulation with its existing color printing technology; "Tabasco" promised "8 pages of the Earth's best wit, fancy, folly and satire. Cartoons in color, free with every copy."[76] The *Recorder* was actually on its last legs, and "Tabasco" was issued only once, in the paper's penultimate Sunday edition. Upon its demise, the *New York Tribune* purchased the bankrupt *Recorder*'s subscription list and equipment—and inherited its color comic supplement. Although the comic supplement got a new name, "Twinkles," it could not escape the emerging backlash against Hearst and Pulitzer.[77] It had been twenty-five years since Horace Greeley had edited the *Tribune*, but competitors on Park Row wasted no time mocking the move: "It is a light-headed and ill-balanced management which is swept off its base by the frantic struggle now in progress between the journalistic Anarchists who have recently invaded our noble profession. . . . In getting itself, or any part of itself, down to *The Recorder* level, *The Tribune* incurs a moral injury. Imbecility is sometimes almost as immoral as positive indecency."[78] Opinions in literary magazines followed suit about the "fall from grace" of "the dignified of Sunday papers, now it has taken on a Recorder annex."[79] The comic weeklies had their digs too: "In Greeley's time *The Tribune* thundered; now it 'Twinkles'" (see plate 10).[80]

"Yellow journalism" soon displaced "new journalism" as the denigration of populist sensationalism, now combined with profuse illustrations and color comic supplements. "Twinkles" actually made the *Tribune* one of the targets of ridicule. Over the next few months, an outright backlash against comic supplements gained momentum, with dozens of libraries and clubrooms banishing both the *World* and the *Journal*.[81] Unsurprisingly, the *Tribune* abandoned "Twinkles" in favor of a stapled halftone magazine. With such vocal detractors, a comic supplement was still sometimes introduced only as a hesitant short-term experiment. The *Boston Herald* separated its color magazine features from its comics and humor in March 1897 by creating a fold-and-tear section called "The Jester." Lasting just a few months, this effort seems to be licensed or syndicated from the *Philadelphia Press*, which had started its own short-lived tabloid comic section, "Jester," in January.[82] These same months in Kentucky, the *Louisville Courier-Journal* (a frequent experimenter with novel forms and supplements) issued a tabloid color comic supplement on fine paper—for just five weeks early in 1897, replaced by a halftone supplement—the same outcome as the *New York Tribune*. A halftone "magazine" supplement was more befitting of the high-class tone such papers were aiming to produce. This middle-brow path was first expertly paved by the *New York Times*, under a new owner, Adolph Ochs. Back in September 1896, the *Times* had also introduced a new illustrated supplement at the same time as many other newspapers, but from its start it employed halftone photographs in black-and-white and avoided color and comics, which helped the paper to avoid being castigated for bending to popular sensationalism.

Many of the most prominent newspapers steered clear of separate comic sections until the very end of the 1890s. Until the new century, the *New York Herald* mixed all of its comic, political, and poster-worthy color art in one color section notable in its layout and design mainly for its lucrative placement of full-page ads on back pages. Similarly, the *Chicago Tribune* stepped forward only tentatively into comic strips, introducing a halftone section in 1897 and taking it color in 1900, but still using only the compiled collections of cartoons from other sources (although two full pages of them) until it launched a color comic strip section late in 1901. The *Philadelphia Inquirer* turned to comic strips comparatively early, as part of its first color section in 1898, but the comic material it printed was limited to a single page until it began to ink its own comic section in June 1901. And the *San Francisco Call* labeled its new color section with the explicitly hybrid "Comic and Half-Tone Section" when it first launched in July 1900.[83]

Sometimes it seems the clout and popularity of a newspaper's editorial cartoonist could determine the position and design of its comics. The *Cleveland Plain Dealer* gave its star cartoonist, James H. "Hal" Donahey, its cover when it started a color section in 1901, as did the *Minneapolis Journal* in 1902 for its celebrity sketch artist, Charles Lewis "Bart" Bartholomew (who had done tours and published books of his comics). Both illustrators soon turned to comic strip designs, allowing these papers to avoid drawing upon syndicated material for color comic sections for several years longer than other papers. Such cases were exceptions; a long-standing staff illustrator shepherding the transition from small black-and-white editorial cartoons to color comic strips with continuing characters was rare. The *New Orleans Item* launched a color comic cover in February 1901, but it was nixed quickly after just three months. The *Item* explained, "It has outlived its usefulness," noting that a canvass of subscribers found too few of them cared for it to justify the expense.[84] Just a year later, the paper introduced a permanent color section, but instead of scenic covers of its own design, it now relied on the more affordable, accessible, and popular form of syndicated comics.

One of the first unabashed comic supplements outside New York came from the *St. Louis Republic*, which introduced a four-page broadsheet "Funny Weekly" section in June 1897 with an elaborate cartoon cover by its own illustrators and a banner of its own design. In the years before syndicated comics, the *Republic*'s comic section was one of the most elaborate and enduring, drawn entirely in-house. The effort, in a sense, precipitates the turn to syndicated color comics, or at least presages them. In response, Pulitzer's provincial sister paper, the *St. Louis Post-Dispatch*, began to reprint the *New York World*'s "Comic Weekly" with a St. Louis masthead. For years already, the *Post-Dispatch* had been redrawing black-and-white versions of the popular comics from New York. Reprinting the *World*'s color originals began just a few weeks after the new competition from the *Republic*. "Next Sunday's *Post-Dispatch*," boasted the advance publicity, "The Colored Comic Supplement will be the biggest and best issued by any newspaper in the world"—true enough, considering it was the *World* that was issuing it rather than the *Post-Dispatch*. The color comics promised to be "a revelation to St. Louis and the West and South as to what can be accomplished in colored newspaper illustration."[85] Starting with its Fourth of July issue, "The Comic Weekly" began to appear in two newspapers simultaneously, the twin version with a St. Louis masthead inelegantly replacing that of the *World*.

Not that accuracy would be expected in such promotional rhetoric, but Pulitzer's sister paper claimed that "no newspaper outside of New York will or can have such a colored cover for its Sunday issue," ignoring how color comic sections had already come to Boston, to Philadelphia, and to the Pacific Coast.[86] Hearst's sister paper, his *San Francisco Examiner*, had installed color presses and began printing a "Weekly Humorist" section in April 1897 after a couple of experimental color covers for Christmas and New Year's 1896. Initially titled the "Colored Art Supplement," it did not at first employ *New York Journal* material but instead profiled full-page sketches by Hearst's long-standing California illustrator, Jimmy Swinnerton, and his famous Little Bears. A step toward syndication came when the popular comic strips of the *New York Journal* were immediately added to the first Sunday edition of Hearst's *Chicago American* in July 1900. By the end of the year, syndicated Hearst comics became the norm, simultaneously published in various newspapers across the continent in addition to Hearst's own chain of Sunday papers.

THE POPULARITY OF
EARLY COMIC CHARACTERS

Early in the new century, the *New York Herald* lost a copyright lawsuit that may have sparked the turn to formal syndication of comic strips. Its publisher, James Gordon Bennett, sued the *Boston Traveler* for reprinting a comic cut without permission. Although the entire issue of the *Herald* had been registered for copyright protection as a periodical, the judge ruled in March 1900 that each illustration had to be registered separately in the distinct category for engravings, cuts, and prints.[87] The ruling added clarity to the question of who owned the copyright to popular columns and comics. Unless the publisher specifically registered a particular illustration, the artist owned the rights to reproductions. By the end of 1900, the verdict pushed the *New York Herald* and Hearst to begin registering each of their Sunday comics as a uniquely copyrighted item. Consequence or coincidence—shift in the legal details or cultural norms—the ruling came at the same time as comics became formally syndicated, published using a day-and-date release strategy in licensed newspapers beyond those directly owned by the publisher. The outcome of the court case coincided with the launch of a new cartoon character in the *Herald*, Carl "Bunny" Schultze's *Foxy Grandpa*, which debuted on the first Sunday of the new century in January 1900.[88] The strip was an immediate hit, with old grandpa trading hoaxes, gags, and pranks back and forth with his two young grandkids. Since the Yellow Kid, other comic characters had become popular, especially the roster of Hearst Sunday comics, which included Rudolph Dirks's *Katzenjammer Kids*, Frederick Opper's *Happy Hooligan and His Brother Gloomy Gus*, and Jimmy Swinnerton's *Little Bears* and *Little Tigers*. Unlike these previous color comic strips, *Foxy Grandpa* immediately appeared simultaneously in the *Boston Herald*, day-and-date with its home base at the *New York Herald*. By the end of the year, the strip was also appearing in the *Chicago Times-Herald*. The modest syndication in Boston and Chicago wasn't really any different from Hearst or Pulitzer comics being reprinted in sister publications. All of these weekly comic strips still appeared just once, in the color supplements. The change in handling the copyright of cartoons coincided with Hearst comics starting to appear in syndication beyond his own chain of papers in December 1900 (see plate 11). As if Hearst shone a light on an unknown path, several new comic syndicates came forward almost simultaneously in 1901 to compete.

The comic supplement became a cultural phenomenon and a mass medium in and of itself, apart from the Sunday paper as much as a part of it. The new medium—the funnies—almost always increased circulation by appealing especially to children, even those who couldn't yet read. The syndicated supplement was a single solution to a twin problem: how to fully exploit the weekly market for the most popular comic strips and how to provide the new medium to smaller circulation papers—even those in small towns—that did not have their own color printing presses. Newspapers with color presses could contract for licensed permission to reproduce Hearst or *Herald* comic strips in a noncompeting territory day-and-date with their New York brethren. This came at a great expense, but few such endeavors were short-lived. Popular comics in syndication boosted circulation enough to merit the cost.

There were cheaper supplements available for those who sought the form without the most popular characters. Even Hearst offered a cheaper alternative of a black-and-white compilation of comics from the daily *New York Evening Journal*. Cheapest of all for small newspapers was the option of a preprinted color comic supplement on which the local masthead could be stamped, often crudely. All of these options became available more or less simultaneously between December 1900 and November 1901. By the end of 1901 there were at least forty-one newspapers in eighteen different states, offering readers one of five nationally syndicated comic supplements. A year earlier there were none except for those with direct connections to a New York paper. A new medium had been institutionalized, coast-to-coast. Altogether the comic syndicates formed a single national market for Sunday funnies in general, especially for the most popular recurring characters and their absurd, predictable mayhem.

The color comic supplement's first popular star was Mickey Dugan, aka the Yellow Kid, who made a celebrity out of its illustrator, Richard Felton Outcault. The character was the youngest waif in a crew of comically rambunctious kids in a primarily Irish urban tenement, "Hogan's Alley" in its Pulitzer days and then "McFadden's Flats" in its Hearst days. East Side tenement gamins, urchins, and newsboys had been a cornerstone of American humor for over a decade already, notably in E. W. Townsend's "Chimmie Fadden" columns for the *New York Sun*.[89] "Chimmie" and his gang offered an appealing ironic mix of knowing naiveté, "not perhaps immoral but certainly unmoral."[90] The emphasis fell on their innocent wonderment in a distinctly worldly dialect: "Hully Gee!" became the Yellow Kid's catchphrase, but it predated him, as did the stock of humorous stories and jokes about city kids.[91] Outcault drew *Hogan's Alley* in a single-panel cartoon, up to a full page, rather than a strip of sequential scenes. The kids would conduct their own working-class variation of some urban activity each week, putting on a vaudeville show or a parade; going to Coney Island, the circus, or a baseball game; or the scene would show a tenement version of a high-class New York ritual like the Easter Parade, a horse show, or playing tennis. The chaotic scenes were always packed with written signs and messages embedded in every nook of the action, most notably painted onto Mickey Dugan's own yellow shirt, speaking for him.

Within a year of his first yellow-shirted appearance in the *Sunday World*, the character's popularity was a true craze. An upstate New York newspaper noted late in 1896 how the boys of the town had a fever for the color comic supplements: "That grotesque and grinning youngster is held in the most profound esteem by the Hogan's Alley club, and he is spoken of but in awe-stricken whispers. His doings are read of and scanned with feverish interest in the New York Sunday papers by 'de gang' who do a sprint for the newsstands the minute the bulky bundles get in."[92] New York's Sunday editions were distributed widely down to Washington, D.C., up to New England and beyond, but these thousands of copies circulating weekly beyond metropolitan New York do not in themselves explain how the Yellow Kid and other early comic characters established the notoriety and fame of popular appeal on a continental scale. Their popularity beyond the metropolis depended especially upon intermedial entertainment networks in popular music, book publishing, lithographic posters, the new product of moving pictures, and, above all else, commercial stage productions that radiated out of New York through touring productions that crisscrossed North America, reaching every regional metropolis and nearly every small city across the continent.

By Labor Day 1896, Outcault himself had scripted and sketched a live reproduction of his *Hogan's Alley* characters on stage as part of a revue at Weber and Fields's Broadway Music Hall.[93] Just a week later, comedians Barney Gilmore and John F. Leonard debuted their latest touring show, *Hogan's Alley*, which drew raves and standing-room-only audiences for its starring depiction of the little yellow-clad urchin who was taking the country's imagination by storm that year. Wherever it played, the show sold out, and "the crush was tremendous. A number were standing and hundreds were turned away. Hogan's Alley is the farce comedy made so famous in the sketches in *The New York Sunday World*, and as there are very few Scrantonians who had not read of it, the desire to witness the performance is easily accounted for."[94] Even a big-city Philadelphia reviewer acknowledged how the show was "a side-splitting laugh from beginning to end. There is not a dull moment in it."[95] This show reached nearly every town on the continent's theatrical circuit, even as at least three other stage reviews and plays followed on its heels. Yellow Kid songs, marches, and dances proliferated in music copyright registrations: "Down in Hogan's Alley," by Harry S. Miller as early as April 1896, and then "Yellow Kids on Parade," by C. E. Vandersloot, and "The Yellow Kid Schottische," by C. Baker, among at least a dozen others up to July 1897. Puzzles, lithographs, and photographs were copyrighted, based on depictions of Outcault's character. Impersonators of the Yellow Kid led a preelection "Junior McKinley" parade in New Jersey, appeared at an election night rally in Pennsylvania, and headed a massive bicycle rally in Virginia.[96] His likeness was used in newspapers' ads for clothing stores, such as W. W. Morgan in Kansas City and Strouse and Bros. in Evansville, Indiana. By Christmas shopping season, the Yellow Kid was nearly as ubiquitous as Santa Claus. A Canal Street shoe store in New Orleans had the "original" Yellow Kid, direct from Hogan's Alley, New York, holding court and distributing presents to every purchaser.

When Outcault switched to the *New York Journal*, he did more than accept Hearst's reported hundred-thousand-dollar offer to defect from Pulitzer.[97] He also, if belatedly, commercialized his own creations outside Sunday supplements with a short-lived biweekly *Yellow Kid Magazine*—the first issue "48 pages of fascinating original and copyrighted sketches, and a wealth of humor, profusely illustrated. 5 cents per copy."[98] Outcault also inked a book version, *The Yellow Kid in McFadden's Flats*, coauthored by E. W. Townsend (who had already transformed his own *New York Sun* "Chimmie Fadden" columns into books). The book received appreciative reviews—for example, in the *Philadelphia Times*, which noted how "the story of the Yellow Kid's young life will probably while away many a weary moment and bring smiles to many a serious countenance."[99] That book review was also an opportunity to explain the logic of novelty behind popular culture crazes: "From time to time the public takes up fads literary or artistic, and presses them to the last degree until a later novelty crowds them into oblivion."[100] The degree of popular craze was perhaps never again matched by a comic supplement character, but the most popular strips were well exploited through similar forms of merchandise.

Rudolph Dirks's *Katzenjammer Kids* had begun appearing in Hearst's *New York Journal* in 1897 and by the fall of 1899 had become a touring play starring the comedy duo Blondell and Fennessy. The same theatrical group then toured with a show of another popular Hearst comic, Frederick Opper's *Happy Hooligan*, even as Edwin S. Porter produced films in 1901 for Edison Manufacturing Co. based on the cheerful tramp and his brother, Gloomy Gus. Book versions of these and other Hearst comics came just in time for Christmas 1902, selling for fifty cents each at bookstores and department stores across the continent. This was two years after the publication in book form of compiled Sunday strips from the *New York Herald's Foxy Grandpa*, by Carl "Bunny" Schultze. A stage version of *Foxy Grandpa* debuted in 1901 by R. Melville Baker and starring Joseph Hart. By the time syndicated comic supplements had taken on a recognizable form, another play, *Looping the Loop*, brought the supplement itself to life in colorful form, with a full range of characters taking turns in the spotlight. The highlight of the show was a bicycle stunt by the Happy Hooligan, doing the titular feat of looping the loop on stage. This was followed in 1902 by Reilly and Wood Comedy Co.'s *The Funny Page*, depicting all of the Hearst characters in a single production.

These comic supplement stage shows were mass popular culture for the entire country, but only appearing for one or two nights at local "opera houses" across North America. In the last years of the nineteenth century, the popularity of the comic supplement's first star characters still relied on circulation through touring stage variety shows and moving pictures and songs. The original comic strip illustrations were available only after the fact through book compilations, which whetted the public appetite to see and read the very latest antics on the very day they were published in the New York Sunday papers. And yet there was no means to circulate the material form of the Sunday "funnies" beyond their original source as supplements to New York's yellow journals and their handful of directly owned partners. The solution was licensed syndication of reproductions. Beginning in 1900, first with Hearst's famous comic characters, newspapers in noncompeting metropolitan markets began to include copyrighted color comic strips through formal syndication. As we noted above, within a year there were three new syndicated comic supplements, including companies that preprinted color sections so that even small-city Saturday papers without their own color press could include the new century's latest popular media sensation: the funny pages. By the end of the century, comics had helped change the very meaning of the word syndicate.

THE MEANING OF SYNDICATED STORIES

As late as 1871, the British term "syndicate" was still of debatable meaning among U.S. journalists, who felt compelled to explain that it referred to councils of church or university dignitaries, but "when used in financial affairs it degenerates into slang."[101] In the 1870s the notion of a "newspaper syndicate" still referred to coordinated editorial interference in politics, applied as late as 1883 to raise suspicions around Joseph Pulitzer's expanding his control from St. Louis to include the *New York World*.[102] We began this book by looking at Sabbatarian objections to selling and reading the Sunday paper, and we have noted how this objection carried forward to the years of protests against the vulgarity and slang of syndicated comic supplements and their cartoon violence. Business syndicates had been a parallel target of sermonizing since the 1880s, casting aspersions on the modern structure of big business operating at a national and transnational scale. Not until 1884 is the copublication of copyrighted leisure reading cast as a matter of syndication, for the launch of "an interesting newspaper enterprise . . . the formation of a newspaper syndicate for the purchase and publication of short stories by the best American authors." This short-lived run of "New American Stories" was initiated by Charles A. Dana of the *New York Sun*, who fronted the payment to the authors and only tepidly sought other papers to take advantage of simultaneous Sunday edition circulation "of conspicuous journals in different large cities . . . combined."[103]

Three early syndicated stories in the series were also included in the *Chicago Tribune*, the *St. Louis Globe-Democrat*, the *Philadelphia Times*, the *San Francisco Chronicle*, and five other papers. Despite the past aspersions of "syndicates" conducting nefarious collusion, other papers expressed optimism and immediately noted the benefit of higher pay for famous writers. The *Detroit Free Press*, for example, remarked that "the newspaper is steadily advancing to the front as the exponent and expression of literary work. . . . A syndicate of newspapers are about publishing in successive Sunday issues original stories from Henry James, [W. D.] Howells and Bret Harte. . . . It is not improbable that before long the American daily paper will have its daily 'feuilleton' like its French contemporaries, with the very best literature of the day in its pages."[104] Brooklyn journalist Addison Irving Bacheller had launched the American Bureau of Fiction just weeks earlier, first offering Joseph Hatton's "London Letter" to subscribing publishers starting in May 1884.[105] None of those newspapers explicitly promoted their participation in a syndicate, whereas all of those printing the *Sun*'s "New American Stories" made their networked collaboration part of the publicity. The *Philadelphia Times* boasted of "a new era of authorship" resulting from higher payment and greater circulation through its "concurrent publication of a new series of stories in nine newspapers having a combined circulation of quite half a million copies, reaching every section of the country at the same time and bringing simultaneous pleasure and profit to not less than two and a half million readers."[106]

By the end of 1884, Mark Twain was interviewed and explained how the new model of combined newspaper circulation was a clear benefit over magazines for a writer seeking a larger readership:

> The trouble is that the two or three magazines which are a good market for a writer and which can aid him in his work for fame are overcrowded. *The Century* has perhaps $100,000 worth of accepted articles in its vault which may not appear for years. They are pushed aside by articles on timely topics which cannot be delayed . . . [but] these combinations of newspapers which print stories and sketches once a week will, it seems to me, give rising and capable writers the field they desire as well as the market. One of these syndicates . . . has written to me and has offered me handsome terms for articles. He seems to think I am a magazine writer, but I really am not.[107]

The contrast with magazines was put into action as part of the value to the newspaper reader, as the latest fiction and features could now be obtained in a Sunday paper. In Massachusetts the *Springfield Republican* explicitly staked a claim to the literary territory of magazines because its Sunday stories, published "in common with a number of other newspapers of corresponding reputation in various parts of the country, deserve especial attention for their manner of publication, for that is a sign of the times. The daily newspaper is assuming the function of the magazine, just as the magazine is becoming steadily newspapery. . . . The readers of *The Sunday Republican* must observe that they are offered the literature of the first-class magazines."[108]

Into this mix of experimentation, Samuel Sidney McClure began providing newspaper publishers another option to syndicate, starting in mid-November 1884 with a new story by H. H. Boyesen, "A Daring Fiction." Early adopters of the McClure service included the *Boston Globe* and the *New York Commercial Advertiser*, the latter noted as its originating source when anthologized, but other simultaneous publications included papers in smaller cities, such as the *Lancaster New Era* in Pennsylvania.[109] Joining just a week later, the *Buffalo Express* explained how its "fresh attraction" would be the centerpiece of its Sunday supplement and described how connecting with other papers ensured the popularity of the feature: "By clubbing together, this newspaper syndicate secures stories of the same grade and by the same writers as the best which appear in *The Century* and *Harper's Magazine*. It is a new and brilliant development of the principle of association."[110] The *Express* continued to spotlight its weekly publication of S. S. McClure's "original copyright stories" as exclusive to the region and "fully up to the highest magazine standard."[111] For months, display ads for the Sunday edition noted how the stories ensured that "every number of *The Sunday Express* is in fact a weekly magazine of choice literature."[112] Within six months, a synopsis noted in May 1885, "Mr. McClure has published in his syndicate as many short stories as the popular magazines combined have published within the same period. The formation of a syndicate is like the founding of a new magazine."[113] Recounting the now-familiar logic of how a syndicate could afford to pay the best writers higher amounts for their latest stories, the *Express* ultimately framed its advantage over magazines as a fight between the two print forums: "Newspapers vs. Magazines! In much of the domain hitherto sacred to the magazine, the newspaper is bound to take the lead! . . . This is effected by combination. . . . *The Express* can print the same story simultaneously with *The Louisville Courier-Journal* and *The Chicago Tribune*, and the readers of all the papers be as well served as if each paper had an exclusive story."[114]

Criticism of syndicates focused on the concentration and conglomeration in big business, if not exactly the practice of print syndication. A small-town editorial from Kansas in 1887 observed how "this is the age of syndicates; great associations and monopolies, vast enterprises, millions of dollars' worth of property, and in many cases whole branches of business are under the control of a few men who regulate prices and dictate rules as though they had the authority of a monarch."[115] This particular editorial pinpointed means of communication as special instances of that tendency—telegraph, telephone, and railroads—but the criticism was cast to modern business in general terms. A news article reporting on the pooling of iron ore and coke producers commented, "Verily, this is an age of syndicates and combinations."[116] Just a few months later, an aphorism was widely reprinted escalating the sentiment to a lament that "this is a wicked age—the age of syndicates."[117] By the turn of the century, John F. Carson had extended the point explicitly to encompass the demoralizing effects of mass culture: "Ours is an age of combinations, an age of syndicates and trusts and corporations. All these bulk mankind. . . . This massing of men belittles man and makes life cheap. In the presence of this universal tendency to deal with men in the mass, the church must put her emphasis upon the individual."[118] Carson's sermons contrasted the mechanized approach of syndicated systems with religion's recognition of people in their own right: "This is an age of syndicates and corporations and the tendency is to deal with men as a mass and shout out all personality. Then men become part of a machine or a system. The Church must put her emphasis on the value of life and she must reach out and hold the individual in such reverence that the outside world will do likewise."[119] Syndicated popular culture used mechanical, corporate distribution to speak meaningfully to individuals—as part of a modern mass public.

Long before antitrust investigations into Hollywood's vertical integration, mass entertainment was already explicitly linked to big business practices and their criticism in the formation of theater syndicates, including the conglomeration of key commercial theater interests into a theatrical trust that was known informally simply as "the Syndicate." The deleterious effect on the quality of stage productions was noted at least once in terms that drew direct parallels between mass production, mass entertainment, and syndicated writing:

> Great actors have died off and their places are taken by those manikins made great by billboards and the dreary efforts of writers in the rear pages of 10-cent magazines. But why should we care? At any rate, it is inevitable. This is the age of syndicates. Syndicates in art, literature, science and industry. Poets will yet be syndicated. They are now, some of them, mainly by their own efforts, and humorists have long been so. All are thus guaranteed bread, while the public is guaranteed so many yards of poetry, painting, sculpture, humor, acting, steel rails, sausages, calico and spaghetti."[120]

Extended to motion pictures and radio broadcasting, by 1922 Jesse Lee Bennett, writing as "The Skeptic" in the *Baltimore Sun*, speculated a profound impact on journalism: "The nature and character of newspapers have changed amazingly in the past generation. And there are now tremendous forces at work—motion pictures, the radical press, ever-increasing standardization and 'syndication,' as well as radio and great social and political changes—which are bound to affect the newspapers."[121]

To a great extent, the cause and effect were arguably reversed, with newspapers' own ever-increasing standardization and syndication practices impacting motion pictures and radio. By the 1920s syndicated magazine-style material filled a good portion of weekday newspapers as Sunday features were transformed into smaller but daily versions; comic strips, serial stories, puzzles, women's columns, and pages of photographs all became everyday features in the early twentieth century. The daily compilation of news and leisure features was similar, if reversed in balance, with the 1920s "picture palace" program of a newsreel, a comic short, and a musical overture before the feature film story. The Sunday paper set the stage for daily radio programming to offer a continual stream of variety in a weekly periodical schedule.

6

THE "CONTINUOUS PERFORMANCE EXTRA" OF POPULAR LEISURE

In the early twentieth century, syndicated Sunday comic supplements and magazines achieved combined circulations far higher than any single New York paper. Identical issues of Sunday supplements were distributed in a dozen or more metropolitan regions to a truly national, simultaneous readership. The mass market was now a mass culture—the syndicated age had arrived—and the circulation of newspapers was an overt conduit for the transmission of popular entertainment. Striving to achieve ever higher circulation was no longer merely a matter of asserting local competitive advantage. In syndicated networks, North America's Sunday supplements—and their advertising—could simultaneously address the mass public as a single body of readers of the same Sunday newspaper magazines and supplements. The blending of newspapers and magazines in syndication transfigured the aims of circulation.

In this chapter we connect the history of syndicated Sunday comics and magazines to the role of newspapers in emerging commercial network radio by arguing that syndicates and networks mutually constitute each other through the common pursuit of circulating national popular culture. Through the 1890s, newspapers and magazines had likewise come to borrow and steal techniques and forms from each other—repurposing and refunctioning aspects of each other while engaging with and helping to grow the nascent mass market. They collectively constituted an emerging mass culture along with other media forms, such as popular music, books, artworks, and film. We refer to this process as a "transfiguration" to call particular attention to moments of encounter when a cultural object enters into a new mediated environment. In the process a media form establishes new relationships with those who encounter it, but it also undergoes profound changes.[1] In the specific process of syndication, the reading public was also transfigured, like the newspaper itself, becoming more national and inter-regional through simultaneous entertainment and leisure. We propose that the late 1920s process of transfiguring print newspaper features into commercial radio networks can be traced back to 1884 with the introduction of syndicated Sunday stories. As we noted in chapter 5, new fiction stories by American authors were among the first newspaper features overtly promoted as simultaneously published in a network of metropolitan Sunday newspapers.

In 1929 a strident writer in *Radio Digest* predicted syndication for the future of radio: "Why produce things in studios, entailing great expense, countless rehearsals, only to broadcast them once? . . . Why not record it, and then send the 'program' on its way to station after station? . . . And so, I say, 'Syndicate!' . . . Follow the precedent already set by the motion pictures, phonograph records, magazines and newspapers."[2] Something of this idea is also apparent in the introduction of a 1929 Universal Pictures "Talking Newsreel." Production was undertaken in conjunction with a team of forty (and later up to eighty) newspapers, including early broadcasting partners of the National Broadcasting Corporation (NBC) and the Radio Corporation of America (RCA). The announcer chosen for the newsreel was Graham McNamee, by then the celebrity news voice of NBC. Although newsreel producers had tried syndicated affiliation with metropolitan newspapers before, the link to network radio distinguished this effort from filmed Hollywood news weeklies.

By 1930 NBC's founding president, Merlin H. Aylesworth, used the notion of syndication to emphasize the centrality that Rockefeller Center would have as a media hub for all American society. "The broadcasting center," Aylesworth said, "will be joined in a vast artery of communication with the dramatic stage, with opera, with variety, with talking-motion pictures, with the symphony hall."[3] The complex contained a symphony hall where RCA artists could be recorded, movie palaces that played Radio-Keith-Orpheum (RKO) "talkies," and NBC broadcast studios that are still in use nearly a century later. For Aylesworth, network radio had become "the recognized means for the *syndication* of entertainment, education and information upon a nation-wide, and, on occasion upon a world-wide, scale."[4]

Although the two forms of media distribution have rarely been considered in tandem, networks and syndicates share a common pursuit of simultaneity in the sense that they are the product of, and rely on, coordinated action. Conventional accounts of media history assume a clear divide between material circulation and ethereal broadcast, reifying evident differences in technological and regulatory systems. To emphasize the continuities between print syndication and network radio, we pay more attention in this chapter to the factor of simultaneity, stretching the meaning somewhat to emphasize synchronized geographic circulation instead of strict temporal liveness. Accounts of the history of networked live radio prioritize the technological hookup apparatus over mass listening to the same content.[5] Asynchronous circulation of radio programs existed and was tested, but alternatives that truly syndicated radio had to rely on the coordinated distribution of prerecorded programming (not unlike syndicated radio and television today, a century later).

Syndicated radio recordings worked in a fashion directly parallel to syndicated print features, but early broadcasting largely rejected this alternative, perhaps because it lacked any spark of technological novelty but also because telephone and telegraph lines were owned by American Telephone & Telegraph Co., itself a radio broadcaster. As a result, live "hook-ups" or chains of radio broadcasts were relayed through a "net-work" of dedicated AT&T telephone lines. In the 1920s, these new terms were often still hyphenated to convey the technical actions involved. Networking local radio transmitters was a newsworthy technical feat that received heaps of publicity, downplaying the advance planning and coordinated collaboration between AT&T, RCA, and local stations that facilitated the simultaneity. In other ways, however, radio networks were organized according to the same logic as newspaper syndicates. The appeal and popularity of nationally networked popular programming was built upon a chain of previous forms of national mass entertainment, from touring theatricals and vaudeville to nationally distributed dime novels and magazines. The direct antecedent for radio networks, though, was syndicated Sunday newspaper supplements and daily newspaper features.

"THE RIGHTS TO REPRODUCE": HEARST'S SYNDICATED COMICS

Newspapers routinely presented the adoption of syndicated comic supplements as a way to connect regional and small cities to an emerging metropolitan network of popular commercial culture. Because of syndication, small regional papers could provide the very same famous characters simultaneously with big-city Sunday papers rather than having to resort to a partial or diminished form. More than any other novel feature in a weekend edition, this made the comic supplement a tangible means of keeping a regional or provincial public current with the emerging national popular culture. In the case of syndicated comics in particular, this process of keeping readerships up to date could be reduced to the technique of simply mentioning already famous artists, the titles of their comic strips, or the names of the characters who were up to their weekly serial antics.

The *Philadelphia Times* was among the first group of newspapers to include Hearst feature comics in December 1900. To drum up excitement, it only had to list what to expect: "The Greatest Comic Section ever issued in Philadelphia, including the famous Katzenjammer Kids, Gus Dirks's laughable conception of insect life, Swinnerton's funny Tigers. You can't help laughing at them" (see plate 11).[6] An elaborate promotion introducing Hearst features to Atlanta even included pictures of famous syndicated comic illustrators alongside their literary and journalistic columnist counterparts. "The Magazine Section of *The Sunday Constitution* will contain a superb array of humorous pictures, fiction of the highest order and articles of best literary merit on the topics of great interest . . . Gus Dirks, The Bugville Artist. R. Dirks, 'The Katzenjammer Artist.'"[7] New comic strips became popular and old ones changed syndicates—Schultze's *Foxy Grandpa* left the *New York Herald* and joined Hearst in 1902—but the names of cartoon characters were a constant shorthand for the currency of commercial popular culture. For example, the people of Cleveland were owed praise when a local newspaper began offering syndicated Hearst comics: "The 'Alphonse and Gaston' and 'Foxy Grandpa' pages for next Sunday will create many laughs. *The Leader* congratulates its readers that it has been able to secure these popular features."[8] Soon enough, the fine-print copyright qualifier at the bottom of the syndicated comic strips could itself be cast as a brand of distinction: "Happy Hooligan, The Katzenjammer Kids, Alphonse and Gaston. Copyrighted, 1903, by W. R. Hearst. A Dozen Live Departments and All The News."[9]

In more than one case, enterprising upstarts attempted to mark the novelty of their syndication with Hearst as a form of progressive reform in the new century. The *Denver Post* was one of the original papers to adopt Hearst comics in December 1900, promoted with a manifesto smack in the middle of the front page, illustrated with a depiction of itself as a youthful uniformed town crier–style postal carrier, combating the nepotism and collusion of competing papers. "So the People May Know," was the cry against old-hat competitors, who "at the beginning of the new *Post*, and even now, never hesitated a moment to attempt to throttle its progress."[10] The fledgling paper's publishers, F. G. Bonfils and H. H. Tammen, had created a mid-continent specimen of the new journalism in just five years, purchasing new presses, new buildings, new typesetting machines, and direct wires from Chicago and San Francisco, along with hiring new editors and new staff. The expense of adopting syndicated Hearst columns and comic strips in 1900 was cast as equivalent to the capital outlay of a new press, except that the new facility was a connection to the great continental network of modern mass communications: "*The Post* has formed a partnership with W. R. Hearst, the editor and proprietor of the *New York Journal*, *Chicago American*, and *San Francisco Examiner*, to print simultaneously with those great journals (which, including *The Post*, make a link from ocean to ocean) the writings and pictures of the celebrated and famous litterateurs, specialists and picture makers of these three great journals. . . . We are starting the Twentieth Century right, with a Twentieth Century *Denver Post*."[11]

Another upstart publisher attempting to mark out a niche of providing the new journalism to a regional public applied the same logic two years later. In 1902 the new owners of the *Fort Worth Telegram* claimed that the city was "metropolitan enough to have as good a newspaper as there is published in the state."[12] A new Sunday morning edition was created, replacing the Saturday evening paper, and included serial stories, fashion and a women's page, puzzles and a children's page. New linotypes and other mechanical equipment were installed.[13] Circulation boomed and Hearst syndication followed. The exclusive character of the syndicate's continental network was explained in detail: "*The New York Journal* and *Chicago American* are owned by W. R. Hearst, and to a few newspapers in the country—and only a few that do not circulate in territory reached by his own publications—he has sold the rights to reproduce the most desirable of the articles used by him. . . . Exclusively through *The Telegram*, Texas people can enjoy the articles that are making the Hearst papers great, on the same day that they are published in New York, Chicago, Denver, and San Francisco."[14] Adopting Hearst features and comics was positively cast as attending to the local needs of the frontier public as part of a national mass public: "Everybody, practically, in the whole country has heard of the Katzenjammer Kids, of Foxy Grandpa, of Happy Hooligan, of Alphonse and Gaston, of Lulu and Leander. . . . And why does *The Telegram* add all this heavy expense? Because the present management recognizes the popularity of the Hearst papers and the features that have made these papers popular" (see table 2).[15]

William Randolph Hearst himself was by now metonymic for the novelty of the new century's popular culture and populism. Like a real-life newspaper mascot, his own corporeal and corporate existence embodied the spirit of the previous

TABLE 2. A Sample of Sunday Circulation, 1905 to 1925

	1905	1910	1915	1918	1920	1923	1925
Boston Advertiser / American*	—	250,000	307,447	375,641	300,828	427,217	495,843
Boston Globe	297,400	321,671	279,583	302,592	327,924	322,907	332,063
Chicago (Herald and) Examiner / American*	512,835	598,717	508,881	495,946	596,851	729,735	1,039,624
Chicago Tribune	200,000	300,000	459,728	645,612	666,496	807,945	941,047
New York American (and Journal)*	800,000		752,004	728,923	930,233	1,061,841	1,090,440
New York Daily News						348,711	807,279
New York Times	100,000	175,000	259,675	392,535	546,728	542,039	576,321
New York World	436,830	459,663	463,280	500,000	561,592	598,437	574,452
Philadelphia Inquirer	142,660	205,647	280,942	305,140	350,634	385,072	402,330
St. Louis Post-Dispatch	218,798	262,067	313,675	357,638	335,401	367,932	383,314

Source: Selected N. W. Ayer and Sons, *American Newspaper Annuals* (indicating changing titles; * Hearst chain)

decade's Globe Man and other figurative representations of circulatory mastery. Hearst and his syndicated features connoted the emerging voracious appetite for popular culture, but Hearst, the man, was seeking popularity and was vilified for it. If anything, the person of Hearst masked the cultural process of national syndicated culture at play even as he exposed and personified it. He turned to politics in 1902, successfully winning election as a congressional representative from New York, leading up to a failed bid for the Democratic presidential nomination in 1904.[16] Scrutiny and ridicule followed, such as this viciously satirical editorial in the *New York Herald*, published on Hearst's election to Congress in 1902:

> Enfant terrible of American journalism; inventor of the Continuous Performance Extra, and proprietor of an endless chain system of newspapers . . .
>
> Invented the method of dating his paper four weeks ahead, in order to reach the uttermost parts of the earth on time . . .
>
> Established wireless telegraphy connections between his own person and every other point of interest in the world, which enables him to get the news while it is happening, and sometimes even before that . . .
>
> His little manual "How to Bring Up Children, by Mrs. Katzenjammer," is a work of sterling value in promoting the truest sentiments of a sweet home life. His study of the submerged classes in his picturesque volume, "The Recollections of Happy Hooligan," is regarded as a standard . . .
>
> Has been mentioned for the vice-presidency 946,738,621 times, and for the governor of New York twice, but prefers the retirement of private life which the editorship of 963 newspapers of the first rank affords.[17]

This lampooning of Hearst's reach and influence inadvertently characterizes the overall effect of the turn to syndication: a simultaneous, all-encompassing network of popular culture reaching everybody and everywhere in North America. Disguised as disgust over Hearst's infamous and well-known ferment and interventions in the 1898 Spanish-American War, the connection between technologies of circulation and spheres of influence pinpoints the escalation of variety and distraction as the quintessential commodity of the new century. Subtract the hyperbole of the lampoon of Hearst as a figure, and what remains is a description of the new mass culture, paradigmatically conveyed through the Sunday paper across the entirety of the United States and beyond.

"THE CHILDREN CRY FOR IT":
SUNDAY FUNNIES EVERYWHERE

William R. Hearst was far from the only supplier of the new material for the syndicated funny pages. Indeed, the *New York Herald* expanded its syndicate in 1903 after it began publishing one of the most popular new characters, R. F. Outcault's latest creation, "Buster Brown." Aside from the *Herald*, however, the main opponents to Hearst's early dominance were not the closest competitors of his own metropolitan newspapers. The in-house comics of competing newspapers in San Francisco, Chicago, and Boston were not syndicated. Even in New York, Joseph Pulitzer's Press Publishing did not begin to syndicate its *New York World* comics widely until 1904. Instead, Philadelphia provided the first metropolitan Sunday paper to give Hearst real competition by syndicating its color comic supplement as a package.

The *Philadelphia North American* had never issued a Sunday edition before 1901, but it launched full steam ahead with its new color presses at the end of September 1901. The turn to color supplements in a Sunday edition was an effort to mark the *North American* as the modern vanguard among Philadelphia papers. Walt McDougall was now the paper's cartoonist; years had passed since he had been the star illustrator at the *New York World*, and it had been even longer since he'd drawn the illustrations for Bill Nye's column. He had drawn some of the first newspaper cartoons ever printed in color, and now he was charged with creating a new syndicated comic supplement from scratch.

For the *North American*, McDougall drew a weekly full-page comic—sometimes a full-page panel, sometimes multipaneled—and he also introduced a new continuing strip, *Fatty Felix and the Flipp Boys*. Other illustrators contributed new strips too: Frank Crane's *Muggsy* and *Willie Westinghouse*, and Jean Mohr's *Sallie Slick*. The new comic supplement quickly replaced Hearst comics in both the *Boston Post* and the *Denver Post* and were added to the *Chicago Record-Herald*'s in-house strips. The *North American* comics were soon syndicated to newspapers in Cleveland, New Orleans, and Baltimore, as well as papers in decidedly smaller markets such as the *Richmond Times* and the *Salt Lake Herald*. While the comic characters in the *North American* syndicated supplement are now forgotten by all but the collector of classic comics, at the time its characters were popular on a national scale, if on a second tier. Another new syndicated comic supplement was named after T. C. McClure, at the time heading the long-established syndicate company his brother founded.[18] The McClure syndicate began its own color comic supplement in April 1901, anchored by its inclusion in the *New York Press* (see fig. 27). Before long it was a supplement to Sunday papers like the *Cleveland Leader*, the *Baltimore Herald*, and the *Philadelphia Press*. Regional papers such as the *Augusta Chronicle* in Georgia latched on to it, boasting that its new comic supplement had caused a stir up along the railway line through South and North Carolina: "The Most Talked About Things in Three States . . . The Children Cry for It."[19] In distant Hawaii it was a point of pride that syndication's national features connected the geographic periphery to the metropolis. In response to the *Honolulu Hawaiian Star*'s launching color comics, the competing *Honolulu Bulletin* announced it had "completed arrangements with the McClure Newspaper

FIGURE 27. "Great Prize Picture Puzzle" and "Little Bobby Bleecker," *New York Press*,
April 28, 1901, T. C. McClure syndicated color comics.

Syndicate of New York for the publication of their colored comic supplement . . .
similar to that supplied by McClures to the leading metropolitan dailies of the
mainland and is certain to make a hit with the Honolulu public."[20]

Even new and less familiar comic strip characters were announced in the brightest of showman's puffery, as if a circus were coming to town: "Boys and Girls!
Did you know that Billy Bounce was coming to Colorado Springs? And Professor Hypnotizer? And Smiling Simon? And the Teasers, Bobby and Marjorie?
. . . The illustrations will all be printed in colors and will present one of the jol-
liest comic supplements that can be found anywhere" (see plate 12).[21] McClure
copyrighted its individual comic strips weekly and in 1903 added a second set
of comics under the copyrighted imprimatur of editor C. J. Hirt. To exploit the
popularity of its color comics, McClure even issued its comic supplement on its
own as a newsstand or home delivery item, with no need to also buy the local
newspaper's weekend edition. *Our Weekly Magazine* began with some bang in
May 1904, advertising prominently throughout the Midwest seeking to hire one

thousand boys to sell subscriptions and deliver the adventures of its characters: "Billy Bounce, Simon Simple, and all the funny fellows with the most beautiful color work ever printed. Write for particulars and clubbing terms. The McClure Newspaper Syndicate. 116 Nassau St., New York."[22]

There was even a third-tier comic supplement, offering preprinted pages to papers in small cities and towns. In later decades World Color Printing became the largest publisher of comic books, but it began as a marginal player in the fledgling business of newspaper comics. The St. Louis company grew out of producing the color comics for the *St. Louis Star*, which dated back to Christmas 1896 as part of its color section, but it had grown gradually more distinct in form. Even after these *St. Louis Star* comics became syndicated in 1901, they were never copyrighted. In any case, they so lacked popular impact that they probably never risked being copied. Purchasing World Color's "patent outside" supplement—with a local nameplate stamped on the front—allowed even small-circulation newspapers in cities well off the beaten path to claim that they were providing their readers a slice of twentieth-century fun. The *Evansville Courier* in Indiana began the new feature in March 1901, introduced as a "metropolitan" item that signified how the paper (and, by extension, its readers) was "always in advance, always abreast of the times. You are not up-to-date unless you take *The Courier*."[23] In Fort Wayne, Indiana, the World Color comics promised to be the "equal of any issued anywhere in the country. This is done at considerable expense, but it won't cost the readers of *The Journal-Gazette* any more, and it will add greatly to their pleasure and entertainment."[24] A paper in Rockford, Illinois, boasted that its World Color supplement provided color comics not found in any Chicago paper: "*The Register-Gazette* will be in the swim with one of the best from now on."[25] The strips in these funny pages included such long-forgotten, arguably forgettable, titles as *Billy the Bell Boy*, *Bug McNutt*, and *Truthful Thomas*. Given the absence of any truly popular comic strips—no *Buster Brown*, no *Katzenjammer Kids*, no *Foxy Grandpa*—the point was providing the form of a color comic sheet as a marker of an "up-to-date" Sunday paper that would keep a small city and its reading public "in the swim" with a distinctly twentieth-century, distinctly American art form.

As with other commercial pastimes, especially those aimed at children, there was a moralistic backlash against the comic supplement. As early as 1904, civil and educational associations began to call on parents to spurn comic sections. Magazines were quick to espouse these arguments, noting how Sunday paper cartoons "are not art nor even decent caricature, but a low order of horseplay fitted to the barroom rather than the family circle. . . . It teaches the language and manners of the slums, and it begets a flippancy of mind."[26] Even some newspaper editors climbed aboard the bandwagon to cast aside the growing influence of comic supplements. An editorial in small-town Ohio asked about big-city Sunday newspapers: "Why is it necessary that it be wrapped in a 'supplement' of rainbow colors, covered with atrocious drawings and filled with labored efforts—seldom successful—to be funny?"[27] In an exceptional move, the *Boston Herald* stopped including color comics in October 1908, announced boldly as judgment of the passing fad: "We discard it as we would throw aside any mechanism that had reached the end of its usefulness, or any 'feature' that had ceased to fulfill the purpose of attraction. Comic supplements have ceased to be comic. They have become as vulgar in design as they are tawdry in color."[28] In another example, when the *Washington Herald* introduced a new Sunday paper to the nation's capital in 1906, its niche was a simple "compact" edition without supplements that would "appeal to the intelligent and discriminating clientele of Washington. . . . It will have no freak features. It will not be made simply to catch the eye."[29] The back-to-basics promise became its logo—no color, no comic—presented as a new approach to journalism. Lacking funny pages as a mark of distinction lasted only until February 1911, when a cartoon section began and the mandate of "no color, no comic" was abandoned. The effort to distinguish the *Washington Herald* by having no special supplements was in fact abandoned earlier, when a syndicated magazine, the *Literary Magazine Section*, was included along with the Sunday edition.

NATIONAL ADVERTISING AND NEWSPAPER MAGAZINES

Despite the new attraction of color comics, the popularity of the Sunday paper had primarily been due to its leisure-reading features, dating back to the 1880s when syndicated serial fiction or humor columns would fill the additional few supplementary pages. Already by the mid-1890s—even before color and magazine inserts—the feature section (or "supplement" in its original sense) began to multiply and eventually dwarf the Sunday news section. In the 1900s, with comic strips fully standardized, the same logic was applied to syndicated magazines, appearing in every metropolitan region simultaneously under a network of mastheads. When the *Seattle Times* struck a deal to run new syndicated features, the details of the contract negotiations were divulged like a treaty resulting from skilled diplomacy: "Mr. C. B. Blethen, managing editor . . . has been in New York for some days purchasing features for *The Sunday Times* for 1905 and the acquisition of 'Buster Brown' is considered by him to be one of the most important changes. . . . Each week will also see the publication of some of the most brilliant short stories yet produced by any American Sunday magazine."[30] In addition to popular comics, Blethen had arranged for syndicated magazine features. Unlike early comic supplements, magazine inserts included advertising, and a national magazine supplement could thus include national ads for mass-marketed products.

Before exploring the emergence of syndicated magazines, it's worth underscoring the centrality of national advertising in their logic. A syndicated magazine distributed with the Sunday editions of a dozen or more newspapers across the United States could instantly and simultaneously provide a circulation of over a million copies (some claimed over four million) at a time when the circulations of even the most popular magazines were less than half a million copies. Collective magazine supplements allowed networks of powerful major newspapers to formally pool their circulations and deal cooperatively with advertisers through a single contract. By the 1920s national advertising contracts were so crucial that a cabal of newspaper publishers was created that simply provided syndicated advertising through its network of newspapers, entirely jettisoning the production of a national magazine as a container for the ads.

National Newspapers Incorporated was created in January 1922, initially as a network of seventeen newspapers as charter members.[31] The first executive group included representatives from the *New York World*, the *Chicago Tribune*, the *Detroit News*, and the *Pittsburg Post*, and the first president was Col. C. B. Blethen of the *Seattle Times*—the very same publisher who had so proudly boasted of securing syndicated comics and magazine features for his progressive newspaper. National Newspapers took out full-page advertisements in its member publications, explaining in detail, and in big type, the service it was offering. Four members were added after the inaugural meeting, bringing the collective up to "twenty-one publishers of twenty-one great Sunday newspapers . . . one of the greatest selling forces ever known in business. . . . For the first time, the National Advertiser has brought to him through the Sunday Magazine Sections of these twenty-one newspapers a great National Newspaper force as one single unit extending over the entire United States—4,600,000 unduplicated Sunday Newspaper circulation."[32]

It is remarkable how the constituent newspapers were, by and large, those that continued to dominate their regional markets for the rest of the twentieth century: the *Cincinnati Enquirer*, *Philadelphia Inquirer*, *San Francisco Chronicle*, and *Cleveland Plain Dealer*, in addition to those mentioned above as represented on the first executive group. Further, many of the members were those who had earlier adopted Hearst color comic supplements as a self-proclaimed progressive move, such as the *Fort Worth Telegram* (now *Star-Telegram*) and the *Atlanta Constitution*. The irony is that as an advertising syndicate, National Newspapers had the growing Hearst chain of newspapers as its primary commercial rival for providing national advertising coast-to-coast through a single contract. After the twin launch of the *Los Angeles Examiner* late in 1903 and the *Boston American* early in 1904, Hearst's chain had remained steady for nearly a decade, with morning and evening editions published in just five cities, represented late in 1906 as five fingers curled into a powerful fist in advertising for "the natural market for your goods" with their combined Sunday circulation of just over two million copies.[33] In the decade between 1912 and 1922, however, Hearst had expanded swiftly into five more markets by purchasing and developing existing newspapers in Atlanta (the *Georgian*, added to the chain in 1912), Washington and Milwaukee (the *Times* and the *News*, respectively, added in 1919), and Detroit (the *Times*, added late in 1921). And yet newspaper chains were not the originators of coordinated, syndicated advertising. The circulatory ad-buying power of networks of newspapers had initially focused on high-quality, fine-paper Sunday magazines syndicated among a network of independent papers rather than across a formal chain.

As with color comic supplements, the first magazine inserts to be distributed in multiple newspapers simultaneously were the "American Magazine" sections of Hearst papers. The title "American Magazine" was first given to the illustrated feature section of the *New York Journal* in October 1896, just weeks before the introduction of the "American Humorist" with the Yellow Kid's new locale at McFadden's Flats. From its start in 1900, this magazine section was part of Hearst's *Chicago Sunday American*. It was soon added to the *San Francisco Examiner* and then other papers as they became part of the chain. In the early years of the new century, this magazine was printed on broadsheet newsprint, just like the color comics and the "American Women's Weekly" section. This enhanced a trend of calling illustrated feature sections of Sunday newspapers "magazine supplements," as in the *New York World* late in 1895 and the *Philadelphia Inquirer* early in 1896.

A high-quality halftoned, stapled "true" magazine insert was an expensive alternative, used by high-class establishment newspapers to distance themselves from the tainted tints of lurid color comic supplements. Under its new publisher Adolph Ochs, the *New York Times'* created a *Sunday Magazine* supplement in September 1896 as a high-class tabloid-size publication with halftone photography on glossy quality paper stock. The paper's new motto "All the News That's Fit to Print" was actually introduced on billboards and spot ads promoting the magazine supplement before the phrase became a fixture on the front page. The price of the *Sunday Times* was the same five cents as its "cheap" competition, but its supplements were "true" magazines in form as well as content: "printed upon fine book paper of such quality as to permit the use of half-tone photographic illustrations and portraits . . . as will, *The Times* hopes, commend it to intelligent readers."[34] Within a month, the famous *New York Times* "Book Review" (initially "Review of Books and Art") was launched as a supplement to the Saturday edition—a cultural review of the highest aspiration at a bargain price of just one cent. (The book review section did not join the Sunday edition until January 1911.) All classes—of readers and of papers—were provided a Sunday supplement, but the high-class version was a proper magazine instead of color comics.

The six-day *New York Mail and Express* called its weekend supplement an "illustrated magazine" in 1897; readers were instructed not to accept the Saturday paper without the magazine and vice versa. As noted in chapter 5, the *New York Tribune* introduced a magazine-format "Illustrated Supplement" of highest-quality printing and halftoned photography in May 1897, after being excoriated for its brief dabbling with a color comic supplement inherited from the defunct *New York Recorder*. At the end of the year, the *Los Angeles Times* launched "something unique in newspapers." The new magazine section was printed on a recently installed new printing press, the Columbia II, which could print tabloid-size magazines "bound with wire staples, folded to page size, counted in parcels and delivered at a running speed of 24,000 per hour."[35] Another example came on New Year's Day 1898 when the *Boston Journal* launched its own Sunday supplement, giving it a moniker of its own: "*The New England Home Magazine*: It is an Entirely New Feature. It is a Complete Magazine. It is a Bound Volume. It is Very Fully Illustrated. It is as Good as Any Monthly. It is a Sunday Necessity."[36]

Despite the distinct contrast with comic supplements in cultural tone and material form, the purpose of a magazine insert was nevertheless to boost circulation and, inseparable from that pursuit, to provide the reading public with a weekly sample of popular culture. A few years later, the idea of a high-class magazine supplement was standardized on a national scale through syndication. When the *Philadelphia North American* began publishing its first Sunday paper in 1901, it issued its own color magazine on broadsheet pages with illustrated features. A decade later, when the *Baltimore Sun* greatly expanded its Sunday edition for New Year's Day 1911, rather than its own magazine, it included a twenty-page syndicated supplement, mentioned by name: *Associated Sunday Magazines*.

ASSOCIATED, ILLUSTRATED NATIONAL SUNDAY MAGAZINES

Begun late in 1903, *Associated Sunday Magazines* was the first and paradigmatic specimen of the form. Together with the *Chicago Record-Herald*, the *St. Louis Republic*, the *Philadelphia Press*, and the *Pittsburg Post*, it was a venture of Joseph P. Knapp's American Lithographic Company. All papers agreed to distribute the exact same general magazine in their Sunday editions; only the hometown nameplate changed from one paper to another. Knapp was, in fact, well familiar with lithographed color supplements in Sunday newspapers and intimately knew the affordances of the form for creating increased circulation and popularity. As discussed in chapter 1, he was a key partner in creating the *New York Recorder*, in particular its giveaways of color lithograph prints in each *Sunday Recorder*. In a sense, the lithographed art supplements of the 1890s were a precedent for the quality magazine supplements of the new century, and Knapp's company originated a syndicated version. By 1910 there were several other syndicated Sunday magazines competing against Knapp's on a weekly, semimonthly, or monthly basis for newspapers in cities of all sizes.

In this one aspect of the typical elements of a Sunday paper, Hearst was actually last to capitulate to the trend. His five-fingered fisted chain of multicolored journals did not include a stapled, high-quality "true" magazine until the *American Monthly Magazine* was launched in October 1911, years after other dozens of Sunday papers introduced one of several glossy magazine inserts: the *Illustrated Sunday Magazine*, the *Literary Magazine Section*, the *National Monthly Magazine*, or the long-dominant *Associated Sunday Magazines*. The typical cover design for all of them was an utterly conventional profile or portrait of a fashionable, beautiful woman—a "Gibson Girl"—although there were dozens of artists churning out these pictures weekly. Even today, the newspaper magazines of this period are collected primarily for these female portrait covers (see plate 13).

Associated Sunday Magazines promoted itself to prospective advertisers in a remarkable series of advertisements in newspapers across the country from June to August 1907. Each of the eleven ads offered what they called a "kernel" of wisdom about the mass market and the logic of national syndication. One of the kernels explained how its newspapers' eight metropolitan markets included almost 90 percent of the American population (see fig. 28). Collectively, the kernels made the case that a syndicated newspaper magazine was the best choice for national advertising because it provided a readership that was larger and more committed than any single newspaper or magazine, placed within a product that was better than any single newspaper or magazine. In "editorial strength," the *Associated Sunday Magazines* showed an "application of the modern idea of co-operation to publishing."[37] Quality printing extended to its audience, since "the reader of a daily newspaper may or may not be a subscriber to independent weekly and monthly magazines, while everyone who reads the latter will never be without his Sunday paper."[38] Another kernel claimed that more than 80 percent of copies of *Associated Sunday Magazines* were delivered straight to the home by subscription, a figure no magazine of comparable circulation could claim, as they primarily relied on newsstands. Yet another explained how every copy was delivered to a home within easy traveling distance of a major city's shopping district, thus eliminating the magazine problem of "waste circulation" to small towns, rural readerships, and regions outside the densely-populated Northeast and Midwest.[39] Finally, a marketing survey of eight thousand subscribers verified how nearly all of the magazines were read thoroughly and kept in the home long afterward. Half reported they kept the magazine supplements permanently; another 39 percent kept it until it was entirely read through.

All of these kernel advantages allowed *Associated Sunday Magazines* to offer a lower advertising rate of just $0.60 for 224 agate lines, or a page per thousand circulation—significantly lower than $0.75 for the *Saturday Evening Post,* the *Ladies' Home Journal* at $0.93, and less than half the cost of advertising in *Harper's* at $1.28. One thing no kernel mentioned is how little newspaper magazines helped increase

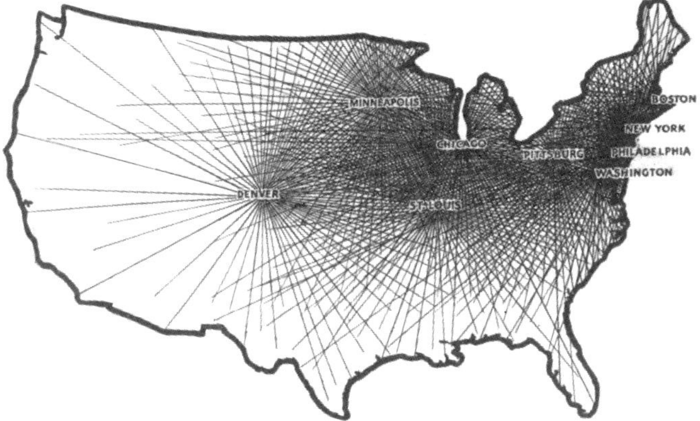

FIGURE 28. Syndicated distribution of *Associated Sunday Magazines.*
"The Area of Concentration," *Everybody's Magazine*, March 1907, 77.

circulation for the papers that adopted them—a crucial difference from comic
supplements. Shortly after the *Minneapolis Journal* adopted it late in 1905, an ad
promoted how the *Associated Sunday Magazines'* total circulation had soared past
the 1.1 million mark in circulation, but the figure remained at that plateau until
1910 when several more newspapers were added to the roster.

Perhaps the motivation behind the "Kernels" national ad campaign was to
counteract a politically tricky situation. In February 1907, just months before

the campaign, the U.S. Postal Commission had begun efforts to regulate and prevent including such newspaper inserts, at least in subscription copies sent by mail. Several proposals were under consideration to redefine newspapers, which would result in reclassifying a modern Sunday paper as requiring parcel post rates, losing its second-class mail subsidy. If an object were to be considered a "newspaper," only half the space could be used for advertising or literary matter, and there could be no pieces or sections of card, cloth, or any substance other than paper, nor paper of greater weight than the rest of the publication.[40] Advertising had to be "germane to the regular issue and supplied in order to complete matter left incomplete in the main body of the publication."[41] The commission also claimed that literary fiction was an "unhealthy exaggeration of the modern newspaper" because "although periodical in its form, [it] has no true periodicity in its essence."[42] Indeed, the commission wrote a wholesale attack on the Sunday paper as a source of leisure: "The newspaper is rapidly being extended into the magazine field at the sacrifice both of the postal revenue and the true mission of the newspaper. . . . You would have no longer one publication, a newspaper, but you have a newspaper plus a weekly magazine."[43] For over a decade already, Sunday newspapers themselves had made the same claim as precisely their appeal and attraction. Of course, there was a distinctly Sabbatarian effort underneath the legislative discourse, as the comic strips and magazines of Sunday editions were described as "muddling the minds with the conglomeration of sensationalism and literary trash."[44] Newspaper publishers struck back hard within their own editorials and news columns, not only proclaiming the postal commission's efforts a form of press censorship but also naming the real problem to be the graft influence of the railroad subsidy rather than the second-class mail subsidy.[45] The threat of censorship mixed with hints of political corruption meant nothing came of the issue at this time.

Rotogravures and Syndicated Photos

In 1907 these concerns about wasteful supplements were linked explicitly to the specific conditions that allowed preprinted syndicated magazines and supplements to flow across the country—a media network atop the railway and postal networks that had long enabled commercial theater and vaudeville, magazines and books, branded consumer goods, and passengers themselves to cohere into a continental mass market. Although syndicated magazines continued for the remainder of the twentieth century—*Parade* and *This Week* are long-running titles from more recent decades—the first several introduced between 1903 and 1910 were more or less defunct by the end of the First World War, due partly to increased wartime prices and shortages of paper. Their wasteful character was, ironically, the source of their decline but in purely material and economic terms rather than sparked by moralistic legislation.

Another reason for their passing was a new trend in Sunday supplements that began late in 1913—the rotogravure, or "photogravure," a high-quality photographic section. Early intaglio sections were first introduced by distinctly highbrow papers, which had denigrated the vulgar daubs of color in the comic supplement, among other cries against lowbrow Sunday papers. The *New York Sun* began perhaps the first intaglio section in October 1913, followed in 1914 by the *Philadelphia Public Ledger* in January, the *Boston Herald* in March, and the *New York Times* in April (increasing the space and quality of its "pictorial" halftoned section, begun in 1905). The content of most rotogravure sections was edited at each individual newspaper's offices, but their selection of photographs was remarkably similar: "a pictorial presentation of world events, the newest war pictures, people in the limelight and prominent movie stars,"[46] or "new fashion models—new society pictures—new pictures of the movie stars."[47] As a result, specialty publishers soon introduced syndicated rotogravure supplements. In 1917 the "Rotogravure Section of the Picture Press" was used by the *Washington Post* and the *Cincinnati Enquirer* but was also included in the *Albert Lea Tribune* in Minnesota and the *Cobb County Times* in Marietta, Georgia, among other small-city and even small-town papers.

To be sure, syndicated rotogravures were rare, and one result of that rarity is the absence of national-brand advertising in the turn to pictorial news sections. Enter Hearst, atypically late to the rotogravure game but in a position to offer something novel—a halftoned newswire service that was, effectively, a photo syndicate. By this point during the First World War, the Hearst media empire had now vastly diversified into magazine publishing, and the *Hearst-Pathé Weekly* newsreel was a key player in the new moving-picture news service (discussed in chapter 3). Hearst International News Service was a key factor in the global circulation of timely news photography, which was especially important and profitable during the war years. Indeed, most of the rotogravure sections had been publishing photographs supplied on a weekly basis by the International News Service for years, before Hearst newspapers began including their own *Pictorial Gravure* section. Launched in March 1918, the "Newspaper Without Words" gave the Hearst chain an opportunity to address advertisers nationally, exhorting them to tap into the new technique for addressing readers: "We have become a nation of photo gazers—reading the lurid story from week to week in the photographic reproductions of the news. . . . You, big national advertisers have been barred from this most effective form of advertising because it gave you small circulations only. The Hearst newspapers have put the multiplication table to the pictorial gravure section."[48] Hearst's address to the public was no less bombastic. In Chicago, for example, the great pictorial news supplement was announced as "the latest addition to the great Super-Sunday *Chicago Examiner.* . . . Remember, these are not the ordinary newspaper pictures; the new photogravure process lays every minute detail before you on the paper—nothing is lost."[49] It was hardly the first venture joining Sunday newspapers and pictures, as the world of moving pictures had already become a central feature each week. But the phrase "We have become a nation of photo gazers" augured further transfigurations to come.

FILM SERIALS AND MOVIE COLUMNISTS

Between 1910 and 1914, the American film industry found its footing as a big business, and moviegoing became a new pastime in its own right. Rather than remaining on the periphery of society, in fairgrounds, arcades, and summer amusement parks, the film industry now had a place of its own in the center of modern life: the movie theater. To achieve its mass public of viewers, the film industry forged key partnerships with newspapers and became an especially prominent and enduring part of the Sunday paper. One key part of becoming institutionalized as "Hollywood" was that the film industry's distribution branch took charge of nationally coordinated publicity and advertising, relying especially on syndicated material in Sunday papers continent-wide.

The culmination of the process was a craze for serial films that began early in 1914 with *The Adventures of Kathlyn*. Each episode on-screen or installment in the paper ended with a suspenseful cliff-hanger—sometimes literally—resolved with next Sunday's installments. Serial film stories in print were accompanied by lists of where to see each episode, charted out on a regional scale, from the downtown metropolitan first run of each episode to small-town or neighborhood theaters showing an episode ten or more weeks behind the city center's movie palace. Sunday newspaper ads and directories displayed the film industry's twist on the logic of syndication: you could pay more and get it immediately in a metropolitan downtown movie palace, and those on the periphery or without the time or means would eventually be included—but later, in a more marginal location, at a lower price. Serial films used newspapers to teach the mass public how to go to the movies, to inform them that "everybody" was going to the movies—eventually, somewhere—encompassing all classes of readers under the umbrella of the newspaper's leisure readership on Sundays. And newspapers, in turn, solidified and expanded their logic of syndication to now take stewardship for the new form of mass entertainment.

One early connection between newspapers and moving pictures drew upon the great popularity of the comic strip form. In November 1911 in the *Chicago Sunday Tribune*, moving picture stories were depicted in pictorial form using photographs from a series of scenes to tell the film's story, laid out in sequence like a comic strip. The *Tribune*'s moving picture stories were a direct collaboration with Chicago-based studios: Selig Polyscope Co., Essanay Film Manufacturing Co., and American Film Manufacturing Co. rotated through the weekly feature. The

Boston Traveler ran a similar but more modest version for several months early in 1912, drawing upon East Coast studios such as Kalem Co. and Edison Manufacturing Co. Of the Chicago studios that had worked with the *Tribune*, American Film syndicated its pictorialized film stories for several months in 1912 in more than seventy-five newspapers spanning the continent, including a few in metropolitan areas, such as the *San Francisco Call* and the *Pittsburg Press*. Despite being only sporadically successful and short-lived, the wide circulation of American Film's syndicated version hinted at the proliferation of film publicity features to come in 1913 with the serial film and its syndicated stories, and it was prescient of the great possibilities that would be realized in that different genre and form.

Responding to the growing importance of cinema, the Scripps-McRae League of newspapers supplied a regular column bannered "The Movies," written by Gertrude M. Price, beginning in November 1912. Many of these papers were published in decidedly second-tier cities, such as the *Des Moines News* and the *Wilkes-Barre Times Leader*, although the feature did run in its tabloid "adless" newspaper, the *Chicago Day Book*.[50] Each of the papers introduced Price to local readers as "a member of our staff" in identical ads, simply inserting its own publication name: "*The Daily News*" (or the *Times Leader* or the *Day Book*, as the case may be), "recognizing 'the movies' as the biggest, most popular amusement in the world, will tell you all about it from every angle."[51] Price's expertise provided newspaper readers, who were also moviegoers, with the knowledge they needed to become *expert* moviegoers, skilled enthusiasts: "Read the first 'movie' story in today's paper—and keep your eyes open right along for the appearance of Your Favorites."[52] The call to read about the movies *first* in the paper before going to see them would be the central trope of metropolitan newspapers' embrace of the film industry. Another such page of syndicated movie material was likewise designed for weekend newspapers in smaller markets. The Syndicated Publishing Company had been providing smaller newspapers with premium prizes and giveaways such as souvenir books and almanacs. In February 1913 the company began issuing a stereotyped illustrated feature page titled "News of the Photoplays and Photoplayers" for Saturday and Sunday editions of small-market newspapers such as the *Milwaukee Sentinel* in Wisconsin, the *San Antonio Light* in Texas, and *The State* in Columbia, South Carolina, among many others.

After seeing the fantastic escalation of moving picture publicity in newspapers throughout 1913, film studios themselves began to devise direct collaborations with newspapers on a continental scale. Mutual Film Corporation purchased a series of newspaper ads late in 1913 featuring a winged clock and the company's slogan, "Mutual Movies Make Time Fly." The ads were arranged locally by Mutual's local film exchanges so that each display contained regionally specific directories of movie theaters showing its films. The campaign was widely heralded within the film trade press as a reason for local showmen to switch to Mutual's film service. The necessity of such regional fine-tuning meant the ads appeared only in select cities, but these included New York in the *Sunday World* and Chicago in the Sunday *Tribune*, as well as other cities in the Midwest.

The Mutual ads were immediately followed by the serial film phenomenon. Perhaps best known for Hearst newspapers' collaboration with Pathé Frères subsidiary Eclectic Film Co.'s *Perils of Pauline*, but the serial craze had actually begun with the syndication of Selig Polyscope Co.'s *Adventures of Kathlyn* in a wide swath of newspapers across North America: the *Chicago Tribune, New York Sun*, and dozens of others in smaller markets.[53] Ads supporting the serial film stories routinely listed where to see which episode across the entire metropolitan region of the newspaper. With *Kathlyn's* serial film promoted concurrently with syndicated stories of each episode, other film studios followed just a few months behind. Pathé worked exclusively with Hearst newspapers as a chain to bring *The Perils of Pauline* to both page and screen in March. Universal had its serial *Lucille Love: The Girl of Mystery* in print and on screen in April, widely syndicated by McClure's to the *Chicago Record-Herald* and dozens of other Sunday papers, sometimes cut down into six smaller daily pieces for newspapers without a Sunday edition. These three collaborations had already begun two or three serial stories each by the end of 1914. Hardly any metropolitan newspaper on the continent remained on the sidelines for the serial film craze in its first few faddish years.

Daily Stories about Moving Pictures

The "serial queen" stories had such a lasting impact and high profile that it is routinely overlooked that Pathé's venture with Hearst, and Universal's with McClure's, had actually begun slightly earlier, in the somewhat different form of a *daily* moving picture story—a twist that prompted the *Chicago Tribune* to quickly react to introduce its own movie stories first by a few days. These daily movie stories began with a bang early in February 1914, exactly one month after the first installment of *The Adventures of Kathlyn*. First, the *Chicago Record-Herald* published a full-page announcement of its novel collaboration with Universal and McClure's: "Read the story in the morning. See it in moving pictures at night. . . . The biggest deal in the history of moving pictures to amuse, entertain and educate Chicago."[54] Acting fast to imitate and start earlier, the *Tribune's* twist was independent judgment, having a journalist choose "Today's *Best* Moving Picture Story" and write a critical synopsis instead of reproducing film studio copy: "To more than half [a] million Chicagoans moving picture plays present the drama of daily life," but again, "the story may be read in the morning. The picture may be seen in the afternoon or at night."[55] The *Tribune's* daily film story continued for months, and in July the reviewer was given a byline, Kitty Kelly. In the meantime, yet another imitator sprang to life, as Hearst and Pathé Films began a direct copy of the idea throughout its newspaper chain: "Read the Story Here—See it in the

Moving Pictures Tonight.... The story may be seen at the moving picture theatres transformed into photoplays by the famous Pathé players."[56]

Within three days of each other, there were now three different versions of daily moving picture stories running in Chicago, with syndication already begun across the country. Within a month, the *Tribune's* independent daily stories were running, for example, in the *Cleveland Leader* and the *Philadelphia Telegraph*; the Pathé stories across the Hearst chain; and the *Record-Herald's* collaboration with Universal had been distributed by the McClure syndicate to at least eight other major newspapers, including the *New York Globe and Commercial Advertiser*, the *Detroit Free Press*, and the *Atlanta Journal*.[57] The connection between seeing movies that one first read about in the paper had been explicitly part of the earlier weekly Sunday pages in various city newspapers since 1911, as well as Gertrude Price's columns for Scripps-McRae and such experiments as American Film's syndicated pictorial versions of its films since 1912. Now, early in 1914, with the well-known serial film craze and the lesser-known daily film story, the instruction to "Read it in the Morning, and See it in the Evening" had become an everyday message across the entire continent.

The rivalry in Chicago escalated another step with the introduction in March 1914 of color Sunday magazine pages devoted to moving pictures and their celebrity players. The *Tribune* announced this feature a week in advance for the benefit of its Sunday-only regional subscribers: "Right Off the Reel! . . . It will be different. It will be dignified. It will abound in color and pictures, humor and romance. . . . This department will be entitled Film and Screen. It will take you into its confidence, ask your wishes about what you want to read and see in it, and give you any and all information you desire concerning moving pictures and their people."[58] The first "Film and Screen" page in the *Tribune's* halftone magazine section featured a portrait in color of Kathlyn Williams, the star of *The Adventures of Kathlyn*, within a filigreed "Frame of Public Favor."[59] Readers could clip out vouchers to nominate those movie stars they wanted to see inside the frame in future Sunday pages. The *Record-Herald* simultaneously began its Sunday page "Reel Drama," and Hearst's *Chicago Examiner* ran a page called "The Motion Pictures" until its serial story *The Perils of Pauline* began the following week. Similar pages began even in many of the highbrow establishment newspapers across the country. Many were already running serial film story tie-ins or were about to embark on the fad.

The newspaper movie directory also became a tool for organizing leisure time—a tool transformed into a technology of great efficiency for its ability to chart an amusement "menu" of the selections available across the entire city that could be sampled and selected without requiring the time of travel: "*The Tribune* places before you an exceedingly appetizing motion picture menu every day in the week—a menu that gives you the widest possible range of choice, with something in it to suit every fancy and every mood."[60] The "menu" motif, as Richard Abel has thoroughly documented, displaced the product of movie-mad culture with the preference of consumer choice, making it a matter of taste rather than appetite.[61] "Which photo-play today," asked the *Chicago Tribune*, explaining how "people of taste and ideas, with likes and dislikes, no longer wander down the street and take their entertainment from the first movie [marquee] they see. They want to know *beforehand* who the leading player is. . . . Get the habit of consulting *The Tribune's* Motion Picture Directory every day and see the best there is."[62] The point was that the newspaper could offer anticipation and excitement to replace the effort and uncertainty of inquiring about what was available to see tonight. The simple act of listing the movie directory of showtimes, unlike the theater and music listings that predated them, was in continuity with newspapers' own fascination with technologically-driven communication, as we discussed in chapter 3. The movies were a halfway point between the embodied theatrical performance of the nineteenth century and the mediated broadcast transmissions of the twentieth century that were not quite yet at hand:

> Where is that Star to-night? Actual stars have a fixed place in the heavens, and few people care where they are. . . . But with stars of the motion picture play . . . among the marvels of this new dramatic art that the genius of the player is freed from the trammels of space and time. The "movie" star is visible at one and the same time in different theaters and on both sides of the globe. The "movie" star that is thrilling an audience to-day may thrill another long after his (terrestrial) light is extinguished.[63]

As we noted above, movie star photographs were as central to rotogravures as war photographs from the battlefields and training camps of the First World War. By 1914 the public of film fans couldn't get enough pictures of its movie stars, and the rotogravure supplement was happy to oblige. The *Milwaukee Sentinel*, for example, offered a poster of Theda Bara: "8 by 11 inches in size, loose in the folds of an inside section. . . . You can frame them and have a gallery of beautiful young women of the screen."[64] In May 1917 the *Chicago Tribune* turned to movie stars as an anchor for its rotogravure section, where one full-page photograph of Charlie Chaplin filled the back page of the supplement, doubling as a poster. Movie star photos were such a fixture of the rotogravure that a syndicated movie fan supplement, *Motion Play Magazine*, was created in 1920 by the Alco Gravure Company, partnering with distributors National Gravure Circuit Inc. As its name indicates, "A. L. Co." Gravure was yet another outgrowth of the American Lithographic Company, which was never too far off stage. The venture followed its forays into art supplements and magazine sections, as discussed in earlier chapters. This specific division was headed by G. H. Buek, who had pioneered cutout paper doll supplements back in 1895. Alco Gravure was the printer of magazines such as *Woman's Home Companion* and the rotogravure section of the *Baltimore Sun* when it began in 1917. *Motion Play Magazine* was one of many magazines for movie fans, but this one was unique by virtue of being a newspaper supplement distributed free with such Sunday papers as the *Washington Herald* and the *Philadelphia Record*, along with a half dozen others. While relatively short-lived (it was defunct by 1922), the movie rotogravure magazine supplement provided a spotlight on the previous decade's special intermedial relation between the Sunday paper and the movies. In 1922, on the other hand, broadcast wireless radio was just taking hold of the public to complement the silent pictures at the movies. A new partnership with the Sunday paper was at hand and in the air.

THE SYNDICATED LOGIC OF BROADCASTING

Betty Crocker, the fictional home cooking instructor, began radio cooking shows in October 1924 on WCCO in Minneapolis. Later the local NBC network affiliate, the station had just received new call letters after being purchased by the Washburn Crosby Company, nationally famous for its Gold Medal brand of flour. By September 1925 triweekly Betty Crocker morning shows were broadcast on twelve stations in AT&T's New York WEAF hookup.[65] One writer joked that if "the menus of six million American families are identical, it will be because radio has added its force to the mass movement which is rapidly making this a syndicated nation."[66] While it was not accompanied by a syndicated newspaper column, the national launch of Betty Crocker's *Gold Medal Flour Home Service Talks* was framed in terms that conflated syndication, simultaneity, and standardized daily routines. As we noted in chapter 5, since the 1880s metropolitan newspapers had collectively delivered syndicated content to millions of Americans. By the 1910s the exact same Sunday magazines and funny pages were circulating to places where at least 90 percent of the population of the United States lived, directly into subscribers' homes on Sunday mornings. The syndicated age was under way.

Syndication's logic of corporate cooperation established a foundation for the synchronous broadcasts of network radio in the 1920s. With radio, the material limitations of newspaper circulation were finally entirely eclipsed. As we reviewed in chapter 3, news publishers had collaborated with new technologies to extend their journalistic reach; with radio, too, newspapers continued to play a key role. When broadcast licenses were first issued in 1921, only a small number of households owned amateur-built receiving sets to listen at home. Nevertheless, newspapers jumped aboard early with bannered radio pages and tabloid radio supplements. Early radio columns—especially Sunday feature pages and sections—advertised equipment and supplies and catered to early listeners, generally characterized as young and enthusiastic "fans."

Newspapers were also some of the first and most prominent radio broadcasters. By the end of 1922, less than a year into the era of licensed commercial radio broadcasting, twelve newspaper-owned stations had installed half of the first twenty-five powerful Western Electric transmitters, but not one of these was located near New York or the Northeast coast.[67] Not even the legacy players of the metropolitan Sunday supplement ventured into radio in the Northeast to compete directly against RCA and AT&T; Pulitzer's *St. Louis Post-Dispatch* began KSD in March 1922, and Hearst launched the *San Francisco Examiner*'s KUO and *Los Angeles Examiner*'s KWH in May 1922, but neither owned stations in New York.

Given a virtual clear channel to develop commercial broadcasting on their own terms, RCA and AT&T took up syndicated circulation as a proven paradigm but in the technological form of rebroadcasting by remote-controlled hookup. AT&T's New York station WEAF forged the way with an experimental hookup to Boston's WNAC early in January 1923, noted then as the first time two broadcast stations were controlled by one studio. "From a technical standpoint," the *Boston Globe* explained how the simultaneous broadcast was "a most delicate problem. Special filter circuits and repeater equipment, carefully adjusted and tested by a corps of engineers, are necessary to eliminate entirely all distortion from the wire circuits. The announcement of the New York Studio will be required to state that this program is being broadcasted through two radio stations."[68] Allow us to continue this brief detour reviewing early radio hookups before NBC was created in 1926. We will juxtapose this facet of radio history below when recounting a failed alternative based explicitly on newspaper syndication.

A hint of the formally networked future for radio came with the launch of a new Washington, D.C., station, WCAP, owned by the regional AT&T subsidiary. From its start, WCAP rebroadcast AT&T's New York WEAF programs.[69] The radio cooperation between telephone companies meant its very first broadcast "was received in Washington over the wires of the Bell system. . . . This, in effect, was to move WEAF to Washington by telephone."[70] In general, AT&T was barred from sublicensing or syndicating its New York–broadcast shows, but it could charge fees for the use of its telephone wire connections, so it devised the concept of "toll broadcasting," where stations could pay a fee for onetime or regular use of WEAF and Bell phone line connections. The first station to begin a toll broadcasting contract was WMAF, an experimental station in Massachusetts owned by radio pioneer Col. E.H.R. Green. Regular hookups to WEAF in New York began on July 1, 1923, with one of Samuel "Roxy" Rothafel's concert programs from the Capitol Theater on Broadway.[71] Green explained, "It is not easy to get the artists to come here and so to overcome this obstacle I made the New York arrangements so that we can get the program over the wires to this station."[72] The regular hookup of three stations along the Atlantic Coast was cast as a sign of AT&T's leadership in forging the future of radio, studying what pleased the listening public: "A special effort is being made to determine the preference of the radio audience with regard to programs."[73]

For variety and amusement, New York was already the center and origin of radio entertainment. The occasional political or newsworthy event demonstrated the value of being able to reverse the direction of the transmission, sending the odd but interesting program by telephone line back to New York. One such moment pushed AT&T to test an early coast-to-coast hookup, broadcasting a speech by President Warren G. Harding from San Francisco across the country. Set for the end of July 1923, the broadcast had to be canceled when Harding took ill and died, but plans widely anticipated how "the transcontinental lines of the Bell telephone system will carry the President's voice to six powerful broadcasting stations located in different sections of the country": WEAF; WMAF; WCAP; the *Chicago Daily News*'s station, WMAQ; as well as WOAW in Omaha and KPO in San Francisco (later co-owned by the *Chronicle*).[74] The idea was revived after Calvin Coolidge became president, when he addressed the nation from Congress in December 1923. This time, links across the Midwest and South came from stations owned by newspapers: the *St. Louis Post-Dispatch* (KSD), the *Kansas City Star* (WDAF) and the *Dallas News* (WFAA).[75] The importance of cooperation with newspaper-owned stations in extending the network idea across the continent is clear from their predominance outside the Northeast.

The network of stations subscribing to AT&T's toll broadcasts expanded throughout 1924 until the "telephone group" included up to twenty stations for special news events. By the spring of 1925, a dozen stations networked for a regular three-hour block of programs nightly.[76] Against AT&T's emerging toll network paradigm, RCA began an alternative hookup from its WJZ New York broadcasting station, using Western Union's telegraph lines to create a network of stations owned by Westinghouse and General Electric, both manufacturers of radio receivers and transmitters.[77] The "radio group" affiliated to RCA's WJZ, using its broadcasting facilities for free because RCA aimed "solely to stimulate consumer demand for its founders' products."[78] While AT&T charged fees for studio time, RCA offered it free of charge; long-distance telephone wires were better for simultaneous hookups than telegraph wires. Both networks were unprofitable, and this phase of competition lasted only a couple of years before all parties joined forces to create the National Broadcasting Corporation in 1926. Cooperation was already evident in earlier simultaneous broadcasts, such as President Coolidge's inauguration in March 1925, transmitted on stations in both the WEAF telephone group and in the WJZ radio group of stations, with moments of the broadcast offered to each network's announcers.[79] In the meantime, AT&T's WEAF network kept growing. In May 1925, radio links were extended permanently to Minneapolis–St. Paul, Kansas City, Atlanta, and Dallas–Fort Worth, now linking nineteen stations whose broadcasts could simultaneously cover the entire eastern half of the United States.[80]

MID-CONTINENT BROADCASTING ASSOCIATES

A short-lived alternative approach to network radio was fleetingly attempted in 1925. This failed effort—this dead media format—spotlights the lost potential radio had to develop as a direct audio copy of newspaper print syndication.[81] A venture aiming to counter the hookup model had Chicago as its nexus. The first step in launching Mid-Continent Broadcasting Associates came when William Hale Thompson, former mayor of Chicago, announced the eponymous WHT early in 1925, a new "radio super-station" with studios in the Wrigley building. Thompson was quoted justifying how "'the slogan of the station will be 'Boost Chicago.' Every effort will be made to keep the programs of general national interest.'"[82] Unlike the previous few years of early radio start-ups, WHT was overt about its plan to sell advertising for profit. H. H. Maier, treasurer, explained how WHT regarded itself as the pioneer in the field of commercial ad-driven radio. He predicted that "within another year, all broadcasting stations will go after advertising just like newspapers do."[83]

The upstart Chicago station soon announced the formation of Mid-Continent Broadcasting Associates, a new chain combining WHT with five locally domi-nant, newspaper-owned stations: KSD, the *St. Louis Post-Dispatch*; WBAP, the *Fort Worth Star-Telegram*; WHAS, the *Louisville Courier-Journal* and *Louisville Times*; WDAF, the *Kansas City Star*; and WJR, the Jewett Phonograph and Radio Company, associated with the *Detroit Free Press* (see fig. 29). H. J. Bligh, WHT's secretary and commercial manager, explained that Mid-Continent Broadcasting Associates had no connection with the AT&T chain and indeed was formed to respond to demand from national advertisers for broadcasts reaching farther across the country than the WEAF network, at the moment still limited to the Northeast. Located mid-continent, the group of six stations reached 85 percent of the territory of the United States. When an advertiser's sponsored program was broadcast, "all sections of the country will have an opportunity to hear it. This is not now possible by simultaneous broadcasting with telephone hook-ups.'"[84] In addition to geographic reach beyond the Northeast, Mid-Continent's networked newspaper-based knowledge of syndicated features and standard-ized advertising was supposed to provide an advantage: "A broadcasting station like a daily newspaper has many things in common. . . . Firms have purchased time on the air similar to space in newspapers and magazines. The time on the air is comparable with the running of advertisements in various editions of publications."[85]

Without access to expensive telephone or telegraph wires, and wanting to avoid shortwave hookups, the Mid-Continent chain hatched a plan for syndi-cated programming that simply relied on the six different transmitters as if they were printing presses, using the same scripts and music to reproduce the same

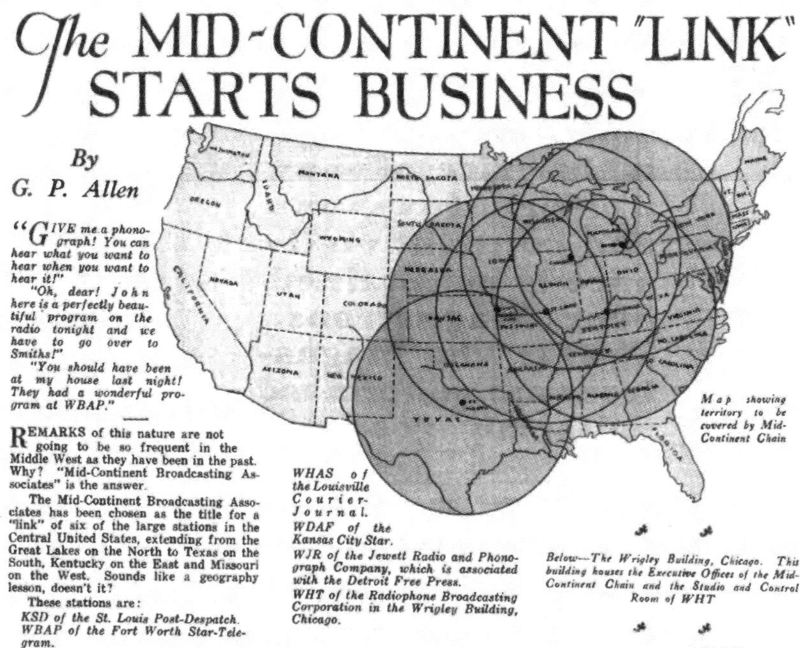

FIGURE 29. G. P. Allen, "The Mid-Continent 'Link' Starts Business," *Radio in the Home,* November 1925.

shows separately in six different metropolitan areas, as if syndicating circulation of a print supplement:

> In simultaneous broadcasting of a program by a number of stations, you have to be at home at a certain time or you miss the program entirely. . . . Thanks to Mid-Continent you are not going to miss the program at all! Pick up your daily paper, and in it you will find that from either WHT, WDAF, WHAS or one of the other stations in the chain, there is being broadcast at the same hour, the same program by an orchestra trained by the same director. . . . Instead of one chance to hear a program, you now are going to have six.[86]

Admittedly, the Mid-Continent idea had none of the technological wizardry of simultaneous broadcasting. Perhaps the idea was presumed to be more appealing to advertisers accustomed to the logistics and extended reach of print syndication.

There is little evidence from newspaper promotion or program listings that the Mid-Continent plan actually succeeded in gaining national advertisers. Only a couple of the firms signed to the network had more than regional recognition: the Borden Company and U.S. Light and Heat of Niagara Falls.[87] In any case, the telephone-line hookup of WEAF reached the Midwest exactly as Mid-Continent launched. At best, the venture pushed AT&T to connect farther west sooner, recalling how hookups to these cities (and several of these very same stations) had already been successfully tested. On the other hand, perhaps the entire venture was a ruse. The Mid-Continent plan may have been adopted from an idea also sketched in 1925 by Westinghouse: a closed-door backup plan laid out as the company participated in conferences that ended up creating NBC. Although there is no explicit mention of any links to Westinghouse in publicity and news reporting at the time, Amy Graban Crawford has recovered correspondence in the company's archives from July to November 1925 about the strategic plan, which would have created the same idea, using exactly the same name.[88]

Westinghouse vice president Harry P. Davis, "the father of radio broadcasting," planned his own Mid-Continent Radio Chain by looking "at the organization of a press association or wire service. . . . He proposed that radio stations could work under the same organizational structure. . . . The Mid-Continent Radio Chain would cull programming from its affiliate members and then share this programming among members through the week. The Mid-Continent Radio Chain would consist of six powerful, well-established stations in the Midwest, each affiliated with a newspaper."[89] The stations contacted to be part of Westinghouse's hypothetical Mid-Continent chain were WMAQ (*Chicago Daily News*), WWJ (*Detroit News*), WBAP (*Fort Worth Star-Telegram*), WDAF (*Kansas City Star*), WHAS (*Louisville Courier-Journal*), and KSD (*St. Louis Post-Dispatch*)—the same six cities and four of the five stations that actually partnered with WHT in the real Mid-Continent Broadcasting Associates. Crawford's research confirms that Westinghouse corresponded with the same newspapers that partnered with WHT at the very same time. Maybe WHT pilfered the idea and put it into action in a low-technology, low-stakes way, but perhaps the WHT venture was a front for Westinghouse raising the stakes in its talks with RCA. According to Crawford, "Talks with the newspaper stations never did resume, and Westinghouse pursued a different route to chain broadcasting," partnering formally with RCA, which a year later formed NBC.[90]

While the actual existence of the Mid-Continent chain was brief, the threat of powerful newspapers coordinated to create syndicated radio as an alternative to network radio may have played a small part in inking the final deals to create NBC. With its ideas for establishing truly syndicated radio programs distributed for local broadcast circulation rather than simultaneous networked broadcast, the Mid-Continent experiment is not only a twin footnote in both newspaper and radio history but also an important spotlight of how the ideals of syndication were setting the terms of the discourse. Soon after the formal launch of NBC, the newspaper trade journal *Editor and Publisher* cast the network radio hookup idea explicitly in terms of the prior decades' centralization and standardization of practices of news gathering and print circulation: "The day of syndicated programs, supplied by several large broadcasting stations, and non-dependent on the advertiser, is near at hand."[91] The slippage between simultaneous networked broadcasting and syndicated programs is striking for the way it is framed in terms of techniques from the newspaper business. Perhaps the prediction about the diminished dependence on sponsored advertising was relying on the presumed separation in a newspaper office between the editorial decisions of the newsroom and the advertising and publicity concerns of the circulation manager. As is well known, commercial radio and, later, television were instead increasingly driven by advertising.

RADIO SPONSORS' NEWSPAPER ADVERTISING

Network radio was built upon a foundation of sponsored programs originating from WEAF and WJZ in New York. National-brand products contracted advertising agencies to produce radio shows—effectively treating broadcasts as supplements to the same companies' existing creative work producing print publicity campaigns.[92] N. W. Ayer and Son had been handling AT&T advertising since 1908—recall from chapter 5 the importance of the company's annual newspaper directory with its lists of verified circulation. The agency gained a new client in September 1923 with the National Carbon Company subsidiary of Union Carbide.[93] One of National Carbon's key brands was Eveready Batteries, an essential product for radio listening. The "Eveready Entertainers" made their WEAF debut on December 4, 1923, linked to WCAP in Washington by January 1924. A weekly hookup of six stations was established for the *Eveready Hour* in October 1924, and the network for the show continued to expand, still serving as a national anchor during NBC's early years in the late 1920s.[94]

From the first days of radio, orchestras and musicians from movie palaces, department store recital halls, and hotel dance floors contributed a type of sponsored entertainment, if you will, because their venue or acts would be mentioned by name. Newspapers and magazines, too, contributed spoken bulletins to the first radio stations, as did libraries, museums, and government agencies. However, the idea of brand-name consumer products sponsoring variety and musical entertainment was a less obvious fit between form and content—unless it was framed as an extension of advertising.[95] One of the first, and for many years most prominent, on WEAF and NBC nationally was the American Tobacco Company's Lucky Strike Dance Orchestra, which began Saturday evening dances on July 14, 1923. Recall from chapter 1 how the American Tobacco Company founded the *New York Recorder*, transforming the concept of collectible cigarette cards into Sunday art supplements. Curiously for a national brand sponsor, the radio show was not initially promoted in Lucky Strike newspaper advertising.[96] Another early brand sponsor was United Cigar Stores, which sponsored daily sports talks on WEAF starting on September 11, 1923. Although the show lasted just a year, it has the distinction of being networked from its first broadcast, on WCAP and WMAF; here, too, the program was not mentioned in local print advertising.

National Carbon, on the other hand, began referring to broadcasts in its print advertising for the November 1924 election night *Eveready Hour*. Subsequently, ads appeared nationally every Tuesday starting in December 1924, listing all of the show's networked stations, regardless of the newspaper where it was printed.[97] Likewise, the A&P Gypsy String Ensemble was included in the chain grocery store's ads from its start on WEAF in March 1924, promoting the weekly iteration of the show: "To the Radio Fans! Tune In!" Notices for Uneeda Biscuits and Lifebuoy soap appeared next to calls to listen to the A&P entertainments on the emerging national brand of WEAF radio.[98] For the rest of the 1920s, newspaper readers planning grocery lists across much of the United States could find notes about the latest A&P Gypsies records, live shows, and weekly broadcasts embedded in the store's local ads.[99] From January 1, 1925—for some, the beginning of "a new radio era"—the *Victor Hour* featured the music company's recording artists, launched biweekly on a network of eight stations to an audience of eight million.[100] The broadcast with the list of affiliated stations was promoted in newspapers on New Year's Day, within nationally syndicated full-page ads for Victrolas and His Master's Voice records. Local dealers immediately began to advertise the *Victor Hour* program details in their regional newspaper ads.[101] Although the *Brunswick Hour of Music* had begun a few months earlier—Tuesdays on RCA's WJZ network starting in November 1924—when faced with the new competition, in February 1925 the phonograph company conducted a nationwide "music memory" contest linked to the program, with full-page ads run nationally in metropolitan Sunday newspapers.[102]

The creation of NBC involved a combination of AT&T's telephone group and RCA's radio group, with AT&T agreeing to retreat from production. WEAF was handed over to RCA in return for free use of long-distance telephone wires as the conduit for network rebroadcasting. *Variety* magazine took to the habit of calling the network "the NBC syndicate" and observed "the growing list of stations who are being absorbed," casting NBC as "the greatest amusement syndicate in the world."[103] By early 1926, the *Eveready Hour* would be promoted with the phrase "It's happening everywhere tonight."[104] A new sponsored show, the *Philco Hour*, expanded NBC's hookup to include the Pacific Coast with thirty stations in September 1927.[105] With the formation of formal network radio, sponsored programs such as the *Philco Hour* gained truly national circulation with two versions in a night, three hours apart for the Atlantic and Pacific and covering everywhere in between. The *Eveready Hour* and others followed suit. The creation of NBC relied especially on newspaper-owned radio stations to link their New York studios for national reach into the South and West. Among NBC stations playing the Philco shows in October 1927, none of the six in the Northeast were newspaper-owned, but nearly half the affiliates in the rest of the country were linked to newspapers—ten out of the remaining twenty-four stations—including all five that had been in the short-lived Mid-Continent syndicated network plan.

Admittedly, the parallel between print syndication and radio networks usually stayed implicit. Occasionally, however, writers would slip and refer to network radio as "syndication." This was even a deliberate choice for the radio columnist of the *Minneapolis Tribune*'s "List'ning Post," who consistently referred to New York WEAF programs in the hookup to WCCO as "syndicated" shows, albeit always within quotation marks.[106] Soon the word "syndicated" was substituted for all the brand names of sponsored network programs in order to avoid providing free publicity to national brands that were not advertising in the *Tribune*. The decision was justified as a matter of journalistic principle to clearly separate ads from news content: "The radio should be a medium of entertainment; the press is the medium of news and advertising. . . . It's the advertising crammed into our ears that spoils otherwise good radio programs."[107] This principled stance was a curious adaptation of wider debates over the commercialism of radio.[108]

Many newspapers were nonetheless eager to ride the popularity of the emerging radio network. When WEAR in Cleveland began the "rebroadcasting of New York radio programs" early in 1925, the *Plain Dealer* printed photographs of a "host of new radio personalities," including Graham McNamee, chief announcer of AT&T's WEAF station, "posed especially for *The Plain Dealer*."[109] When the *Dallas News*'s own station formally joined NBC early in 1927, the newspaper published a full-page advertisement, cosponsored by local radio dealers, booming, "New York radio programs now over WFAA for Dallas and the Southwest."[110] An expanded Pacific Coast hookup in 1928 meant the *Oregonian*'s own KGW station would now broadcast "the Lucky Strike Hour, produced in the WEAF studios, New York City."[111] NBC president Merlin Aylesworth was quoted about the new routine, which meant "Maine and Oregon now can dance to the same music."[112] The argument curiously ignores the need for performing twice, three hours apart—syndicated across time zones, if you will. There were also intermedial connections between network radio and newspaper syndication, such as nationwide print supplements and syndicated columns to accompany popular shows. One early example was Roxy Rothafel's concerts from the Capitol Theater, which began on WEAF in November 1922 and were among the first hookup broadcasts in 1923. Capitalizing on the growing network of stations carrying Roxy and His Gang, Rothafel had a syndicated column for five months in 1925 in the *New York Daily News* and at least four other metropolitan papers.[113] The "impresario of the air" had "joined the staff of New York's greatest newspaper" to "broadcast a daily message of good cheer."[114]

AMOS 'N' ANDY'S "RADIO COMIC STRIP"
AND THE BLACK PRESS

Early connections between radio and newspapers were fleeting and brief experimentations compared to the 1928 package that accompanied the debut of *Amos 'n' Andy*. In the show, white actors voiced stereotypical African American dialect, leading Karen Cox to argue that their comic antics revolved around "the story of the Great Migration of southern blacks to northern cities and the difficulties of that adjustment."[115] The radio program itself, Cox emphatically clarified, was blackface performance. The minstrel duo, played by Charles J. Correll and Freeman F. Gosden, had begun at the *Chicago Tribune's* WGN in 1926 as a "radio comic strip" called *Sam 'n' Henry*, although the *Tribune* did not run an actual comic in print. Not unlike Hearst's hiring R. F. Outcault and the Yellow Kid out from under Pulitzer, Correll and Gosden were pinched by the *Chicago Daily News's* WMAQ but had to change the names of their characters. *Amos 'n' Andy* began in March 1928, accompanied by a comic strip syndicated by the *Daily News*.[116] The paper explained how the daily radio skit was "synchronized with a cartoon strip . . . giving illustration to the events that transpire before the microphone."[117] Listening readers were assured that the combination of comic strip and radio show would be "doubly enjoyable since it will not only permit the characters to be visualized, but heard as well."[118] The plan was lauded as "the first direct radio-amusement-newspaper circulation tie-up."[119] The *Chicago Daily News* also sold *Amos 'n' Andy* to a "record syndicate" of affiliated radio stations, distributing weekly phonograph recordings of parts of the original nightly show on WMAQ: "The hinterland stations, hungry for good programs, are the contemplated market for this type of canned entertainment."[120] The syndicated show was especially popular in western states, although WNAC Boston and WEAN Providence played the "canned" versions of the show too.

The racist stereotyping and blackface minstrelsy of *Amos 'n' Andy* was controversial in the black press, although there are indications that the show was perhaps as popular among African Americans as with the mainstream. In the *Chicago Defender*, a prominent African American newspaper with national reach, *Sam 'n' Henry* records were prominently advertised in 1926, while letters and comments in 1928 noted how folks were listening in.[121] Early in 1930, however, a high-profile sermon by Bishop William Jacob Walls of the African Methodist Episcopal Zion Conference was widely reported as a critique of how young African Americans were "laughing themselves into semi-slavery" because the radio show "was part of the extensive system of furthering segregation by making the race seem different. . . . His sufferings are laughed at, his clamors for justice winked at and his whole cause sold as stock for game-makers and joy mongers."[122] The black press also noted that in the case of *Amos 'n' Andy*, racism and exploitation of black intellectual property went hand in hand. The slang and characters of Amos and Andy were strikingly similar to the long-standing vaudeville act of Flournoy Miller and Aubrey Lyles, two black performers, leading to a copyright lawsuit.[123] Despite the allegation, African American newspapers such as the *New York Age* and the *Pittsburgh Courier* continued to report on *Amos 'n' Andy* regularly.

In April 1931 the *Courier* spearheaded a bold-type headlined "Campaign for Self-Respect," calling for readers to petition and lobby to cancel the popular radio show.[124] An editorial argued that the popularity of *Amos 'n' Andy* cast a shadow across a racial color line: "The people reaping the financial gain from the characterization are all white. But the people who are getting the black eye out of it all are the Negroes of this country," using another term of the day.[125] The paper asked readers to write answers to the question "Do you consider Amos 'n' Andy a reflection upon your race?" which was followed by "Do you know any other race of people who would allow themselves to be so exploited?"[126] The campaign continued for months, culminating in "Self-Respect Sunday" when fifteen hundred ministers agreed to preach sermons supporting the *Courier*'s drive to collect one million signatures.[127] Perhaps the most cutting attacks of the "Campaign for Self-Respect" were editorial cartoons by Wilbert L. Holloway (see fig. 30), but this prompted at least one comment that Holloway's own comic strip, *Sunny Boy Sam*, peddled some of "the very same stereotypes which we now oppose."[128]

In Chicago, where the radio show originated, the *Defender* took an entirely different stance. The stars of *Amos 'n' Andy*, doing their act in person, were the headline guests of the 1931 Bud Billiken *Defender* Picnic, an annual festival and parade for Chicago's black community that continues nearly a century later. It was a great irony that Amos 'n' Andy, the blackface stars of the "radio comic strip," were hosted by Bud Billiken, the personified newspaper mascot of the *Defender*, who was even briefly himself transformed into a comic strip in the mid-1920s.[129] Billiken was introduced as the moniker for the *Defender*'s "Junior" page editor in 1921, when the paper began printing clip-out coupons to join a young reader's page "Bud Billiken Club" with contests, prizes, and special events, such as the annual picnic in Washington Park. In 1931 an immense crowd of thirty-five thousand people gathered for the Billiken picnic, when the blackface radio stars appeared in person: "Amos 'n' Andy mounted chairs with megaphones, but you couldn't hear your ears. . . . When it was over the crowd let out a salvo of applause that could be heard for miles. Gosden and Correll, the men, were immensely interested and impressed. . . . They saw a sight that opened their eyes wide in unaffected pleasure."[130] Perhaps having Amos 'n' Andy in person at the 1931 picnic was a defensive maneuver against the criticism of the *Courier*'s campaign to have the show canceled. To be stars of the rival African American newspaper's main annual community event would certainly counteract the criticism.

The above cartoon by our Mr. Holloway tells the "Amos 'n' Andy" story as it should be. After two years of recklessly assaulting a helpless people, the machine of propaganda runs into a stubborn opposition in the form of Negro self respect.

No one will respect us more than we respect ourselves. It was some time before Negroes really caught the real harm we are suffering because of the ridicule heaped upon us. At the "trial" of Andy, Madam Queen was shown to be a Negro woman with three husbands. She was shown to be a bigamist. The Negro lawyers Andy picked out to defend him were shown to be "crooks" and most unfit to practice the profession. But the lawyer finally selected to go to Court—they were afraid to ridicule the Court—was a white man, Mr. Collins, whose attitude toward his client was most condescending. This was a slap at the Negro lawyers, and Madam Queen's bigamy was an insult to all Negro women. There are intelligent lawyers of the Negro race. Why did not the pair select one to represent the profession? Not so. The Negro lawyer was presented to the listening world as a crook unfit to go to any Court. And yet we sit still and allow this insult to be sent all over the radio world. What sort of stuff are we made of when we can laugh at ourselves outraged?

It is time this insult closed. The air must be free of insult as far as we are concerned. Self respect will do more to stop the insult than anything else. Every home must be a HOME of Self Respect. Start at your own home today. Out with the insult—and we must wreck the machine of dirty propaganda.

FIGURE 30. The "Campaign for Self-Respect" against *Amos 'n' Andy.* Wilbert L. Holloway, "After Two Years of Reckless Driving!" *Pittsburgh Courier,* May 16, 1931, 11.

The commingling of blackface comics Amos 'n' Andy with Bud Billiken, the African American cartoon character, demonstrates the immense draw of Sunday color comics as a cornerstone of popular culture. The *Courier* organized its readers against the latest popular iteration of racist blackface popular culture. But the radio stars' enthusiastic reception at the *Defender*'s picnic indicates a more complex relation with African American readers, a contradiction often noted at the core of black popular culture.[131] Jean Lee Cole's reflection on "the comic sensibility" at the turn of the twentieth century proposed that we can "think of black caricature in the early comic strip as a negotiated site of meaning. ... A space thereby opens for black readers to become active readers of the comics, solidifying and even empowering a black comics-reading audience that would eventually produce comic strips that were by, about, and for blacks."[132] And, to be sure, the black press had developed its own comic strips, such as the *Defender*'s long-standing cornerstone comic *Bungleton Green*, which was expanded to a color comic in 1928 as the back cover for its new magazine supplement.[133] In her overview of black newspaper comic strips, Sheena Howard explains that "blacks could turn to the *Bungleton Green* strip for comic relief and a sense of escapism."[134] She hastens to point out how this escapism served a social purpose that was different from that of mainstream popular entertainment. For African Americans, "the use of humor provided a small, yet significant, form of relief from the brutality and hardships of slavery" and the legacies of discrimination in the twentieth century.[135] The *Courier* too had its own comics, including several comics that were syndicated across a number of black newspapers.[136] And the *Courier* launched a small-size tabloid illustrated features magazine, also a syndicated supplement that began the same time in the *Baltimore Afro-American* and perhaps other papers.[137] An editorial in the *Courier* in 1923 took stock of the "great strides" that African American newspapers had made in their "bid for circulation ... feature writers, funny-sides, red-ink headlines have all made their debut." Specifically listing the new comic strips by name, the writer concluded, "The diversion from the more or less unbending and inflexible editorial content is appreciated by readers."[138] As Kim Gallon notes in her review of African American newspapers' coverage of sexuality, black newspapers "regularly featured serial and short stories, book reviews, comic strips, and crossword puzzles ... [that] editors knew satisfied the twin objectives of racial uplift and entertainment."[139] Even for the African American press, the mechanism of using popular culture and magazine features to gather a national public was the very same as the one that had been developed by the mainstream Sunday paper decades earlier.

In our two chapters on syndication, we have considered how the Sunday paper's supplements became standardized through syndicated features, especially color comic sections and literary feature magazines. We began the book with the example of the *Philadelphia North American*, which launched a first Sunday edition in 1901, entirely of its own making. It printed its own color comic section and halftone magazine section on its own machinery in a new pressroom in a brand-new head office building. In some respects this launch of a new Sunday paper from scratch was the culmination of the previous decade of innovation among a select and limited number of metropolitan Sunday newspapers. In the decade after the *New York Morning Journal* introduced art poster supplements in 1889 and tabloid-size fiction magazines in 1890, a cascade of invention led the publishers of Sunday papers in the largest metropolitan cities to experiment with Sunday supplements of a wide variety of forms and contents. With syndication in the early 1900s, the form became accessible and replicable. Dozens, then hundreds, of Sunday papers in small cities across the United States began to include color comics and illustrated magazines in a form that remained more or less the same for the rest of the twentieth century.

Throughout the 1920s, when small cities adopted Sunday supplements in standardized syndicated form, they boasted about offering a local version of a "metropolitan Sunday paper." Adding new supplements in 1923, the *Lancaster News-Journal* in Pennsylvania, promised "the best Sunday paper for newspaper readers . . . Pages and pages of live local news . . . Telegraphic news of the outside world . . . Complete Sports . . . Magazine Section equals Metropolitan Sunday paper. Full page Colored Comics section on first release."[140] Newswire items and sports coverage were daily fare; the magazine and comics distinguished the Sunday edition. In 1929 the *Owensboro Messenger-Inquirer* gave its small city new syndicated supplements and offered "a metropolitan Sunday newspaper for only 5 cents . . . Kentucky's greatest nickel's worth."[141] Starting up a new Sunday edition in 1924, *The Bee* in Fresno, California, gave its small city "a real metropolitan Sunday newspaper to which she has long been entitled and which she has never had—sensational in that it will comb the world for news, purchase the best features, give the children colored comics and the grown-ups a colored magazine . . . a Sunday newspaper with all the news, the color of life, and the entertainment that can be crammed into one paper."[142] Well into the era of chains of Hollywood movie palaces and even after the introduction of network radio sponsored by national-brand products, what had begun as a unique innovation in the largest-circulation Sunday papers was still being boasted about as a metropolitan medium, even as the form became standard in more than five hundred Sunday papers across the country.

Recall how by 1903 there were already six companies offering color comics on a continental scale. The early names of the companies changed over the course of the century, but Hearst's King Features Syndicate and E. W. Scripps's United Feature Syndicate remained central to the business for over a hundred years. To be clear, those syndicates sold only the copyrighted popular characters of the comics. As we noted earlier in this chapter, a network of the largest-circulation newspapers had formed an advertising-buying network, National Newspapers Incorporated, to collectively leverage national-brand advertising contracts in their cumulative circulations. In 1932 a new company, Metropolitan Sunday Newspapers, was created to do something similar for color advertising in comic supplements and high-quality ads in rotogravure magazine inserts. The venture was launched initially in eleven major newspapers with full-page advertisements: "For Philadelphia . . . *The Inquirer*," or "For Baltimore . . . *The Sun*," and others, each of which explained how "big metropolitan newspapers have joined forces to develop a gigantic power for the sale of volume merchandise at low cost. . . . To do a real job in America's metropolitan areas, where sales and profit are on speaking terms, you need the power of Metropolitan Sunday Newspapers."[143] One genuinely new result of the Metropolitan Sunday Newspapers venture was to infuse comic sections with advertising, much of it taking the form of comic strips. Newspapers and magazines had typically been laden with advertising, but early color comic supplements had actually been free of this commercial basis. In the 1930s, however, ads for chocolate bars, kids' cereals, and toys were presented by cartoon characters alongside animated promotions for tobacco, cosmetics, and automobiles. For example, advertisements filled almost a third of the space of a twelve-page comic section in the *Chicago Tribune* in March 1938. Only the first page had no ads, while half-page color comics sold Camel cigarettes, Oxydol detergent, Colgate dental cream, and other products; Shirley Temple ate Quaker Puffed Wheat; and every second page had a chocolate bar banner: Oh Henry! Nestlé, Butterfinger, and Baby Ruth.[144]

By 1920, and for the remainder of the twentieth century, the form of the Sunday paper was remarkably stable and standard. Some metropolitan papers had high-profile book review supplements and published their own magazines (some also offered a syndicated *Parade* or *This Week*). The *New York Times* truly stands out as the exception for never including a color comic section, especially since, as we noted, New York Sunday papers were first to syndicate their comics in the very first years of the twentieth century, joined by a group of comic syndicates. But the importance of standard forms and syndicated content for Sunday supplements goes well beyond economies of scale. Syndication cannot be reduced to efficient assembly lines for the mass production of leisure reading, nor should the impetus behind decisions to adopt syndicated features be taken merely as the display of a managerial "visible hand" on the part of publishers. Those economic factors need to be seen through the emergence of a new mass society, with popular culture as its foundation—admittedly commercial, secular, and crass but accessible and inclusive in its way. As is most evident with the inclusion of "menus" of movie directories, the Sunday paper allowed local readers to navigate the stars of mass culture, aware that thousands would join them at a particular show, itself just one of thousands across North America. If the newspapers' new features in the 1890s delivered participation on a metropolitan scale, then the subsequent syndicated features of the 1900s cast the net more broadly to cover the entire country and beyond.

For African Americans and other racialized readers, the systemic racism of syndicated humor opened a fraught form of inclusion, replicated and then transfigured as it was debated and critiqued within the ethnic and community presses. Popular culture's dominance grew from the kernel of circulation growth—spelled out in *Associated Sunday Magazines'* "Kernels" campaign—conflating the public's attention with public interest. Advertisers were interested in inserting their own direction upon this conflation of the public and the popular, but the Sunday paper—as an object, as a habit, as a business—continued to mediate consumer and commercial culture under its aegis. Nonetheless, publishers' corporate goals overlapped with advertisers' aims to achieve the widest possible circulation, which syndication achieved, linking markets with coordinated content of commercial amusements and popular culture. Radio networks of synchronous broadcasts went one step further, and circumstances conspired to upend the relation between content and advertising. Network radio programs were named after advertisers, produced by advertising agencies. The syndicated world of popular leisure had always served the interests of advertisers, but with network radio, popular culture became advertising's servant. Radio transformed the metropolitan promise of being "in the swim" into a more literal experience of being "in sync" on a continental scale.

CONCLUSION

"Newspaper Reading" without a Newspaper

In a BBC radio broadcast on March 21, 1943, the science fiction author and futurist H. G. Wells proclaimed, "One profound conviction that I have is that what we have known hitherto as the newspaper is as dead as mutton. And it will never come back."[1] Wells goes on to suggest that just as he does not consult the newspaper when he wants to know the time, he should not consult the newspaper when inquiring after the news. Instead, like the British T.I.M. telephone exchange he would ring to know the precise time, there ought to be a N.E.W.S. exchange to provide the news, since, after all, the newspapers were no longer doing it. Wells's prophetic statement about other media doing a better job at carrying news than the old technology of paper anticipates the anxieties that contemporary newspaper observers have had for decades regarding the changing form of the newspaper in a networked digital milieu. His comments speak to the precise dilemma newspaper editors faced with each introduction and expansion of new media forms: "what we have known hitherto as the newspaper" must change.

This process began, in many ways, more than a century ago, as this book has charted. As we suggested throughout this book, with each introduction of new media to its assemblage, the newspaper sought to reenvision what it does for and in response to society. The form of the newspaper was the central battleground for this continual reimagining of its pages, its manufacturing, its operations, and, most significantly for the Sunday newspaper, how it operated within culture. The Sunday newspaper, with its connection to leisure, to the home, and to other media technologies, offered readers new ways of experiencing and knowing the world around them. The weekend edition taught new techniques of reading and produced new kinds of reading subjects. The twenty-first-century newspaper, in crisis for decades now, is no less in search of new ways of connecting with its readers, offering them new meanings and new ways of learning about the world—and once again producing new kinds of reading subjects as it is transfigured in the process.

When the *New York Times* unveiled its virtual reality (VR) documentary film *The Displaced* as a 360 video supplement to the Sunday edition's *New York Times Magazine* in November 2015, it was just one of a flurry of new media ventures undertaken that year in an effort to seek novel ways of engaging with its readers.[2] In 2015 alone, the *Times* launched new Instagram and Facebook pages as well as new apps for Android and iPhone, Apple Watch, and other interactive reading platforms. The *Times* followed its VR video venture with Op-Docs documentaries by, for example, Oscar-winner Errol Morris; a top-rated podcast of its *Modern Love* column in conjunction with Boston public radio's WBUR; a food-themed Pinterest board working with celebrity chef Nigella Lawson; a joint investigative story and broadcast with National Public Radio's *This American Life*; a custom crossword collaboration with the SAT College Board; a VR music concert series as part of the SXSW festival; its own *Minecraft* world as part of a magazine feature on the video game; and plans for a Daydream app using Google's Jump camera technology. The wild success of the *Times*'s award-winning podcast, *The Daily*, was then still a year away. By posing the rhetorical question "Are we on the brink of a new form of journalism?" *Times Magazine* editor Jake Silverstein put the new multimedia ventures in historic context:

> One hundred nineteen years ago, the inaugural issue of this magazine published the first photographs ever to appear in *The New York Times*.... Now, more than 6,000 Sundays later, the magazine is proud to introduce another visual innovation.... It is hard to know whether readers of the magazine's issue on Sept. 6, 1896, were as transported by the newspaper's first photographs as I hope the readers of today will be by "The Displaced." But we are proud to carry on a tradition—one as old as journalism itself—of *pressing new technologies into the service of storytelling*.[3]

This juxtaposition of journalism's present with its past is striking for the way it epitomizes why the history we outline in *The Sunday Paper* is timely and relevant for twenty-first-century eyes. Many of the efforts to discover new forms of online engagement originate in Sunday magazine supplements, even in a paper of record like the *New York Times*. As the *Times* explained in launching *The Displaced*, an augmented reality feature alongside a print story about refugees, it opted to use this filming technique because it "enables an uncanny feeling of connection with people whose lives are far from our own."[4] This Sunday supplement feature, like countless others for one hundred years before it, not only used other media technology to create "the experience of being present within distant worlds," but it also presumed the whiteness and Americanness of its readers, sustaining the now well-recognized "'us-them' binary."[5] Engaging readers' interest in habitually enjoying the newspaper is rooted less in the hallowed legacies of journalism than in the commercial history of circulation, subscription, and syndication, which still happens through the Sunday paper and its supplements, even if those are now digital or otherwise. In an era when digital content has a seemingly shorter and shorter shelf life, the continued availability of the series on the *Times*'s website is not surprising in light of the cultural import and the presumptions about readers assigned to the story.

As this book details, metropolitan Sunday papers from the 1880s to the 1920s introduced new forms of engagement with readers, whose attention was concurrently lured by the introduction of other mass culture and media, such as magazines, vaudeville, film, and radio. In other words, incorporating new media forms as supplements to news reading has a long history, dating back to the beginnings of the commercialization and rapid expansion of the press. The early period of Sunday expansion in the 1890s not only saw corporate conglomeration of news organizations (such as the emergence of chain papers and syndication), but their market also expanded into a mass audience including women and children, albeit as members of the patriarchal family. News readers became more than simply readers; they became members of mass society by virtue of their multimodal media consumption. Their habits as listeners and viewers were largely structured through a subscription to a metropolitan Sunday paper, which organized their participation in mass society, popular culture, and the democratic public sphere. In the twenty-first century, as the *Washington Post*'s director of product put it in a 2015 Nieman Lab post, the key to building connected readers has always been to ask, "How might we use the time-honored traditions of news design to *create oases for news reading* in this increasingly distracting world?"[6] As we have argued throughout this book, the drive for circulation growth historically lay behind such oases for reading, which we cast, following Michel Foucault, as a technique for the production of new kinds of modern subjects.

The *New York Times*'s present-day push to find new forms of engagement is anchored in this history. In 1896, when it added a Sunday illustrated magazine and a book review supplement, the *Times* itself was one of many papers jumping on a bandwagon that was hardly limited to Hearst's and Pulitzer's yellow journals. As we have demonstrated, newspapers used the innovative new media technologies they developed in and for their Sunday papers to position themselves as all-encompassing conduits for storytelling, building relationships with readers through a variety of audiovisual as well as print forms and formats.

This process predates electric media. Perhaps none took the ideal of the God's-eye perspective so literally heavenly as Joseph Pulitzer's repeated turns to hot air ballooning as an amusing and visually spectacular way of animating the *Sunday World*. Recall how in 1887 the *World* sent a reporter in a balloon from St. Louis to just outside New York, "searching the firmament," to bind Pulitzer's two sister papers into a national network of observation and spectacle over the landscape itself. The balloon expedition was intended to demonstrate that newspapers—especially illustrated Sunday newspapers—could bring fantastic fiction to life and "give to our readers a story which shall be after the manner of Verne, wonderful and entrancing except only with the difference that every word of *The World* narrative will be truth from an experienced eye-witness."[7]

Recall the rush of articles about transmitting pictures a thousand miles by telegraph in Hearst's *New York Journal* in collaboration with the Edison laboratories in 1896, just months after cinema's debut. As with moving pictures, reporting from a hot air balloon—and for that matter, the present-day use of *New York Times* online supplements—the basis of the breakthrough was the capacity of yet another news machine to mimic what could be perceived and experienced through technology—in this case the electrified reproduction of unbroken line drawings reproduced mechanically as minuscule dots transmitted by telegraph. Other newspapers reimagined the future of "visual telegraphy" through scenes prescient of live television broadcasting or video-linked teleconferencing that were strikingly similar to today's Zoom and FaceTime calls.[8] Like a concert video extra, embedded in an online entertainment news page today, Pulitzer's *World* illustrated "how pictures may be transmitted a thousand miles" with an etching across the top of two adjacent pages, showing an audience in a Chicago theater looking onto a panorama of Madison Square in New York, with the two cities linked by telegraph wires.[9]

CIRCULATING ENGAGEMENT: "NEWSPAPER READING" IN THE DIGITAL AGE

The clear parallels between these historical and contemporary examples demonstrate how the concept of media engagement deserves its own media archaeology, which we have only just begun with this book.[10] We see affinities particularly between contemporary engagement strategies and the historical innovations introduced with the Sunday paper over a century ago.[11] A wide range of printed forms and circulation practices structured "reading" as more than reading print on a page but, more broadly, as participation in culture and society as well. Cutting coupons for the Sunday poster supplement prepared women and children for consumption or art appreciation. Cutting out toy stages and paper dolls reminded children that the family newspaper was a key element in their daily lives. Guessing contests invested readers in the growth of their newspapers as an everyday object that could be known from front to back and inside out. The supplement and all of its various reading technologies and practices disciplined readers into connected and engaged communities together, even as its astonishing formal variety implicitly recognized that people read the paper for different reasons at different times and for different purposes. Though we often think of the twentieth-century newspaper as the monolithic hallmark of mass communication, it was just as much an atomized object with separate sections for all segments of the heteronormative family structure.

In the late nineteenth century, confronted by changing readerships in light of mass immigration, expanding literacy, and other demographic shifts, the newspaper radically repositioned its role and function. The contemporary newspaper faces a similar challenge, although the shift away from the stable medium of paper to online platforms—only sometimes owned by news organizations—poses different challenges, ushering in a new era of gatekeeping dependent on circumstances other than the authority of the newspapers themselves.

The history of the Sunday paper is instructive here. Each of the proliferating sections and supplements functioned almost like its own "product," despite the stability of the medium of print. When supplements were introduced in the newspaper, recall how the postal commission had to settle its legal status: Was it a separate mailing? Was it entitled to the same postage rates as newspapers? With the rise of digital products and the rise of a host of engagement strategies, practices, and technologies that are also "off the page," we see a similar concern with what newspapers are, what their function should be, and what to call the people who consume their features, in whatever form. Martin Conboy asks, "Trust? Ethics? What distinguishes journalism from mere 'content'?"[12] Here we might push further still and ask, "What distinguishes the newspaper in the twenty-first century, when it is no longer connected to the rich forms that were once its hallmark: supplements, comics, and magazines but also flyers and advertising inserts (the key print elements that fed much-needed revenue to the corporate newspaper)?" This book provides historical context for understanding how a shifting hybrid assemblage of networked media forms, including print, permits the nature of the relationship between journalism, communication technologies, news organizations, and readerships to remain meaningful and connected.[13] If the focus within digital journalism at the moment is on *user* and *audience* engagement, not *citizen* engagement, and if, "instead of participation *through* news, the focus is on participation *in* news," then the history of engagement will have taught us nothing.[14]

As in the late nineteenth century, the news industry today lacks a standardized way of measuring or even defining what engagement means. Previous measures of circulation that were developed and standardized through advertising agents N. W. Ayer and Son counted copies sold, ad rates, political affiliations, and other useful bits of information about the industry in North America. Independent audits were critical for establishing rates of advertising and thus systematizing profits. Circulation was at the heart of how the economic system worked. And subscription was a mechanism for building the cultural practices that would sustain that circulation: reading the news, to be sure, but also cutting coupons, collecting supplements, attending events, doing puzzles, and so on. Subscription transformed the commitment of buying a paper into a social and cultural relation that helped build mass leisure.[15] Much like the relationship between circulation and subscription, engagement is not merely the sum total of time spent with a particular news product. In recent years, following the well-established mechanism for engaging readers through a variety of new technology, the *New York Times* invested in online supplements. In the same recent period, the *Chicago Tribune* began committing to a full range of in-person events with readers, only some of which centered on media technologies. It called this "Trib Nation," positioning newspaper reading as a form of citizenship and a way of life. What united these strategies, both online and in person, was a preoccupation with getting readers to imagine their news organizations as taking up more space in their lives and linking with cultural and social relations.

Crafting "personal connections," the *Tribune* cast an explicit relationship between the paper's journalism and the relations it builds with readers. The paper saw events in particular as "a new platform for publishing . . . journalism."[16] Beginning in 2010, the *Tribune*, like many other newspapers struggling to maintain readership and revenue, took seriously the idea of using face-to-face meet-ups of all kinds as a way of reflecting its editorial mission.[17] Meet-ups of mutually engaged readers, and other attempts at transparency and responsiveness, were the hallmark of Trib Nation, the paper's initiative to build social relations with its audience. In 2012 alone, the paper organized one hundred news events, including talks with authors, monthly "Community Conversations," cooking competitions, craft brewing events, and a sold-out tour of the paper's printing facilities. Though many of those initiatives were short-lived (Trib Nation survived only a few years), similar initiatives long ago likewise connected readerships beyond the merely imagined community. Recall how Joseph Pulitzer opened the circulation books of the *Sunday World* to public scrutiny, offered competitors tours of his pressroom, and published illustrated features reviewing the technologies behind the Sunday paper. When his new skyscraper building was opened in 1890, it featured a viewing gallery specifically installed for public tours, with free admission.[18] Although the *Chicago Tribune* charged its attendees twenty-five dollars for the twenty-first-century printing facilities tour, the age-old draw was the same expectation of being dazzled by the technology in exactly the same fashion as had held the fascination of readers and city dwellers in the 1890s. The technology and form of the paper has changed, but the practices and techniques that produce engagement are remarkably consistent.

INTERMEDIALITY AND
THE DEATH OF NEWSPRINT

If the turn-of-the-twentieth-century Sunday edition introduced a paper that was *more than* a paper, the turn-of-the-twenty-first-century newspaper is a sad end as the conclusion of that trajectory some one hundred years later. The newspaper is now dislodged from its centrality in culture: *less than* a paper used to be—in many cases, *no longer even a paper*. Utterly consumed by the daily paper's ethos of functioning as an information machine, displaced first by "breaking news" radio and television broadcasts and then by Twitter and other social media, the newspaper form has withered because it can no longer fulfill even its own desires. Magazines, books, toys, radio broadcasts, newsreels, plays—the Sunday newspaper claimed to be all of it and now is usually none of it. As the story has been told by many observers and scholars, changes to reading and consumption habits as work and cultural life changed—alongside increased newsprint costs and the stagnant or declining circulation that comes with changing demographics—all marked the decline of the daily newspaper and the Sunday paper with it.[19] Changes in the rhythms of leisure, acutely transformed under late capitalism and rearranged anew within pandemic times, have occasioned a recursive look to what worked in the past.

The ascendancy of the Sunday paper was, of course, deeply connected to an economics of newspaper production that led to its eventual demise. As the Sunday paper form stabilized in the first decades of the twentieth century, the general feeling was that "quality" editorial content was the surest way to secure "quality" readers (*read*: white, middle-class families) who were most sought by advertisers. Arguing against the inclusion of circulation boosters like giveaways and coupons, W. F. Herron of the *Pittsburg Gazette-Times* suggested that the "best way to build up the Sunday edition" was through the hallmark features of Sunday reading: "[The advertiser] has no use for the man who buys the paper merely to secure a coupon that is printed in it. The advertiser knows that the subscriber of value to him is the man who buys the paper for the information or entertainment it affords him."[20] By the early part of the twentieth century, the familiar formula of Sunday features supporting circulation and acting as a draw for advertising was widely recognized as crucial to the political economy of the newspaper, as our chapters on syndication show: "If the circulation men are dependent upon the editors, the advertising men are more dependent upon the circulators. The advertising manager at times entirely forgets or ignores the fact that it is the quality and quantity of the circulation that enables him to make any showing whatever. Without a good circulation to back him up, the greatest advertising solicitor in the world would be helpless."[21] The reliance on advertising and the selling of the audience to advertisers would become the hallmark of all mass media in the United States.

Advertising and the Sunday Newspaper

The primary change in the form of the Sunday paper as the century progressed was the ballooning importance and eventual centrality of advertising. As we noted in chapter 6, syndicated magazines had always included national brand advertising. In 1907 *Associated Sunday Magazines'* "Kernels" campaign honed the logic of national market coverage through the combined circulation of a dozen or more metropolitan Sunday papers. Hearst's *American Weekly Magazine* section, too, explained the power of "intensive selling" through its chain of six Sunday papers in 1917.[22] The chain would soon expand to take over many more papers—a foreshadowing of the vast newspaper chains that would follow in later decades.[23]

Syndicated magazines became more common than ever in the latter half of the twentieth century. *This Week* was launched in 1935, *Parade* in 1941, and *Family Weekly* in 1953, all as preprinted supplements to Sunday papers across the country.[24] By 1958 they were carried by 42, 64, and 182 papers, respectively.[25] As a defensive move against this competition for Sunday magazine ad revenues, the independently produced magazines in major papers, represented by Metropolitan Sunday Newspapers, collectively renamed themselves *Sunday*, "locally edited and published" but branded in a standardized format and sold as a package to national advertisers.[26] Many of the largest-circulation newspapers simply ended up including both their own magazines and one of the syndicated options.

By 1985 *Parade* was being included in 275 papers weekly, with a combined circulation of more than 30 million.[27] At the same time, *USA Weekend* (successor to *Family Weekly*) was carried in another 267 papers, with another 13.5 million circulation.[28] Meanwhile, the number of Sunday newspapers that were editing and publishing their own magazines in-house was declining sharply. The president of Metropolitan Sunday Newspapers reported a half-million-dollar deficit at the 1985 annual general meeting, facing off against the intensified competition. He tried to stress the "indefinable sense of quality" that came from a newspaper publishing its own Sunday magazine. "'Like the news pages,' he said, 'Sunday magazines should not be viewed as profit-makers.'"[29] The same could not be said of the Sunday paper on the whole.

By 1990 a typical Sunday edition of the *Chicago Tribune* was eight hundred or more pages, and about half of the bulk was pure advertising—whole sections of ads in the form of flyers. Noted as a novelty in 1952 when Macy's purchased a sixty-four page Christmas catalog insert in a Sunday edition of the *New York Times*, flyers were really the only new form of Sunday supplement in the entire latter half of the twentieth century.[30] Indeed, the strategy of "total market coverage" allowed metropolitan newspapers to gather up all the flyers—with barely any news or editorial content—and deliver those advertising-only supplements to all nonsubscribers in the circulation zone (permitted by computerized zip code cross-referencing of subscriber lists against post office routes).[31] In this context, the Sunday newspaper reached the end of the millennium riding a wave of creeping commercialization, inflated reliance on advertising inserts, and the general decline of that 1890s ideal of "quality circulation," as opposed to "'mere circulation,' 'cheap circulation,' 'worthless circulation,' . . . readers who were unlikely to be good consumers."[32] It is perhaps no wonder that total Sunday circulation reached a cumulative peak in 1990 of 62 million papers nationwide, even before the emergence of digital subscriptions and online news aggregators. Even the stalwart *New York Times* peaked in the print circulation of its hallowed Sunday edition in the early 1990s (see table 3). It would take another decade before digital subscriptions made up for the decline, even for this exception to the twenty-first-century rule of the death of the newspaper.[33]

Death of ~~Newsprint~~ the Newspaper

As we write these final pages, the Sunday paper faces an uncertain future, if a future at all. What began as a decline in the reliance on its print format came to undermine the entire economic structure upholding the newspaper itself. An estimate of Sunday newspaper circulation in 2018—including digital subscriptions—put the figure at a total of 30 million, half of the peak of 1990; so low a figure had not happened since 1938, with far less than half the current population.[34] Thomas

TABLE 3. A Sample of Sunday Newspaper Circulation, 1977 to 2012

	1977	1983	1992	1998	2006	2012 (Print)	2012 (Digital)
Boston Globe	630,061	778,876	808,251	748,726	604,068	332,208	33,304
Chicago Tribune	1,155,572	1,127,778	1,133,249	1,034,440	957,212	755,265	24,175
Dallas News		406,893	744,714	795,030	649,709	321,592	41,537
Detroit News (and Free Press)	826,304	855,461	1,191,790	809,479	669,315	458,963	5,811
Los Angeles Times	1,300,260	1,342,720	1,531,527	1,385,373	1,231,318	850,267	102,494
New York Daily News	2,752,739	2,004,835	938,240	856,042	795,153	480,131	155,007
New York Times	1,479,862	1,563,531	1,773,876	1,650,179	1,683,855	1,265,839	737,408
Philadelphia Inquirer	861,600	1,036,717	977,684	871,659	705,965	413,371	72,137
San Francisco Examiner and Chronicle	664,251	695,898	709,201	617,708	451,504		
Washington Post	766,241	1,005,468	1,177,004	1,110,703	960,684	688,576	30,725

Source: Selected Audit Bureau of Circulations Biannual reports of Top 25 Sunday Newspapers (for the six months ending March 31), from *Editor and Publisher*.

Leonard pinpointed the decline in influence and circulation to the displacement of the primary goal of reporting "news for all" by what had always been a secondary task: delivering advertising. Writing in 1995, he fondly recounted the history of "the old-fashioned circulation drive" and even esteemed the humble innovation of the coupon as "one of the unheralded revolutions of news in print during the twentieth century."[35] On the other hand, he deemed later developments of sending flyers to nonsubscribers "not news for all, it is ads for all. . . . A newspaper that uses its resources to supply non-news to its non-readers is almost certainly in a bad business, no matter how much money comes in the short run."[36] Leonard offered the drastic polemic that "the modern news corporation has moved into the junk mail business."[37] As we have seen above, now that flyers are a thing of the past, along with so many of the print editions of Sunday papers that once contained them, newspapers like the *New York Times* and the *Chicago Tribune* have spent much of the past decade attempting to rebuild "quality circulation" through online and intermedial engagement. If that process succeeds, the newspaper will be barely recognizable.

The newspaper's transfiguration from print to website was already under way in 1996, when *Wired* magazine published an apocalyptic declaration that print would be dead within ten years. At the time, Jon Katz rightly pointed out that the internet would only hasten the decline that the U.S. newspaper industry was already experiencing with its shrinking number of readers.[38] Its continued decline over the last twenty-six years has been staggering to watch. By the turn of the century, almost all dailies and most larger weeklies had created electronic versions of their papers.[39] The rise of the corporate newspaper removed much of the multivocality that existed in the newspaper as we describe it in this book;[40] it also ensured a particular political economy that would make it very susceptible to a shrinkage in audiences and advertising revenues; economic crises (beginning in 2007 several economic crises have hit media industries particularly hard); technological changes (the shift in journalism scholarship's discussion of "digital journalism" from referring to online newspapers is only one indicator of its impact); and cultural changes that make the idea of a "mass society" hopelessly antiquated and rightfully problematic. In a rare shimmer of hope, Mark Jacob recently posited that the Sunday paper may survive precisely because of the turn to digital-only publication—for those publications that survive at all, that is, as the sobering statistics indicate (see table 3).[41] In the same report, Leonard Woolsey, president of the Southern Newspapers chain, speculated that for their papers, the Sunday paper is the most likely to survive "because I think it's a product people appreciate, the experience of sitting down with a physical newspaper and walking through. And I think there's a terrific model out there for having a powerful print weekend product and then digital for the rest of the week."[42]

Documenting changes in industry over the course of more than a century is well beyond the scope of a book largely focused on the emergence of a historically contingent form of the Sunday newspaper, but it is worthwhile pausing in conclusion to consider the enormity of change to the news publishing industry that had made that form possible. Scholars such as Pablo Boczkowski have been researching "innovation in online newspapers" for two decades, as some newspapers ceased paper publication of their papers while continuing to publish online.[43] Importantly, between 2004 and 2015, eighteen hundred American print newspaper outlets closed. As Margaret Sullivan recounts, with more than two thousand closures of newspapers across the United States since 2004, hundreds of American towns and cities now have no local newspaper or news outlet, a distinct change from the period we studied in this book.[44] Starker yet is the 2019 finding that between 2008 and 2018, newspaper advertising revenue dropped by 68 percent.[45] As Clara Hendrickson suggests, local newspapers especially have been hit hard by the capture of their advertising markets by Google and Facebook. Characteristic of their parasitic relationship with content providers, the technology behemoths offer newspapers greater reach to new audiences, but they do so by draining newspapers' key revenue source, advertising. As Hendrickson puts it, "While the two companies account for 58% of digital advertising revenue nationally, the two companies account for 77% in local markets—squeezing local news publishers."[46]

The consequence of the closures and changed economics extends to the profession of journalism too. Pew Research reports that between 2008 and 2019, newsroom employment in newspapers specifically has dropped by more than half.[47] Since the beginning of the COVID-19 pandemic in 2020, *Poynter*'s website has tried to keep count of the "newsroom layoffs, furloughs and closures," despite the difficulty of tracking categories of workers like freelancers.[48] Those layoffs and furloughs eventually led to full closures of newsrooms too, with more than ninety of them closing in the first eighteen months of the pandemic.[49] Notwithstanding these sobering statistics, Michael Delli Carpini offers an important reminder that this moment in time also begs for historicization: "The crisis in journalism is perhaps better thought of as an historical moment in which journalism worldwide is in a state of major transition, the implications of which remain very much in doubt."[50]

Perhaps the only logical conclusion to the story of the printed newspaper occurred a year after *Harper's Magazine* declared "The Final Edition" of the newspaper on its cover in December 2009. Soon after, McSweeney's, the online humor site and literary quarterly known for experimenting with form, took the conventional idea of a Sunday paper as a dense (but ultimately and purposefully consumable) object of leisure, and created . . . an utterly fetishized collectible. Witness *McSweeney's* 2010 print publication of the "fake" *San Francisco Panorama*. Simultaneously everything the nineteenth-century Sunday paper was and everything it wasn't, the publication was intended as a demonstration of not only how print newspapers might survive but also how they might expand their reach. At 320 pages printed on broadsheet, in full color, with a 112-page magazine, 96-page book section, and pull-out posters, it is enormous. Yet this newspaper sold for US$16.00 a decade ago and sold out immediately. The copy shipped to us in Canada arrived three months late. Neither cheap nor timely, it was never really a newspaper, though it remains everything a fetish object should be. Back issues now cost US$250.00, while copies available on amazon.com began at the relatively affordable price of US$85.29. Despite its claim to offer a "21st-century newspaper prototype," the *Panorama* borrows not only from the history of the form but also from the discourse of offering something for everyone. Answering why the paper is called the *San Francisco Panorama*, it proclaims, "It's from here, but it's for everybody." Exactly what made it impossible to produce on the internet is what made it impossible to continue publishing: its "luxurious broadsheet" size of 15" by 22".[51] Stretched to its most extreme, this leisure print object seems almost a joke—it was published by *McSweeney's*, after all—or at least a spectacle of itself, recalling the newspaper mascots discussed in chapter 5. Like the poster art supplements from more than a century before, it is meant to be collected and peered upon with curiosity—all the more so for contemporary audiences a decade later—rather than consumed and tossed away.

The Recursive Return of Audio

Since 2010 the foray of newspapers into podcasting has had an interesting reverberation with the earlier history of the newspaper's entry into radio broadcasting. Among the many newspapers that launched podcasts in the last decade are *The Guardian's Today in Focus*; the *Washington Post's Post Reports*; the *New York Times's The Daily*; and in Canada, the *Toronto Star's This Matters* and the *Globe and Mail's The Decibel*. Stripped of the massive burden of broadcasting licenses and incredible investments in transmission towers and equipment, newspaper podcasting accomplished what radio did for newspapers some one hundred years earlier by extending the reach of the newspaper. And yet if radio in the 1920s extended the paper's reach into entertainment and leisure, newspaper podcasting in the 2020s has largely relied on providing a deeper dive into its mainstay commodity: news. Offering episodes Monday through Friday, free of charge through other apps and platforms, these podcasts typically offer greater insights into the production of the story, including interviews with the journalists behind the reporting and the frequent reminder to support the "journalism" with a paid subscription to the hosting newspaper. In a call to the history of newspaper-radio partnerships of the

1920s explored in chapter 6, partnerships with public radio stations are offering some news outlets a new life. As the *Chicago Sun-Times* negotiates a sale offer from Chicago Public Media, (which owns WBEZ, broadcaster of the popular podcasts *Wait Wait . . . Don't Tell Me!* and *This American Life*), attention returns to alternative corporate and financial arrangements. For the *Sun-Times*, a merger with a nonprofit public media offers opportunities for new audiences, reach and generating revenue differently.[52]

The *New York Times* website formally recognizes its podcasts as "columns," much like it lists its video content. The website for *The Daily* perhaps expresses the cultural ambition best, describing the podcast as "how news should sound." A pop-up prompt to subscribe is inescapable, not unlike virtually all intermedial integration from the past century and more. In another striking corollary to the residual forms and formats of the early twentieth-century newspaper, *The Daily* was also transformed into a radio show, initially syndicated on 16 radio stations but eventually broadcast from over 250 stations.[53] In its radio transmission, the show is a standardized twenty-two minutes long, while the podcast varies in length from twenty to thirty-odd minutes.[54]

Beginning in 2020, the *New York Times* introduced *The Sunday Read*, a weekend podcast supplement to *The Daily*. These Sunday podcast supplements appear on the newspaper's website under the heading of *The Sunday Read* alongside a selection of *Sunday Magazine* feature stories that include audio podcast supplements so that you can "listen to this article" while you read it—or instead of reading it. Using *The Sunday Read* to simultaneously supplement *The Daily* podcast and *Sunday Magazine* features offers a compelling example of how the *Times* is following this century-old practice of capitalizing on additional weekend leisure time to supplement the daily subscription to the newspaper. *New York Times* executive audio producer, Lisa Tobin, explained the rationale soon after the new feature launched: "Every Sunday morning on *The Daily* feed, we're sharing some of our favorite magazine stories and long-form journalism from around *The Times*, read aloud. Intimate essays. Gripping capers. Fascinating profiles. The perfect weekend stories to escape to while making breakfast, walking the dog or just sitting on the couch."[55] *The Sunday Read* podcast episodes do not have a recurring host and are typically introduced by the journalist providing the background, but the story itself is often read by an actor, with occasional music and effects adding a compelling soundscape in the retelling. As a retelling of something written for print, it demands attention in different ways than "chattier" podcasts that use a talking heads format (like *The Daily*, for one). Typically thirty to fifty minutes (sometimes more than an hour), these Sunday supplements to the daily podcast and main news media draw upon the same performative styles of pen-picture storytelling established over a century ago, asking readers to let themselves be immersed in a story via an even older practice of reading aloud the news from the newspaper.[56]

After two decades of many newspapers no longer printing paper versions of their news, it seems almost inevitable for the *New York Times* to announce it will no longer use the term "op-ed"—a term coined in the habitual publication of opinion articles *opposite* the *editorial* page in the printed newspaper. For online readers, the navigational experience of finding a feature of the newspaper always in the same place, opposite another, the reference no longer makes sense. As opinion editor Kathleen Kingsbury rightly points out, "It is a relic of an older age and an older print newspaper design."[57] After market research with readers, it has been replaced with "Guest Essay," a term meant to signal inclusiveness by removing "clubby newspaper jargon" and by inviting more diverse opinions into the paper: "Opinion writing in 2021 is a collaborative project, one that is dynamic and not static." And while the move is as much a response to the "fake news" era where opinion and journalism have become less distinguishable, this subtle shift also speaks to a need to continually redefine the shape of the newspaper—what Kingsbury describes as its geography and what we have described as its form and format.

Ending *The Sunday Paper* with a glimpse at these digital online forms may seem a curious place to end our book. These cases seem to belie desperate attempts to sustain an entire industry with a broken business model. Yet our historical view of media practices and technologies across the newspaper's history, especially within its popular efforts, finds the newspaper using the familiar tactic of assembling and reassembling in order to stake out new cultural importance for itself. Recent efforts are sustained by networks of connections to other technologies and media, precisely at a moment when the form and format of newspapers are being transfigured by new production, distribution, and reading practices along with the cultural imperative to strive for a more inclusive address of a diverse readership. In earlier times, too, newspapers used other media to extend their reach beyond the map of how far they circulated and the count of how many copies were printed. Now the understanding of the very constitution of the newspaper has shifted yet again, moving us increasingly further away from thinking of it as a paper object—or even as media—at all.

NOTES

INTRODUCTION

1. "The People's Exchange," *Chicago Inter-Ocean*, May 7, 1893, 13.

2. "The Literary Features," *Chicago Inter-Ocean*, October 31, 1891, 12.

3. "The Sunday World," *New York World*, August 8, 1896, 16.

4. "The Sunday World's Stage," *New York World*, August 28, 1897, 11.

5. "All the World's a Stage," *San Francisco Examiner*, May 7, 1922, E9.

6. "Making 'Movie' History," *Chicago Record-Herald*, February 16, 1914, 12.

7. "Everybody's Going!" *Chicago Record-Herald*, February 23, 1914, 12.

8. Many volumes of original print newspapers, including illustrated color supplements of the *New York World*, have been preserved and archived at the Duke University Library's American Newspaper Repository. The project of rescuing these newspapers from the possible dustbin is recounted in Nicholson Baker and Margaret Brentano's illustrated oversized book, *The World on Sunday: Graphic Art in Joseph Pulitzer's Newspaper 1898–1911* (New York: Bulfinch Press, 2005). The book was no small catalyst for us, and our earliest archival trip in 2007 was to visit the collection in North Carolina.

9. "Sunday Magazine and Woman's World," *New York World*, March 13, 1898, S-1.

10. Marshall McLuhan, *Understanding Media: The Extensions of Man* (1964; Cambridge, MA: MIT Press, 1994).

11. Kevin G. Barnhurst and John C. Nerone, *The Form of News: A History* (New York: Guilford Press, 2001), 3.

12. Ibid.

13. The idea that metropolitan popular culture was "socially prismatic" is developed by William R. Taylor, *In Pursuit of Gotham: Culture and Commerce in New York* (New York: Oxford University Press, 1992), 82–83.

14. On the relation between early cinema and modernity, see Ben Singer, *Melodrama and Modernity: Early Sensational Cinema and Its Contexts* (New York: Columbia University Press, 2001). On the social experience and structure of modernity more generally, see Marshall Berman, *All That Is Solid Melts into Air: The Experience of Modernity* (New York: Verso, 2010); Zygmunt Bauman, *Liquid Modernity* (Malden, MA: Polity Press, 2001); David Frisby, *Fragments of Modernity* (Cambridge, MA: MIT Press, 1986).

15. "Ideology represents the imaginary relationship of individuals to their real conditions of existence." Louis Althusser, "Ideology and Ideological State Apparatuses (Notes toward an Investigation)," in *Mapping Ideology*, ed. Slavoj Žižek (New York: Verso, 1994), 123.

16. Lisa Gitelman, *Paper Knowledge: Toward a Media History of Documents* (Durham, NC: Duke University Press, 2014), 12.

17. Jonathan Sterne, "The MP3 as Cultural Artifact," *New Media and Society* 8, no. 5 (2006): 825–42.

18. Dick Higgins, "Intermedia," *Leonardo* 34, no. 1 (2001): 49–54; Éric Méchoulan, "Intermédialités: le temps des illusions perdues," *Intermédialités / Intermediality* 1 (2003): 9–27; Clive Scott, "From the Intermedial to the Synaesthetic: Literary Translations as Centrifugal Practice," *Comparative Critical Studies* 8, no. 1 (2011): 39–50; Carol Steen, "Visions Shared: A Firsthand Look into Synaesthesia and Art," *Leonardo* 34, no. 3 (2001): 203–208.

19. Caroline Sumpter, "The Cheap Press and the 'Reading Crowd': Visualizing Mass Culture and Modernity, 1838–1910," *Media History* 12, no. 3 (2006): 233–52; Charles Johanningsmeier, "Welcome Guests or Representatives of the 'Mal-Odorous Class'? Periodicals and Their Readers in American Public Libraries," *Libraries and Culture* 39, no. 3 (2004): 260–92.

20. Magazines, especially women's magazines, were likewise hard at work inculcating their readers into modern life. Matthew Schneirov, for instance, describes the imbrication of readers of American magazines into a specifically urban and consumerist sensibility, in *The Dream of a New Social Order: Popular Magazines in America 1893–1914* (New York: Columbia University Press, 1994). Likewise, Helen Damon-Moore notes that the *Ladies Home Journal* "connected gender and commerce" in its pages, in *Magazines for the Millions: Gender and Commerce in* The Ladies Home Journal *and* The Saturday Evening Post, *1880–1910* (Albany: State University of New York Press, 1994), 189. Further, Ellen Gruber Garvey concludes that contests were used specifically to train female readers' attention to the advertisements in American magazines, in *The Adman in the Parlor: Magazines and the Gendering of Consumer Culture, 1880s to 1910s* (New York: Oxford University Press, 1996), 51–79.

21. Julia Guarneri, *Newsprint Metropolis: City Papers and the Making of Modern Americans* (Chicago: University of Chicago Press, 2017).

22. Joseph W. Campbell, *Yellow Journalism: Puncturing the Myths, Defining the Legacies* (Westport, CT: Praeger, 2001). See also Joseph W. Campbell, *The Year That Changed American Journalism: 1897 and the Clash of Paradigms* (New York: Routledge, 2005).

23. John Nerone, "The Historical Roots of the Normative Model of Journalism," *Journalism* 14, no. 4 (2012): 446–58. Reminders by journalism historians to contextualize the value of objectivity date back, for example, to Michael Schudson, *Discovering the News: A Social History of American Newspapers* (New York: Basic Books, 1981); Michael Schudson, "Public Spheres, Imagined Communities, and the Underdeveloped Historical Understanding of Journalism," in *Explorations in Communication and History*, ed. Barbie Zelizer, 181–89 (New

York: Routledge, 2008); Richard L. Kaplan, *Politics and the American Press: The Rise of Objectivity, 1865–1920* (New York: Cambridge University Press, 2002); Richard L. Kaplan, "Press, Paper, and the Public Sphere: The Rise of the Cheap Mass Press in the USA, 1870–1910," *Media History* 21, no. 1 (2015): 42–54.

24. The *North American* gained this moniker from its roots in the *Pennsylvania Packet* in 1771. The *Philadelphia Inquirer* retains this distinction, since the *North American* was later absorbed into the *Public Ledger*, which was absorbed in turn by the *Inquirer.*

25. "First Issue To-Morrow," *Philadelphia North American*, September 28, 1901, 5.

26. "Boys and Girls!" *Detroit News*, February 17, 1922, 24.

27. Charles Musser, *Before the Nickelodeon: Edwin S. Porter and the Edison Manufacturing Company* (Berkeley: University of California Press, 1991).

28. Tom Gunning, "The Cinema of Attractions," in *Early Cinema: Space, Frame, Narrative,* ed. Thomas Elsaesser, 56–62 (London: British Film Institute, 1990); André Gaudreault, *Film and Attraction: From Kinematography to Cinema* (Urbana: University of Illinois Press, 2011).

29. "Programme of the High Class Entertainment," *New York Herald*, October 14, 1899, 18.

30. Eric Hobsbawm, *The Age of Empire, 1875–1914* (New York: Abacus Books, 1994); Susan Strasser, *Satisfaction Guaranteed: The Making of the American Mass Market* (New York: Pantheon, 1989).

31. Aurora Wallace, *Media Capital: Architecture and Communications in New York City* (Urbana: University of Illinois Press, 2012), 68–73.

32. "The Corner Stone, Impressive Exercises at Mr. Joseph Pulitzer's New Building," *New York World*, October 11, 1889, 1.

33. Gunther Barth, *City People: The Rise of Modern City Culture in Nineteenth-Century America* (New York: Oxford University Press, 1980).

34. Guarneri, *Newsprint Metropolis*, 54–101.

35. Robert E. Park, "The Natural History of the Newspaper," *American Journal of Sociology* 29 (1923): 273–89; Richard Wohl and Anselm Strauss, "Symbolic Representation and the Urban Milieu," *American Journal of Sociology* 63, no. 5 (1958): 523–32. Collections of Chicago School work on urbanism in general include Robert E. Park, Ernest W. Burgess, and Roderick D. McKenzie, eds., *The City* (Chicago: University of Chicago Press, 1967); and Robert E. Park, *The Crowd and the Public and Other Essays*, ed. H. Elsner Jr. (Chicago: University of Chicago Press, 1972). See also Lyn Lofland, "History, the City, and the Interactionist: Anselm Strauss, City Imagery, and Urban Sociology," *Symbolic Interactionism* 14, no. 2 (1991): 205–223.

36. Jackson Lears, *Rebirth of a Nation: The Making of Modern America, 1877–1920* (New York: HarperCollins, 2009), 252.

37. Henry Louis Gates Jr., *Stony the Road: Reconstruction, White Supremacy, and the Rise of Jim Crow* (New York: Penguin, 2019), 132.

38. Jean Lee Cole, "Laughing Sam and Krazy Kats: The Black Comic Sensibility," *Canadian Review of American Studies* 47, no. 3 (2017): 374.

39. Kerry Soper, "From Swarthy Ape to Sympathetic Everyman and Subversive Trickster: The Development of Irish Caricature in American Comic Strips between 1890 and 1920," *Journal of American Studies* 39, no. 2 (2005): 261.

40. Anonymous, "How They Publish the Comic Supplement in the Jungle," *New York Journal and Advertiser*, December 5, 1897, "American Humorist," 7. The unsigned comic may

have been inked by Gus Dirks, who penned several subsequent "Jungle" panels and takes aim specifically at E. W. Kemble's hideous "coon" comics, which were also appearing weekly in the *Journal* at the time, as well as compiled into books. See Francis Martin Jr., "To Ignore Is to Deny: E. W. Kemble's Racial Caricature as Popular Art," *Journal of Popular Culture* 40, no. 4 (2007): 655–82.

41. The phrase cites a 1918 article from the *Chicago Broad Ax* that chastised black audiences for enjoying "patronizing films that ridiculed the race." See Jacqueline N. Stewart, *Migrating to the Movies: Cinema and Black Urban Modernity* (Berkeley: University of California Press, 2005), 93–95.

42. Jean Lee Cole, "Ethnic Caricature and the Comic Sensibility," in *Handbook of American Literary Realism*, ed. Keith Newlin, 249–67 (New York: Oxford University Press, 2019).

43. Carrie Tirado Bramen, *The Uses of Variety: Modern Americanism and the Quest for National Distinctiveness* (Cambridge, MA: Harvard University Press, 2000).

44. Neil Harris, *Cultural Excursions: Marketing Appetites and Cultural Tastes in Modern America* (Chicago: University of Chicago Press, 1990), 19.

45. Ibid., 26.

46. William R. Taylor, "The Launching of a Commercial Culture: New York, 1860–1930," in *Power, Culture, Space: Essays on New York City*, ed. John Mollenkopf, 107–135 (New York: Russell Sage Foundation, 1988); William R. Taylor, *In Pursuit of Gotham: Culture and Commerce in New York* (New York: Oxford University Press, 1992).

47. Taylor, "Launching of a Commercial Culture," 107.

48. Ibid.

49. Taylor, *In Pursuit of Gotham*, 83.

50. James W. Carey, "Technology and Ideology: The Case of the Telegraph," in *Communication as Culture: Essays on Media and Society* (Boston: Unwin-Hyman, 1989), 201–230; John Durham Peters, "Technology and Ideology: The Case of the Telegraph Revisited," in *Thinking with James Carey: Essays on Communications, Transportation, History*, ed. Jeremy Packer and Craig Robertson, 137–58 (New York: Peter Lang, 2006).

51. Richard B. Kielbowicz, "Electrifying News! Journalists, Audiences, and the Culture of Timeliness in the United States, 1840–1920," *Time and Society* 28, no. 1 (2016): 200–230.

52. William R. Scott, *Scientific Circulation Management for Newspapers* (New York: Ronald Press Company, 1915), 51.

53. "The Sunday News," *New York Evening World*, March 29, 1890, 4.

54. David C. Smith, "Wood Pulp and Newspapers, 1867–1900," *Business History Review* 38, no. 3 (1964): 334.

55. Harold Innis, "Technology and Public Opinion in the United States," *Canadian Journal of Economics and Political Science* 17, no. 1 (1951): 13. These ideas in Innis date back, for example, to "The Newspaper in Economic Development," *Journal of Economic History* 2, Supp. (December 1942): 1–33, and are at the core of *The Bias of Communication*, 2nd ed. (1951; Toronto: University of Toronto Press, 2008). For a recent reevaluation of this work, see Michael Stamm, *Dead Tree Media: Manufacturing the Newspaper in Twentieth-Century America* (Baltimore: Johns Hopkins University Press, 2018).

56. "The New York World Where It Circulates," *New York World*, May 7, 1893, 39.

57. Bruno Latour, *Reassembling the Social: An Introduction to Actor-Network Theory* (New York: Oxford University Press, 2005); see also Bruno Latour, "On Recalling ANT," in *Actor*

Network Theory and After, ed. John Law and John Hassard, 15–26 (Malden, MA: Blackwell, 1999).

58. John Durham Peters, *Speaking into the Air: A History of the Idea of Communication* (Chicago: University of Chicago Press, 1999); Jeffrey Sconce, *Haunted Media: Electronic Presence from Telegraphy to Television* (Durham, NC: Duke University Press, 2000).

59. Sandra Gabriele, "Cross-Border Transgressions: The American Sunday Newspaper, the Lord's Day Alliance, and the Reading Public, 1890–1916," *Topia* 25, no. 2 (2011): 115–32; Ronald R. Rodgers, *The Struggle for the Soul of Journalism: The Pulpit versus the Press, 1833–1923* (Columbia: University of Missouri Press, 2018).

60. Few Sabbatarians protested the fact that producing a Monday morning paper required news workers' labor on Sundays. As late as the 1890s, news readers in cities in the Deep South and on the Pacific Coast unproblematically accepted Sunday delivery as a routine consequence of Saturday's news work but had to forgo Monday's edition as the result of giving the newspaper office a day of rest on Sunday.

61. "Sunday Observance, Discussion of Methodist Ministers," *Chicago Tribune*, March 18, 1884, 8; W. H. Gillam, "The Sunday Newspaper," *Western Methodist* (Wichita, KS), July 31, 1890, 1; "Concluding Sessions," quoting Rev. J. F. Moyer, *Altoona (PA) Tribune*, February 16, 1895, 1.

62. Rodgers, *Struggle for the Soul of Journalism*, 59–60. See also Alfred McClung Lee, *The Daily Newspaper in America: The Evolution of a Social Instrument*, vol. 1 (New York: Macmillan, 1937), 68; Charles Johanningsmeier, "The Devil, Capitalism, and Frank Norris: Defining the 'Reading Field' for Sunday Newspaper Fiction, 1870–1910," *American Periodicals* 14, no. 1 (2004): 93; John P. Ferré, "Sunday Newspapers and the Decline of Protestant Authority in the United States," *American Journalism* 10, no. 1 (1993): 8.

63. Horace Greeley explained his choice to discontinue Sunday editions because "there has been only one occasion when the news was of such moment as to render indispensable the appearance of the paper on Sunday. . . . Though its circulation has fully equaled our expectations, we have determined to bring it now to a close." *New York Tribune*, September 15, 1861, 4. And yet Greeley's 1861 test of Sunday issues was noted when starting a regular Sunday *Tribune*, December 6, 1879, 4. The 1861 "Start of the Sunday Edition" was recalled by *Chicago Tribune* for a Fiftieth-Anniversary Edition, June 10, 1897, 5. As Rodgers notes in his conclusion, by 1901 an anniversary issue of the *New York Times* could reflect back upon the "alarms and anxieties of the civil war [that] created a state of public feeling out of which were born the modern theory and practice of newspapermaking. . . . At the close of the war the press of the city had gained tens of thousands of new readers. The people of this city had acquired the habit of newspaper reading." *New York Times*, October 20, 1901, Jubilee supplement, 6, as cited in Rodgers, *Struggle for the Soul of Journalism*, 60.

64. "First Number of the Sunday Edition," *Philadelphia Times*, September 21, 1878, 2.

65. "A Sunday Tribune," *New York Tribune*, December 6, 1879, 4.

66. "The Inter-Ocean, A Sunday Edition," *Chicago Inter-Ocean*, April 15, 1883, 1.

67. "The Inquirer's Sunday Edition," *Philadelphia Inquirer*, November 27, 1889, 4.

68. S.N.D. North, *History and Present Condition of the Newspaper and Periodical Press of the United States* (Washington, DC: Government Printing Office, 1881), 124.

69. Ibid.

70. Ibid.

71. Henry Jenkins, *Convergence Culture: Where Old and New Media Collide* (New York: New York University Press, 2008); Jay David Bolter and Richard Grusin, *Remediation: Understanding New Media* (Cambridge, MA: MIT Press, 2000).

72. In our focus on form and design, we follow Barnhurst and Nerone, *Form of News*, which argues for greater foregrounding of design issues in journalism history. See also Barnhurst and Nerone, "Design Trends in U.S. Front Pages, 1885–1895," *Journalism and Mass Communication Quarterly* 68, no. 4 (1991): 796–804.

73. Pablo J. Boczkowski, Eugenia Mitchelstein, and Facundo Suanzo, "The Smells, Sights, and Pleasures of Ink on Paper: The Consumption of Print Newspapers during a Period Marked by Their Crisis," *Journalism Studies* 21, no. 5 (2020): 565–81; Rachel Plotnick, "Rubbing Readers the Wrong Way? Materiality and the Case of Ink Rub-Off," *American Journalism* 32, no. 2 (2015): 221–32.

74. James Mussell, *The Nineteenth-Century Press in the Digital Age* (New York: Palgrave-Macmillan, 2012).

75. Lisa Gitelman, *Always Already New* (Cambridge, MA: MIT Press, 2006), 4.

76. Ibid., 7.

77. Tony Bennett, "Making Culture, Changing Society," *Cultural Studies* 21, no. 4 (2007): 617.

78. Stuart Hall, "Signification, Representation, Ideology: Althusser and the Post-Structuralist Debates," *Critical Studies in Mass Communication* 2, no. 2 (1985): 91.

79. Jennifer Daryl Slack and J. Macgregor Wise, *Culture + Technology: A Primer*, 2nd ed. (New York: Peter Lang, 2015), 146.

80. Bruno Latour, "On Recalling ANT," in Law and Hassard, *Actor Network Theory and After*, 17.

81. "Scenes from a New England Home on a Sunday Morning," *Boston Globe*, April 7, 1922, 19.

82. "Scenes from a New England Home on a Sunday Morning—No. 2," *Boston Globe*, April 8, 1922, 10.

83. "Scenes from a New England Newsstand," *Boston Globe*, April 15, 1922, 8.

84. Durham Peters, *Speaking into the Air*, 16–17.

PART I. SUBSCRIPTION

1. Bruno Latour, "Technology Is Society Made Durable," in *A Sociology of Monsters: Essays on Power, Technology, and Domination*, ed. John Law (New York: Routledge, 1991), 108.

2. John Law and Annemarie Mol, "Notes on Materiality and Sociality," *Sociological Review* 43, no. 2 (1995): 274.

3. Bruno Latour, "Where Are the Missing Masses? The Sociology of a Few Mundane Artifacts," in *Shaping Technology / Building Society: Studies in Sociotechnical Change*, ed. Wiebe E. Bijker and John Law (Cambridge, MA: MIT Press, 1992), 257n15.

CHAPTER 1. SUBSCRIBING TO THE SUNDAY PAPER

1. "A Cabinet Possibility," *St. Louis Post-Dispatch*, November 15, 1896, 25.

2. Ibid.

3. Laurel Brake, "Lost and Found: Serial Supplements in the Nineteenth Century," *Victorian Periodicals Review* 43, no. 2 (2010): 111–18.

4. Robert Bernasconi, "Supplement," in *Derrida: Key Concepts*, ed. Claire Colebrook, 19–22 (New York: Routledge, 2015).

5. Jacques Derrida, *Of Grammatology*, trans. Gayatri Chakravorty Spivak (Baltimore: Johns Hopkins University Press, 1976), 144.

6. Ibid., 145.

7. Michel Foucault, *Ethics: Subjectivity and Truth, Essential Works of Michel Foucault, 1954–1984*, vol. 1, ed. Paul Rabinow (New York: New Press, 1997), 87.

8. Ibid., 95.

9. Roy Rosenzweig, *Eight Hours for What We Will: Workers and Leisure in an Industrial City, 1870–1920* (New York: Cambridge University Press, 1983).

10. Michael Warner, *Publics and Counter Publics* (New York: Zone Books, 2002); Benedict Anderson, *Imagined Communities: Reflections on the Origin and Spread of Nationalism* (1983; New York: Verso, 2006). Specific to the premediated mass reading public of cinema, see Paul S. Moore, "Advance Publicity for the Vitascope and the Mass Address of Cinema's Reading Public," in *A Companion to Early Cinema*, ed. André Gaudreault, Nicolas Dulac, and Santiago Hidalgo (Malden, MA: Blackwell, 2012), 381–97.

11. Harry G. Cocks and Matthew Rubery, "Margins of Print: Ephemera, Print Culture, and Lost Histories of the Newspaper," *Media History* 18, no. 1 (2012): 2.

12. Ibid., 3.

13. Charles Johanningsmeier, *Fiction and the American Literary Marketplace: The Role of Newspaper Syndicates in America, 1860–1900* (New York: Cambridge University Press, 1997).

14. James Mussell, "Elemental Forms: The Newspaper as Popular Genre in the Nineteenth Century," *Media History* 20, no. 1 (2014): 8.

15. James Guillory, "The Memo and Modernity," *Critical Inquiry* 31, no. 1 (2004): 110. See also Lisa Gitelman, *Paper Knowledge: Toward a Media History of Documents* (Cambridge, MA: MIT Press, 2014).

16. Terhi Rantanen, *When News Was New* (Malden, MA: Blackwell, 2009), 17.

17. Laurel Brake, "The Longevity of 'Ephemera': Library Editions of Nineteenth-Century Periodicals and Newspapers," *Media History* 12, no. 1 (2012): 7–20.

18. Engin F. Isin, "Theorizing Acts of Citizenship," in Engin F. Isin and Greg M. Nielsen, *Acts of Citizenship* (New York: Zed Books, 2008), 15–43.

19. Miriam Hansen, "Room-for-Play: Walter Benjamin's Gamble with Cinema," *October* 109 (2004): 3–45.

20. Frank Luther Mott, *American Journalism: A History of Newspaper in the United States, 1690–1940* (New York: Macmillan, 1941), 436–39.

21. The phrase "new journalism" was used in reference to "society journalism in England" by 1883 and was the subject of much debate in 1889. "Society Journalism in England," *Philadelphia Times*, April 9, 1883, 2; "Stead on Journalism, The Coming Great Newspaper," *Philadelphia Times*, August 25, 1889, 6. The link to sensational reporting in the United States was made as early as 1891—for example, in "Items of Interest," *Savannah (GA) News*, August 15, 1891, 7: "The central idea of the new journalism of New York, represented entirely by the new journals, was stolen from Coney Island. It is here that Mr. Pulitzer got his inspiration. Hysterios—noise, blow, frenzy. 'I'm the Dandy Jim of newspapers; Hooray!' 'Got another subscriber; Whoop!' 'This way gents, the only real, live whoop-'er-up newspaper in the world!' The phrase became more common in 1896, leading up to the "yellow journalism"

discourse linked to Hearst and Pulitzer. See Joseph W. Campbell, *Yellow Journalism: Puncturing the Myths, Defining the Legacies* (Westport, CT: Praeger, 2001), 32. See also Joseph W. Campbell, *The Year That Changed American Journalism: 1897 and the Clash of Paradigms* (New York: Routledge, 2005), 42–44.

22. Alice Fahs, *Out on Assignment: Newspaper Women and the Making of Modern Public Space* (Chapel Hill: University of North Carolina Press, 2011); Jean Marie Lutes, *Front-Page Girls: Women Journalists in American Culture and Fiction, 1880–1930* (Ithaca, NY: Cornell University Press, 2006); Sandra Gabriele, "Gendered Mobility, the Nation, and the Woman's Page: Exploring the Mobile Practices of the Canadian Lady Journalist," *Journalism* 7, no. 2 (2006): 174–96.

23. "Behind Asylum Bars," *New York World*, October 9, 1887, 25–26.

24. Lutes, *Front-Page Girls*, 13.

25. "The New *World*'s Birthday: A Chapter of Achievements," *New York World*, May 10, 1887, 9.

26. This manifesto was reprinted many times for anniversaries—for example, in "*The World*'s Corner Stone Principles," *New York World*, May 6, 1894, 30. The principles printed in the first edition under Pulitzer were widely reprinted across the country—for example, in "*The World*," *St. Louis Post-Dispatch*, May 11, 1883, 1; "Greeting of the 'New World,'" *Boston Globe*, May 11, 1883, 1; and "New York *World*," *Philadelphia Times*, May 12, 1883, 4.

27. "The New World's Sixth Birthday," *New York World*, May 11, 1889, 5.

28. "*The World*'s Corner Stone Principles," *New York World*, May 6, 1894, 30.

29. "We Must Raise the Money!" *New York World*, March 16, 1885, 1. See also Martin Conboy, *The Press and Popular Culture* (Thousand Oaks, CA: Sage, 2002), 53.

30. "No Funds for the Pedestal," *New York Herald*, March 13, 1885, 9.

31. "The Still Unfinished Pedestal," *New York Times*, March 13, 1885, 8.

32. "Popular Subscriptions," *New York World*, July 1, 1885, 5.

33. "The Statue's Good Cause," *New York World*, July 1, 1885, 9.

34. "One Hundred Thousand Dollars!" *New York World*, August 11, 1885, 1.

35. Promotions for "The Idea Contest" span from "That $1,000 Idea!" *New York Evening World*, October 19, 1889, 1, to November 1889.

36. "Ideas at a Premium," *St. Louis Post-Dispatch*, January 12, 1890, 7, and then a syndicated boiler-plate column, e.g. "*New York World* Prize Winners," *Marion (OH) Star*, February 1, 1890, 2.

37. "25,000! Ideas Already Submitted in the Contest of Brains," *New York World*, October 27, 1889, 21.

38. "The Idea Contest," *New York World*, November 3, 1889, 21.

39. "The Newsboys' Fund," *Philadelphia Item*, December 18, 1887, 1.

40. "Welcomed!" *San Francisco Examiner*, December 29, 1889, 11.

41. Ibid., 11.

42. Tiago de Luca, "Global Visions: Around-the-World Travel and Visual Culture in Early Modernity," in *Journeys on Screen: Theory, Ethics, Aesthetics*, ed. Louis Bayman and Natalia Pinazza, 19–35 (Edinburgh: Edinburgh University Press, 2019).

43. "Around the World," *New York World*, November 14, 1889, 1.

44. "Nellie Bly Guessing Match," *New York World*, November 29, 1889, 6.

45. Ibid., 6.

46. "Likes Globe-Trotting," *New York World*, January 27, 1890, 1.

47. "All O.K. Meaning *The Enquirer's* Guessing Enterprise," *Cincinnati Enquirer*, November 12, 1890, 1, and wire story widely printed same day.

48. "How Many Words in a Twenty-Eight-Page Chronicle?" *San Francisco Chronicle*, September 15, 1895, 1.

49. "The Winner of the Chronicle World Contest," *San Francisco Chronicle*, October 20, 1895, 12.

50. "Winner of the Word Contest," *San Francisco Examiner*, October 27, 1895, 17.

51. "Coupon Journalism," *Wilkes-Barre News-Dealer*, April 11, 1893, 4; widely reprinted from *Buffalo Courier*.

52. "The Sunday Edition of *The Times*, The Great Family Newspaper," *Philadelphia Times*, January 7, 1888, 2. Note also how promoting "Prizes for Children" had been on one of the front-page ears of the nameplate that day.

53. "For Young Readers," *Philadelphia Times*, January 8, 1888, 12.

54. Ibid.

55. "The Model Sunday Newspaper," *Philadelphia Times*, January 23, 1888, 2.

56. "Children's Corner: The P. D. Puzzlers' Club," *St. Louis Post-Dispatch*, January 15, 1888, 17.

57. "The Winning Words," *St. Louis Post-Dispatch*, February 19, 1888, 20.

58. "$1,000 in Gold," *New York World*, March 9, 1895, 5.

59. "Prize Novel Awards," *New York World*, April 22, 1895, 6.

60. "$100 in Gold," *Boston Post*, May 2, 1895, 5; "Prize Story Solutions," *Boston Post*, June 9, 1895, 17.

61. "Our Prize Story," *Chicago Inter-Ocean*, November 17, 1895, 7.

62. "The Mill of Silence," *San Francisco Examiner*, April 27, 1896, 14.

63. "$10,000 Prize for Film Story Won by St. Louis Girl," *St. Louis Post-Dispatch*, February 20, 1915, 1. See also Ilka Brasch, *Film Serials and American Cinema, 1910–1940* (Amsterdam: Amsterdam University Press, 2018), 81–83.

64. Early coupon voting contests include Most Popular Schoolteacher, with coupons on the "Children's Corner" page of the *St. Louis Post-Dispatch* starting February 19, 1888; Most Popular Veteran of the Grand Army of the Republic, with coupons daily in the *Boston Globe* starting July 5, 1890; and a "Grand Christmas Voting Carnival" with a dozen prizes, including a trip to Europe for the most popular person or organization in New England, again in the *Boston Globe* starting October 18, 1890.

65. "Swindling the Advertiser," *Nebraska State Journal* (Lincoln), February 4, 1890, 4.

66. "Most Popular Newsdealer," *New York Morning Journal*, March 9, 1890, 1.

67. "Pushing Forward: Albert Pulitzer Enlarges the New York Journal," *Fourth Estate*, April 18, 1895, 3; "On Newspaper Row," *Bookseller and Newsman*, January 1896, 19.

68. "Gotham's 'Morning Journal': Five Years of Newspaper Prosperity," *The Journalist*, December 3, 1887, 1; James Palmer, "Albert Pulitzer: Notes on the Lesser-Known Pulitzer Brother," The Pulitzer Prizes, www.pulitzer.org/page/albert-pulitzer-notes-lesser-known-pulitzer-brother/.

69. Reports that Joseph Pulitzer was behind the *Morning Journal* initially outnumber stories naming Albert as early as "Gotham Gossip," *New Orleans Picayune*, October 11, 1882, 9; "A New Daily," *Chicago Tribune*, October 22, 1882, 6; "A Penny Paper to Be Started in

New York," *New Orleans Picayune*, October 22, 1882, 2; "News and Notes," *Literary World*, November 18, 1882, 404.

70. "Our New York Letter: The Other Pulitzer," *St. Paul Globe*, May 12, 1884, 5, alleges that Albert Pulitzer's fortune was an ill-gained result of inside connections to the elevated railway companies while reporting for the *New York Herald*: "He published for the companies that which he ought to publish and left unpublished that which he ought not to publish and there was no journalistic honesty in him. They gave him of shares galore and in a few years found himself worth $25,000. He started the *Journal* . . . great is its gospel of gush."

71. *The Journalist*, July 12, 1884, 4, cited in George Juergens, *Joseph Pulitzer and the New York World* (Princeton, NJ: Princeton University Press, 1966), 9.

72. Kenneth Whyte, *The Uncrowned King: The Sensational Rise of William Randolph Hearst* (New York: Random House, 2009).

73. "A Newspaper Shakeup," *Buffalo News*, June 14, 1891, 6.

74. "Our New York Letter: The Other Pulitzer," *St. Paul Globe*, May 12, 1884, 5; "Americans in Paris: Two New York Journalists' Ideas of French Newspapers," *Philadelphia Times*, June 5, 1887, 11.

75. Whyte, *Uncrowned King*.

76. Press coverage of the upper class for the entertainment of the hoi polloi had become a routine part of the fame of wealth in the Gilded Age. See Lori Lyn Bogle, "Pandering to the Crowd: The American Governing Elite's Changing Views on Mass Media and Publicity during the Nineteenth Century," *Journalism History* 43, no. 2 (2017): 62–74.

77. "28 Pages To-Morrow," *New York Morning Journal*, September 14, 1889, 1.

78. "To-Morrow's Journal," *New York Morning Journal*, January 18, 1890, 1.

79. Henry Kellett Chambers, with an introduction by Lawrence Pratt, "A Park Row Interlude: Memoir of Albert Pulitzer," *Journalism Quarterly* 40, no. 4 (1963): 541.

80. "Topic of the Day XVIII—The Secret of Success in Journalism, by One Who Succeeded," *Pall Mall Budget*, May 30, 1884, 15.

81. "Gotham's 'Morning Journal': Five Years of Newspaper Prosperity," *The Journalist*, December 3, 1887, 1.

82. "By-the-bye," *The Journalist*, November 19, 1887, 9.

83. "Topic of the Day XVIII—The Secret of Success in Journalism, by One Who Succeeded," *Pall Mall Budget*, May 30, 1884, 15; "New York Morning Journal," *Printers' Circular*, April 1886, 25.

84. R. Louis Stevenson's "Treasure Island" launched the *Sunday World*'s "Midsummer Library" of weekly unabridged novels printed as broadsheet sections. See advance promotion—for example, "A Library for the Million, Newspaper and Book for 4 cts," *New York Evening World*, July 7, 1888, 2. These continued on Sundays through September 1888.

85. An illustrated banner collecting Sunday humor began with "The World's Funny Side," *New York World*, December 9, 1888, 28.

86. "Novel Supplements" begin in the *Morning Journal* by September 1888—for example, advertised in "The Irish Hurlers," *New York Evening World*, September 29, 1888, 1. See also Robert Buchanan's "That Winter Night or Love's Victory," *New York Morning Journal*, January 6, 1889, 17–20.

87. Printed anonymously, the winner turned out to be Miss May Belle Gregory of Tennessee, her crowning celebrated at home in Nashville. "Queen of Beauties," *Nashville Tennessean*,

April 28, 1889, 1; "Miss May B. Gregory, The Nashville Beauty," *Memphis Public Ledger*, May 2, 1889, 1.

88. "Our Prize Beauty Show: Group No. One," *New York Morning Journal*, November 24, 1889, 17.

89. "Our Manly Beauties," *New York Morning Journal*, January 26, 1890, 12.

90. "An Art Jewel," *New York Morning Journal*, November 9, 1889, 1.

91. "Picture Gallery No. 1," *New York Morning Journal*, November 10, 1889, 1.

92. "Picture Free of Charge To-Morrow," *New York Morning Journal*, December 14, 1889, 1.

93. "Two Beautiful Pictures," *New York Morning Journal*, January 11, 1890, 1.

94. "Next Sunday," *New York Morning Journal*, January 23, 1890, 1.

95. "Next Sunday's Picture," *New York Morning Journal*, February 21, 1890, 1.

96. "Next Sunday's Journal," *New York Morning Journal*, March 7, 1890, 1.

97. "Vestal Virgin," *New York Morning Journal*, May 17, 1890, 1.

98. "Deserted," *New York Morning Journal*, May 11, 1890, 2.

99. Fergus Hume, *Miss Mephistopheles*, "Morning Journal Library," *New York Morning Journal*, June 1, 1890.

100. Special supplements began in the *New York News* as "complete novels" in its two-cent Sunday edition from May 1890 to February 1892. See advertising in "People Wonder," *New York Evening World*, May 9, 1890, 3. The *New York World* brought back its "complete novel" summer Sunday supplements in July 1892. See advertising in "Don't Fail to Buy To-Morrow *The World's* Summer Novel," *New York Evening World*, July 23, 1892, 5. Discussed in more detail in the next section, art supplements begin, for example, in the *New York Sunday World* in September 1892 with special posters of Grover Cleveland and his wife. See advertising, "An Art Supplement," *New York Evening World*, August 30, 1892, 1.

101. Ann Colbert, "Philanthropy in the Newsroom: Women's Editions of Newspapers, 1894–1896," *Journalism History* 22, no. 3 (1996): 90–99.

102. "The New Newspaper," *The Newsman*, January 1891, 2. At the time, W. Duke, Sons & Co. had entered into a merger only a year earlier and J. P. Knapp would soon lead a similar amalgamation of lithographers. "Cigarette Nabobs Form a Huge Trust," *New York Herald*, January 22, 1890, 8; "A New Trust: Organization of the American Lithographic Company," *New York Times*, February 6, 1892, 3.

103. "The New York Recorder," *The Newsman*, March 1891, 10.

104. "Local Lines," *Boston Globe*, March 21, 1891, 5.

105. "Every Sunday Edition," *Greensboro (NC) North State*, April 9, 1891, 4.

106. "The Art Supplement," *York (PA) Daily*, April 24, 1891, 1.

107. "News of the Week Illustrated," *New York Recorder*, July 12, 1891, 1.

108. "Starting a New York Newspaper," *New York Sun*, July 12, 1891, 15.

109. "A New Idea in Newspapers!" *New York Press*, April 11, 1891, 1.

110. "Ready for Music, Castle Garden Watered and Made to Blossom," *New York Morning Journal*, August 30, 1891, 2. Several front-page illustrated articles in the *Morning Journal* spotlighted the festivities throughout September.

111. "The City," *Bismarck (SD) Tribune*, September 13, 1891, 3.

112. "Parnell's Life-Romance," *New York Morning Journal*, November 29, 1891, Library supplement; "The Rabbi's Spell: A Russo-Jewish Romance," *New York Morning Journal*, December 6, 1891, Library supplement.

113. "Delilah, in rich colors, by the finest art process. Also a great book, which will fascinate the readers. Both free with the paper and costing only 5 cents." "With Next Sunday's *Journal*," *New York Morning Journal*, November 26, 1891, 7.

114. "Announcement Extraordinary," *Philadelphia Inquirer*, April 2, 1893, 8.

115. "Three Great Gems," *Boston Post*, September 16, 1893, 1.

116. "A Faint Idea," *Washington Times*, November 8, 1894, 2.

CHAPTER 2. APPRECIATING THE ART OF THE SUPPLEMENT

1. Walter Benjamin, *The Work of Art in the Age of Its Technological Reproducibility, and Other Writings on Media* (Cambridge, MA: Belknap Press of Harvard University Press, 2008).

2. "Do You Want a Frame for Your *Chicago Tribune* Picture Free?" *Chicago Tribune*, May 27, 1894, 26.

3. "In the Nursery," *Buffalo News*, August 8, 1894, 3.

4. "A Free Binder," *Chicago Inter-Ocean*, April 29, 1893, 16.

5. For example, "The Inquirer's Great Offer," *Philadelphia Inquirer*, September 24, 1893, 24.

6. "*The Inquirer* Portfolios," *Philadelphia Inquirer*, October 1, 1893, 4.

7. The promotional ad "A Clamoring Multitude" appears with local coupons offering the portfolios in, for example, the *Memphis Commercial*, October 1, 1893, 7; *Buffalo News*, October 14, 1893, 4; *Denver Rocky Mountain News*, October 16, 1893, 3; and *Evansville (IN) Courier*, January 30, 1894, 6, among others.

8. "Came in Throngs," *St. Louis Post-Dispatch*, December 4, 1893, 6.

9. "The Golden Wedding of Those Twin Spirits of the Ages," *St. Louis Post-Dispatch*, December 6, 1893, 6.

10. "The Elevation of the Masses," *Philadelphia Inquirer*, March 4, 1894, 13.

11. "Pictures Flashed by Ocean Cable To-Morrow," *Philadelphia Inquirer*, April 28, 1895, 28.

12. "Wild Flowers of America," *Boston Post*, July 22, 1894, 24.

13. "Great Music Offer," *Boston Globe*, December 17, 1893, 23.

14. "Of Course," *Chicago Inter-Ocean*, May 7, 1894, 12.

15. "*The Republic's* Music Supplement," *St. Louis Republic*, May 5, 1894, 10.

16. "*Boston Globe* Cut Paper Patterns," *Boston Globe*, October 22, 1893, 28.

17. "Patterns for the Ladies," *St. Louis Republic*, November 26, 1893, 31.

18. "Prima Donnas as Christmas Dolls," *New York Herald*, December 23, 1894, 4.

19. "Dolls Who Are Also Men of Mark," *New York Herald*, December 30, 1894, 7.

20. "Delight the Children," *Chicago Herald*, January 4, 1895, 5.

21. Ibid.

22. "Thousands of Children," *Detroit Free Press*, January 27, 1895, 28.

23. "The Colored Doll Supplements," *Detroit Free Press*, February 18, 1895, 3.

24. "Always Something New," *San Francisco Chronicle*, November 17, 1895, 12.

25. "Of Interest to Every Lady," *Boston Herald*, March 23, 1895, 12.

26. "Why Not Be Up to Date on Fashions?" *San Francisco Chronicle*, November 17, 1895, 24.

27. Ibid.

28. "Dolls and Doll Dresses by the Hundred Given Away with the Sunday Globe," *Boston Globe*, May 29, 1895, 4.

29. "They Give Pleasure to Many," *New York Herald*, January 9, 1895, 11.

30. "Dolls and Doll Dresses by the Hundred Given Away with the Sunday Globe," *Boston Globe*, May 29, 1895, 4.

31. "$250 in Gold. A Man You All Know Becomes a Doll," *Boston Globe*, August 9, 1895, 4.

32. "Something New!" *Boston Globe*, August 30, 1895, 8.

33. "A Yacht Free," *Boston Globe*, September 6, 1895, 4.

34. "Going to the Fire," *Boston Globe*, November 8, 1895, 6.

35. "A Whole Theatre Free," *Boston Globe*, December 7, 1895, 5.

36. "Little Red Riding Hood," *Boston Globe*, December 11, 1895, 4.

37. "Next Sunday's Christmas Present to *Inquirer* Readers," *Philadelphia Inquirer*, December 15, 1895, 20.

38. "Tremendous Rush for Sunday *Inquirers*," *Philadelphia Inquirer*, December 23, 1895, 1.

39. "The Joy of the Children," *Washington Times*, February 9, 1896, 5.

40. "No Dull Sundays Now!" *Washington Evening Times*, February 29, 1896, 5.

41. "Inaugural Announcement Boston Herald Opera House," *Boston Herald*, February 25, 1896, 7.

42. "A Real Theater with Moving Figures," *Philadelphia Press*, February 23, 1896, 38.

43. "*The Sunday Inquirer* Souvenir Fairy Theater," *Philadelphia Inquirer*, February 23, 1896, 24.

44. "Base Ball at Home," *Philadelphia Inquirer*, May 10, 1896, 12.

45. "An Unending Wonder. Newspaper of Novelties," *Boston Herald*, April 4, 1896, 4.

46. "See *The Globe*'s Biggest Press at Work!" *Boston Globe*, August 15, 1896, 6.

47. "Order! In Advance To-Morrow's *Sunday World*," *New York Evening World*, November 18, 1911, 5.

48. "A Sunday Newspaper Magazine Free," *New York Evening World*, September 26, 1912, 11.

49. "A Development in Sunday Newspapers," *Boston Herald*, October 6, 1912, 30.

50. The term "tabloid" was embraced in the United Kingdom by Alfred Harmsworth, proprietor of the *London Mail*, who spotlighted the idea in the United States when invited by Joseph Pulitzer to edit the New Year's Day 1901 edition of the *New York World*: "condensed, tabloid journalism . . . all the news in sixty seconds . . . the busy man's paper," a novelty for "the Twentieth or Time-Saving century." See the facsimile of the "Title Page of Harmsworth's Edition of *New York World*," *Fourth Estate*, January 5, 1901, 6, and "In Deference to Mr. Harmsworth's Ideas," *Fourth Estate*, January 5, 1901, 2. See also Frank Luther Mott, *American Journalism: A History of Newspapers in the United States, 1690 to 1940* (New York: Macmillan, 1941), 666–67.

51. "Don't Fail to Read 'Midget' in To-Morrow's *Sunday Post-Dispatch*," *St. Louis Post-Dispatch*, December 30, 1893, 3.

52. "Your Little Paper," *St. Louis Post-Dispatch*, January 13, 1894, 2.

53. "The Christmas *Inter-Ocean*," *Chicago Inter-Ocean*, December 23, 1893, 8.

54. "Great Prize Picture Puzzle," *New York Press*, April 28, 1901, Magazine supplement, 16. In the early twentieth century, Samuel S. McClure's bother, Thomas Carlyle, was charged with managing McClure Newspaper Syndicate, including the launch of color comics. "T. C. McClure is Dead; Managed Syndicate," *Editor and Publisher*, November 3, 1934, 36.

55. "Winners in the Sunday Republic's Prize Color Page Contest," *St. Louis Republic*, April 20, 1902, 29.

56. Ibid.

57. Ibid.

58. Ibid.

59. "Name Puzzles," *San Francisco Call*, January 3, 1904, 16.

60. For example, "Magic for the Little Ones," *New York Times*, February 8, 1902, 1.

61. "Magic Color Pictures," *Mount Carmel (PA) News*, March 7, 1902, 4.

62. "Directions," *Cleveland Plain Dealer*, April 6, 1902, Color supplement, 8.

63. "The New Era Transformation Magazine Supplement," *Indianapolis Journal*, December 20, 1901, 2.

64. "Watch for Next Surprise that is Different," *Buffalo Times*, February 12, 1902, 2.

65. Among the other newspapers who promoted, including the New Era Transformation Magazine, were the *Elyria (OH) Chronicle*, December 30, 1901, 2, and the *Owensboro (KY) Inquirer*, March 12, 1902, 2, the latter including many preserved copies between March 1902 and April 1903. See also "'The' Supplement," *Newspaperdom*, September 18, 1902, 13.

66. "Special Christmas Attractions with Tomorrow's Boston Sunday Journal," *Boston Journal*, December 21, 1901, 2.

67. "Not Now but Next Sunday," *Boston Journal*, January 2, 1902, 2.

68. "Hidden Pictures, Rub Blank Spaces with Bowl of a Spoon," *Pittsburg Press*, March 2, 1902, Comic supplement and subsequent Sundays; Rachel Plotnick, "Rubbing Readers the Wrong Way? Materiality and the Case of Ink Rub-Off," *American Journalism* 32, no. 2 (2015): 221–32.

69. "Develop the Negative," *Boston Post*, February 7, 1902, 5; "The Great Hidden Pictures, Instructions," *Boston Post*, February 9, 1902, 1.

70. Matthew Solomon, "Review of Georges Méliès: First Wizard of Cinema, 1896–1913," *Moving Image* 12, no. 2 (2012): 187–92.

71. Charles Musser and Carol Nelson, *High-Class Moving Pictures: Lyman H. Howe and the Forgotten Era of Traveling Exhibition, 1880–1920* (Princeton, NJ: Princeton University Press, 1991); see one of Howe's posters, featuring "New Magic Pictures," at Library of Congress, online at www.loc.gov/item/97520513/.

72. "With Tomorrow's Sunday Examiner," *Riverside (CA) Press*, December 17, 1904, 5; "Plastograph and Anaglyph," *San Francisco Examiner*, January 24, 1905, 16, and subsequent weeks.

73. "Special Announcement," *Lexington (VA) Gazette*, February 1, 1905, 3.

74. *Syracuse Herald*, January 2, 1905.

75. *Boston Herald*, May 12, 1905. The same product had been earlier linked to coupons in the *Buffalo Enquirer*, from October 5, 1904, and the *Detroit Free Press*, from October 27, 1904.

76. "Book of Magic" supplement, *Washington Times*, December 4, 1921, S-5, and same in *San Francisco Examiner*, December 11, 1921.

77. A "Fairy Color Section" was launched in the *Cleveland Plain Dealer*, April 23, 1922, promoted regionally, for example, in "New!! Wonderful!! First Time!!" *Mansfield (OH) News*, April 21, 1922, 2.

78. "Not Second-Class Matter," *Washington Post*, April 12, 1905, 10.

79. 45th Congress of the United States, *Statutes at Large*, Chapter 180 (An Act making appropriations for the service of the Post Office Department), Section 16 (Second-Class Matter, Supplements), March 3, 1879. The definition of a publication's supplement was intro-

duced in December 1878 and passed in March 1879. See "A Proposed New Postal Law," *New York Times*, December 18, 1878, 1; "The Postal System," *Chicago Tribune*, March 11, 1879, 1.

80. "Not Second-Class Matter," *Washington Post*, April 12, 1905, 10.

81. Ibid.

82. "Not a Square Deal," *Frederick (MD) News*, January 6, 1906, 6.

83. "New Journalistic Wrinkles," *Waco (TX) Examiner*, December 22, 1881, 1, reprinted from the *St. Louis Republican.*

84. According to Michael Stamm, newspapers in the United States in the 1930s pioneered the techniques of media convergence and the multimedia conglomerate precisely through operating radio stations, by 1940 owning fully one-third of the nation's stations, a trend that "continued into newly licensed FM stations after 1941 and television stations after 1948." Stamm, *Sound Business: Newspapers, Radio, and the Politics of New Media* (Philadelphia: University of Philadelphia Press, 2011), 5.

85. Anne F. MacLennan, "Learning to Listen: Developing the Canadian Radio Audience in the 1930s," *Journal of Radio and Audio Media* 20, no. 2 (2013): 331–26.

86. "Demand for Trained Radio Editors Growing," *Editor and Publisher*, February 23, 1924, 11, quoting an interview with E. L. Bragdon, radio editor of the *New York Herald.*

87. Michele Hilmes, *Radio Voices: American Broadcasting, 1922–1952* (Minneapolis: University of Minnesota Press, 1997), 72.

88. Gene Allen, "Old Media, New Media, and Competition: Canadian Press and the Emergence of Radio News," in *Communicating in Canada's Past: Essays in Media History*, ed. Gene Allen and Daniel J. Robinson (Toronto: University of Toronto Press, 2009), 51.

89. Hilmes, *Radio Voices*, 69.

90. Hans V. Kaltenborn's 1927 remarks to the American Society of Newspaper Editors are cited in Alf Pratte, "Going Along for the Ride on the Prosperity Bandwagon: Peaceful Annexation Not War between the Editors and the Radio, 1923–1941," *Journal of Radio Studies* 2, no. 3 (1993): 129–39.

91. Stamm, *Sound Business*, 14.

92. Mary Vipond, *Listening In: The First Decade of Canadian Broadcasting, 1922–1932* (Montreal: McGill-Queen's University Press, 1992), 44.

93. "The News Radiophone to Give Vote Results," *Detroit News*, August 31, 1920, 1.

94. "Radio Carries Voice and Band," *Detroit News*, December 21, 1921, 35.

95. "Florida Dances by News Radio, Powerful Apparatus Installed," *Detroit News*, February 12, 1922, 1.

96. Hilmes, *Radio Voices*, 54–63.

97. "Entire State Responds to KUO Call," *San Francisco Examiner*, March 24, 1922, 6.

98. Oliver W. Tuttle, "Concert Wins High Praise for Examiner," *San Francisco Examiner*, April 2, 1922, 1.

99. "High-Powered Station Will Send Thrills," *San Francisco Examiner*, April 1, 1922, 8.

100. "Entertainment Program Sent Out from Radio Station at *Post-Dispatch*," *St. Louis Post-Dispatch*, March 12, 1922, 1.

101. "K.S.D. Program is Heard in Iowa," *St. Louis Post-Dispatch*, April 5, 1922, 3.

102. "Read Jack Binns Radio Articles Every Sunday," *New York Tribune*, February 4, 1922, 9. Binns's illustrated feature page began the next day.

103. "Radio Phone Service Column," *New York Evening World*, January 14, 1922, 4. The column soon gained a byline, Capt. Robert Schofield Wood, "former commander 167th Squadron, Royal Air Force."

104. "A Radio Magazine Free with *The Globe*," *New York Herald*, February 17, 1922, 9.

105. "*The Evening Mail*, A 16-Page Illustrated Radio Magazine," *New York Tribune*, March 11, 1922, 9.

106. Lloyd C. Greene's page, "Citizen Radio Broadcasts," begins with the *Boston Globe*, February 12, 1922, 40.

107. Joe Toye, "Sunday Herald Radio Department," *Boston Herald*, February 19, 1922, D-9.

108. G. R. Entwistle, "Citizen Wireless," *Boston Traveler*, March 18, 1922, 4; "An Afternoon Broadcast of News Daily, furnished by *The Boston Traveler*," *Boston Herald*, March 31, 1922, 19.

109. "$10 Prize for Best Photo of Radio Family," *San Francisco Examiner*, March 23, 1922, 1.

110. "Citizen Wireless Prize Contest," *Boston Traveler*, March 20, 1922, 11.

111. "Examiner's Going to Give Radiophones to Live Wires!" *San Francisco Examiner*, March 25, 1922, 7, and full-page ad with details on page 18.

112. "1000 Radio Receiving Sets Offered FREE," *St. Louis Post-Dispatch*, April 9, 1922, 31, with the subscribers' information needing to be submitted by June 1. This offer was repeated in September.

113. "Everyone Can Win a Radio Receiving Set Free," *San Francisco Chronicle*, April 12, 1922, C-12.

114. "Listening In Outside the Studio," *Kansas City Star*, June 25, 1922, C-16.

115. "Radio Equipped Photoplay Houses," *Kansas City Star*, June 4, 1922, 11.

116. "Fashion Chat from WDAF," *Kansas City Star*, July 7, 1922, 1.

117. Margery Wells, "Good Taste in Modern Dressing," *New York Evening World*, February 13, 1922, 19. First broadcast announced by Capt. Robert Scofield Wood, "Fashion Chats by Wireless," *New York Evening World*, February 11, 1922, 4.

118. Program listings for WJZ, week March 19–25, 1922, *New York Herald*, March 19, 1922, 29.

119. "Here Is Tonight's Program of News Service by Radio," *Chicago Tribune*, February 1, 1922, 1. The *Tribune*–Westinghouse Radio News Service began a week earlier. "Radio to Carry Resume of News," *Chicago Tribune*, January 24, 1922, 1.

120. "WGN's Daily Entertainment Is Designed to Please Everybody!" *Chicago Tribune*, January 10, 1926, part 5, p. 2.

121. "Radio Programs for Today," *Chicago Tribune*, January 12, 1926, 21.

122. Quin A. Ryan, WGN announcer, "Inside the Loud Speaker," *Chicago Tribune*, February 14, 1926, part 5, p. 4.

123. "Radio Programs for Today," *Chicago Tribune*, January 20, 1926, 19.

124. Vanessa Schwartz, *Spectacular Realities: Early Mass Culture in Fin-de-Siècle Paris* (Berkeley: University of California Press, 1998).

125. "Radio Photo Trip Ready," *Chicago Daily News*, September 26, 1924, 1. See also Katie Day Good, "Listening to Pictures: Converging Media Histories and the Multimedia Newspaper," *Journalism Studies* 18, no. 6 (2017), 691–709.

126. "Many 'See' Game," *Wisconsin State Journal* (Madison), November 5, 1922, 5.

127. "Radio Truck Gives Ball Game Play by Play," *Dallas News*, August 7, 1922, 7.

128. Ibid.

129. "World Series Returns to Be Flashed by Radio," *San Antonio News*, October 3, 1922, 1. See also Will Mari, "Technology in the Newsroom: Adoption of the Telephone and the Radio Car from c. 1920 to 1960," *Journalism Studies* 19, no. 9 (2018): 1366–89; Sandra Gabriele and Paul S. Moore, "Old Media, New Media, Intermedia: The Toronto Star and CFCA, 1922–1933," in *Cultural Industries.ca: Making Sense of Canadian Media in the Digital Age*, ed. Ira Wagman and Peter Urquhart (Toronto: Lorimer, 2012), 220–38.

130. "Radio Car Is Novelty for Party Guests," *San Antonio News*, October 26, 1922, 9.

131. "Hundreds Introduced to Wonders of Radio," *Rochester Democrat and Chronicle*, October 8, 1922, C-18.

132. "WGN, Tribune Radio, Starts Tonight," *Chicago Tribune*, March 29, 1924, 1.

133. "How It's Done by Radio Seen in News Reel," *Chicago American*, April 28, 1922, 12.

134. Michael Warner, *Publics and Counter Publics* (New York: Zone, 2002); Miriam Hansen, "Room-for-Play: Walter Benjamin's Gamble with Cinema," *October* 109 (2004): 3–45.

135. "How It's Done by Radio Seen in News Reel," *Chicago American*, April 28, 1922, 12.

PART II. CIRCULATION

1. Though the list here could be long, we note only two important references: Theodor Adorno and Max Horkheimer, *The Culture Industry: Selected Essays on Mass Culture* (New York: Routledge, 1991); and Dallas Smythe, "On the Audience Commodity and Its Work," in *Dependency Road: Communications, Capitalism, Consciousness, and Canada*, (Norwood, NJ: Ablex, 1981), 22–51.

2. Lisa Gitelman, *Paper Knowledge: Toward a Media History of Documents* (Durham, NC: Duke University Press, 2014), 163.

3. Lisa Gitelman, *Always Already New* (Cambridge, MA: MIT Press, 2006); Will Straw, "The Circulatory Turn," in *The Wireless Spectrum: The Politics, Practices, and Poetics of Mobile Media*, ed. Barbara Crow, Michael Longford, and Kim Sawchuk, 17–28 (Toronto: University of Toronto Press, 2010).

4. Michael Warner, *Publics and Counterpublics* (New York: Zone, 2002), 88.

5. David M. Henkin, "On Forms and Media," *Representations* 104, no. 1 (2008): 36.

6. Lawrence Grossberg, *Bringing It All Back Home: Essays in Cultural Studies* (Durham, NC: Duke University Press, 1997); Stuart Hall, "On Postmodernism and Articulation: An Interview with Stuart Hall," in *Stuart Hall: Critical Dialogues in Cultural Studies*, ed. David Morley and Kuan-Hsing Chen, 131–50 (New York: Routledge, 1996); Stuart Hall, "The Toad in the Garden: Thatcherism among the Theorists," in *Marxism and the Interpretation of Culture*, ed. Carol Nelson and Lawrence Grossberg, 35–73 (Urbana: University of Illinois Press, 1988); Stuart Hall, "Signification, Representation, Ideology: Althusser and the Post-Structuralist Debates," *Critical Studies in Mass Communication* 2, no. 2 (1985): 91–114; Jennifer Daryl Slack, "The Theory and Method of Articulation in Cultural Studies," in *Stuart Hall: Critical Dialogues in Cultural Studies*, ed. David Morley and Kuan-Hsing Chen, 112–30 (New York: Routledge, 1996); and Jennifer Daryl Slack and John M. Wise, *Culture + Technology: A Primer*, 2nd ed. (New York: Peter Lang, 2015).

7. Alexandra Boutros and Will Straw, eds., *Circulation and the City: Essays on Urban Culture* (Montreal: McGill-Queen's University Press, 2010), 3–22; Alan Blum, *The Imaginative Structure of the City* (Montreal: McGill-Queen's University Press, 2003).

8. Bruno Latour, *Reassembling the Social: An Introduction to Actor-Network Theory* (New York: Oxford University Press, 2005); John Law and John Hassard, *Actor-Network Theory and After* (Malden, MA: Blackwell, 1999); W. E. Bijker, T. P. Hughes, and T. J. Pinch, *The Social Construction of Technological Systems: New Directions in the Sociology and History of Technology* (Cambridge, MA: MIT Press, 1987); Gilles Deleuze and Félix Guattari, *A Thousand Plateaus: Capitalism and Schizophrenia* (Minneapolis: University of Minnesota Press, 1987).

9. Benjamin Lee and Edward LiPuma, "Cultures of Circulation: The Imaginations of Modernity," *Public Culture* 14, no. 1 (2002): 191–213.

CHAPTER 3. THE INTERMEDIAL IDEALS OF THE SUNDAY EDITION

1. *New York Journal*, December 19, 1896, 19.

2. *Philadelphia Press*, April 25, 1903, 13.

3. André Bazin, *What Is Cinema?* trans. Timothy Barnard (Montreal: Caboose, 2009).

4. Lisa Gitelman, *Scripts, Grooves, and Writing Machines: Representing Technology in the Edison Era* (Stanford, CA: Stanford University Press, 1999); Lisa Gitelman, *Always Already New* (Cambridge, MA: MIT Press, 2006).

5. Steve J. Wurtzler, *Electric Sounds: Technological Change and the Rise of Corporate Mass Media* (New York: Columbia University Press, 2007).

6. Laurel Brake and Marysa Demoor, eds., *The Lure of Illustration in the Nineteenth Century: Picture and Press* (New York: Palgrave Macmillan, 2009); Gerry Beegan, *The Mass Image: A Social History of Photochemical Reproduction in Victorian London* (New York: Palgrave Macmillan, 2008).

7. "Wonders of the Newspaper Color Press," *San Francisco Examiner*, April 18, 1897, 4.

8. Ibid. The same wonder and fascination was true of the quest for color film. See Joshua Yumibe, *Moving Color: Early Film, Mass Culture, Modernism* (New Brunswick, NJ: Rutgers University Press, 2012).

9. Jonathan Crary, *Techniques of the Observer: On Vision and Modernity in the Nineteenth Century* (Cambridge, MA: MIT Press, 1990); Jonathan Crary, *Suspensions of Perception: Attention, Spectacle, and Modern Culture* (Cambridge, MA: MIT Press, 2000).

10. "A Marvel of Modern Mechanism," *New York World*, February 26, 1898, 16.

11. Dilip Gaonkar and Elizabeth Povinelli, "Technologies of Public Forms: Circulation, Transfiguration, Recognition," *Public Culture* 15, no. 3 (2003): 385–97.

12. For example, "Toasts of the Typographical Society," *Philadelphia Spirit of the Press*, November 16, 1805, 2; "New York Typographical Society," *New York Spectator*, July 10, 1827, 2.

13. John Nerone, *The Media and Public Life: A History* (Malden, MA: Polity Press, 2015). See also John Nerone, "Newswork, Technology, and Cultural Form, 1937–1920," in *Explorations in Communication and History*, ed. Barbie Zelizer (New York: Routledge, 2008), 141.

14. For example, "New Publications," *New York Mirror*, June 12, 1855, 3, or "Books and Stationery," *Philadelphia Inquirer*, July 6, 1855, 3.

15. "'The Item' Telephone," *Philadelphia Item*, September 4, 1887, 15.

16. "Vitascope Pictures," *Washington Post*, October 18, 1896, 6.

17. "The Vitascope," *Washington Post*, December 6, 1896, 4.

18. Will Mari, "Technology in the Newsroom: Adoption of the Telephone and the Radio Car from c. 1920 to 1960," *Journalism Studies* 19, no. 9 (2018): 1366–89.

19. The phrase "from an instantaneous photograph" was used to caption eyewitness illustrations as early as 1871 in *Frank Leslie's Illustrated Newspaper* (e.g., "Our Wandering Minstrels," November 25, 1871, 165). In use by 1885 to accompany amateur photographs (e.g., "Artists in Sun Pictures," *New York World*, October 4, 1885, 4), the phrase was attached to capture the actions of sports (e.g., "How Men Pitch Ball," *St. Louis Post-Dispatch*, September 2, 1886, 5; "We Win, Mayflower Beats the Galatea," *Boston Herald*, September 8, 1886, 1).

20. N. S. Shaler, "The Process of Storms," *Boston Herald*, June 9, 1889, 21.

21. Phillip Prodger, ed., *Time Stands Still: Muybridge and the Instantaneous Photography Movement* (New York: Oxford University Press, 2003).

22. "The Flood on the Sacramento River," *San Francisco Examiner*, December 15, 1889.

23. An earlier instance of a "photographic interview" came in Paris in *Le Journal Illustré* in 1886. With pictures by famous photographer Nadar, the novelty received comment in the United States and among journalistic circles and was repeated again late in 1889, which may have more directly inspired the *New York World* to copy the idea. Thierry Gervais, "Interview of Chevreul, France, 1886," in *Getting the Picture: The Visual Culture of News*, ed. Jason E. Hill and Vanessa R. Schwartz, 35–37 (New York: Bloomsbury, 2015).

24. Frank Luther Mott, *American Journalism: A History of Newspaper in the United States, 1690–1940* (New York: Macmillan, 1941), 502–503.

25. "A Photographic Interview," *New York World*, April 13, 1890, 19–22; "Talmage the Unique," *New York World*, May 4, 1890, 17–20.

26. Advance promotion for the photographic interview with Senator Ingalls. "Read It and Preserve It for Your Children's Children," *New York Evening World*, April 11, 1890, 1.

27. Ibid.

28. "Newspaper Illustrations," *New Haven (CT) Register*, April 15, 1890, 2.

29. Ibid.

30. Ibid.

31. "Talmage the Unique," *New York World*, May 4, 1890, 17–20.

32. Ibid.

33. "That New York Interview," *Kansas City Star*, August 17, 1900, 2; see also John James Ingalls, *A Collection of Writings: Essays, Addresses, Orations*, ed. William E. Connelly (Kansas City: Hudson-Kimberly, 1902).

34. "Dainty Della Fox!" *New York Morning Journal*, May 25, 1890, 24.

35. "King of Pugilists, John L. Sullivan," *New York Morning Journal*, June 15, 1890, 17.

36. "Bellamy's Boston, He Slept a Century," *Boston Globe*, May 4, 1890, 25.

37. The novelty was revived by the *Boston Journal* in the last months of 1896 to illustrate interviews with Boston society figures with actual halftoned photographs in its Sunday photographic supplement. The move was briefly followed by the *Boston Herald* in February 1897.

38. "Last and First Photograph of McKinley and His Cabinet," *New York World*, May 16, 1897, M-1; "Veriscope Records Fight," *New York World*, May 22, 1897, 4–5; "Loie Fuller Defines Pantomime," *New York World*, May 23, 1897, 29.

39. The sprawling headline for the double-page illustration ran "Exact Reproduction of the Scene at Grant's Tomb Yesterday When the First Division of 54,000 Uniformed Men Passed in Review Before President McKinley, the Vice President, The Governor of the State, Gen. Grant's Widow, and Countless Spectators," *New York World*, April 28, 1897, 5–6.

40. Another double-page headline topping the illustration ran "The Land and Naval Parades in Honor of Gen. Grant, as They Will Appear Next Tuesday Passing the Tomb of America's Greatest Military Hero, and the Immense Concourse of Citizens that Will Witness the Dedication of the Tomb," *New York World*, April 25, 1897, 22–23.

41. "Bryan Poses for the Inter-Ocean's Moving Picture Machine," *Chicago Inter-Ocean*, July 15, 1900, 37.

42. "Bryan in a Moving Picture," *Kansas City Star*, May 24, 1898, 1.

43. "Bryan Poses for the Inter-Ocean," *Chicago Inter-Ocean*, July 15, 1900, 37.

44. "Moving Pictures Which Governor Roosevelt Declined to Pose For at St. Paul," *Chicago Inter-Ocean*, July 22, 1900, 37.

45. Ibid.

46. For example, "Gets Ahead of Roosevelt, Picture Man Steals a March on the 'Rough Rider,'" *Sioux City (IA) Journal*, July 21, 1900, 6, from "Moving Picture Man Steals March on Gov. Roosevelt in St. Paul," *Chicago Tribune*, July 19, 1900, 5.

47. "A New Terror to Public Men," *Chicago Tribune*, July 10, 1900, 6.

48. Juliette De Maeyer and John Delva, "When Computers Were New: Shifts in the Journalistic Sensorium, 1960s-1990s," *Digital Journalism* 9, no. 6 (2020): 1–18, doi.org/10.1080/21670811.2020.1780143.

49. "Searching the Firmament," *New York World*, May 1, 1887, 11. On the public media spectacles of "aerial theatre," including fireworks and balloon ascensions, see Erkki Huhtamo, "The Sky Is (not) the Limit: Envisioning the Ultimate Public Media Display," *Journal of Visual Culture* 8, no. 3 (2010): 329–48.

50. "Searching the Firmament," *New York World*, May 1, 1887, 11.

51. Ibid.

52. Ibid.

53. "The Balloon Is in the Sky," *New York World*, June 18, 1887, 1.

54. "Imitation Is the Sincerest Flattery," *New York Graphic,* May 20, 1887, 660–61.

55. "A Real Flying Machine at Last!" *New York World*, August 4, 1895, 21.

56. Ibid.

57. "*The Sunday World* Discovers a Flying Machine that Really Flies," *New York World*, May 16, 1897, 30.

58. "*The Sunday World*'s Balloon for Photographing Greater New York 1,000 Feet Above the Ground," *New York World*, May 2, 1897, 31. On the drive to make maps always more engaging, see Brooke Belisle, "Nature at a Glance: Immersive Maps from Panoramic to Digital," *Early Popular Visual Culture* 13, no. 4 (2015): 313–35.

59. "Bird's Eye Map of New York Made from Photographs Taken from *The Sunday World*'s Balloon," *New York World*, May 23, 1897, 32.

60. "Greater New York Photographed from *The Sunday World*'s Balloon," *New York World*, May 23, 1897, 34–35.

61. "Exact Reproductions by Wire," *New York Journal*, October 25, 1896, 31.

62. Ibid.

63. Ibid.

64. "How Pictures May be Transmitted a Thousand Miles and Friends Brought Face to Face," *New York World*, October 18, 1896, 24–25.

65. Ibid.

66. Ibid.

67. "A Very Interesting Discovery of Science," *San Francisco Examiner*, November 1, 1896, 34.

68. Ibid.

69. Noah Arceneaux, "News on the Air: The *New York Herald*, Newspapers, and Wireless Telegraphy, 1899–1917," *American Journalism* 30, no. 2 (2013): 160–81.

70. "The Telediagraph, The Century's Latest Wonder," *New York Herald*, April 23, 1899, D-1.

71. "Newspaper Illustration Sent By Wire," *Boston Herald*, April 23, 1899, 40.

72. "Wreck on the Reading Railroad in Exeter," *New York Herald*, May 14, 1899, 2.

73. "Wireless Telegraphy Saves Lives," *San Francisco Call*, May 7, 1899, 19.

74. "Visitors Delighted," *Boston Herald*, April 25, 1899, 12. See also "Newspaper Illustrations Sent by Wire," *Boston Herald*, April 23, 1899, 40.

75. "Flashing Pictures Around the World," *San Francisco Call*, April 3, 1898, 25.

76. "Moving Pictures By Wire," *Detroit Free Press*, April 3, 1898, D6.

77. "Flashing Pictures Around the World," *San Francisco Call*, April 3, 1898, 25.

78. "A Boy Wizard to Flash *The World*'s Motto from London to Paris Without Wires," *New York World*, August 8, 1897, 29.

79. Ibid.

80. "Official Wireless War News Under Water Demonstrated by *The World*," *New York World*, May 8, 1898, 25.

81. "To Whisk *The World* from Here to India in a Day by Unseen Hands," *New York World*, May 16, 1897, 33.

82. "Marvelous Work of Wireless Telegraphy," *San Francisco Call*, October 4, 1899, 2.

83. "Crowds in Front of the *Inquirer* Building Listening to the *Bulletin* Announcer and Watching the Progress of the Ariel Yachts," *Philadelphia Inquirer*, October 4, 1899, 7.

84. "Lake and Land Stations of Wireless Telegraph System," *Toronto Star*, August 10, 1903, 1.

85. "Success Crowns *The Call*'s Efforts in Behalf of Wireless Telegraphy," *San Francisco Call*, January 4, 1904, 7.

86. Charles Musser, *Before the Nickelodeon: Edwin S. Porter and the Edison Manufacturing Company* (Berkeley: University of California Press, 1991).

87. "The Evolution of the Comic Picture and the Comic Artist," *San Francisco Call*, November 12, 1905, M-4.

88. "Film Newspaper Shown," *Oregonian* (Portland), August 8, 1911, 10. For a comprehensive overview of the classical newsreels of later decades, see also Joseph Clark, *News Parade: The American Newsreel and the World as Spectacle* (Minneapolis: University of Minnesota Press, 2020); and Mark Garrett Cooper, Sara Beth Levavy, Ross Melnick, and Mark Williams, eds., *Rediscovering U.S. Newsfilm: Cinema, Television, and the Archive* (New York: Routledge, 2018).

89. "Film Newspaper Shown," *Oregonian* (Portland), August 8, 1911, 10.

90. Paul S. Moore, *Now Playing: Early Moviegoing and the Regulation of Fun* (Albany: State University of New York Press, 2008).

91. Richard Abel, *Menus for Movieland: Newspapers and the Emergence of American Film Culture, 1913–1916* (Berkeley: University of California Press, 2015); Paul S. Moore, "Sub-

scribing to Publicity: Syndicated Newspaper Features for Moviegoing in North America, 1911–1915," *Early Popular Visual Culture* 12, no. 2 (2014): 260–73; Paul S. Moore, "'Everybody's Going: City Newspapers and the Early Mass Market for Movies," *City and Community* 4, no. 4 (2005): 339–57.

92. Andrew A. Erish, *Col. William N. Selig: The Man Who Invented Hollywood* (Austin: University of Texas Press, 2012).

93. Louis Pizzitola, *Hearst over Hollywood: Power, Passion, and Propaganda in the Movies* (New York: Columbia University Press, 2002).

94. Andrée Lafontaine, "The Rise and Fall of Cosmopolitan Productions: William Randolph Hearst's Cross-Promotional Strategies," *Journal of Cinema and Media Studies* 60, no. 2 (2021): 32–55.

95. For example, "Pathé Pictures and the Hearst Newspapers," *Moving Picture World*, February 28, 1914, 1056–57.

96. Jennifer Bean, "Technologies of Early Stardom and the Extraordinary Body," *Camera Obscura* 16, no. 3 (2001): 8–57.

97. "Hearst-Selig News Pictorial," *Moving Picture World*, March 14, 1914, 1351.

98. "Head and Shoulders above them all!" *Moving Picture World*, July 31, 1915, 775.

99. "*Daily Pioneer* to Show Its Own Motion Pictures," *Bemidji (MN) Pioneer*, September 30, 1915, 4. See also "Weekly Events Film Proves Popular in Northwest," *Motion Picture News*, May 29, 1915, 75; "Northwest Film Weekly Shows Current Events," *Minneapolis Tribune*, May 7, 1915, 12; and "The Northwest Weekly," *Grand Forks (ND) Herald*, August 8, 1915, 6.

100. "Reel Newspaper for Duluth," *Duluth (MN) News-Tribune*, September 5, 1915, 12.

101. "Golden Gate Weekly," *Moving Picture World*, December 27, 1913, 1570–71; "New York Weekly," *Moving Picture World*, February 7, 1914, 725.

102. See "*The Item's* News to be Shown in Movies," *New Orleans Item*, February 19, 1914, 5, and, for example, "Police Chief and His 'Family' on Film," *New Orleans Item*, June 28, 1914, 4.

103. "*Item* Pictures Are Alive with News," *New Orleans Item*, March 18, 1914, 3.

104. "*The Item's* News to be Shown in Movies," *New Orleans Item*, February 19, 1914, 5.

105. Ray H. Leek, "Here are the 'Herald Movies,'" *Chicago Herald*, July 5, 1914, E-1.

106. Ibid.

107. Ibid.

108. Ibid.

109. Ibid.

110. "Pictures in the Future," *Variety*, July 10, 1914, 18.

111. Cooper C. Graham and Ron van Dopperen, "Edwin F. Weigle: Cameraman for *The Chicago Tribune*," *Film History* 22, no. 4 (2010): 389–407.

112. "Extra! Extra! Somewhere New History is in the Making," *Chicago Tribune*, December 26, 1915, G-4.

113. Ibid.

114. "Pathé and International Weeklies Combine," *Motion Picture News*, January 20, 1917, 386; "Hearst Buys Universal Weekly and Mutual's Screen Telegram," *Exhibitors Herald and Motography*, November 16, 1918, 21.

115. "25 Great News Journals Combine with World Film to Make National Weekly," *Moving Picture World*, August 7, 1915, 952–53.

116. "Movie Weekly to be Filmed for Enquirer," *Buffalo Enquirer*, July 31, 1915, 1.

117. "Cincinnati Happenings Will Be Depicted on Movie Screens," *Cincinnati Enquirer*, August 1, 1915, 3. See also "A New Kind of Weekly," *Moving Picture World*, July 17, 1915, 470.

118. "Metro to Release News Weekly," *Moving Picture World*, October 9, 1915, 262.

119. The collaboration with the *Plain Dealer* lasted just over two years through two name changes—to the *Plain Dealer Screen Magazine* in May 1918 and then to the *Plain Dealer Film Topics* in June 1919.

120. "Don't Miss *The Plain Dealer*'s Motion Pictures," *Cleveland Plain Dealer*, June 10, 1917, 10. On local films, see Martin L. Johnson, *Main Street Movies* (Bloomington: Indiana University Press, 2018).

121. "*The Plain Dealer*'s Moving Pictures of Cleveland," *Cleveland Plain Dealer*, July 8, 1917, 5.

122. "*Plain Dealer* Takes Aerial Pictures," *Cleveland Plain Dealer*, November 23, 1918, 10.

123. Late in 1914, at least briefly, the *Dallas Times and Herald* released the *Times-Herald Weekly* in Texas theaters (ad for the Old Mill theater, *Dallas News*, December 27, 1914). In 1915 the *Milwaukee Journal* created the newsreel "The Journal's Weekly News ("'Certainly on the Job,' See the News," *Milwaukee Journal*, October 2, 1915). And the *Oakland Tribune* combined with that city's most-prestigious movie palace to briefly create the *Tribune-Kinema Weekly* in 1919 ("Read it in The Tribune. See it in pictures at the Kinema," *Oakland Tribune*, June 5, 1919). See also Richard Abel, "The Circulation of Local Newsreels in the Silent Period: The Case of Detroit," in *Rediscovering U.S. Newsfilm: Cinema, Television, and the Archive*, ed. Mark Garrett Cooper, Sara Beth Levavy, Ross Melnick, and Mark Williams, 133–54 (New York: Routledge, 2018).

124. David E. Nye, *American Technological Sublime* (Cambridge, MA: MIT Press, 1996); David E. Nye, *America as Second Creation: Technology and Narratives of New Beginnings* (Cambridge, MA: MIT Press, 2003).

CHAPTER 4. THE SPECTACLE OF SUNDAY DELIVERY

1. Paul S. Moore, "Advance Publicity for the Vitascope and the Mass Address of Cinema's Reading Public," in *A Companion to Early Cinema*, ed. André Gaudreault, Nicolas Dulac, and Santiago Hidalgo, 381–97 (Malden, MA: Blackwell, 2012); Charles Musser, "The May Irwin Kiss: Performance and Early Cinema," in *Visual Delights 2: Exhibition and Reception*, ed. Vanessa Toulmin and Simon Popple, 96–115 (Eastleigh, UK: John Libbey); Linda Williams, *Screening Sex* (Durham, NC: Duke University Press, 2008).

2. Kate McGuirk, "The Anatomy of a Kiss," *New York World*, April 26, 1896, 21.

3. Ibid.

4. Ibid.

5. "An Amazing Scientific Analysis of a Kiss," *New York World*, October 24, 1897.

6. Ibid.

7. The mobility of the stunt-girl journalist in this and other stories contradicts the typical "tethering" of female columnists to their typewriters as opposed to the idea of male reporters on the beat. See Rachel Plotnick, "Tethered Women, Mobile Men: Gendered Mobilities of Typewriting," *Mobile Media and Communication* 8, no. 2 (2020): 188–208. See also Sandra Gabriele, "Gendered Mobility, the Nation, and the Woman's Page: Exploring the Mobile Practices of the Canadian Lady Journalist," *Journalism* 7, no. 2 (2006): 174–96.

8. Kate McGuirk, "Rides a Mile in Thirty-Two Seconds," *New York World*, October 24, 1897, 33.

9. Stephen Bottomore, "The Panicking Audience? Early Cinema and the 'Train Effect,'" *Historical Journal of Film, Radio, and Television* 19, no. 2 (1999): 177–216; Kristen Whissel, *Picturing American Modernity: Traffic, Technology, and the Silent Cinema* (Durham, NC: Duke University Press, 2008).

10. David E. Nye, *American Technological Sublime* (Cambridge, MA: MIT Press, 1996); David E. Nye, *America as Second Creation: Technology and Narratives of New Beginnings* (Cambridge, MA: MIT Press, 2003); Marshall McLuhan, *Understanding Media: The Extensions of Man* (1964; Cambridge, MA: MIT Press, 1994).

11. The journalism trade press (*Newspaperdom, Newspaper Maker, Printers' Ink*, etc.) confirms, in general, that the discourse presented to the news-reading public was remarkably similar and parallel with internal trade discourse, which indeed often merely summarizes news and publicity first published on newspapers' pages themselves.

12. "*The World* Woman on the Fast Mail" and "Exciting Ride on the Fast Newspaper Train," *New York World*, May 3, 1896, 26. This stunt was almost certainly the same as one conducted and published at the same time by Grace Carew Sheldon for the *Buffalo Times*, as noted in advance in *Buffalo Courier*, April 26, 1896, 18, and promoted in *Buffalo Commercial*, May 2, 1896, 14. Sunday issues of the *Buffalo Times* are not archived, and it may not be possible to confirm whether Sheldon was indeed "*The World* Woman."

13. "Exciting Ride on the Fast Newspaper Train," *New York World*, May 3, 1896, 26.

14. John Durham Peters, *Speaking into the Air: A History of the Idea of Communication* (Chicago: University of Chicago Press, 1999); James W. Carey, "Technology and Ideology: The Case of the Telegraph," in *Communication as Culture: Essays on Media and Society* (Boston: Unwin-Hyman, 1989), 201–230; Harold A. Innis, *The Bias of Communication*, 2nd ed. (1951; Toronto: University of Toronto Press, 2008).

15. "Exciting Ride on the Fast Newspaper Train," *New York World*, May 3, 1896, 26.

16. Henry Jenkins, *Convergence Culture: Where Old and New Media Collide* (New York: New York University Press, 2008).

17. Note here that the well-known concepts of remediation and premediation are both anchored in a relatively linear temporal relation of old media to new media. We instead continually point out the intermediation of all media, the continuation of older media in relation to newer, and not merely in diminished form as "residual media" or nostalgic repurposing. Jay David Bolter and Richard Grusin, *Remediation: Understanding New Media* (Cambridge, MA: MIT Press, 2000); Richard A. Grusin, "Premediation," *Criticism* 46, no. 1 (2004): 17–39; Charles R. Acland, ed., *Residual Media* (Minneapolis: University of Minnesota Press, 2007).

18. James Carey, *Communication as Culture: Essays on Media and Society*, rev. ed. (New York: Routledge, 2009).

19. Laurel Brake and Marysa Demoor, eds., *The Lure of Illustration in the Nineteenth Century: Picture and Press* (New York: Palgrave-Macmillan, 2009); Gerry Beegan, *The Mass Image: A Social History of Photochemical Reproduction in Victorian London* (New York: Palgrave-Macmillan, 2008).

20. Elizabeth L. Eisenstein, *The Printing Press as an Agent of Change* (New York: Cambridge University Press, 1979), 8.

21. Jennifer Daryl Slack, "Contextualizing Technology," in *Rethinking Communication: Paradigm Exemplars*, ed. B. Dervin, L. Grossberg, J. O'Keefe, and E. Wartella (Thousand Oaks, CA: Sage, 1989), 332–33.

22. Lawrence Grossberg, *Bringing It All Back Home: Essays in Cultural Studies* (Durham, NC: Duke University Press, 1997); Stuart Hall, "On Postmodernism and Articulation: An Interview with Stuart Hall," in *Stuart Hall: Critical Dialogues in Cultural Studies*, ed. David Morley and Kuan-Hsing Chen, 131–50 (New York: Routledge, 1996).

23. John Law and John Hassard, eds., *Actor-Network Theory and After* (Malden, MA: Blackwell, 1999), 4.

24. Bruno Latour, "Is Re-Modernization Occurring—And If So, How to Prove It?: A Commentary on Ulrich Beck," *Theory Culture Society* 20, nos. 3–5 (2003): 36.

25. Bruno Latour, "On Actor-Network Theory; A Few Clarifications Plus More Than a Few Complications," in *Literary Theory: An Anthology*, 3rd ed., ed. Julie Rivkin and Michael Ryan (Malden, MA: Blackwell, 2017), 1463.

26. John R. G. Hassard, *The Wonders of the Press* (New York: Tribune Association, 1878), 13.

27. "See *The Globe*'s Biggest Press at Work!" *Boston Globe*, August 15, 1896, 6.

28. Ibid.

29. "*Globe*'s Big Presses. Famous 'Quad' Reproduced in Art Supplement," *Boston Globe*, August 16, 1896, 24.

30. "*The Globe*'s New Color Press," *Boston Globe*, January 20, 1895, 1.

31. Ibid.

32. Ibid.

33. Ibid.

34. Vincent Mosco, *The Digital Sublime: Myth, Power, and Cyberspace* (Cambridge: MIT Press, 2004).

35. Susan Buck-Morss, *The Dialectics of Seeing: Walter Benjamin and the Arcades Project* (Cambridge, MA: MIT Press, 1991); Walter Benjamin, *The Arcades Project*, ed. Rolf Tiedermann (Cambridge, MA: Belknap Press of Harvard University Press, 2002); Walter Benjamin, *The Work of Art in the Age of Its Technological Reproducibility, and Other Writings on Media* (Cambridge, MA: Belknap Press of Harvard University Press, 2008).

36. Alfred D. Chandler Jr, *The Visible Hand: The Managerial Revolution in American Business* (Cambridge, MA: Belknap Press of Harvard University Press, 1977).

37. R. Hoe, "How I Built the First High Speed Printing Press," *Denver Post*, June 11, 1899, 14.

38. Aurora Wallace, *Media Capital: Architecture and Communications in New York City* (Urbana: University of Illinois Press, 2012), 5.

39. "Better than . . ." from "First Issue To-Morrow," *Philadelphia North American*, September 28, 1901, 5, referring to "The New Home of the North American," *Philadelphia North American*, September 29, 1901, section 2.

40. Ibid.

41. "The Cyclorama of a Great City," *Philadelphia North American*, September 29, 1901, section 2, 16. The significance of cycloramas and other "techniques of the observer" in the nineteenth century is at the core of early histories of media and modernity and its development into the field of media archaeology—for example, Vanessa Schwartz, *Spectacular Realities: Early Mass Culture in Fin-de-Siecle Paris* (Berkeley: University of California Press, 1998); Jonathan Crary, *Suspensions of Perception: Attention, Spectacle, and Modern Culture* (Cambridge, MA: MIT Press, 2000); and more recently and more comprehensively, Erkki Huhtamo, *Illusions in Motion: Media Archaeology of the Moving Panorama and Related Spectacles* (Cambridge, MA: MIT Press, 2013).

42. "The Bullock Perfecting Printing Press," *Chicago Inter-Ocean*, September 30, 1876, 3.

43. "A Stride in Advance," *Chicago Inter-Ocean*, June 2, 1877, 6.

44. The notion of opening circulation books to inspection originates in 1885 when *The World* began boasting sales of over a million copies a week. "A Million a Week, Largest Circulation in America," *New York World*, July 19, 1885, 1. Soon after came the invitation to "advertisers and the editors and publishers of all newspapers . . . to visit *The World's* pressroom, examine the books and satisfy themselves of the correctness of these facts." "Nearly 5 Million copies a month!" *New York World*, September 14, 1885, 4. By April 1887 the phrase "Open to All!" was part of the masthead, transformed to "Circulation Books Open to All" by January 1888 and then transferred to the front-page nameplate across the logo in May 1889. It remained one of the mottos of the paper for decades. In later years, competitors reveled in exposing Pulitzer's "bogus circulation," such as an article in the *Sun* that exposed how tons of unsold copies of the *World* were being pulped at paper mills. "*The World's* practice is to supply dealers with all the copies they can be induced to order and then to take back the unsold papers at the price received for them. The basis for the circulation claims is the alleged number of papers printed and sent out. Of course a great many of these come back the next day." "Tons of Unsold *World*s," *New York Sun*, October 20, 1895, 5.

45. "41,110,606 'Worlds,'" *New York World*, November 8, 1885, 12.

46. "Cordially Invited!" *New York World*, November 9, 1885, 1.

47. "The Magic of Modern Days," *New York World*, December 6, 1885, 2.

48. "The Mastodon of Printing Machines," *New York World*, May 10, 1887, 11.

49. Aurora Wallace, "A Height Deemed Appalling: Nineteenth-Century New York Newspaper Buildings," *Journalism History* 31, no. 4 (2006): 178–89. On the waning importance of Park Row in the early twentieth century, see Dale Cressman, "From Newspaper Row to Times Square: The Dispersal and Contested Identity of an Imagined Journalistic Community," *Journalism History* 34, no 4 (2009): 182–93.

50. "The Pulitzer Building Erected by the Pennies of an Appreciative Public for the People's Newspaper," *New York World*, December 10, 1890, souvenir supplement, 3.

51. "'The World's' Gigantic Presses," *New York World*, November 6, 1892, 32.

52. Ibid.

53. Viewing galleries were installed at the *Chicago Herald* in 1891, the *San Francisco Call* in 1892, and the *Philadelphia Inquirer* in 1894, as well as the aforementioned gallery at the *Boston Globe*.

54. Wallace, *Media Capital*, 75–77. On the role of the Herald Building in the shift away from Park Row, see Cressman, "From Newspaper Row to Times Square."

55. R. Hoe, "How I Built the First High Speed Printing Press," *Denver Post*, June 11, 1899, 14.

56. "Over 433,000 Circulation per Day," *New York World*, March 4, 1894, 1.

57. "Greatest Circulation in America," *New York Morning Journal*, October 26, 1889, 2; "Circulation per Day during the Last Six Months," *New York World*, October 31, 1889, 1.

58. "*The Journal* First of All," *New York Morning Journal*, November 24, 1889, 1.

59. Ibid.

60. Ibid.

61. "$100 for the Most Popular Newsdealer," *New York Morning Journal*, March 9, 1890, 1.

62. "Sold 208 Copies," *New York Morning Journal*, March 15, 1890, 1.

63. "*Journal* 50, *Herald* 30, *World* 30," *New York Morning Journal*, March 16, 1890, 1.

64. "And Still We Boom!" *New York Morning Journal*, May 3, 1890, 1.

65. "Chapter 1," *San Francisco Examiner*, January 27, 1891, 1.

66. "Newspaper Honesty," *San Francisco Examiner*, February 20, 1891, 6.

67. Ibid.

68. "May: 1,774,750," *San Francisco Examiner*, July 1, 1891, 6.

69. "Progress of *The Examiner*," *San Francisco Examiner*," January 1, 1893, 35.

70. "In the Senate," *San Francisco Examiner*, January 25, 1893, 2.

71. "An Act," *San Francisco Examiner*, March 14, 1893, 6.

72. "A Curb for Newspapers," *New York World*, March 22, 1893, 1.

73. "A Just Measure," *New York World*, March 22, 1893, 4.

74. "Passed *The World*'s Bill," *New York World*, April 20, 1893, 1.

75. "375,000 per Day. A Testimonial," *New York World*, April 20, 1893, 4.

76. "World-Famed Advertisers Certify to *The Journal*'s Supremacy," *New York Journal*, November 8, 1896, 13.

77. Dawn Spring, *Advertising in the Age of Persuasion: Building Brand America, 1941–1961* (New York: Palgrave-Macmillan, 2011).

78. Lincoln Steffens, "The Business of a Newspaper," *Scribner's*, October 1897, 447–67.

79. Tim Wu, *The Attention Merchants: The Epic Scramble to Get Inside Our Heads* (New York: Vintage, 2016).

80. "'The Item' Wagons," *Philadelphia Item*, May 1, 1887, 10.

81. Articles about various "automatic" newspaper machines include "The Automatic Newsboy," *Boston Journal*, April 4, 1890, 4; "Newsies and Shines," *Pittsburgh Dispatch*, June 12, 1892, 21; and "Drop in a Nickel and Get a Paper," *New York Sun*, March 5, 1893, 10.

82. Michael Stamm, *Dead Tree Media: Manufacturing the Newspaper in Twentieth-Century America* (Baltimore: Johns Hopkins University Press, 2018).

83. Menahem Blondheim, *News over the Wires: The Telegraph and the Flow of Information in America, 1844–1897* (Cambridge, MA: Harvard University Press, 1994); David Hochfelder, *The Telegraph in America, 1832–1920* (Baltimore: Johns Hopkins University Press, 2012); Richard John, *Network Nation: Inventing American Telecommunications* (Cambridge, MA: Harvard University Press, 2010).

84. Alfred McClung Lee, *The Daily Newspaper in America: The Evolution of a Social Instrument*, vol. 1 (New York: Macmillan, 1937), 261.

85. Ibid.

86. David Nasaw, *Children of the City: At Work and At Play* (New York: Oxford University Press, 1986). An unsigned article in *The Newsman* in 1891 notes that even before the turn of the century, conditions for some had changed: "Newsdealers hire boys to help them. These boys might be newsboys, but the distributing of newspapers has gone through a process of development and concentration just as other lines of business have, and instead of being independent capitalists they have become employees." "The Newsboy Supplanted," *The Newsman* 8, no. 1 (January 1891): 3; Vincent DiGirolamo, *Crying the News: A History of America's Newsboys* (New York: Oxford University Press, 2019).

87. McClung Lee, *Daily Newspaper in America*, 262.

88. Ibid., 263. McClung Lee had earlier used the term "newsboy giant" in "The A.N.P.A. and Its Predecessors," *Editor and Publisher*, April 21, 1934, 74, a history of the American News-

paper Publishers Association. See also discussion of the "newsboy giant" in DiGirolamo, *Crying the News*, 153.

89. F. M. Somers, "American News Company," *Current Literature: A Magazine of Record and Review*, October 1888, 283.

90. "A Vast System of Distribution," *New York Herald*, October 1, 1893, C-6.

91. "Sinclair Tousey, Wholesale Newsdealer," *New York Times*, June 21, 1862, 5.

92. "The oldest house dealing in books, monthly magazines, daily and weekly newspapers in the United States, and in the amount of business done, second to none in the world. Established 1840 . . . We are the General Agents for and take the whole edition of a large number of leading publications, all of which we supply at Publishers' lowest prices. . . . Publishers of books, magazines and newspapers who may desire a reliable house in this city to act as agents for their publications are requested to communicate with us. Our facilities for pushing any work are unequaled, as we have customers in all the principal cities in the United States, to whom we ship goods daily." See "H. Dexter, Hamilton & Co.," *New York Times*, November 3, 1863, 5, and others, e.g., *Philadelphia Inquirer*, November 14, 1863, 3.

93. Madeleine B. Stern, "Dissemination of Popular Books in the Midwest and Far West during the Nineteenth Century," in *Getting the Books Out: Papers of the Chicago Conference on the Book in America*, ed. Michael R. Hackenberg (Washington, DC: Library of Congress, 1987), 87–88, citing fn 46, *American Bookseller*, July 1, 1887, 7.

94. "Sketches of the Publishers: The American News Company," *The Round Table*, April 21, 1866, 250.

95. "To the Trade," *Chicago Tribune*, April 13, 1866, 1; "The Western News Company," *Chicago Inter-Ocean*, April 26, 1866, 2.

96. "American News Company, How Newspapers Are Circulated," *St. Paul Dispatch*, May 28, 1869, 1. This article is reprinted from *The Ledger*, which may be a Boston publication that was an early key to Tousey's success, as its New York newsagent. See "A Vast System of Distribution," *New York Herald*, October 1, 1893, C-6, reprinted in "The American News Company Up to Date," *American Newsman*, November 1893, 4.

97. Leander Richardson, "How Big Monopolies Work," *Boston Herald*, January 28, 1886, 8.

98. DiGirolamo, *Crying the News*, 153.

99. Richardson, "How Big Monopolies Work."

100. "Newsdealers Meet," *Boston Globe*, July 13, 1887, 2.

101. Ibid.

102. Actress Marie Prescott sued the American News Company for libel in 1882 and initially won damages of $12,500, which was overturned on a technicality only because the prosecution had failed to include evidence that any specific person had actually read the magazine. The legal liability for distributing libelous material stood as the law in most jurisdictions for decades. See "A Libel Suit," *Canaan (CT) Western News*, October 25, 1882, 1, for contemporary news coverage of the case, and Samuel Merrill, *Newspaper Libel: A Handbook for the Press* (Boston: Ticknor and Company, 1888), 139.

103. Standard Oil's target was the latest 1904 monthly installment of Thomas W. Lawson's "Frenzied Finance" in *Everybody's Magazine*, which had been promoted nationally with full-page newspaper "advertorials." See "Stop the Press. Standard Oil Will Not Allow Distribution," *Los Angeles Times*, December 20, 1904, 1.

104. Somers, "American News Company," 284.

105. Samuel Merrill, *Newspaper Libel: A Handbook for the Press* (Boston: Ticknor and Company, 1888), 140.

106. Ibid., 141, quoting *The Journalist*, April 12, 1884.

107. "A Vast System of Distribution," *New York Herald*, October 1, 1893, C-6.

108. Ibid.

109. "After a Great Newspaper Is Printed a Great Task Remains," *New York Herald*, October 8, 1899, 12.

110. Ibid.

111. All details and quotations in the synopsis in this paragraph and the next are taken from "Catching an Express," *New York World*, December 7, 1885, 1.

112. "Express Extraordinary," *Brooklyn Eagle*, April 9, 1860, 6.

113. "A Hickory Ham Competitor," *New York Herald*, July 23, 1874, 5, quoting *Saratoga (NY) Sentinel*.

114. "Niagara Falls' Sunday Train," *New York Herald*, June 13, 1875, 15.

115. "The Sunday Newspaper Train," *Chicago Tribune*, July 24, 1874, 4; "Railway News: The Sunday Milwaukee Newspaper Train," *Chicago Inter-Ocean*, July 27, 1874, 8; "The Globe Special," *Boston Globe*, May 18, 1880, 4. *The Globe* and other Boston papers were similarly sent up to Bangor, Maine, on summer Sundays from 1880 and later gained a competitive advantage in upstate New York because the Boston newspaper train reached Saratoga fifteen minutes before the train from New York. See "Flying over the Rails," *Boston Herald*, August 3, 1885, 2.

116. "The Times' Fast Train," *Kansas City Times*, November 23, 1889, 1.

117. "Two Kinds of 'Flyers,'" *Los Angeles Times*, February 24, 1892, 1.

118. Ibid.

119. "Too Few Newspaper Trains," *New York Times*, July 29, 1893, 8.

120. Ibid.

121. "Scattering Sunday Suns," *Philadelphia Times*, June 29, 1886, 4.

122. "Railway News: Won a Great Race Easy," *Cleveland Plain Dealer*, February 14, 1898, 5.

123. "*The World* Beat," *Wilkes-Barre Times*, March 16, 1898, 8.

124. "Keep Your Eye on To-Morrow's Great *New York Sunday World*," *Philadelphia Press*, March 5, 1898, 7.

125. "*Inquirer* Beats in Race to Sea," *Philadelphia Inquirer*, November 17, 1901, 12.

126. "*Post's* Big Baby, It Weighed 32,478 Pounds," *Boston Post*, September 11, 1893, 1.

127. Ibid.

128. Ibid., 2.

129. All details and quotations in the rest of this paragraph are from "After a Great Newspaper Is Printed a Great Task Remains," *New York Herald*, October 8, 1899, 12.

130. Nasaw, "Newsies," in *Children of the City*, 62–87.

131. DiGirolamo, *Crying the News*, provides an excellent accounting of the diversity of newsboys as well, including immigrant children (pp. 315–20), black newsboys (pp. 320–26), and even newsgirls (pp. 327–34).

132. McClung Lee, *Daily Newspaper in America*, 262.

133. Ibid., 264.

134. "The Newsboy Supplanted," *The Newsman* 8, no. 1 (January 1891): 3.

135. Somers, "American News Company," 283.

136. Nasaw, *Children of the City*, 67–69.

137. DiGirolamo, *Crying the News*, 378.

138. Oenone Kubie, "Reading Lewis Hine's Photography of Child Street Labour, 1906–1918," *Journal of American Studies* 50, no. 4 (2016): 873–97.

139. "A Strike!" *St. Louis Dispatch*, August 9, 1876, 1.

140. "Young Strikers," *St. Louis Globe-Democrat*, August 10, 1876, 8.

141. Ibid.

142. "Dispatch Difficulties," *St. Louis Globe-Democrat*, August 11, 1896, 4.

143. "The Newsboys Strike Too," *Brooklyn Standard Union*, July 20, 1899, 12.

144. "Newsboys on Strike," *Brooklyn Standard Union*, May 9, 1898, 8.

145. "Boycott by Newsboys," *Brooklyn Eagle*, May 9, 1898, 16.

146. "Looking for 'Scabs,'" *Hartford (CT) Courant*, May 12, 1898, 8.

147. "An Infantile Boycott," *Brooklyn Eagle*, August 12, 1889, 4.

148. "Newsboys Win the Day," *Chicago Tribune*, August 13, 1889, 5.

149. "Newsboys on Strike," *New York Times*, August 13, 1889, 8.

150. "Newsboys Out on a General Strike," *San Francisco Examiner*, October 16, 1896, 5.

151. "Went to the Council," *San Francisco Call*, October 17, 1896, 11.

152. "Table Talk," *Buffalo Commercial*, August 3, 1887, 2. At least one earlier item speculated that "automated newsboys" would soon appear when stamp-dispensing boxes were installed in Brooklyn in 1886: "Do You Want a Postage Stamp?" *Newport (PA) News*, December 18, 1886, 7, from *Newsdealer and Stationer*.

153. "An Automatic Newsboy," *Cherryvale (KS) Bulletin*, October 20, 1888, 4; "The Automatic Newsboy," *Boston Journal*, April 4, 1890, 4.

154. "Table Talk," *Buffalo Commercial*, August 3, 1887, 2.

155. "A Silent Newsboy," *Seattle Post-Intelligencer*, March 12, 1892, 5.

156. Ibid.

157. "The Silent Newsboy, *Chronicle* Delivered by a Machine," *San Francisco Chronicle*, May 12, 1892, 12.

158. Ibid.

159. "Machine Newsboys," *San Francisco Call*, May 13, 1892, 8.

160. "Angry Newsboys," *San Francisco Call*, May 14, 1892, 8.

161. "The Silent Newsboy," *San Francisco Chronicle*, May 17, 1892, 6.

162. George J. Southwick, "The Pacific Coast, California," *The Journalist*, May 28, 1892, 2.

163. "Newsies and Shines," *Pittsburgh Dispatch*, June 12, 1892, 21.

164. "An Automatic Newsboy," *Buffalo Express*, July 21, 1892, 2.

165. "Automatic Newsboys," *Cimarron (KS) Gray County Jacksonian*, July 29, 1892, 2; "A Valuable Invention," *Phoenix Republic*, March 21, 1893, 8.

166. "An Automatic Newsboy," *Fourth Estate*, November 5, 1896, 10.

167. "The Automatic Newsboy," *Publishers' Weekly*, December 19, 1896, 1190.

168. *New York Sun*, March 5, 1893, 10.

169. *Philadelphia Inquirer*, August 5, 1919, 5.

170. McClung Lee, *Daily Newspaper in America*, 266.

171. Ibid.

172. "The New York World Where It Circulates," *New York World*, May 7, 1893, 39.

173. Lisa Gitelman, "On the Status of Print at the Origin of Recorded Sound," in *New Media, 1740–1915*, ed. Lisa Gitelman and Geoffrey Pingree (Cambridge: MIT Press, 2003), 163.

PART III. SYNDICATION

1. James W. Carey, "Technology and Ideology: The Case of the Telegraph," in *Communication as Culture: Essays on Media and Society* (Boston: Unwin-Hyman, 1989), 201–230.

2. Alfred D. Chandler Jr., *The Visible Hand: The Managerial Revolution in American Business* (Cambridge, MA: Belknap Press of Harvard University Press, 1977).

3. Walter Benjamin, *The Work of Art in the Age of Its Technological Reproducibility, and Other Writings on Media* (Cambridge, MA: Belknap Press of Harvard University Press, 2008).

4. Siegfried Kracauer, *The Mass Ornament: Weimar Essays*, trans. Thomas Y. Levin (Cambridge, MA: Harvard University Press, 1995); Max Horkheimer and Theodor W. Adorno, *Dialectic of Enlightenment* (1944; New York: Continuum, 1995).

CHAPTER 5. THE CORPOREAL CHARACTER OF CIRCULATION

1. "How the Journal Has Grown in Twelve Months," *New York Journal*, November 8, 1896, 15.

2. Ibid.

3. For a critical history of the commercial character of newspaper comics, see Ian Gordon, *Comic Strips and Consumer Culture, 1890–1945* (Washington, DC: Smithsonian Institute, 1998). For a history of cartooning that culminates in newspaper comics, see Thierry Smolderen, *The Origins of Comics: From William Hogarth to Winsor McCay*, trans. Bart Beaty and Nick Nguyen (Jackson: University Press of Mississippi, 2014). For a small sample of color newspaper comics, reproduced broadsheet size, see Peter Maresca, ed., *Society Is Nix: Gleeful Anarchy at the Dawn of the American Comic Strip* (Palo Alto, CA: Sunday Press Books, 2013), and *Forgotten Fantasy: Sunday Comics, 1900–1915* (Palo Alto, CA: Sunday Press Books, 2011). An encyclopedic reference guide of details about newspaper comics is given by Allan Holtz, *American Newspaper Comics* (Ann Arbor: University of Michigan Press, 2012); Holtz's *Strippers Guide* blog (www.strippersguide.blogspot.com) explores hundreds of case studies further.

4. Menahem Blondheim, *News over the Wires: The Telegraph and the Flow of Information in America, 1844–1897* (Cambridge, MA: Harvard University Press, 1994).

5. The earliest *Catalogue of Title-Entries* (Washington, D.C.: Government Printing Office, 1891), no. 1, lists individual headlined newspaper stories under copyrighted "books" registered by James Gordon Bennett (*New York Herald*) and the Sun Print and Publishing Co. (*New York Sun*). Entire newspaper editions are not registered as copyrighted "periodicals" until the *Sun* is listed for the entire week of May 23–28, 1892, in *Catalogue of Title-Entries*, 1892, no. 47.

6. Pulitzer's Press Publishing Co. began registering "The World's Sunday Magazine" as an entity unto itself, first under "books" for the issue of Decmeber 29, 1895 (*Catalogue of Title-Entries*, 1896, no. 235), and then under "periodicals" for the issue of June 7, 1896 (*Catalogue of Title-Entries*, 1896, no. 258). At this time in 1896, Press Publishing was still listing specific copyrighted stories as "books" instead of whole issues of the *New York World*, although six other New York newspapers were then registering entire editions as copyrighted "periodicals," as well as papers in Buffalo, Philadelphia, and Pittsburgh.

7. "Will It Come to This?" *New York World*, December 15, 1889, 1.

8. N. W. Ayer and Son, *American Newspaper Annual* (Philadelphia: N. W. Ayer and Son, 1880), 4.

9. Ayer and Son, *American Newspaper Annual* (1888), 15.

10. "The Books Wide Open," *New York World*, May 11, 1889, 1. See also "The Books Wide Open: An Absolutely Conclusive Inquiry into '*The World's*' Circulation," *Printers' Ink*, June 1, 1889, 563–64.

11. Joseph Pulitzer Papers, MSS 37044, Manuscript Division, Library of Congress. lccn.loc.gov/mm78037044/.

12. "One Hundred and Four Millions!" *New York World*, January 1, 1889, 1.

13. "The Ladder of Prosperity," *New York World*, January 1, 1889, 1.

14. Ibid.

15. Ibid.

16. Ibid.

17. Ibid.

18. Alison Hedley, "Data Visualization and Population Politics in *Pearson's Magazine*, 1896–1902," *Journal of Victorian Culture* 23, no. 3 (2018): 421–41.

19. "*The Chicago Times-Herald*, Consolidated March 4th 1895," *Chicago Herald*, March 3, 1895, 39.

20. "Scorching!" *New York World*, May 9, 1897, comic supplement, 1.

21. "News of the Week Illustrated," *New York Recorder*, July 19 1891, 1.

22. "*The Inter-Ocean* Prize Cartoons," *Chicago Inter-Ocean*, March 20, 1892, 1.

23. "Won the Prizes," *Chicago Inter-Ocean*, March 16, 1892, 1; "The Boodlers and The Boodled," *Chicago Inter-Ocean*, March 27, 1892, 17.

24. "The Boodlers and The Boodled," *Chicago Inter-Ocean*, March 27, 1892, 17; "I Will Guarantee Emancipation from Boss Slavery," *Chicago Inter-Ocean*, April 3, 1892, 9.

25. "Won the Prizes," *Chicago Inter-Ocean*, March 16, 1892.

26. "The Sunday Globe in Colors!" *Boston Globe*, November 24, 1894, 6.

27. "The Seven Ages of The Globe," *Boston Globe*, November 25, 1894, 1.

28. "At the Telephone" began in the *Boston Globe*, October 6, 1883, 2, and started using "The Globe Man" as one of the mixed-wire speakers on October 30, 1883, 4.

29. See promotion for the return of the feature "The Globe Telephone Man," *Boston Globe*, September 29, 1883, 2.

30. "The Sunday Globe," *Boston Globe*, July 24, 1886, 4.

31. "The Globe Man Gets All the News from Everywhere," *Boston Globe*, October 16, 1886, 4.

32. "Nothing Will Escape Him! The Busiest Man in Boston Election Night," *Boston Globe*, November 1, 1896, 33. On the use of media in election night newspaper-sponsored festivals, see Carolyn Marvin, *When Old Technologies Were New: Thinking about Electric Communication in the Nineteenth Century* (New York: Oxford University Press, 1990), 218–21; and Charles Musser, *Politicking and Emergent Media: US Presidential Elections of the 1890s* (Berkeley: University of California Press, 2016).

33. "The Way the Great Journalistic Race in Boston Now Looks," *Boston Globe*, February 2, 1887, 1.

34. "The Great Newspaper Race in Boston—The Globe Rapidly Gaining the Lead," *Boston Globe*, June 24, 1883, 16. Interim versions of "The Great Journalistic Race" also appeared

on January 31, 1886, 4, and April 6, 1886, 4, both showing the *Globe* taking the lead but still without the Globe Man as the running figure.

35. "There's Plenty of Room at the Top," *Boston Globe*, September 23, 1894, 1.

36. Ibid.

37. "Circulation Talks," *Boston Globe*, April 7, 1893, 4, and continuing with the masthead for years.

38. "$250 in Gold. A Man You All Know Becomes a Doll," *Boston Globe*, August 9, 1895, 4.

39. "The Globe Man Introduces to His Readers Metcalf's Water White Vanilla," *Boston Globe*, May 1, 1893, 1.

40. "The Women Delighted," *Boston Globe*, October 27, 1894, 6.

41. "What *The Globe* Recipes Did for One Family," *Boston Globe*, December 2, 1894, 36.

42. Ibid.

43. The first recurring, self-described "Colored Supplement" of the *New York World* appeared on May 21, 1893, featuring a Walt McDougall cartoon titled "Broadway Cable Car Possibilities." Several special supplements had appeared earlier with color covers.

44. The first recurring color section of the *New York Herald* appeared on June 10, 1894, featuring a full-page art supplement called "Picturesque New York." See "Interesting Everybody, To-Morrow's Sunday Herald," *New York Herald*, June 9, 1894, 16, and "We All Rub Elbows in Madison Square," *New York Herald*, June 10, 1894, C-1.

45. Jean Lee Cole, *How the Other Half Laughs: The Comic Sensibility in American Culture, 1895–1920* (Jackson: University Press of Mississippi, 2020).

46. "The 'New Journalism,'" *New York Press*, January 9, 1897, 4.

47. Joseph W. Campbell, *Yellow Journalism: Puncturing the Myths, Defining the Legacies* (Westport, CT: Praeger, 2001), 25–49.

48. Advance promotions for the Yellow Kid starting in the *Journal* began a week ahead in "Out Next Sunday," *New York Journal*, October 11, 1896, 8, and on October 16, 1896. They also appeared in the *Brooklyn Eagle, Buffalo News, Washington Times, Atlanta Constitution*, and other papers.

49. "The Colossus of Sunday Newspapers," *New York World*, February 29, 1896, 14.

50. "Giant of Sunday Newspapers, The Great Sunday World, All Others Are Pigmies," *New York World*, April 3, 1896, 12.

51. "Magazine, Newspaper and Comic Weekly Combined in the Great Sunday World," *New York World*, April 10, 1896, 16.

52. "Out Next Sunday," *New York Journal*, October 11, 1896, 8; "Get Your Order Early," *New York Journal*, October 16, 1896, 5.

53. Wm. H. Friday, words, and Homer Tourjée, music, "The Yellow Kid, The Latest and The Greatest," *New York Journal*, November 8, 1896, "American Humorist" supplement, 7–8. See also Jean Lee Cole, "Rising from the Gutter: Rudolph Block, the Comic Strip, and the Ghetto Stories of Bruno Lessing," *MELUS: Multi-Ethnic Literature of the United States* 41, no. 2 (2016): 27–54; and Christina Meyer, "Media Transgressions: Comics–Sheet Music–Theatre–Toys," *Journal of Graphic Novels and Comics* 7, no. 3 (2016): 293–305.

54. "The Kittikat Klub Enters Politics," *Boston Globe*, September 27, 1896, 37; also October 18, 1896, 33; November 15, 1896, 33; and recurring just once on November 18, 1900, 46.

55. "*The Recorder's* Rag-Tags," *New York Recorder*, September 17, 1896, 8, and nearly daily until October 6, 1896, 6.

56. "The Bumpkins Out Foraging for a Trip to San Francisco," *San Francisco Call*, September 26, 1897, 26, and continuing for over a year on the "Boys and Girls Page" every Sunday.

57. Swinnerton's bears originated in October 1893 as a mascot in the *Examiner*'s daily publicity for the forthcoming Mid-Winter Exposition. See "The Building of the Million-Dollar Midwinter City," *San Francisco Examiner*, October 14, 1893, 4. The bears were a subject of the illustrated article "The Men and the Cartoons," *San Francisco Examiner*, November 18, 1894, 26, and became a recurring feature on the children's page in June 1895.

58. Early books linked to newspaper comic illustrators include Annie Laurie and Jimmy Swinnerton, *The Little Boy Who Lived on the Hill* (San Francisco: William Doxey, 1895); and E. W. Townsend and R. F. Outcault, *The Yellow Kid in McFadden's Flats* (New York: G. W. Dillingham, 1897). Books compiling Sunday comics include the *New York Herald*'s *Foxy Grandpa by Bunny* (New York: Foxy Grandpa Co., 1900) and five books collecting Hearst's *New York Journal* strips in December 1902.

59. An illustrated banner collecting Sunday humor began with "The World's Funny Side," *New York World*, December 9, 1888, 28. The bottom of this and subsequent pages noted that "all humorous articles sent for The Funny Page must have price affixed. Rejected MSS will not be returned unless addressed stamped envelope is sent."

60. Walt McDougall, "Looking Backwards on 1889," *New York World*, December 29, 1889, 17.

61. See Steven H. Gale, *Encyclopedia of American Humorists* (New York: Routledge, 1988), 279–80 (on M. Quad) and 340–42 (on Bill Nye).

62. "The Comic Sketch Club: A Syndicate Which Furnishes Drawings," *Newspaper Maker*, August 29, 1895, 3.

63. Ibid.

64. "Instead of Reading a Novel on Sunday," *New York World*, September 29, 1893, 5.

65. "The Comic Sketch Club," *Boston Post*, September 10, 1893, 19.

66. An additional eight-page section began in the *Philadelphia Inquirer* on April 9, 1893, including a column (later a page) called "With the Wits."

67. "*Enquirer* Supplement," *Cincinnati Enquirer*, July 7, 1895, 25–28.

68. "Humor of the Week," *Philadelphia Times*, July 5, 1896, illustrated supplement, 3.

69. "A Little Humor Now and Then, etc.," *Washington Times*, August 4, 1895, 12.

70. "Something for Everyone, A Paper for Everybody," *Washington Times*, August 24, 1895, 1.

71. "Christmas Fun," *New York Herald*, December 20, 1896, F-6.

72. "Contemporary Opinion as Expressed in the Best Cartoons," *New York World*, August 9, 1896 and August 23, 1896, both on page 2 of the "Comic Weekly."

73. Color covers in the *St. Paul Globe* start with "The Voice of the American People," November 8, 1896, and end with "The Christmas Globe," December 20, 1896.

74. "Funny Fancies," *Philadelphia Inquirer*, February 23, 1896, 36.

75. "Funny Fancies," *Philadelphia Inquirer*, April 5, 1896, 40.

76. "A Peach! Given Free with Every Copy of the Big Sunday Recorder!" *New York Recorder*, October 2, 1896, 5.

77. "Twinkles, Serio-Comic Supplement" was a sixteen-page quarto color section, first published in the *New York Tribune* on October 25, 1896, and last published on May 23, 1897.

It was replaced by a sixteen-page tabloid "real" magazine with halftoned photographs on Memorial Day, May 30, 1897.

78. "Notes on the New Journalism," *New York Sun*, October 21, 1896, 6.

79. *The Critic*, quoted in "Shade of Horace Greeley!" *Los Angeles Herald*, November 8, 1896, 18.

80. *Truth*, quoted in "Humor of the Week," *Los Angeles Herald*, November 21, 1896, 2.

81. "The Duty of the Press," *New York Times*, January 26, 1897, 12, recounts efforts to ban the comic supplements from libraries. "A General Revolt," *New York Sun*, March 22, 1897, 5, collected more than two dozen opinions from other newspapers across the country.

82. The same double-page center color cartoon, "Mr. New-Rich" by Jay Hambidge, appears in both the *Philadelphia Press* "Sunday Press Jester" of February 14, 1897, and also the *Boston Herald* "Sunday Jester" of March 14, 1897.

83. "Comic and Half-Tone Section," *San Francisco Call*, July 22, 1900, a new eight-page tabloid section. See "Next Sunday's *Call*," *San Francisco Call*, July 19, 1900, 11.

84. "New *Item* Features," *New Orleans Item*, May 26, 1901, 1.

85. "Sunday's Colored Cover," *St. Louis Post-Dispatch*, July 3, 1897, 1.

86. "Sunday's Colored Cover," *St. Louis Post-Dispatch*, July 1, 1897, 3.

87. Arthur S. Hamlin, *Copyright Cases, 1893–1903* (New York: Putnam's, 1904), 166–68.

88. *Foxy Grandpa! New York Herald*, January 7, 1900, Colored Section, 4.

89. For example, "You Done I'm Brown, Chimmie," *New York Sun*, September 25, 1892, 13.

90. "Chimmie, Some Not Unpleasant Traits of His," *New York Tribune*, March 27, 1892, 15.

91. For example, "What We Are All Talking About," *New York Sun*, June 5, 1890, 6.

92. "Admirers of the Yellow Kid, Watertown Has Its Hogan's Alley Gang and Its Yaller Youngsters," *Watertown Times*, December 12, 1896, 5.

93. R. F. Outcault, "*The Sunday World*'s Hogan Alley Folk on the Stage at Weber and Fields's Broadway Music Hall," *New York World*, September 6, 1896, 27.

94. "Amusements," *Wilkes-Barre News-Dealer*, October 6, 1896, 5.

95. "Three New Plays Shown Last Night," *Philadelphia Inquirer*, December 8, 1896, 11.

96. "Young Patriots, Unique Street Parade," *Jersey City Journal*, October 24, 1896, 2; *Charleston News and Courier*, October 29, 1896; "Pleased with the Yellow Kid," *Wilkes-Barre Times*, November 5, 1896, 6; "Wheelmen in Line," *Richmond Dispatch*, November 22, 1896, 11.

97. *Hogan's Alley* continued in the *World* but was inked by George B. Luks. See Christina Meyer, "George Benjamin Luks and the Comic Weeklies of the Nineteenth Century," *Journal of Graphic Novels and Comics* 3, no. 1 (2012): 69–83.

98. "Just Published, The Yellow Kid Magazine," *Cincinnati Enquirer*, March 20, 1897, 5; and on the same day in *Boston Post* and *St. Louis Globe-Democrat*.

99. Advertisement for *The Yellow Kid in McFadden's Flats*, *Philadelphia Times*, March 20, 1897, 7.

100. Ibid.

101. "The 'Syndicate' Question," *Baltimore Sun*, August 29, 1871, 2, quoting the *New York Post*. See also "Miscellaneous," *Chicago Tribune*, August 22, 1871, 2.

102. "A Newspaper Syndicate," *Freeport (IL) Journal and Republican*, May 18, 1883, 2.

103. "An Interesting Newspaper Enterprise," *St. Louis Globe-Democrat*, May 28, 1884, 6; "Short Sunday Stories by the Best Authors," *Chicago Tribune*, May 29, 1884, 4. Also sub-

scribing to these syndicated stories were the *New Orleans Times-Democrat*, the *Springfield (MA) Republican*, the *Cincinnati Enquirer, Syracuse Standard*, and *Savannah (GA) News*, which began featuring the stories in their regional advertising, e.g. *Conecuh-Escambia Star* (Evergreen, AL), June 19, 1884, 2. The series began with "Pandora" by Henry James, followed by "A Blue Grass Penelope" by Bret Harte, then "Georgina's Reason" by James, and also promised stories from Mark Twain, W. D. Howells, and other distinguished authors. See "New American Stories," *San Francisco Chronicle*, July 19, 1884, 1.

104. Editorial, *Detroit Free Press*, June 1, 1884, 4.

105. Charles Johanningsmeier, "The Heyday of American Fiction Syndication: Irving Bacheller, S. S. McClure, and Other Early Syndicators," in *Fiction and the American Literary Marketplace: The Role of Newspaper Syndicates in America, 1860–1900* (New York: Cambridge University Press, 1997), 64–98. The first of Hatton's "London Letters" appeared on Saturday, May 10, 1884, in the *Brooklyn Times* (where Bacheller was employed), *Chicago Daily News*, and *Cincinnati Commercial-Gazette*, and on Sunday, May 11, in the *Boston Herald* and the *Philadelphia Inquirer*, perhaps others, continuing weekly until February 1885. A rare contemporaneous remark about Bacheller's announced new endeavor was amused by the name "American Bureau of Fiction," joking how it would find "the more valuable selections from the local columns of Boston." *New York Graphic*, January 19, 1884, 4.

106. "The New Era for Authorship," *Philadelphia Times*, August 3, 1884, 4.

107. "American Literature, an Interview with Mark Twain," *Philadelphia Times*, December 31, 1884, 2, reprinted from the *Pittsburgh Chronicle-Telegraph*. Twain referred to Allen Thorndyke Rice, editor of *North American Review*, who launched a fourth syndicate in 1884, which fizzled within a year. A summary of the first years of competition in the field was offered by S. S. McClure, "Newspaper 'Syndicates,'" *The Critic*, July 23, 1887, 42–43.

108. "The New American Stories," *Springfield (MA) Republican*, July 20, 1884, 4.

109. Hjalmar H. Boyesen, "A Daring Fiction," *Lancaster (PA) New Era*, November 15, 1884, 3; and *Boston Globe*, November 16, 1884, 16. See also advertising for the *Commercial Advertiser*'s "supplement of today … Good Stories for 3 cents," *New York Tribune*, November 15, 1884, 5.

110. "A Fresh Attraction," *Buffalo Express*, November 23, 1884, 4.

111. "The Express Stories," *Buffalo Express*, December 27, 1884, 4.

112. "Original Copyright Stories," *Buffalo Express*, January 20, 1885, 8.

113. "Writers of Short Stories," *Buffalo Express*, May 29, 1885, 7, reprinted from the *New York Commercial Advertiser*.

114. "Express Stories," *Buffalo Express*, August 12, 1885, 4.

115. "This Is the Age of Syndicates," *Eskridge (KS) Star*, March 17, 1887, 2.

116. "Ore Producers Combine," *Pittsburgh Press*, February 15, 1888, 1.

117. "Lemon Seltzer," *Rush Centre (KS) Gazette*, October 18, 1888, 2, reprinted from *Pittsburgh Chronicle-Telegraph*.

118. Quoting John F. Carson, "Three Sermons at the Dedication of Duryea Church," *Brooklyn Eagle*, October 29, 1906, 7.

119. Quoting John F. Carson, "Open Rich Churches to Poor and Humble," *Brooklyn Citizen*, May 22, 1911, 6.

120. "These Theater Syndicates," *St. Louis Globe-Democrat*, November 9, 1907, 8.

121. Jesse Lee Bennett, "The Skeptic," *Baltimore Sun*, June 29, 1922, 8.

CHAPTER 6. THE "CONTINUOUS PERFORMANCE EXTRA" OF POPULAR LEISURE

1. Dilip Gaonkar and Elizabeth Povinelli, "Technologies of Public Forms: Circulation, Transfiguration, Recognition," *Public Culture* 15, no. 3 (2003): 396.

2. Maurice Wetzel, "What Innovations Portend in Our Radio of Tomorrow?" *Radio Digest*, March 1929, 58–59.

3. M. H. Aylesworth, "This Month's Most Spectacular Announcement," *What's on the Air*, August 1930, 15.

4. Ibid.; emphasis added.

5. Michael Socolow, "A Wavelength for Every Network: Synchronous Broadcasting and National Radio in the United States, 1926–1932," *Technology and Culture* 49, no. 1 (2008): 89–113.

6. "The Christmas Number of *The Times*," *Philadelphia Times*, December 12, 1900, 13.

7. "The Magazine Supplement of *The Sunday Constitution*," *Atlanta Constitution*, December 29, 1900, 10.

8. "*The Sunday Leader* Continues to Come," *Cleveland Leader*, August 1, 1902, 7.

9. "Next Sunday's *Enquirer*," *Cincinnati Enquirer*, August 22, 1903, 4. Also "Lulu and Leander and Pussy Pumpkin. Copyright, 1903, by W. R. Hearst" is noted in "Next Sunday's *Enquirer*," *Cincinnati Enquirer*, September 12, 1903, 4.

10. "So the People May Know," *Denver Post*, December 14, 1900, 7.

11. Ibid.

12. "*Mail-Telegram* to Push to the Front, Contemplated Re-Organization Is Perfected," *Fort Worth Mail-Telegram*, July 10, 1902, 8. The name of the paper soon changed to *Telegram and Mail* on Monday, July 28, 1902, then dropped the word "Mail" entirely on August 17.

13. "Announcement, Beginning Next Sunday," *Fort Worth Telegram and Mail*, August 7, 1902, 5.

14. "The Hearst Syndicate," *Fort Worth Telegram*, January 4, 1903, 4.

15. "The Hearst Service Now in *The Telegram*," *Fort Worth Telegram*, January 15, 1903, 5.

16. David Nasaw, *The Chief: The Life of William Randolph Hearst* (New York: Houghton Mifflin, 2000).

17. Reprinted in "Who's What and Why in America," *Galveston (TX) News*, November 2, 1902, 16, and others.

18. In 1892, when Samuel S. McClure launched his eponymous magazine, management of the newspaper syndicate was handed to his brother, Thomas Carlyle, who oversaw two decades of expansion, including the launch of syndicated color comics. "T. C. McClure is Dead; Managed Syndicate," *Editor and Publisher*, November 3, 1934, 36.

19. "The Colored Comic Supplement," *Augusta (GA) Chronicle*, August 27, 1903, 1.

20. "Comic Supplement Feature with Saturday *Bulletin*," *Honolulu Bulletin*, December 18, 1903, 1. See also "A New Thing in Honolulu Journalism," *Honolulu Hawaiian Star*, December 19, 1903, 1.

21. "Hi There, Boys and Girls," *Colorado Springs Gazette*, February 16, 1904, 6.

22. For example, "The McClure Newspaper Syndicate," *Mansfield (OH) News*, May 21, 1904, 6.

23. "Be Sure to Get a Copy," *Evansville (IN) Courier*, March 10, 1901, 4.

24. "To the Public," *Fort Wayne Journal-Gazette*, November 8, 1903, 1.

25. "Here's One for the Children," *Rockford (IL) Register-Gazette*, September 19, 1904, 4.

26. "The Court of Last Resort, The Sunday Paper Cartoons," *Ladies Home Journal*, June 1904, 22.

27. "Pernicious Literature," *East Liverpool (OH) Review*, October 24, 1905, 4.

28. "*The Herald's* Advance," *Boston Herald*, October 25, 1908, 36.

29. "A Few Words to Readers," *Washington Herald*, October 13, 1906, 2.

30. "Buster Brown for Seattle," *Seattle Times*, December 4, 1904, 1.

31. "Newspapers Join for Advertising, News Features," *Oakland Tribune*, February 1, 1922, 3.

32. "National Newspapers Incorporated," *Buffalo Courier*, May 21, 1922, 11, and others, as well as subsequent advertisements.

33. "If the Great Cities," *Chicago American*, November 17, 1906, 6.

34. "*The Times* Has Begun," *New York Times*, September 12, 1896, 4.

35. "Something Unique in Newspapers," *Los Angeles Times*, December 3, 1897, 9.

36. "New England Home Magazine, Free with *The Sunday Journal*," *Boston Journal*, January 1, 1898, 2.

37. "Kernels No. 1, Editorial Strength," *Detroit Free Press*, June 4, 1907, 2. Other newspapers where the "Kernels" series was printed were not identical to the papers including the *Sunday Magazine* as a supplement. The ads appeared in the *New York Tribune* (carrying the insert) but also the *New York Sun*; the *Pittsburg Post* and *Denver Rocky Mountain News* were listed in the ads they printed, but the campaign also ran in the *Cleveland Plain Dealer* and the *Cincinnati Enquirer*, among others.

38. "Kernels No. 4, Quality," *Detroit Free Press*, June 25, 1907, 12, and others.

39. "Kernels No. 6, Distribution," *Detroit Free Press*, July 9, 1907, 10, and others.

40. "Reforms Suggested in Postal Service, Newspapers and Other Publications Defined," *Chicago Inter-Ocean*, January 28, 1907, 10.

41. Ibid.

42. *Report of the Postal Commission on Second-Class Mail Matter* (Washington, DC: Government Printing Office, 1907), 39, and reported widely—for example, "To Banish Fiction from the Newspapers," *Rockford (IL) Republic*, February 7, 1907, 3.

43. *Report of the Postal Commission on Second-Class Mail Matter* (Washington, DC: Government Printing Office, 1907), 39.

44. "Press Censorship," *Quincy (IL) Herald*, January 30, 1907, 4; reprinted as "The Proposed Press Censorship," *Rock Island (IL) Argus*, February 4, 1907, 4.

45. "Freak Legislation for Post Office," *San Francisco Call*, February 10, 1907, 24.

46. "Free with the Rotogravure Section," *Chicago Tribune*, February 10, 1918, G-12.

47. "Next Sunday," *Cleveland Plain Dealer*, February 2, 1922, 7.

48. "The Giant of Gravure Publications, Hearst's *Pictorial Gravure*," *New York Evening World*, February 5, 1918, 9.

49. "16 Big Pages of Rotogravure in Next Sunday's Examiner," *Chicago Examiner*, February 24, 1918, C-6.

50. Duane C. S. Stoltzfus, *Freedom from Advertising: E. W. Scripps's Chicago Experiment* (Urbana: University of Illinois Press, 2007).

51. "Here You Are Folks! All about 'The Movies,'" *Chicago Day Book*, November 11, 1912, 24, and others, including *Des Moines News*, as discussed in Richard Abel, *Americanizing the*

Movies and "Movie-Mad" Audiences, 1910–1914 (Berkeley: University of California Press, 2006), 231–51. See also Diana Anselmo-Sequeira, "Screen-Struck: The Invention of the Movie Girl Fan," *Cinema Journal* 55, no. 1 (2015): 1–28.

52. "Oh, There's That Smiley Golden-Haired Girl Again," *Sacramento (CA) Star*, November 18, 1912, 1, and others.

53. Ilka Brasch, *Operational Detection: Film Serials and the American Cinema, 1910–1940* (Amsterdam: Amsterdam University Press, 2018); Josh Lambert, "Wait for the Next Pictures: Intertextuality and Cliffhanger Continuity in Early Cinema and Comic Strips," *Cinema Journal* 48, no. 2 (2009): 3–25. Of course, radio serials continued in similar fashion in later years. Anne F. MacLennan, "Women, Radio, and the Depression: A 'Captive' Audience from Households to Story Time and Serials," *Women's Studies* 37, no. 6 (2008): 616–33. See also Roger Hagedorn, "Doubtless to Be Continued: A Brief History of Serial Narrative," in *To Be Continued . . : Soap Operas around the World*, ed. Robert C. Allen, 27–48 (New York: Routledge, 1995).

54. "Read the Story in the Morning, See It in Moving Pictures at Night," *Chicago Record-Herald*, February 4, 1914, 5.

55. "Today's Best Moving Picture Story," *Chicago Tribune*, February 5, 1914, 5.

56. For example, "Read the Story Here—See It in the Moving Pictures Tonight," *Chicago Examiner*, February 7, 1914, 8.

57. This list of papers syndicating the Universal moving-picture stories was given by just one of the papers. See "In *The Herald* This Morning," *Washington Herald*, March 9, 1914, 6.

58. "Right off the Reel!" *Chicago Tribune*, February 22, 1914, 6.

59. Advance promotion, "Right off the Reel!" *Chicago Tribune*, February 22, 1914, H-6, and started with "In the Frame of Public Favor," *Chicago Tribune*, March 1, 1914, Color Section, 3.

60. "High Class Motion Picture Theaters," *Chicago Tribune*, April 24, 1915, 9 and 17.

61. Richard Abel, *Menus for Movieland: Newspapers and the Emergence of American Film Culture, 1913–1916* (Berkeley: University of California Press, 2015).

62. "Which Photo-Play Today?" *Chicago Tribune*, January 10, 1916, 14.

63. "Where Is That Star To-Night?" *Chicago Daily News*, December 4, 1915, 13.

64. See regional promotion for the *Sunday Milwaukee Sentinel*—for example, "A Gallery of Beautiful Young Women of the Screen," *Wisconsin State Journal* (Madison), June 22, 1916, 7.

65. "Betty Crocker to Give Home Service Talks," *Pittsburgh Press*, August 25, 1925, 22. See also Ann V. Bliss, "Visiting on the Air: Radio Homemakers and the Professionalization of Domesticity," *Journal of American Studies* 50, no. 4 (2016): 999–1019.

66. "Promise Real Service to Nation's Housewives," *Buffalo Times*, September 20, 1925, 65.

67. "Western Electric Broadcasting Stations in the U.S.," *Radio Broadcast*, January 1923, 265.

68. "Simultaneous Broadcasts by WNAC, Boston, and WEAF, New York," *Boston Globe*, January 2, 1923, 12.

69. "Big C. & P. Radio Station Is Ready," *Washington Star*, July 3, 1923, 2.

70. "WCAP, the New Washington Radio Station," *Washington Star*, July 8, 1923, B-15.

71. "Millionaire Radio Fan Brings Broadway Talent to Easterners," *Asbury Park (NJ) Press*, July 17, 1923, 14.

72. "Round Hills Radio Station Broadcast," *Fall River (MA) News*, July 2, 1923, 4.

73. "Radio Gossip," *Washington Star*, August 12, 1923, B-13.

74. "President Harding in Continental Broadcast," *Boston Globe*, July 29, 1923, 53. See also "3,000,000 Radio Fans Will Hear Harding's Speech on Tuesday," *St. Louis Globe-Democrat*, July 29, 1923, B-12.

75. "Coolidge Message to Be Broadcast," *Philadelphia Inquirer*, December 1, 1923, 4.

76. Michelle Hilmes, "NBC and the Network Idea: Defining the 'American System,'" in *NBC: America's Network*, ed. Michelle Hilmes (Berkeley: University of California Press, 2007), 13.

77. General Electric's WGY in Schenectady began routine rebroadcasting of WJZ in July 1924, with RCA's WRC in Washington often added by October 1924. Westinghouse stations KDKA in Pittsburgh and KYW in Chicago joined them for the launch of the *Brunswick Hour* in December, and General Electric's WBZ in Springfield and Boston joined in March 1925.

78. Michael Socolow, "'Always in Friendly Competition': NBC and CBS in the First Decade of National Broadcasting," in *NBC: America's Network*, ed. Michelle Hilmes (Berkeley: University of California Press, 2007), 26.

79. "Nation Will Hear Inaugural," *Baltimore Sun*, March 1, 1925, C-10.

80. David Dietz, "Nineteen Cities Included in WEAF Radio Link," *Wilmington (DE) Journal*, May 9, 1925, 7.

81. On Bruce Sterling's "Dead Media Project," see deadmedia.org and Tara Brabazon, "Dead Media: Obsolescence and Redundancy in Media History," *First Monday* 18, no. 7 (2013), online at doi.org/10.5210/fm.v18i7.4466. On the methodology of paying dead media close attention, see Erkki Huhtamo and Jussi Parikka, eds., *Media Archaeology: Approaches, Applications, and Implications* (Berkeley: University of California Press, 2011).

82. "Thompson's New Station, WHT, Takes Air Soon," *Chicago Tribune*, February 15, 1925, H-11.

83. Roy J. Gibbons, NEA service writer, "Radio Ads a Business with WHT," *Madison (WI) Capital Times*, July 3, 1925, 9, and syndicated widely.

84. "Mid-Continent Link Starts in Midwest," *Radio Digest*, September 19, 1925, 18.

85. "WHT, Showplace of the Wrigley Building," *Radio Digest*, October 31, 1925, 6.

86. G. P. Allen, "The Mid-Continent 'Link' Starts Business," *Radio in the Home*, November 25, 1925, 20–21.

87. "WHT, Showplace of the Wrigley Building," *Radio Digest*, October 31, 1925, 7.

88. Amy Graban Crawford, "A Universal Speaking Service: The Role of Westinghouse Electric and Manufacturing Company in the Development of National Network Broadcasting, 1922–1926," *Journal of Broadcasting and Electronic Media* 51, no. 3 (2007): 516–29.

89. Ibid., 521.

90. Ibid., 522.

91. E. M. Boyd, "Radio Program Syndication Seen as Solution of Air Muddle," *Editor and Publisher*, November 13, 1926, 22.

92. Cynthia B. Meyers, *A Word from Our Sponsor: Admen, Advertising, and the Golden Age of Radio* (New York: Fordham University Press, 2014).

93. "Agency Appointments by Union Carbide Subsidiaries," *Printers' Ink*, September 20, 1923, 12; "National Carbon Company Spending More Than a Million Dollars in Advertising Support for Their Country Dealers," *Rural Trade*, December 1923, 9; Noel L. Griese, "AT&T: 1908 Origins of the Nation's Oldest Continuous Institutional Advertising Campaign," *Advertising History* 6, no. 3 (1977): 18–23.

94. "Pioneer Radio Hour Goes Off the Air," *Lansing (MI) State Journal*, December 2, 1930, 14. This Associated Press story states that the Eveready Entertainers debuted on WEAF on July 6, 1923, a onetime special, and returned December 23, 1923, with their continuous weekly show, lasting exactly seven years.

95. Cynthia B. Meyers, "Commerce and Culture: Histories of Radio Sponsorship Yet to Be Written," *Journal of Radio and Audio Media* 23, no. 2 (2016): 369–80.

96. The Lucky Strike Dance Orchestra was not added to brand advertising until January 1929—for example, in the *Brooklyn Standard Union*, January 8, 1929, 7, and nationally starting the same day.

97. Ads for the *Eveready Hour* election day special, November 4, 1924, were printed, for example, in the *Pittsburg Post*, *Boston Globe*, and *Detroit Free Press*, all noting local radio hookups. Ads for the *Eveready Hour* listing the (then) six-station network playing the *Eveready Hour* began December 9, 1924, in the *Boston Globe* (with local station WEEI on the list) and the *Buffalo Times* (where WGR was listed) but also in the *St. Louis Post-Dispatch, Kansas City Times*, and as far west as the *Fort Worth Record*. National advertising for Eveready every Tuesday continued to list stations for two years until November 1926, when the phrasing switched to "the WEAF network," adding "and associated N.B.C. stations" in November 1927.

98. Ad for the Great Atlantic & Pacific Tea Co., *New York Daily News*, March 6, 1924, 6, and similar versions across New Jersey and northern Pennsylvania.

99. For example, in the *Des Moines Tribune-Capital*, November 18, 1927, and the *Chicago Tribune*, November 20, 1927, noting to tune in to WHO and WGN, respectively.

100. "Concert Seen as New Radio Era, Eight Million Hear Great Artists on Air," *Chicago Tribune*, January 2, 1925, 8.

101. Ad for Victor Talking Machine Company, *New York Daily News*, January 1, 1925, 6, and similar local retailer advertising between December 30 and January 1 across New York and Pennsylvania, by the end of January as far as Lincoln, Nebraska, and Huntsville, Alabama.

102. Full-page ads for the *Brunswick Hour* "Music Memory Contest" ran on Sunday, January 25, 1925, in the *Chicago Tribune, Cincinnati Enquirer, Baltimore Sun*, and others.

103. "Capitol and Roxy Sew Up WEAF and WJZ," *Variety*, March 2, 1927, 4; "Gigantic Artists' Control Agency Seen in Radio's System," *Variety*, April 27, 1927, 29.

104. Ad for the *Eveready Hour, St. Louis Globe-Democrat*, February 2, 1926, 23.

105. "Philco Radio Hour Planned," *Dayton (OH) News*, September 4, 1927, B-6.

106. Night Watchman, "The List'ning Post," *Minneapolis Tribune*, January 19, 1926, 10. The column began on December 15, 1925, and ran to April 1928.

107. Night Watchman, "The List'ning Post," *Minneapolis Tribune*, October 13, 1927, 16. This decision might have been linked to the "agreement" of the *Tribune*, the *Minneapolis Journal*, and the *St. Paul Pioneer Press* "to withdraw from the field" of broadcasting late in 1922, after being among the radio pioneers in the Twin Cities. Winfield Barton, "What Broadcasting Does for a Newspaper," *Radio Broadcast*, February 1924, 346, quoting T. J. Dillon, managing editor of the *Tribune*. See also Ted Curtis Smythe, "The Birth of Twin Cities' Commercial Radio," *Minnesota History* 41 (1969): 327–34.

108. Michelle Hilmes, *Radio Voices: American Broadcasting, 1922–1952* (Minneapolis: University of Minnesota Press, 1997), 11–23.

109. "WEAF's Famed Trio of Announcers," *Cleveland Plain Dealer*, February 15, 1925, E-1.

110. "New York Radio Programs Now over WFAA," *Dallas News*, February 20, 1927, B-5.

111. "Lucky Strike Program to Be Broadcast by KGW through National Radio Network," *Oregonian* (Portland), September 9, 1928, D-8.

112. Ibid.

113. Ross Melnick, *American Showman: Samuel "Roxy" Rothafel and the Birth of the Entertainment Industry* (New York: Columbia University Press, 2012), 244.

114. Ad for "Hello, Everybody!" *Rochester (NY) Democrat and Chronicle*, March 9, 1925, 4, and in dozens of newspapers across New York and New Jersey. See also "Hello, Everybody!" *New York Daily News*, March 4, 1925, 33.

115. Karen L. Cox, *Dreaming of Dixie: How the South Was Created in American Popular Culture* (Chapel Hill: University of North Carolina Press, 2011), 58.

116. "Amos 'n' Andy," *Chicago Daily News*, March 17, 1928, 15.

117. William S. Hedges, "Creators of Sam 'n' Henry on WMAQ Beginning March 19," *Chicago Daily News*, February 25, 1928, 24.

118. Ibid.

119. "Literati: Radio Act for Promotion," *Variety*, March 28, 1928, 29.

120. Mark Quest, "Additional Facts in the Private Life of Amos and Andy," *Radio Digest*, April 1930, 15; "Canned Names on National Scheme of Distribution for All Spots," *Variety*, November 28, 1928, 57. Syndicated recordings of "canned" *Amos 'n' Andy* programs begin to appear late in April 1928—for example on KMOX in St. Louis.

121. Rialto Music House, *Sam 'n' Henry* advertising, *Chicago Defender*, May 22, 1926, 6; "Defender Forum," *Chicago Defender*, September 7, 1929, 1.

122. "Bishop Flays Race Citizens Who Laugh at Amos 'n' Andy," *Pittsburgh Courier*, May 3, 1930, 13; also appears as "Bishop Walls' Criticism of 'Amos 'n' Andy,' *New York Age*, May 10, 1930, 10, and "Bishop Walls Deplores Amos 'n' Andy Chats," *Chicago Defender*, May 3, 1930, 7.

123. "Amos and Andy Sued by Miller and Lyles," *Baltimore Afro-American*, May 10, 1930, 8. Chappy Gardner, "Imposters Steal Race Material," *Pittsburgh Courier*, May 10, 1930, 2, considers the wider success of white actors in blackface. See also Noah Arceneaux, "Blackface Broadcasting in the Early Days of Radio," *Journal of Radio Studies* 12, no. 1 (2005): 61–73.

124. Kim Gallon, *Pleasure in the News: African American Sexuality in the Black Press* (Urbana: University of Illinois Press, 2020), 23.

125. Editorial, "Amos 'n' Andy," *Pittsburgh Courier*, April 25, 1931, 10.

126. "What the People Think!" *Pittsburgh Courier*, April 25, 1931, 12.

127. "Self-Respect Sunday," *Pittsburgh Courier*, October 3, 1931, 10.

128. "Insult for Insult," *Pittsburgh Courier*, July 4, 1931, 12. For more context of *Sunny Boy Sam*, see Sheena C. Howard, "Brief History of the Black Comic Strip: Past and Present," in *Black Comics: Politics of Race and Representation*, ed. Sheena C. Howard and Ronald L. Jackson II (New York: Bloomsbury, 2013), 15.

129. Bud Billiken was the moniker for the mascot of the "Chicago Defender Jr." column, beginning April 2, 1921, and initially appearing on the woman's page, edited by Ethel Gavin. A week later, coupons were available to clip out and submit to join the Bud Billiken Club of young readers, who were referred to as "Billikens." A relatively short-lived comic strip version of Bud Billiken began on January 19, 1924, and ran until September 1925 by Roger L. Powell, and then was briefly drawn by Langdon Abington until January 1926. See Gallon, *Pleasure in the News*, 39.

130. "Crowd of 35,000 Attends Bud Billiken's Big Picnic," *Chicago Defender*, August 22, 1931, 16.

131. Henry Louis Gates Jr., *Stony the Road: Reconstruction, White Supremacy and the Rise of Jim Crow* (New York: Penguin, 2019); Jackson Lears, *Rebirth of A Nation: The Making of Modern America, 1877–1920* (New York: HarperCollins, 2009), 222–75.

132. Jean Lee Cole, "Laughing Sam and Krazy Kats: The Black Comic Sensibility," *Canadian Review of American Studies* 47, no. 3 (2017): 374; Jean Lee Cole, *How the Other Half Laughs: The Comic Sensibility in American Culture, 1895–1920* (Jackson: University Press of Mississippi, 2020).

133. The comic strip *Bungleton Green*, by Leslie M. Rogers, began in the *Chicago Defender* on November 20, 1920, and ran in various forms until 1963. *Bungleton Green* was expanded to a full page in color ink on January 1, 1927, as part of the launch of an illustrated feature section. Rogers was profiled several times and gained some celebrity in his role as illustrator and cartoonist for the *Defender*. See "Bung's Paper on the Job," *Chicago Defender*, December 25, 1926, 8; and "Bung Green's Papa," *Chicago Defender*, March 23, 1929, 10.

134. Howard, "Brief History of the Black Comic Strip," 14.

135. Ibid., 20, citing Dexter B. Gordon, "Humor in African American Discourse: Speaking of Oppression," *Journal of Black Studies* 29, no. 2 (1998): 254–76.

136. The comic strip *Amos Hokum*, by Jim Watson, began in the *Baltimore Afro-American* on March 2, 1923. Noted as copyrighted by Kelly Newspaper Feature Service, the strip soon also began in the *Pittsburgh Courier* on June 2, 1923, but had ceased publication by the end of 1924. The comic strip *Sambo Sims*, by Charles W. Russell, began in the *Pittsburgh Courier* on June 30, 1923. Noted as copyrighted by the Pryce Service Bureau, it also ran in the *Wichita (KS) Negro Star* in October 1923 but ceased publication in both papers by the end of 1923. Another early syndicated comic strip was *As Others See Us*, by Jay Paul Jackson, which ran from 1928 to 1933 in the *Pittsburgh Courier*, the *Chicago Defender*, and the *New York Amsterdam News*.

137. A color-inked tabloid magazine, *The Illustrated Feature Section*, began on November 3, 1928, in both the *Pittsburgh Courier* and the *Baltimore Afro-American*.

138. Floyd J. Calvin, "The Digest," *Pittsburgh Courier*, November 17, 1923, 9.

139. Gallon, *Pleasure in the News*, 39.

140. *Lancaster (PA) News-Journal*, September 28, 1923, 6.

141. *Owensboro (KY) Messenger-Inquirer*, March 1, 1929, 1.

142. *Fresno (CA) Bee*, September 6, 1924, 1.

143. "For Washington . . . The Sunday Star," *Washington Star*, October 25, 1932, 10, among others.

144. The sample of advertising comics is taken from *Chicago Tribune*, March 6, 1938.

CONCLUSION

1. H. G. Wells, *Science and the Citizen* [recording], BBC Archive 1943. Available to listen in the UK online at www.bbc.co.uk/archive/hg-wells—science-and-the-citizen/zmwcpg8/.

2. The term "360 video" refers to an immersive video production technique that records video in all directions, providing viewers with a full 360-degree view of the scene. Interestingly, the *Times* described it as "virtual reality," though one could not interact with objects

in the video. The video provides vignettes of the migration of three children from Eastern Ukraine, Syria, and South Sudan.

3. Jake Silverstein, "Virtual Reality: A New Way to Tell Stories," *New York Times Magazine*, Editor's Letter, November 5, 2015, www.nytimes.com/2015/11/08/magazine/virtual-reality-a-new-way-to-tell-stories.html/ (emphasis added).

4. Jake Silverstein, "The Displaced: Introduction," *New York Times*, November 5, 2015, www.nytimes.com/2015/11/08/magazine/the-displaced-introduction.html/.

5. Prasun Sonwalkar, "Banal Journalism: The Centrality of the 'Us-Them' Binary in News Discourse," in *Journalism: Critical Issues*, ed. Stuart Allan, 261–73 (Berskshire, UK: Open University Press, 2005).

6. Julia Beizer, "When We Start Getting Creative about Engagement," *Predictions for Journalism 2016, Nieman Lab* (2015), www.niemanlab.org/2015/12/when-we-start-getting-creative-about-engagement/ (emphasis added).

7. "Searching the Firmament," *New York World*, May 1, 1887, 11.

8. "A Very Interesting Discovery of Science," *San Francisco Examiner*, November 1, 1896, 34.

9. "How Pictures May be Transmitted a Thousand Miles and Friends Brought Face to Face," *New York World*, October 18, 1896, 24–25.

10. Erkki Huhtamo and Jussi Parikka, eds., *Media Archaeology: Approaches, Applications, and Implications* (Berkeley: University of California Press, 2011); Jussi Parikka, *What Is Media Archaeology?* (Malden, MA: Polity, 2012).

11. In this sense we add to the proposal to resist social media analytics as a simple focus for news engagement. Steen Steensen, Raul Ferrer-Conill, and Chris Peters, "(Against a) Theory of Audience Engagement with News," *Journalism Studies* 21, no. 12 (2020): 1662–80.

12. Martin Conboy, *Journalism Studies: The Basics* (London: Routledge, 2013), 162.

13. Valerie Belair-Gagnon, "News on the Fly: Journalist-Audience Online Engagement Success as a Cultural Matching Process," *Media, Culture, and Society* 41, no. 6 (2019): 757–73.

14. Chris Peters and Tamara Witschge, "From Grand Narratives of Democracy to Small Expectations of Participation," *Journalism Practice* 9, no. 1 (2015): 19–34.

15. Subscription now, of course, works completely differently. Take, for instance, just one example of many we could offer. Recognizing us as Canadian readers, for instance, the *New York Times* was able to offer a "basic digital access subscription" in Canadian dollars once we had hit our limit of "free articles." Interestingly, the fine print lays out that many of its popular features are not included: e-reader editions, "NYT Games" (the crossword puzzle), and "NYT Cooking." A more detailed analysis of digital subscriptions and how they elicit readership is beyond the scope of this project.

16. James Janega, "5 Ways to Engage More with Your Audience—In Person and Online," *Poynter*, February 18, 2013, www.poynter.org/reporting-editing/2013/5-ways-to-better-engage-with-your-audience-in-person-and-online/.

17. Laura Weber, "About Trib Nation Events," September 5, 2014, www.chicagotribune.com/news/chi-trib-nation-events-chicago-tribune-live-events-story.html/; Janega, "5 Ways to Engage More with Your Audience."

18. "The Pulitzer Building Erected by the Pennies of an Appreciative Public for the People's Newspaper," *New York World*, December 10, 1890, souvenir supplement, 3.

19. Though many early observers could be cited here, we are most indebted to Pablo Boczkowski's careful analysis of the early phase of digital newspapers in *Digitizing the News: Innovation in Online Newspapers* (Cambridge, MA: MIT Press, 2004).

20. W. F. Herron, "The Best Way to Build up the Sunday Edition," *Proceedings of the Eleventh Annual Convention of the National Association Managers of Newspaper Circulation*, Cleveland, Ohio, June 22–24, 1909, 48.

21. J. H. Lackey, *Nashville Banner, Proceedings of the National Association of Managers of Newspaper Circulation*, 1909, 25.

22. Advertising for *American Weekly Magazine, San Francisco Examiner*, January 28, 1917, 50.

23. Eli Noam, *Media Ownership and Concentration in America* (New York: Oxford University Press, 2009).

24. *This Week*, published by the United Newspaper Magazine Corporation, began in 1935 and was initially offered in 21 papers, including the *New York Herald-Tribune*. "Innovation in Sunday Magazines Begins," *Editor and Publisher*, February 23, 1935, 20. *Parade* magazine was launched in 1941 by Marshall Field as part of his starting the *Chicago Sun*. The magazine was initially also sold separately on newsstands and built slowly from its launch in only one paper, the *Nashville Tennessean*; however, it grew quickly to 11 papers with nearly a million circulation by the end of the year, when it started four-color printing. "Field Launches 'Parade,' Using Features from PM," *Editor and Publisher*, July 12, 1941, 4; "Parade Starts to Print Advertising," *Editor and Publisher*, November 8, 1941, 3. *Family Weekly* began in 1953, headquartered on Madison Avenue. Serving smaller-market papers, it was carried in many more papers, 153 to start, but with lower total circulation than the other metropolitan pre-printed magazines. "Marriott to Introduce New Sunday Magazine," *Editor and Publisher*, November 1, 1952, 68; "Starting Sunday Sept. 13," *Editor and Publisher*, April 11, 1953, 5.

25. "Sunday Magazines," *Editor and Publisher*, June 27, 1959, 132.

26. "The Spokesman-Review [Spokane, WA] Joins the Sunday Network," *Editor and Publisher*, October 1, 1966, 39.

27. "Atlanta Dailies to Carry Parade," *Editor and Publisher*, October 19, 1985, 4.

28. *USA Weekend* was created when *USA Today* purchased *Family Weekly*. "The Parade to USA Weekend," *Editor and Publisher*, April 19, 1986, front cover advertising.

29. Andrew Radolf, "Metro Sunday Newspapers Complete a Tough Year," *Editor and Publisher*, December 14, 1985, 16.

30. See "Advertising and Marketing News," *New York Times*, November 24, 1952, 34; and "For More Linage Try Mail Order," *Advertising Age*, June 8, 1953, 3 and 72. Color advertising inserts became widely available by the late 1950s. See, for example, "Leighton Forms Color Insert Clearing House," *Editor and Publisher*, August 2, 1958, 16.

31. "Total market coverage" was introduced, for example, by the *Oakland Tribune* in 1967. "Advertiser's Inserts Given Total Delivery," *Editor and Publisher*, August 26, 1967, 20.

32. Thomas Leonard, *News for All: America's Coming-of-Age with the Press* (New York: Oxford University Press, 1995), 166.

33. Sunday circulation peaked in 1993 for the *New York Times* at 1,812,458 and for the *Boston Globe* at 811,409. Earlier, in 1992, Sunday circulation peaked for the *Los Angeles Times* at 1,531,527 and for the *Washington Post* at 1,177,004; in 1991 for *Long Island Newsday* at 875,239; in 1990 for the *Detroit News and Free Press* at 1,270,420; for the *Chicago Tribune* at 1,141,455

(another peak came in 1978 at 1,155,678); and for the *Philadelphia Inquirer* at 994,539. The all-time-high Sunday circulation is perhaps the *New York Daily News* in 1977, at 2,752,739, before its long decline from the highest-circulation newspaper in America. Figures collected from biannual Audit Bureau of Circulation reports of "Top 25 Sunday Newspapers," as reported in *Editor and Publisher*.

34. For U.S. national aggregated circulation, see "Gains and Losses in U.S. Sunday Newspaper Circulations, 1919 to 1958," *Editor and Publisher*, June 27, 1959, 132; and "Total Estimated Circulation of U.S. Daily Newspapers, 1945 to 2018," Pew Research Center for Journalism and Media, www.pewresearch.org/journalism/chart/sotnm -newspapers-total-estimated-circulation-for-u-s-daily-newspapers/.

35. Leonard, *News for All*, 128.

36. Ibid., 194.

37. Ibid., 199.

38. Jon Katz, "Online or Not, Newspapers Suck," *Wired*, September 1, 1994, www.wired .com/1994/09/news-suck/.

39. John Nerone and Kevin G. Barnhurst, "Beyond Modernism: Digital Design, Americanization, and the Future of the Newspaper Form," *New Media and Society* 3, no. 4 (2001): 467–82.

40. Ibid., 474. Nerone and Barnhurst suggest that "web news" has allowed a return to multivocality. Recent scholarship, however, has pointed out that the "representational harms" of journalism have not been undone by a change in form, format, or medium. See especially Candis Callison and Mary Lynn Young, *Reckoning: Journalism's Limits and Possibilities* (New York: Oxford University Press, 2020).

41. Mark Jacob, "Is 24/7 Digital and Sunday-Only Print the Future for Local News?" September 20, 2021, *Local News Initiative*, localnewsinitiative.northwestern.edu/posts /2021/09/20/sunday-only-print/.

42. Ibid.

43. Boczkowski, *Digitizing the News*. Print editions seemed to fall over a precipice early in 2009, with the one-two punch of the closing of the *Denver Rocky Mountain News* and the switch to a digital-only edition of the *Seattle Post-Intelligencer*. See Matt Carlson, "'Where Once Stood Titans': Second-Order Paradigm Repair and the Vanishing US Newspaper," *Journalism* 13, no. 3 (2011): 267–83.

44. Margaret Sullivan, *Ghosting the News: Local Journalism and the Crisis of American Democracy* (New York: Columbia Global Reports, 2020).

45. Clara Hendrickson, "Local Journalism in Crisis: Why America Must Revive Its Local Newsrooms," *Brookings Institute*, November 12, 2019, www.brookings.edu/research/ local-journalism-in-crisis-why-america-must-revive-its-local-newsrooms/.

46. Ibid.

47. Elizabeth Grieco, "U.S. Newspapers Have Shed Half of Their Newsroom Employees since 2008," *Pew Research Center*, July 23, 2021, www.pewresearch.org/fact -tank/2020/04/20/u-s-newsroom-employment-has-dropped-by-a-quarter-since-2008/.

48. Kristen Hare, "Here Are the Newsroom Layoffs, Furloughs, and Closures Caused by the Coronavirus," *Poynter*, April 26, 2020 (updated October 11, 2021), www. poynter.org/business-work/2021/here-are-the-newsroom-layoffs-furloughs-and -closures-caused-by-the-coronavirus/.

49. Kristen Hare, "More than 90 Local Newsrooms Closed during the Pandemic," *Poynter*, October 20, 2021, www.poynter.org/locally/2021/the-coronavirus-has-closed-more-than-60-local-newsrooms-across-america-and-counting/.

50. Michael X. Delli Carpini, "Postscript: The Who, What, When, Where, Why, and How of Journalism and Journalism Studies," *Remaking the News: Essays on the Future of Journalism Scholarship in the Digital Age* (Cambridge, MA: MIT Press, 2017), 273–74.

51. *McSweeney's*, "A Look at the *San Francisco Panorama*," online description at www.mcsweeneys.net/articles/a-look-at-the-san-francisco-panorama/. Another art publishing endeavor that has preserved the Sunday comics as a fetish object is the work of Peter Maresca, publisher of Sunday Press Books, who has curated a series of full-size compilations of color Sunday comics. Descriptions of books made of comics from 1895 onward are available online at sundaypressbooks.com/.

52. Katie Robertson, "Chicago Public Media is set to acquire *The Chicago Sun-Times*," *New York Times*, January 20, 2022, B4; Aria Bracci, "How Public Radio is trying to save Print," *The Verge*, October 19, 2021, www.theverge.com/22732611/wbez-chicago-public-media-sun-times-deal-radio-print-journalism-podcast/. See also Rosalie Westenskow and Edward Carter, "Journalism as a Public Good: How the Nonprofit News Model Can Save Us from Ourselves," *Communication Law and Policy* 26, no. 3 (2021): 336–75.

53. *The Daily*, www.nytimes.com/column/the-daily/.

54. Lauren Jackson, Desiree Ibekwe, and Mahima Chablani, "Radio Nostalgia," *The Daily* (podcast), April 23, 2021, www.nytimes.com/2021/04/23/podcasts/the-daily-newsletter-radio.html/.

55. Lisa Tobin, "The Quarantine Season," *New York Times* online, April 17, 2020, www.nytimes.com/2020/04/17/podcasts/daily-newsletter-quarantine-virus.html/.

56. We likewise note that the *Guardian* now offers *The Long Read*, a reading of long-form journalism produced and republished as a podcast several days or weeks after its text publication. For only a short list of articles that discuss the immersiveness of listening in podcasts, see David Dowling and Kyle Miller, "Immersive Audio Storytelling: Podcasting and Serial Documentary in the Digital Publishing Industry," *Journal of Radio and Audio Media* 26, no. 1 (2019): 167–84; Siobhan McHugh, "How Podcasting Is Changing the Audio Storytelling Genre," *Radio Journal* 14, no. 1 (2016): 65–82; and Richard Berry, "Podcasting: Considering the Evolution of the Medium and Its Association with the Word 'Radio,'" *Radio Journal* 14, no. 1 (2016): 7–22.

57. Kathleen Kingsbury, "Why the New York Times Is Retiring the Term 'Op-Ed,'" *New York Times*, April 26, 2021, www.nytimes.com/2021/04/26/opinion/nyt-opinion-oped-redesign.html/.

INDEX

PAUL MOORE is a professor of sociology at Ryerson University. He is the author of *Now Playing: Early Moviegoing and the Regulation of Fun,* winner of the Gertrude J. Robinson Prize.

SANDRA GABRIELE is Vice-Provost for Innovation in Teaching and Learning and an associate professor of communication studies at Concordia University. She is a coeditor of *Intersections of Media and Communications: Concepts and Critical Frameworks.*

THE HISTORY OF COMMUNICATION

The University of Illinois Press
is a founding member of the
Association of University Presses.

———————————————————

Composed in 10.5/13 Arno Pro
with Adobe Jenson Pro display
by Kirsten Dennison
at the University of Illinois Press
Manufactured by Versa Press

University of Illinois Press
1325 South Oak Street
Champaign, IL 61820-6903
www.press.uillinois.edu